Organizational

Culture and Leadership

Edgar H. Schein

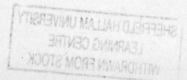

Organizational Culture and Leadership

Fourth Edition

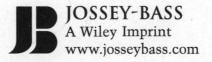

JOSSEY-BASS
A Wiley Imprint
www.josseybass.com

Published by Jossey-Bass
A Wiley Imprint
989 Market Street, San Francisco, CA 94103-1741—www.josseybass.com

Readers should be aware that Internet Web sites offered as citations and/or sources for further information may have changed or disappeared between the time this was written and when it is read.

Limit of Liability/Disclaimer of Warranty: While the publisher and author have used their best efforts in preparing this book, they make no representations or warranties with respect to the accuracy or completeness of the contents of this book and specifically disclaim any implied warranties of merchantability or fitness for a particular purpose. No warranty may be created or extended by sales representatives or written sales materials. The advice and strategies contained herein may not be suitable for your situation. You should consult with a professional where appropriate. Neither the publisher nor author shall be liable for any loss of profit or any other commercial damages, including but not limited to special, incidental, consequential, or other damages.

Jossey-Bass books and products are available through most bookstores. To contact Jossey-Bass directly call our Customer Care Department within the U.S. at 800-956-7739, outside the U.S. at 317-572-3986, or fax 317-572-4002.

Jossey-Bass also publishes its books in a variety of electronic formats. Some content that appears in print may not be available in electronic books.

Library of Congress Cataloging-in-Publication Data has been applied for

ISBN 978-0-470-18586-5 (cloth)
ISBN 978-0-470-19060-9 (paper)

Printed in the United States of America
FOURTH EDITION
HB Printing   10 9 8 7 6 5 4 3 2 1
PB Printing   10 9 8 7 6 5 4 3 2 1

The Jossey-Bass
Business & Management Series

Contents

Preface to Fourth Edition   ix

The Author   xv

Part One: Organizational Culture and Leadership Defined

1. The Concept of Organizational Culture: Why Bother?   7

2. The Three Levels of Culture   23

3. Cultures in Organizations: Two Case Examples   35

4. Macrocultures, Subcultures, and Microcultures   55

Part Two: The Dimensions of Culture

5. Assumptions About External Adaptation Issues   73

6. Assumptions About Managing Internal Integration   93

7. Deeper Cultural Assumptions: What is Reality and Truth?   115

8. Deeper Cultural Assumptions: The Nature of Time and Space   125

9. Deeper Cultural Assumptions: Human Nature, Activity,
   and Relationships   143

10. Culture Typologies and Culture Surveys   157

11. Deciphering Organizational Cultures   177

Part Three: The Leadership Role in Building, Embedding, and Evolving Culture

12. How Culture Emerges in New Groups   197

13. How Founders/Leaders Create Organizational Cultures   219

14. How Leaders Embed and Transmit Culture   235

15. The Changing Role of Leadership in Organizational "Midlife"   259

16. What Leaders Need to Know About How Culture Changes   273

Part Four: How Leaders Can Manage Culture Change

17. A Conceptual Model for Managed Culture Change   299

18. Culture Assessment as Part of Managed Organizational Change   315

19. Illustrations of Organizational Culture Changes   329

Part Five: New Roles for Leaders and Leadership

20. The Learning Culture and the Learning Leader   365

21. Cultural Islands: Managing Multicultural Groups   385

References   401

Index   415

On-line Instructor's Guide is available at www.wiley.com/college/schein.

Preface to Fourth Edition

Organizational culture and leadership have both become very complicated topics. Over the past several decades, organizational culture has drawn themes from anthropology, sociology, social psychology, and cognitive psychology. It has become a field of its own and has connected significantly with the broader cultural studies that have been spawned by the rampant globalism of recent times. The explosion of new tools in information technology and media transmission has made cultural phenomena highly accessible, and some of these phenomena are unique to the information age. Cultural variations around nation, ethnicity, religion, and social class have become highly visible through television and the Internet. Having a certain kind of culture, being a certain kind of culture, and wanting a certain kind of culture have been frequently referred to in the daily press. "Command and control" has become a cultural archetype even as clear descriptions of just what this means have become more elusive when we observe organizations carefully.

We are also increasingly in an age of peril, especially from the potential dangers of rapidly increasing complexity in all of our technologies. And surprisingly, this also begins to focus us on culture. We are in danger of destroying our planet through indifference to the threat of global warming; we have the capacity to genetically engineer various forms of life with unknown consequences; we have a major problem in our health care industry because of high rates of hospital-induced infections, raising the specter of possible bio threats; and we continue to depend on nuclear energy even as we dread nuclear weapons and fear nuclear accidents.

Suddenly we have become aware that the occupations that govern activities in these arenas are themselves cultures about which we know precious little. We know, for example, that doctors strongly value autonomy and that this makes certain kinds of reforms in health care more difficult.

We know that the "executive culture" values returns for the stockholders, which creates problems of social responsibility. We know that the culture of science values exploration and innovation even into ethically dangerous areas such as genetically engineering or cloning humans. Not surprisingly, the peril of further nuclear accidents has created in the nuclear industry a whole new set of concerns about the safety of this technology leading to a preoccupation with and effort to define "safety culture."

The impact of all of this on me as an author is to feel overwhelmed not only by the mass of research and consulting that all of this has spawned in the culture field, but also by the growing difficulty of making sense of the whole field. What I have discovered is that our empirical knowledge of how different cultures interact, how different occupations define tasks, and how multicultural teams function is growing rapidly and is beyond my scope to review systematically. But I have also realized that the basic conceptual model that I articulated in the first three editions is still sound as a way of analyzing cultural phenomena. For this reason, much of the basic material in this fourth edition is similar to its counterparts in the third edition, but it has all been broadened and deepened to reflect the trends I just referred to. I have also added in each chapter some brand new material to reflect what we have learned in the culture field and what new problems have arisen as the field has broadened. And I have added some new chapters to reflect some thinking about culture at different levels of analysis, from national and ethnic macroculture to team-based microculture. This broader perspective reveals the need to think about a few cultural universals, issues that exist at every cultural level, and the need to evolve the concept of "cultural islands" to deal with the dilemma of how to create the ability to work together in very diverse multicultural groups.

What of leadership? Writings about leadership have also exploded, but we are not much clearer today than we were twenty-five years ago about what is a good leader and what a leader should be doing. We have many proposals of what leaders should be and do, and different lists of "core competencies" or traits that leaders should exhibit. Part of the confusion derives from the fact that there is no clear consensus on defining who is a leader—the CEO, anyone at the head of a department, or anyone who takes the initiative to change things. Leadership as a distributed function is gaining ground, which leads to the possibility that anyone who facilitates progress toward some desired outcome is displaying leadership.

I continue to believe that the most important way of staying focused in this sea of possibilities is to keep exploring how leadership and culture are fundamentally intertwined. I will continue to argue (1) that leaders as entrepreneurs are the main architects of culture, (2) that after cultures are formed, they influence what kind of leadership is possible, and (3) that if elements of the culture become dysfunctional, leadership can and must do something to speed up culture change.

I should also note that with the changes in technological complexity, especially in information technology, the leadership task has changed. Leadership in a networked organization is a fundamentally different thing from leadership in a traditional hierarchy. So we will have to examine carefully how the interplay between culture and leadership is evolving as the world becomes more globally interconnected.

How Is This Book Different from the Second Edition of My 2009 *Corporate Culture Survival Guide?*

This fourth edition continues to be a general text that covers most aspects of corporate culture dynamics and their relationship to leadership. The *Survival Guide* is an updated practical roadmap for leaders and managers who want immediate guidance on how to think about culture management. This fourth edition continues to dig deeper into the theoretical and practical issues surrounding the culture field. So, for example, the culture assessment process is presented as eight steps in the *Guide* and as ten steps in this edition because I have elaborated the rationale and broken down a couple of the steps into substeps. Some of the case materials are the same, but I included new cases for this fourth edition and kept the cases that make particularly important theoretical points. The student should read this book; the practicing manager should read the *Guide*.

How This Book Is Organized

In Part I, I will note that the culture and leadership field has differentiated itself and can now be viewed from three different perspectives: the traditional scholar/researcher who is pursuing fundamental theory, the practitioner who is developing tools to help leaders and managers deal with the cultural issues they encounter, and the scholar/practitioner who is concerned about middle-level theory and the translation of that theory into concepts and tools that will help the practitioner even as he or she continues to inform theory.

I have always written from this third perspective because I have had the good fortune of a variety of consulting experiences that provided rich clinical experience from which to build and test theory. What I have labeled "Clinical Research" argues that practical experiences where we are actually helping organizations to solve their problems provide multiple opportunities to observe and inquire, leading to better concepts, models, and tools to be replicated in further experience.

Where social systems and human dynamics are involved, it is difficult to do experiments, and where cultural phenomena are involved, it is hard to gather credible data by survey methods, so I rely more on careful observation, group interviews, and focused inquiry with informants. As a scholar/practitioner, I rely on face validity and on the fact that feedback from readers and clients illuminates the complex phenomena that we are trying to understand. I also rely more on a version of "replication." Would others see the same phenomena that I see if they were to enter the situation?

Part I defines culture and provides some examples and a model for how to think about culture as an abstraction. In Part II, I discuss the major dimensions along which you can analyze culture and review a few of the more salient culture typologies that are being used. In Part III, the focus shifts to leadership and the dynamics of how cultures begin, evolve, and change. Part IV deals with the dynamics of "managed" culture change by reviewing first a general model of change, then a chapter on how to decipher and assess culture, and then a number of cases of organization/culture change. I close in Part V with two chapters that present the challenges of culture management as we see the world becoming more complex, networked, and multicultural. The concept of cultural islands and the use of dialogue are introduced as possible new approaches for leadership in a multicultural world.

The main goal of this edition continues to be to clarify the concept of culture and its relationship to leadership, show how culture works, and enable students to explain organizational and occupational phenomena that might otherwise be puzzling and/or frustrating. With understanding, the student then also acquires the insight and tools needed to demonstrate leadership in creating, evolving, and changing culture.

An updated online Instructor's Guide is available at www.wiley.com/college/schein.

Acknowledgments

In preparing for this edition, I have been helped enormously by the anonymous reviewers of the third edition that were recruited by Jossey-Bass. They provided a useful critique and many suggestions for how to improve the text and the basic message. I owe a special debt to Professor Joan Gallos, who not only reviewed my prior editions but also became very engaged in helping me sort out how to integrate the mass of new information that has become available in the past ten years.

As usual, it is my clients who were and continue to be the chief inspiration for the ideas and concepts I have developed. There is nothing as powerful as empirical observation for building models and theories of how things work. Where possible I will name the organizations and groups from which I learned or else use pseudonyms if confidentiality is required. I am especially grateful to the many members of the Institute of Nuclear Power Operations, the Con Edison Company, and the group of hospital CEOs brought together by Mary Jane Kornacky and Jack Silversin.

Colleagues with whom to discuss these matters are essential to figuring things out, so special thanks to Jean Bartunek, Michael and Linda Brimm, David Coghlan, Scott Cook, Dan Denison, Paul Evans, Marc Gerstein, Mary Jo Hatch, Grady McGonagill, Joanne Martin, John Minahan, Sophia Renda, Otto Scharmer, Majken Schultz, and John Van Maanen.

Finally, some special thanks need to go to a most unusual and valued colleague, Joichi Ogawa, who brought together a small group to represent very different approaches to the question of how to analyze and help organizations; Steve Bond, a Jungian therapist; David Calof, a systemic family therapist who works with organizations; Jon Stokes, a Tavistock-based organizational consultant who works from a psychoanalytic perspective; and Hillel Zeitlin, a Sullivanian family therapist. This group met for several days in each of the past five years and dug deeply into the question of what is an organization, what is culture, and how does one do "therapy" with an organization. The multiple perspectives used in the analysis of our various consulting cases have proved to be invaluable in reconceptualizing the material in this fourth edition. We did not solve the problem of integrating Jung, Freud, family systems theory, and Lewin, but we had a wonderful time trying to do it and produced a short book called *Organizational Therapy* (2009).

Jan. 1, 2010   EDGAR H. SCHEIN
Cambridge, MA

The Author

Ed Schein was educated at the University of Chicago, at Stanford University where he received a master's degree in psychology in 1949, and at Harvard University where he received his Ph.D. in social psychology in 1952. He was chief of the Social Psychology section of the Walter Reed Army Institute of Research while serving in the U.S. Army as captain from 1952 to 1956. He joined MIT's Sloan School of Management in 1956 and was made a professor of Organizational Psychology and Management in 1964.

From 1968 to 1971, Schein was the undergraduate planning professor for MIT, and in 1972, he became the chairman of the Organization Studies Group of the MIT Sloan School, a position he held until 1982. He was honored in 1978 when he was named the Sloan Fellows Professor of Management, a chair he held until 1990. He retired from MIT in 2006 and is currently professor emeritus.

Schein is the founding editor of *Reflections: The Society for Organizational Learning Journal* (1999–2004), which is devoted to connecting academics, consultants, and practitioners around the issues of knowledge creation, dissemination, and utilization.

He has been and continues to be a prolific researcher, writer, teacher, and consultant. Besides his numerous articles in professional journals, he has authored fourteen books, including *Organizational Psychology* (3rd ed., 1980), *Career Dynamics* (1978), *Organizational Culture and Leadership* (1985, 1992, 2004), *Process Consultation* Vol. 1 and Vol. 2 (1969, 1987, 1988), *Process Consultation Revisited* (1999), the *Corporate Culture Survival Guide* (1999, 2009), and a revision of his best-selling *Career Anchors* (2006), which has been widely used in career counseling and coaching. His book *Process Consultation Revisited* (1999) received the Members Choice Award of the

Organization Development Network, 2005. His most recent publication is *Helping: How to Offer, Give, and Receive Help* (2009).

Schein also wrote a cultural analysis of the Singapore Economic Development Board entitled *Strategic Pragmatism* (1997) and has published an extended case analysis of the rise and fall of Digital Equipment Corporation entitled *DEC is Dead; Long Live DEC: The Lasting Legacy of Digital Equipment Corporation* (2003). He was coeditor with the late Richard Beckhard of the Addison Wesley Series on organization development, which has published more than thirty titles since its inception in 1969.

His consultation focuses on organizational culture, organization development, process consultation, and career dynamics, and among his past and current clients are major corporations both in the United States and overseas, such as Alcoa, AMOCO, Apple, British Petroleum, Ciba-Geigy, Citibank, Con Edison, Digital Equipment Corporation, the Economic Development Board of Singapore, EssoChem Europe, Exxon, General Foods, Hewlett-Packard, ICI, Motorola, Procter & Gamble, Saab Combitech, Shell, Steinbergs, and the International Atomic Energy Agency (on the subject of "safety culture").

Schein has received many honors and awards for his writing, most recently the Lifetime Achievement Award in Workplace Learning and Performance of the American Society of Training Directors, February 3, 2000; the Everett Cherington Hughes Award for Career Scholarship from the Careers Division of the Academy of Management, August 8, 2000; the Marion Gislason Award for Leadership in Executive Development from the Boston University School of Management Executive Development Roundtable, December 11, 2002; the Lifetime Achievement Award of the Organization Development Network, 2005; and, most recently, the Distinguished Scholar-Practitioner Award of the Academy of Management, August 2009.

At the present, he serves on the boards of Massachusetts Audubon, Boston Baroque, and Cambridge at Home. He is also on the advisory board of the Institute for Nuclear Power Operations and the Environmental Safety Review Board of ConEdison in New York.

Organizational
Culture and Leadership

Part One

ORGANIZATIONAL CULTURE AND LEADERSHIP DEFINED

In Part I of this book, I will do three things: (1) Define the concept of culture, (2) show the intimate relationship between culture and leadership, and (3) show how both the study of culture and of leadership have evolved in the past decade. To fully understand this evolution, it is first necessary to get a definition of culture that we can all agree on so that when I speak of the initiation, growth, and evolution of culture, you will know what I am referring to. Similarly we have to define leadership because there are now so many definitions running around both in the academic and applied literature, there are so many prescriptions of what a leader should be in terms of basic competencies and what a leader should do in terms of increasing the effectiveness of organizations, that the students and practitioner can't possibly figure out what to believe and what to ignore.

To begin to unscramble these many trends, we need to create a larger conceptual map of the total territory and have a clear set of labels to identify places on the map. The main topic of this book is *organizational culture* focused on all kinds of private, public, government, and nonprofit organizations. When dealing with the private sector, we often call this *"corporate culture."* But throughout this book, I will also be referring to national and

Exhibit I.1.   Categories of Culture.

Culture	Category
Macrocultures	Nations, ethnic and religious groups, occupations that exist globally
Organizational cultures	Private, public, nonprofit, government organizations
Subcultures	Occupational groups within organizations
Microcultures	Microsystems within or outside organizations

ethnic cultures, which I will call *macrocultures*, and to the various occupational groups that make up organizations, which can best be thought of as *subcultures*. Occupations, such as medicine, law, and engineering, transcend organizations and, for some purposes, can also be thought of as macrocultures, but their main impact is in their operation as subcultures within organizations. There is also a growing interest in the cultures of small coherent units within organizations, units such as surgical teams or task forces that cut across occupational groups and are, therefore, different from occupational subcultures. This kind of organizational unit is increasingly being called a *microsystem* and would, therefore, have a *microculture*. These labels are summarized in Exhibit I.1.

Conceptual Approach

My approach is observational and clinical, in the sense that I draw on both academic knowledge and my own lived experience (Schein, 1987a, 2008). For academic knowledge to be useful, it must illuminate experience and provide explanations for what we observe that puzzles or excites us. If experience cannot be explained by what research and theorizing have shown so far, then the scholar/practitioner must develop his or her own concepts and, thereby, enhance existing theory. As we will see, the field of culture provides many opportunities for the development of new concepts because it has not yet been studied enough in group, organizational, and occupational domains to have spawned new theory. It is still an evolving field. The implications of this approach for the student are that you should go out and experience cultures as you read about them. Visit different kinds of organizations, and see what you can observe for yourself.

Culture is both a "here and now" dynamic phenomenon and a coercive background structure that influences us in multiple ways. Culture is constantly reenacted and created by our interactions with others and shaped by our own behavior. When we are influential in shaping the behavior and values of others, we think of that as "leadership" and are creating the conditions for new culture formation. At the same time, culture implies stability and rigidity in the sense that how we are supposed to perceive, feel, and act in a given society, organization, or occupation has been taught to us by our various socialization experiences and becomes prescribed as a way to maintain the "social order." The "rules" of the social order make it possible to predict social behavior, get along with each other, and find meaning in what we do. Culture supplies us our language, and language provides meaning in our day-to-day life. Culture can be thought of as the foundation of the social order that we live in and of the rules we abide by. The culture of macrosystems such as societies is more stable and ordered because of the length of time they have existed. Organizational cultures will vary in strength and stability as a function of the length and emotional intensity of their actual history from the moment they were founded. Occupational cultures will vary from highly structured ones such as medicine to relatively fluid ones such as management. Microcultures are the most variable and the most dynamic and, therefore, provide special opportunities to study culture formation and evolution.

The connection between culture and leadership is clearest in organizational cultures and microcultures. What we end up calling a culture in such systems is usually the result of the embedding of what a founder or leader has imposed on a group that has worked out. In this sense, culture is ultimately created, embedded, evolved, and ultimately manipulated by leaders. At the same time, with group maturity, culture comes to constrain, stabilize, and provide structure and meaning to the group members even to the point of ultimately specifying what kind of leadership will be acceptable in the future. If elements of a given culture become dysfunctional leaders have to surmount their own culture and speed up the normal evolution processes with forced managed culture change programs. These dynamic processes of culture creation and management are the essence of leadership and make you realize that leadership and culture are two sides of the same coin. The vast leadership literature will not be reviewed in this book, but the connection between culture and leadership will be pointed out in every chapter and will be highlighted in Parts III, IV, and V.

As we proceed into this fourth edition, the reader will note that much of the basic conceptual material remains the same, but the context within which it is presented and analyzed has changed considerably in the past seven years, and new material has been added to reflect how organizational culture as a domain has enlarged to encompass occupational subcultures, national/ethnic macrocultures, and a variety of microcultures. There are several reasons for this enlargement of the domain (as summarized in Exhibit I.2). First, all the occupations and disciplines by which the world works are getting more technical and more complex, leading to occupational cultures that are more highly differentiated and, therefore, use different languages and concepts. The immediate implication is that coordination among subcultures within organizations will become more difficult. Second, the explosion of information technology and the ensuing networking of the entire globe are changing the nature of how work is defined, how work is done, and how organizational boundaries are drawn. If the growth and evolution of culture is a function of human interaction, and if human interaction is undergoing fundamental changes, then culture formation and evolution will itself change in unknown ways.

Third, with globalization of both private sector and public sector organizations, multicultural groups will do more work that will involve multiple macrocultures. To understand how an organization such as a merger or joint venture that cuts across several macrocultures can begin to function, we will need to have a much better understanding of the dynamics of microsystems. We have as yet relatively little understanding of how to quickly train a multi-national multi-occupational project team such as a United Nations health team going into a disaster area in an underdeveloped country.

Exhibit I.2.   Forces Influencing Culture Studies.

- Increasing technological/scientific complexity of all functions
- Global networking through information technology
- More multicultural organizations through mergers and joint ventures
- More organizational concern about global warming and sustainability

But a study of organizational culture should provide some guidance on how to think about and implement such training.

Fourth, the crisis around global warming, climate change, and sustainability will influence all levels of culture that have been identified. Not only will this bring into being whole new sets of organizations whose mission will be intimately connected to these global issues, but private sector organizations will increasingly have to consider how environmental responsibility will have to be worked into the concept of core mission and how this will be expressed culturally.

To summarize, understanding culture at any level now requires some understanding of all of the levels. National, ethnic, occupational, organizational, and microsystem issues are all interconnected. In Chapter One, we focus on organizational culture and provide examples of why it is important to understand this aspect of the broad cultural domain. In Chapter Two, the general concept of culture is analyzed structurally to highlight that culture is a complex phenomenon that operates at several different levels of observability. Chapter Three illustrates this complexity by describing the cultures of two organizations, and Chapter Four shows how these organizations are influenced by their location in macrocultures.

1

THE CONCEPT OF ORGANIZATIONAL CULTURE: WHY BOTHER?

Culture is an abstraction, yet the forces that are created in social and organizational situations deriving from culture are powerful. If we don't understand the operation of these forces, we become victim to them. Cultural forces are powerful because they operate outside of our awareness. We need to understand them not only because of their power but also because they help to explain many of our puzzling and frustrating experiences in social and organizational life. Most importantly, understanding cultural forces enables us to understand ourselves better.

What Needs to Be Explained?

Most of us in our roles as students, employees, managers, researchers, or consultants work in and have to deal with groups and organizations of all kinds. Yet we continue to find it amazingly difficult to understand and justify much of what we observe and experience in our organizational life. Too much seems to be "bureaucratic," "political," or just plain "irrational." People in positions of authority, especially our immediate bosses, often frustrate us or act incomprehensibly, and those we consider the "leaders" of our organizations often disappoint us.

When we get into arguments or negotiations with others, we often cannot understand how our opponents could take such "ridiculous" positions. When we observe other organizations, we often find it incomprehensible that "smart people could do such dumb things." We recognize cultural differences at the ethnic or national level but find them puzzling at the group, organizational, or occupational level. Gladwell (2008) in his popular book *Outliers* provides some vivid examples of how both ethnic and organizational cultures explain such anomalies as airline crashes and the success of some law firms.

As managers, when we try to change the behavior of subordinates, we often encounter "resistance to change" at a level that seems beyond reason. We observe departments in our organization that seem to be more interested in fighting with each other than getting the job done. We see communication problems and misunderstandings between group members that should not be occurring between "reasonable" people. We explain in detail why something different must be done, yet people continue to act as if they had not heard us.

As leaders who are trying to get our organizations to become more effective in the face of severe environmental pressures, we are sometimes amazed at the degree to which individuals and groups in the organization will continue to behave in obviously ineffective ways, often threatening the very survival of the organization. As we try to get things done that involve other groups, we often discover that they do not communicate with each other and that the level of conflict between groups in organizations and in the community is often astonishingly high.

As teachers, we encounter the sometimes-mysterious phenomenon that different classes behave completely differently from each other even though our material and teaching style remains the same. If we are employees considering a new job, we realize that companies differ greatly in their approach, even in the same industry and geographic locale. We feel these differences even as we walk in the door of different organizations such as restaurants, banks, stores, or airlines.

As members of different occupations, we are aware that being a doctor, lawyer, engineer, accountant, or manager involves not only learning technical skills but also adopting certain values and norms that define our occupation. If we violate some of these norms, we can be thrown out of the occupation. But where do these come from and how do we reconcile the fact that each occupation considers its norms and values to be the correct ones? How is it possible that in a hospital, the doctors, nurses, and administrators are often fighting with each other rather than collaborating to improve patient care? How is it possible that employees in organizations report unsafe conditions, yet the organization continues to operate until a major accident happens?

The concept of culture helps to explain all of these phenomena and to "normalize" them. If we understand the dynamics of culture, we will be less likely to be puzzled, irritated, and anxious when we encounter the unfamiliar and seemingly irrational behavior of people in organizations, and we will have a deeper understanding not only of why various groups of people or organizations can be so different but also why it is so hard to change them.

Even more important, if we understand culture better, we will understand ourselves better and recognize some of the forces acting within us that define who we are. We will then understand that our personality and character reflect the groups that socialized us and the groups with which we identify and to which we want to belong. Culture is not only all around us but within us as well.

Five Personal Examples

To illustrate how culture helps to illuminate organizational situations, I will begin by describing several situations I encountered in my experiences as a consultant.

DEC

In the first case, Digital Equipment Corporation (DEC), I was called in to help a management group improve its communication, interpersonal relationships, and decision making (Schein, 2003). DEC was founded in the middle 1950s and was one of the first companies to successfully introduce interactive computing, something that today we take completely for granted. The company was highly successful for twenty-five years but then developed a variety of difficulties, which led to its sale to the Compaq Corporation in 1996. I will be referring to the DEC story many times in this book.

After sitting in on a number of meetings of the top management, I observed, among other things: (1) High levels of interrupting, confrontation, and debate, (2) excessive emotionality about proposed courses of action, (3) great frustration over the difficulty of getting a point of view across, (4) a sense that every member of the group wanted to win all the time, and (5) shared frustration that it took forever to make a decision that would stick.

Over a period of several months, I made many suggestions about better listening, less interrupting, more orderly processing of the agenda, the potential negative effects of high emotionality and conflict, and the need to reduce the frustration level. The group members said that the suggestions were helpful, and they modified certain aspects of their procedure, such as lengthening some of their meetings. However, the basic pattern did not change. No matter what kind of intervention I attempted, the basic style of the group remained the same. How to explain this?

(Continued)

Ciba-Geigy

In the second case, I was asked, as part of a broader consultation project, to help create a climate for innovation in an organization that felt a need to become more flexible to respond to its increasingly dynamic business environment. This Swiss Chemical Company consisted of many different business units, geographical units, and functional groups. It was eventually merged with the Sandoz Company and is today part of Novartis.

As I got to know more about Ciba-Geigy's many units and problems, I observed that some very innovative things were going on in many places in the company. I wrote several memos describing these innovations, added other ideas from my own experience, and gave the memos to my contact person in the company with the request that he distribute them to the various business unit and geographical managers who needed to be made aware of these ideas.

After some months, I discovered that those managers to whom I had personally given the memo thought it was helpful and on target, but rarely, if ever, did they pass it on, and none were ever distributed by my contact person. I also suggested meetings of managers from different units to stimulate lateral communication but found no support at all for such meetings. No matter what I did, I could not seem to get information flowing laterally across divisional, functional, or geographical boundaries. Yet everyone agreed in principle that innovation would be stimulated by more lateral communication and encouraged me to keep on "helping." Why did my helpful memos not circulate?

Cambridge-at-Home

This third example is quite different. Two years ago I was involved in the creation of an organization devoted to allowing people to stay in their homes as they aged. The founding group of ten older residents of Cambridge asked me to chair the meetings to design this new organization. To build strong consensus and commitment, I wanted to be sure that everyone's voice would be heard even if that slowed down the meetings. I resisted Robert's Rules of Order in favor of a consensus building style, which was much slower but honored everyone's point of view. I discovered that this consensus approach polarized the group into those who were comfortable with the more open style and those who thought I was running the "worst meetings ever." What was going on here?

Amoco

In the fourth example, Amoco, a large oil company that was eventually acquired by British Petroleum, decided to centralize all of its engineering functions into a single service unit. Whereas engineers had previously been regular full-time members of projects, they were now supposed to "sell their services" to clients who would be charged for these services. The engineers would now be "internal consultants" who would be "hired" by the various projects. The engineers resisted this new arrangement violently, and many of them threatened to leave the organization. Why were they so resistant to the new organizational arrangements?

Alpha Power

In the fifth example, Alpha Power, an electric and gas utility that services a major urban area, was faced with becoming more environmentally responsible after being brought up on criminal charges for allegedly failing to report the presence of asbestos in one of its local units that suffered an accident. Electrical workers, whose "heroic" self-image of keeping the power on no matter what, also held the strong norm that one did not report spills and other environmental and safety problems if such reports would embarrass the group. I was involved in a multi-year project to change this self-image to one where the "heroic" model was to report all safety and environmental hazards even if that meant reporting on peers and even bosses. A new concept of personal responsibility, teamwork, and openness of communication was to be adopted. Reporting on and dealing with environmental events became routine, but no matter how clear the new mandate was, some safety problems continued if peer group relations were involved. Why? What could be more important than employee and public safety?

How Does the Concept of Culture Help?

I did not really understand the forces operating in any of these cases until I began to examine my own assumptions about how things should work in these organizations and began to test whether my assumptions fitted those operating in my client systems. This step of examining the *shared* assumptions in an organization or group and comparing them to your own takes us into "cultural" analysis and will be the focus from here on.

It turned out that in DEC, senior managers and most of the other members of the organization shared the assumption that you cannot determine whether or not something is "true" or "valid" unless you subject the idea or proposal to intensive debate. Only ideas that survive such debate are worth acting on, and only ideas that survive such scrutiny will be implemented. The group members assumed that what they were doing was discovering truth, and, in this context, being polite to each other was relatively unimportant. I become more helpful to the group when I realized this and went to the flip chart and just started to write down the various ideas they were processing. If someone was interrupted, I could ask him or her to restate his or her point instead of punishing the interrupter. The group began to focus on the items on the chart and found that this really did help their communication and decision process. I had finally understood and accepted an essential element of their culture instead of imposing my own. By this intervention of going to the flip chart, I had changed the *microculture* of their group to enable them to accomplish what their organizational culture dictated.

In Ciba-Geigy, I eventually discovered that there was a strong shared assumption that each manager's job was his or her private "turf" not to be infringed on. The strong image was communicated that "a person's job is like his or her home, and if someone gives unsolicited information, it is like walking into someone's home uninvited." Sending memos to people implies that they do not already know what is in the memo, which is seen to be potentially insulting. In this organization, managers prided themselves on knowing whatever they needed to know to do their job. Had I understood this aspect of their culture, I would have asked for a list of the names of the managers and sent the memo directly to them. They would have accepted it from me because I was the paid consultant and expert.

In my Cambridge meetings, different members had different prior experiences in meetings. Those who had grown up with a formal Robert's Rules of Order system on various other nonprofit boards were adamant that this was the only way to run a meeting. Others who had no history on other boards were more tolerant of my informal style. The members had come from different subcultures that did not mesh. In my human relations training culture, I had learned the value of involving people to get better implementation of decisions and was trying to build that kind of microculture in this group. Only when I adapted my style to theirs was I able to begin to shape the group more toward my preferred style.

In Amoco, I began to understand the resistance of the engineers when I learned that their assumptions were "good work should speak for itself," and "engineers should not have to go out and sell themselves." They were used to having people come to them for services and did not have a good role model for how to sell themselves.

In Alpha, I learned that in the safety area, all work units had strong norms and values of self-protection that often over-rode the new requirements imposed on the company by the courts. The groups had their own experience base for what was safe and what was not safe and were willing to trust that. On the other hand, identifying environmental hazards and cleaning them up involved new skills that workers were willing to learn and collaborate on. The union had its own cultural assumption that under no conditions would one "rat out" a fellow union member, and this applied especially in the safety area.

In each of these cases, I initially did not understand what was going on because my own basic assumptions about truth, turf, and group relations differed from the shared assumptions of the members of the organization or group. And my assumptions reflected my "occupation" as a social psychologist and organization consultant, while the group's assumptions reflected in part their occupations and experiences as electrical engineers, chemists, nonprofit organization board members, and electrical workers.

To make sense of such situations requires taking a "cultural perspective," learning to see the world through "cultural lenses," becoming competent in "cultural analysis" by which I mean being able to perceive and decipher the cultural forces that operate in groups, organizations, and occupations. When we learn to see the world through cultural lenses, all kinds of things begin to make sense that initially were mysterious, frustrating, or seemingly stupid.

Culture: An Empirically Based Abstraction

Culture as a concept has had a long and checkered history. Laymen have used it as a word to indicate sophistication, as when we say that someone is very "cultured." Anthropologists have used it to refer to the customs and rituals that societies develop over the course of their history. In the past several decades, some organizational researchers and managers have used it to describe the norms and practices that organizations develop around their handling of people or as the espoused values and credo of an organization. This sometimes confuses the concept of culture with the concept of climate, and confuses culture as what *is* with culture as *what ought to be*.

Thus managers speak of developing the "right kind of culture," a "culture of quality," or a "culture of customer service," suggesting that culture has to do with certain values that managers are trying to inculcate in their organizations. Also implied in this usage is the assumption that there are better or worse cultures, stronger or weaker cultures, and that the "right" kind of culture would influence how effective organizations are. In the managerial literature, there is often the implication that having a culture is necessary for effective performance, and that the stronger the culture, the more effective the organization.

Researchers have supported some of these views by reporting findings that certain cultural dimensions do correlate with economic performance, but this research is hard to evaluate because of the many definitions of culture and the variety of indexes of performance that are used (Wilderom, Glunk, and Maslowski, 2000). Consultants and researchers have touted "culture surveys" and have claimed that they can improve organizational performance by helping organizations create certain kinds of cultures, but these claims are often based on a very different definition of culture than the one I will be arguing for here (Denison, 1990; Sackman and Bertelsman, 2006). As we will see, whether or not a culture is "good" or "bad," "functionally effective," or not, depends not on the culture alone but on the relationship of the culture to the environment in which it exists.

Perhaps the most intriguing aspect of culture as a concept is that it points us to phenomena that are below the surface, that are powerful in their impact but invisible and to a considerable degree unconscious. Culture creates within us mindsets and frames of reference that Marshak (2006) identified as one of a number of important *covert* processes. In another sense, culture is to a group what personality or character is to an individual. We can see the behavior that results, but we often cannot see the forces underneath that cause certain kinds of behavior. Yet, just as our personality and character guide and constrain our behavior, so does culture guide and constrain the behavior of members of a group through the shared norms that are held in that group.

Culture as a concept is thus an abstraction. If an abstract concept is to be useful to our thinking, it should be observable yet increase our understanding of a set of events that are otherwise mysterious or not well understood. From this point of view, I will argue that we must avoid the superficial models of culture and build on the deeper, more complex anthropological models. Those models refer to a wide range of observable events and underlying forces, as shown in the following list.

- **Observed behavioral regularities when people interact:** The language they use, the customs and traditions that evolve, and the rituals they employ in a wide variety of situations (for example, Goffman, 1959, 1967; Jones and others, 1988; Trice and Beyer, 1993; Van Maanen, 1979b).

- **Group norms:** The implicit standards and values that evolve in working groups, such as the particular norm of "a fair day's work for a fair day's pay" that evolved among workers in the Bank Wiring Room in the Hawthorne studies (for example, Homans, 1950; Kilmann and Saxton, 1983).

- **Espoused values:** The articulated publicly announced principles and values that the group claims to be trying to achieve, such as "product quality" or "price leadership" (for example, Deal and Kennedy, 1982, 1999).

- **Formal philosophy:** The broad policies and ideological principles that guide a group's actions toward stockholders, employees, customers, and other stakeholders such as the highly publicized "HP Way" of the Hewlett-Packard Co. (for example, Ouchi, 1981; Pascale and Athos, 1981; Packard, 1995).

- **"Rules of the game":** The implicit, unwritten rules for getting along in the organization, "the ropes" that a newcomer must learn to become an accepted member, "the way we do things around here" (for example, Schein, 1968, 1978; Van Maanen, 1976, 1979b; Ritti and Funkhouser, 1987).

- **Climate:** The feeling that is conveyed in a group by the physical layout and the way in which members of the organization interact with each other, with customers, or with other outsiders (for example, Ashkanasy, and others 2000; Schneider, 1990; Tagiuri and Litwin, 1968).

- **Embedded skills:** The special competencies displayed by group members in accomplishing certain tasks, the ability to make certain things that get passed on from generation to generation without necessarily being articulated in writing (for example, Argyris and Schon, 1978; Cook and Yanow, 1993; Henderson and Clark, 1990; Peters and Waterman, 1982; Ang and Van Dyne, 2008).

- **Habits of thinking, mental models, and/or linguistic paradigms:** The shared cognitive frames that guide the perceptions, thought, and language used by the members of a group and are taught to new members in the early socialization process (for example, Douglas, 1986; Hofstede, 1991, 2001; Van Maanen, 1979b; Senge, Roberts, Ross, Smith, and Kleiner, 1994).

- **"Shared meanings":** The emergent understandings that are created by group members as they interact with each other (for example, Geertz, 1973; Smircich, 1983; Van Maanen and Barley, 1984; Weick, 1995, Weick and Sutcliffe, 2001; Hatch and Schultz, 2004).

- **"Root metaphors" or integrating symbols:** The ways that groups evolve to characterize themselves, which may or may not be appreciated consciously, but that get embodied in buildings, office layouts, and other material artifacts of the group. This level of the culture reflects the emotional and aesthetic response of members as contrasted with the cognitive or evaluative response (for example, Gagliardi, 1990; Hatch, 1990; Pondy, Frost, Morgan, and Dandridge, 1983; Schultz, 1995).

- **Formal rituals and celebrations:** The ways in which a group celebrates key events that reflect important values or important "passages" by members such as promotion, completion of important projects, and milestones (Trice and Beyer, 1993, Deal and Kennedy, 1982, 1999).

All of these concepts and phenomena relate to culture and/or reflect culture in that they deal with things that group members share or hold in common, but none of them can usefully be thought of as *the* culture of a country, organization, occupation, or group. You might wonder why we need the word *culture* at all when we have so many other concepts such as norms, values, behavior patterns, rituals, traditions, and so on. However, the word *culture* adds several other critical elements to the concept of sharing. The concept of culture implies structural stability, depth, breadth, and patterning or integration.

Structural Stability

Culture implies some level of structural stability in the group. When we say that something is "cultural" we imply that it is not only shared but also stable because it defines the group. After we achieve a sense of group identity, which is a key component of culture, it is our major stabilizing force and will not be given up easily. Culture is something that survives even when some members of the organization depart. Culture is hard to change because group members value stability in that it provides meaning and predictability.

Depth

Culture is the deepest, often unconscious part of a group and is therefore less tangible and less visible. From this point of view, most of the categories used to describe culture listed earlier can be thought of as *manifestations* of culture, but they are not the "essence" of what we mean by culture. Note that when something is more deeply embedded that also lends stability.

Breadth

A third characteristic of culture is that after it has developed, it covers *all* of a group's functioning. Culture is pervasive and influences all aspects of how an organization deals with its primary task, its various environments, and its internal operations. Not all groups have cultures in this sense, but the concept connotes that if we refer to "the culture" of a group, we are referring to all of its operations.

Patterning or Integration

The fourth characteristic that is implied by the concept of culture and that further lends stability is patterning or integration of the elements into a larger paradigm or "Gestalt" that ties together the various elements and resides at a deeper level. Culture implies that rituals, climate, values, and behaviors tie together into a coherent whole, and this pattern or integration is the essence of what we mean by "culture." Such patterning or integration ultimately derives from the human need to make our environment as sensible and orderly as we can (Weick, 1995). Disorder or senselessness makes us anxious, so we will work hard to reduce that anxiety by developing a more consistent and predictable view of how things are and how they should be. Thus: "Organizational cultures, like other cultures, develop as groups of people struggle to make sense of and cope with their worlds" (Trice and Beyer, 1993, p. 4).

How then should we think about this "essence" of culture, and how should we formally define it? The most useful way to arrive at a definition of something as abstract as culture is to think in dynamic evolutionary terms. If we can understand where culture comes from, how it evolves, then we can grasp something that is abstract, that exists in a group's unconscious, yet that has powerful influences on a group's behavior.

Any social unit that has some kind of shared history will have evolved a culture. The strength of that culture depends on the length of time, the stability of membership of the group, and the emotional intensity of the actual historical experiences they have shared. We all have a common-sense notion of this phenomenon, yet it is difficult to define it abstractly. The formal definition that I propose and will work with builds on this evolutionary perspective and argues that the most fundamental characteristic of culture is that it is a product of social *learning*.

Culture Formally Defined

The culture of a group can now be defined as a pattern of shared basic assumptions learned by a group as it solved its problems of external adaptation and internal integration, which has worked well enough to be considered valid and, therefore, to be taught to new members as the correct way to perceive, think, and feel in relation to those problems.

Culture by this definition tends toward patterning and integration. But a given group may not have the kind of learning experiences that allow it to evolve a culture in this sense. There may be major turnover in leaders or members, the mission or primary task may change, the underlying technology on which the group is built may evolve, or the group may split into subgroups that develop their own subcultures leading to what Joanne Martin and her colleagues define as *differentiated* cultures and/or *fragmented* cultures (Martin, 2002).

We all know of groups, organizations, and societies where there are beliefs and values that work at cross purposes with other beliefs and values leading to situations full of conflict and ambiguity. But if the concept of culture is to have any utility, it should draw our attention to those things that are the product of our human need for stability, consistency, and meaning. Culture formation, therefore, is always, by definition, a striving toward patterning and integration, even though in many groups, their actual history of experiences prevents them from ever achieving a clear-cut unambiguous paradigm.

Culture Content

If a group's culture is that group's accumulated learning, how do we describe and catalogue the content of that learning? Group and organizational theories distinguish two major sets of problems that all groups, no matter what their size, must deal with: (1) Survival, growth, and adaptation in their environment; and (2) Internal integration that permits daily functioning and the ability to adapt and learn. Both of these areas of group functioning will reflect the macrocultural context in which the group exists and from which are derived broader and deeper basic assumptions about the nature of reality, time, space, human nature, and human relationships. Each of these areas will be explained in detail in later chapters.

The Process of Socialization or Acculturation

After a group has a culture, it will pass elements of this culture on to new generations of group members (Louis, 1980; Schein, 1968; Van Maanen, 1976; Van Maanen and Schein, 1979). Studying what new members of groups are taught is, in fact, a good way to discover some of the elements of a culture, but we only learn about surface aspects of the culture by this means. This is especially so because much of what is at the heart of a culture will not be revealed in the rules of behavior taught to newcomers. It will only be revealed to members as they gain permanent status and are allowed into the inner circles of the group where group secrets then are shared.

On the other hand, *how* people learn and the socialization processes to which they are subjected may indeed reveal deeper assumptions. To get at those deeper levels, we must try to understand the perceptions and feelings that arise in critical situations, and we must observe and interview regular members or "old timers" to get an accurate sense of the deeper-level assumptions that are shared.

Can culture be learned through anticipatory socialization or self-socialization? Can new members discover for themselves what the basic assumptions are? Yes and no. We certainly know that one of the major activities of any new member when she or he enters a new group is to decipher the operating norms and assumptions. But this deciphering can only be successful through the rewards and punishments that are meted out by old members to new members as they experiment with different kinds of behavior. In this sense, there is always a teaching process going on, even though it may be quite implicit and unsystematic.

If the group does not have shared assumptions, as will sometimes be the case, the new members' interaction with old members will be a more creative process of building a culture. But once shared assumptions exist, the culture survives through teaching them to newcomers. In this regard, culture is a mechanism of social control and can be the basis of explicitly manipulating members into perceiving, thinking, and feeling in certain ways (Van Maanen and Kunda, 1989; Kunda, 1992). Whether or not we approve of this as a mechanism of social control is a separate question that will be addressed later.

Can Culture Be Inferred from Only Behavior?

Note that the definition of culture that I have given does not include overt behavior patterns, though some such behavior, especially formal rituals, would reflect cultural assumptions. Instead, this definition emphasizes that the shared assumptions deal with how we perceive, think about, and feel about things. We cannot rely on overt behavior alone because it is always determined both by the cultural predisposition (the perceptions, thoughts, and feelings that are patterned) and by the situational contingencies that arise from the immediate external environment.

Behavioral regularities can occur for reasons other than culture. For example, if we observe that all members of a group cower in the presence of a large and loud leader, this could be based on biological reflex reactions to sound and size, individual learning, or shared learning. Such a behavioral regularity should not, therefore, be the basis for defining culture, though we might later discover that, in a given group's experience, cowering is indeed a result of shared learning and therefore a manifestation of deeper shared assumptions. Or, to put it another way, when we observe behavioral regularities, we do not know whether or not we are dealing with a cultural manifestation. Only after we have discovered the deeper layers that I am defining as the essence of culture can we specify what is and what is not an "artifact" that reflects the culture.

Do Occupations Have Cultures?

The definition provided previously does not specify the size or location of the social unit to which it can legitimately be applied. We know that nations, ethnic groups, religions, and other kinds of social units have cultures in this sense. I called these *macrocultures*. Our experience with large organizations also tells us that even globally dispersed corporations such as IBM or Unilever have corporate cultures in spite of the obvious presence of many diverse subcultures within the larger organization.

But it is not clear whether it makes sense to say that medicine or law or accounting or engineering have cultures. If culture is a product of joint learning leading to shared assumptions about how to perform and relate internally, then we can see clearly that many occupations do evolve cultures. If there is strong socialization during the education and training period and if the beliefs and values learned during this time remain stable as taken-for-granted assumptions even though the person may not be in a group of occupational peers, then clearly those occupations have cultures. For most of the occupations that will concern us, these cultures are global to the extent that members are trained in the same way to the same skill set and values. However, we will find that macrocultures also influence how occupations are defined, that is, how engineering or medicine is practiced in a particular country. These variations make it that much more difficult to decipher in a hospital, for example, what is national, ethnic, occupational, or organizational.

Summary and Conclusions

In this chapter, I have introduced the concept of culture and have argued that it helps to explain some of the more seemingly incomprehensible and irrational aspects of what goes on in groups, occupations, organizations, and other kinds of social units that have common histories. I reviewed the variety of elements that people perceive to be "culture," leading to a formal definition that puts the emphasis on shared learning experiences that lead to shared, taken-for-granted basic assumptions held by the members of the group or organization.

In this sense, any group with a stable membership and a history of shared learning will have developed some level of culture, but a group that either has had a great deal of turnover of members and leaders or a history lacking in any kind of challenging events may well lack any shared assumptions. Not every collection of people develops a culture, and, in fact, we tend to use the terms "group," "team," or "community" rather than "crowd" or "collection of people" only when there has been enough of a shared history so that some degree of culture formation has taken place.

After a set of shared assumptions has come to be taken for granted it determines much of the group's behavior, and the rules and norms that are taught to newcomers in a socialization process that is a reflection of culture. We noted that to define culture, we must go below the behavioral level because behavioral regularities can be caused by forces other than culture. We noted that even large organizations can have a common culture if there has been enough of a history of shared experience.

We also noted that culture and leadership are two sides of the same coin in that leaders first start the process of culture creation when they create groups and organizations. After cultures exist, they determine the criteria for leadership and thus determine who will or will not be a leader. But if elements of a culture become dysfunctional, it is the unique function of leadership to perceive the functional and dysfunctional elements of the existing culture and to manage cultural evolution and change in such a way that the group can survive in a changing environment. The bottom line for leaders is that if they do not become conscious of the cultures in which they are embedded, those cultures will manage them. Cultural understanding is desirable for all of us, but it is essential to leaders if they are to lead.

2

THE THREE LEVELS OF CULTURE

The purpose of this chapter is to show that culture can be analyzed at several different levels, with the term *level* meaning the degree to which the cultural phenomenon is visible to the observer. Some of the confusion surrounding the definition of what culture really is results from not differentiating the levels at which it manifests itself. These levels range from the very tangible overt manifestations that you can see and feel to the deeply embedded, unconscious, basic assumptions that I am defining as the essence of culture. In between these layers are various espoused beliefs, values, norms, and rules of behavior that members of the culture use as a way of depicting the culture to themselves and others.

Many other culture researchers prefer the term *basic values* to describe the deepest levels. I prefer *basic assumptions* because these tend to be taken for granted by group members and are treated as nonnegotiable. Values are open to discussion, and people can agree to disagree about them. Basic assumptions are so taken for granted that someone who does not hold them is viewed as a "foreigner" or as "crazy" and is automatically dismissed.

The three major levels of cultural analysis are shown in Exhibit 2.1.

Artifacts

At the surface is the level of artifacts, which includes all the phenomena that you would see, hear, and feel when you encounter a new group with an unfamiliar culture. Artifacts include the visible products of the group, such as the architecture of its physical environment; its language; its technology and products; its artistic creations; its style, as embodied in clothing, manners of address, and emotional displays; its myths and stories told about the organization; its published lists of values; and its observable rituals and ceremonies.

Exhibit 2.1.   The Three Levels of Culture.

---

1. Artifacts
- Visible and feelable structures and processes
- Observed behavior
  - Difficult to decipher

2. Espoused Beliefs and Values
- Ideals, goals, values, aspirations
- Ideologies
- Rationalizations
  - May or may not be congruent with behavior and other artifacts

3. Basic Underlying Assumptions
- Unconscious, taken-for-granted beliefs and values
  - Determine behavior, perception, thought, and feeling

Among these artifacts is the "climate" of the group. Some culture analysts see climate as the equivalent to culture, but it is better thought of as the product of some of the underlying assumptions and is, therefore, a manifestation of the culture. Observed behavior is also an artifact as are the organizational processes by which such behavior is made routine. Structural elements such as charters, formal descriptions of how the organization works, and organization charts also fall into the artifact level.

The most important point to be made about this level of the culture is that it is both easy to observe and very difficult to decipher. The Egyptians and the Mayans both built highly visible pyramids, but the meaning of pyramids in each culture was very different—tombs in one, temples as well as tombs in the other. In other words, observers can describe what they see and feel but cannot reconstruct from that alone what those things mean in the given group. Some culture analysts argue that among the artifacts, you find important symbols that reflect deep assumptions of the culture, but symbols are ambiguous, and you can only test a person's insight into what something may mean if the person has also experienced the culture at the deeper level of assumptions (Gagliardi, 1990, 1999).

It is especially dangerous to try to infer the deeper assumptions from artifacts alone because a person's interpretations will inevitably be projections of his or her own feelings and reactions. For example, when you see a very informal, loose organization, you may interpret that as "inefficient" if your own background is based on the assumption that informality means playing around and not working. Or, alternatively, if you see a very formal organization, you may interpret that to be a sign of "lack of innovative capacity" if your own experience is based on the assumption that formality means bureaucracy and standardization.

If the observer lives in the group long enough, the meanings of artifacts gradually become clear. If, however, you want to achieve this level of understanding more quickly, you must talk to insiders to analyze the espoused values, norms, and rules that provide the day-to-day operating principles by which the members of the group guide their behavior. This kind of inquiry takes you to the next level of cultural analysis.

Espoused Beliefs and Values

All group learning ultimately reflects someone's original beliefs and values, his or her sense of what ought to be, as distinct from what is. When a group is first created or when it faces a new task, issue, or problem, the first solution proposed to deal with it reflects some individual's own assumptions about what is right or wrong, what will work or not work. Those individuals who prevail, who can influence the group to adopt a certain approach to the problem, will later be identified as leaders or founders, but the group does not yet have any shared knowledge as a group because it has not yet taken a common action in reference to whatever it is supposed to do. Whatever is proposed will only be perceived as what the leader wants. Until the group has taken some joint action and together observed the outcome of that action, there is not as yet a shared basis for determining whether what the leader wants will turn out to be valid.

For example, if sales begin to decline in a young business, a manager may say, "We must increase advertising" because of her belief that advertising always increases sales. The group, never having experienced this situation before, will hear that assertion as a statement of that manager's beliefs and values: "She believes that when one is in trouble it is a good thing to increase advertising." What the leader initially proposes, therefore, cannot have any status other than a value to be questioned, debated, challenged, and tested.

If the manager convinces the group to act on her belief, the solution works, and the group has a shared perception of that success, then the perceived value that "advertising is good" gradually becomes transformed: first into a *shared value or belief* and ultimately into a *shared assumption* (if actions based on it continue to be successful). If this transformation process occurs, group members will tend to forget that originally they were not sure and that the proposed course of action was at an earlier time just a proposal to be debated and confronted.

Not all beliefs and values undergo such transformation. First of all, the solution based on a given value may not work reliably. Only those beliefs and values that can be empirically tested and that continue to work reliably in solving the group's problems will become transformed into assumptions. Second, certain value domains—those dealing with the less controllable elements of the environment or with aesthetic or moral matters—may not be testable at all. In such cases, consensus through social validation is still possible, but it is not automatic. Third, the strategy/goals of the organization may fall into this category of espoused beliefs in that there may be no way of testing it except through consensus because the link between performance and strategy may be hard to prove.

Social validation means that certain beliefs and values are confirmed only by the shared social experience of a group. For example, any given culture cannot prove that its religion and moral system are superior to another culture's religion and moral system, but if the members reinforce each others' beliefs and values, they come to be taken for granted. Those who fail to accept such beliefs and values run the risk of "excommunication"—of being thrown out of the group. The test of whether they work or not is how comfortable and anxiety free members are when they abide by them.

In these realms, the group learns that certain beliefs and values, as initially promulgated by prophets, founders, and leaders, "work" in the sense of reducing uncertainty in critical areas of the group's functioning. And, as they continue to provide meaning and comfort to group members, they also become transformed into nondiscussible assumptions even though they may not be correlated to actual performance. The espoused beliefs and moral/

ethical rules remain conscious and are explicitly articulated because they serve the normative or moral function of guiding members of the group in how to deal with certain key situations, and in training new members how to behave. Such beliefs and values often become embodied in an ideology or organizational philosophy, which then serves as a guide to dealing with the uncertainty of intrinsically uncontrollable or difficult events.

If the beliefs and values that provide meaning and comfort to the group are not congruent with the beliefs and values that correlate with effective performance, we will observe in many organizations espoused values that reflect the desired behavior but are not reflected in observed behavior (Argyris and Schon, 1978, 1996). For example, a company's ideology may say that it values people and that it has high quality standards for its products, but its actual record in that regard may contradict what it says. In U.S. organizations, it is common to espouse *teamwork* while actually rewarding *individual competitiveness*. Hewlett-Packard's highly touted "The HP Way" espoused consensus management and teamwork, but in its computer division, engineers discovered that to get ahead they had to be competitive and political (Packard, 1995).

So in analyzing espoused beliefs and values, you must discriminate carefully among those that are congruent with the underlying assumptions that guide performance, those that are part of the ideology or philosophy of the organization, and those that are rationalizations or only aspirations for the future. Often espoused beliefs and values are so abstract that they can be mutually contradictory, as when a company claims to be equally concerned about stockholders, employees, and customers, or when it claims both highest quality and lowest cost. Espoused beliefs and values often leave large areas of behavior unexplained, leaving us with a feeling that we understand a piece of the culture but still do not have the culture as such in hand. To get at that deeper level of understanding, to decipher the pattern, and to predict future behavior correctly, we have to understand more fully the category of basic assumptions.

Basic Underlying Assumptions

When a solution to a problem works repeatedly, it comes to be taken for granted. What was once a hypothesis, supported only by a hunch or a value, gradually comes to be treated as a reality. We come to believe that nature really works this way. Basic assumptions, in this sense, are different from what some anthropologists called "dominant value orientations" in that such dominant orientations reflect the *preferred* solution among several basic alternatives, but all the alternatives are still visible in the culture, and any given member of the culture could, from time to time, behave according to variant as well as dominant orientations (Kluckhohn and Strodtbeck, 1961).

Basic assumptions, in the sense defined here, have become so taken for granted that you find little variation within a social unit. This degree of consensus results from repeated success in implementing certain beliefs and values, as previously described. In fact, if a basic assumption comes to be strongly held in a group, members will find behavior based on any other premise inconceivable. For example, in a group whose basic assumption is that the individual's rights supersede those of the group, members find it inconceivable to commit suicide or in some other way sacrifice themselves to the group even if they had dishonored the group. In a capitalist country, it is inconceivable that someone might design a business organization to operate consistently at a financial loss or that it does not matter whether or not a product works. In an occupation such as engineering, it is inconceivable to deliberately design something that is unsafe; it is a taken-for-granted assumption that things should be safe. Basic assumptions, in this sense, are similar to what Argyris and Schon identified as "theories-in-use"—the implicit assumptions that actually guide behavior, that tell group members how to perceive, think about, and feel about things (Argyris and Schon, 1974, 1996).

Basic assumptions, like theories-in-use, tend to be nonconfrontable and nondebatable, and hence are extremely difficult to change. To learn something new in this realm requires us to resurrect, reexamine, and possibly change some of the more stable portions of our cognitive structure—a process that Argyris and others have called "double-loop learning," or "frame breaking" (Argyris, Putnam, and Smith, 1985; Bartunek, 1984). Such learning is intrinsically difficult because the reexamination of basic assumptions temporarily destabilizes our cognitive and interpersonal world, releasing large quantities of basic anxiety.

Rather than tolerating such anxiety levels, we tend to want to perceive the events around us as congruent with our assumptions, even if that means distorting, denying, projecting, or in other ways falsifying to ourselves what may be going on around us. It is in this psychological process that culture has its ultimate power. Culture as a set of basic assumptions defines for us what to pay attention to, what things mean, how to react emotionally to what is going on, and what actions to take in various kinds of situations. After we have developed an integrated set of such assumptions—a "thought world" or "mental map"—we will be maximally comfortable with others who share the same set of assumptions and very uncomfortable and vulnerable in situations where different assumptions operate because either we will not understand what is going on, or, worse, we will misperceive and misinterpret the actions of others (Douglas, 1986; Bushe, 2009).

The human mind needs cognitive stability. Therefore, any challenge or questioning of a basic assumption will release anxiety and defensiveness. In this sense, the shared basic assumptions that make up the culture of a group can be thought of both at the individual and group level as psychological cognitive defense mechanisms that permit the group to continue to function. At the same time, culture at this level provides its members with a basic sense of identity and defines the values that provide self-esteem (Hatch and Schultz, 2004). Cultures tell their members who they are, how to behave toward each other, and how to feel good about themselves. Recognizing these critical functions makes us aware why "changing" culture is so anxiety provoking.

To illustrate how unconscious assumptions can distort data, consider the following example. If we assume, on the basis of past experience or education, that other people will take advantage of us whenever they have an opportunity, we expect to be taken advantage of, and we then interpret the behavior of others in a way that coincides with those expectations. We observe people sitting in a seemingly idle posture at their desk and interpret their behavior as "loafing" rather than "thinking out an important problem." We perceive absence from work as "shirking" rather than "doing work at home."

If this is not only a personal assumption but also one that is shared and thus part of the culture of an organization, we will discuss with others what to do about our "lazy" workforce and institute tight controls to ensure that people are at their desks and busy. If employees suggest that they do some of their work at home, we will be uncomfortable and probably deny the request because we will figure that at home they would loaf (Bailyn, 1992; Perin, 1991).

In contrast, if we assume that everyone is highly motivated and competent, we will act in accordance with that assumption by encouraging people to work at their own pace and in their own way. If we see someone sitting quietly at their desk, we will assume that they are thinking or planning. If someone is discovered to be unproductive in such an organization, we will make the assumption that there is a mismatch between the person and the job assignment, not that the person is lazy or incompetent. If employees want to work at home, we will perceive that as evidence of their wanting to be productive.

In both cases, there is the potential for distortion, in that the cynical manager will not perceive how highly motivated some of the subordinates really are, and the idealistic manager will not perceive that there are subordinates who are lazy and are taking advantage of the situation. As McGregor noted many decades ago, such assumptions about "human nature" become the basis of management and control systems that perpetuate themselves because if people are treated consistently in terms of certain basic assumptions, they come eventually to behave according to those assumptions to make their world stable and predictable (1960).

Unconscious assumptions sometimes lead to ridiculously tragic situations, as illustrated by a common problem experienced by U.S. supervisors in some Asian countries. A manager who comes from a U.S. pragmatic tradition assumes and takes it for granted that solving a problem always has the highest priority. When that manager encounters a subordinate who comes from a cultural tradition in which good relationships and protecting the superior's "face" are assumed to have top priority, the following scenario has often resulted.

The manager proposes a solution to a given problem. The subordinate knows that the solution will not work, but his unconscious assumption requires that he remain silent because to tell the boss that the proposed solution is wrong is a threat to the boss's face. It would not even occur to the subordinate to do anything other than remain silent or, if the boss were to inquire what the subordinate thought, to even reassure the boss to go ahead and take the action.

The action is taken, the results are negative, and the boss, somewhat surprised and puzzled, asks the subordinate what he would have done or would he have done something different. This question puts the subordinate into an impossible double bind because the answer itself is a threat to the boss's face. He cannot possibly explain his behavior without committing the very sin he was trying to avoid in the first place—namely, embarrassing the boss. He may even lie at this point and argue that what the boss did was right and only "bad luck" or uncontrollable circumstances prevented it from succeeding.

From the point of view of the subordinate, the boss's behavior is incomprehensible because to ask the subordinate what he would have done shows lack of self-pride, possibly causing the subordinate to lose respect for that boss. To the boss, the subordinate's behavior is equally incomprehensible. He cannot develop any sensible explanation of his subordinate's behavior that is not cynically colored by the assumption that the subordinate at some level just does not care about effective performance and therefore must be gotten rid of. It never occurs to the boss that another assumption—such as "you never embarrass a superior"—is operating, and that, to the subordinate, that assumption is even more powerful than "you get the job done."

If assumptions such as these operate only in an individual and represent her idiosyncratic experience, they can be corrected more easily because the person will detect that she is alone in holding a given assumption. The power of culture comes about through the fact that the assumptions are *shared* and, therefore, mutually reinforced. In these instances, probably only a third party or some cross-cultural experiences could help to find common ground whereby both parties could bring their implicit assumptions to the surface. And even after they have surfaced, such assumptions would still operate, forcing the boss and the subordinate to invent a whole new communication mechanism that would permit each to remain congruent with his or her culture—for example, agreeing that, before any decision is made and before the boss has stuck his neck out, the subordinate will be asked for suggestions and for factual data that would not be face threatening. Note that the solution has to keep each cultural assumption intact. We cannot, in these instances, simply declare one or the other cultural assumption "wrong." We have to find a third assumption to allow them both to retain their integrity.

I have dwelled on this long example to illustrate the potency of implicit, unconscious assumptions and to show that such assumptions often deal with fundamental aspects of life—the nature of time and space; human nature and human activities; the nature of truth and how we discover it; the correct way for the individual and the group to relate to each other; the relative importance of work, family, and self-development; the proper role of men and women; and the nature of the family.

These kinds of assumptions form the core of macrocultures and will be discussed in detail in Part II, The Dimensions of Culture. We do not develop new assumptions about each of these areas in every group or organization we join. Members of any new group will bring their own cultural learning from prior groups, from their education, and from their socialization into occupational communities, but as the new group develops its own shared history, it will develop modified or new assumptions in critical areas of its experience. It is those new assumptions that then make up the culture of that particular group.

Summary and Conclusions

Any group's culture can be studied at three levels—the level of its artifacts, the level of its espoused beliefs and values, and the level of its basic underlying assumptions. If you do not decipher the pattern of basic assumptions that may be operating, you will not know how to interpret the artifacts correctly or how much credence to give to the espoused values. In other words, the essence of a culture lies in the pattern of basic underlying assumptions, and after you understand those, you can easily understand the other more surface levels and deal appropriately with them.

Though the essence of a group's culture is its pattern of shared, basic taken-for-granted assumptions, the culture will manifest itself at the level of observable artifacts and shared espoused values, norms, and rules of behavior. In analyzing cultures, it is important to recognize that artifacts are easy to observe but difficult to decipher and that espoused beliefs and values may only reflect rationalizations or aspirations. To understand a group's culture, you must attempt to get at its shared basic assumptions and understand the learning process by which such basic assumptions evolve.

Leadership is originally the source of the beliefs and values that get a group moving in dealing with its internal and external problems. If what leaders propose works and continues to work, what once were only the leader's assumptions gradually come to be shared assumptions. When a set of shared basic assumptions is formed by this process, it defines the character and identity of the group and can function as a cognitive defense mechanism both for the individual members and for the group as a whole. In other words, individuals and groups seek stability and meaning. Once achieved, it is easier to distort new data by denial, projection, rationalization, or various other defense mechanisms than to change the basic assumption. As we will see, culture change, in the sense of changing basic assumptions, is difficult, time-consuming, and highly anxiety-provoking—a point that is especially relevant for the leader who sets out to change the culture of an organization.

The most central issue for leaders is to understand the deeper levels of a culture, to assess the functionality of the assumptions made at that level, and to deal with the anxiety that is unleashed when those assumptions are challenged.

3

CULTURES IN ORGANIZATIONS: TWO CASE EXAMPLES

In the previous chapter, I indicated in a rather abstract manner how to think about the complex concept of culture as it applies to groups and organizations. I emphasized the need to go beyond the surface levels of artifacts and espoused beliefs and values to the deeper, taken-for-granted shared basic assumptions that create the pattern of cognitions, perceptions, and feelings displayed by the members of the group. Unless we understand what is going on at this deeper level, we cannot really decipher the meaning of the more surface phenomena, and, worse, we might misinterpret them because of the likelihood that we will project our own cultural biases onto the observed phenomena.

In this chapter, I will illustrate this multilevel analysis by describing two companies with whom I worked for some period of time, permitting me to begin to identify some of the deep elements of their cultures. I say elements because it is not really possible to describe an entire culture, but I can describe enough elements to make some of the key phenomena in these companies comprehensible.

The Digital Equipment Corp.

Digital Equipment Corp. (DEC) is a major case running throughout this book because it not only illustrates aspects of how to describe and analyze organizational culture, but it also reveals some important cultural dynamics that explain both DEC's rise to the position of the number two computer company in the world and its rapid decline in the 1990s (Schein, 2003). I was a consultant to the founder, Ken Olsen, and to the various executive committees and engineering groups that ran the company from 1966 to 1992; therefore, I had a unique opportunity to see cultural dynamics in action over a long period of time. DEC was the first major company to introduce interactive computing and became a very successful manufacturer of what came to be called "mini computers." It was located primarily in the northeastern part of the United States, with headquarters in an old mill in Maynard, Massachusetts, but it had branches throughout the world. At its peak, it employed more than 100,000 people, with sales of $14 billion; in the mid-1980s it became the second largest computer manufacturer in the world after IBM. The company ran into major financial difficulties in the 1990s and was eventually sold to the Compaq Corp. in 1998. Compaq was in turn acquired by Hewlett-Packard in 2001.

Artifacts: Encountering the Company

To gain entry into any of DEC's many buildings, you had to sign in with a guard who sat behind a counter where there were usually several people chatting, moving in and out, checking the badges of employees who were coming into the building, accepting mail, and answering phone calls. After signing in, you waited in a small, casually furnished lobby until the person you were visiting came personally or sent a secretary to escort you.

What I recall most vividly from my first encounters with this organization some forty plus years ago is the ubiquitous open office architecture, the extreme informality of dress and manners, a very dynamic environment in the sense of rapid pace, and a high rate of interaction among employees, seemingly reflecting enthusiasm, intensity, energy, and impatience. As I would pass cubicles or conference rooms, I would get the impression of openness. There were very few doors. The company cafeteria spread out into a big open area where people sat at large tables, hopped from one table to another, and obviously were intensely involved in their work even at lunch. I also observed that there were many cubicles with coffee machines and refrigerators in them and that food seemed to be part of most meetings.

The physical layout and patterns of interaction made it very difficult to decipher who had what rank, and I was told that there were no status perquisites such as private dining rooms, special parking places, or offices with special views and the like. The furniture in the lobbies and offices was very inexpensive and functional, and the company was mostly headquartered in an old industrial building that had been converted for their use.

The informal clothing worn by most managers and employees reinforced this sense of economy and egalitarianism.

I had been brought into DEC to help the top management team improve communication and group effectiveness. As I began to attend the regular staff meetings of the senior management group, I was quite struck by the high level of interpersonal confrontation, argumentativeness, and conflict. Group members became highly emotional at the drop of a hat and seemed to get angry at each other, though it was also noticeable that such anger did not carry over outside the meeting.

With the exception of the president and founder, Ken Olsen, there were very few people who had visible status in terms of how people deferred to them. Olsen himself, through his informal behavior, implied that he did not take his position of power all that seriously. Group members argued as much with him as with each other and even interrupted him from time to time. His status did show up, however, in the occasional lectures he delivered to the group when he felt that members did not understand something or were "wrong" about something. At such times, Olsen could become very emotionally excited in a way that other members of the group never did.

My own reactions to the company and these meetings also have to be considered as artifacts to be documented. It was exciting to be attending top management meetings—and surprising to observe so much behavior that seemed to me dysfunctional. The level of confrontation I observed made me quite nervous, and I had a sense of not knowing what this was all about, as I indicated in the example in Chapter One. I learned from further observation that this style of running meetings was typical and that meetings were very common, to the point where people would complain about all the time spent in committees. At the same time, they would argue that without these committees, they could not get their work done properly.

The company was organized as a matrix, one of the earliest versions of this type of organization, in terms of functional units and product lines, but there was a sense of perpetual reorganization and a search for a structure that would "work better." Structure was viewed as something to tinker with until you got it right. There were many levels in the technical and managerial hierarchy, but I sensed that the hierarchy was just a convenience, not something to be taken very seriously. On the other hand, the communication structure was taken very seriously. There were many committees already in existence, and new ones were constantly being formed; the company had an extensive e-mail network that functioned worldwide, engineers and managers traveled frequently and were in constant telephone communication with each other, and Olsen would get upset if he observed any evidence of under-communication or miscommunication. To make communication and contact easier, DEC had its own "air force" of several planes and helicopters. Ken Olsen was a licensed pilot and flew his own plane to a retreat in Maine for recreation.

Many other artifacts from this organization will be described later, but for the present, this will suffice to give a flavor of what I encountered at DEC. The question now is, what does any of it mean? I knew what my emotional reactions were, but I did not really understand why these things were happening and what significance they had for members of the company. To gain some understanding, I had to get to the next level: the level of espoused beliefs and values.

Espoused Beliefs and Values

As I talked to people at DEC about my observations, especially those things that puzzled and scared me, I began to elicit some of the espoused beliefs and values by which the company ran. Many of these were embodied in slogans or in parables that Olsen wrote from time to time and circulated throughout the company. For example, a high value was placed on personal responsibility. If someone made a proposal to do something and it was approved, that person had a clear obligation to do it or, if it was not possible to do, to come back and renegotiate. The phrase "He who proposes, does" was frequently heard around the organization.

Employees at all levels were responsible for thinking about what they were doing and were enjoined at all times to "do the right thing," which, in many instances, meant being insubordinate. If the boss asked you to do something that you considered wrong or stupid, you were supposed to "push back" and attempt to change the boss's mind. If the boss insisted, and you still felt that it was not right, then you were supposed to not do it and take your chances on your own judgment. If you were wrong, you would get your wrist slapped but would gain respect for having stood up for your own convictions. Because bosses knew these rules, they were, of course, less likely to issue arbitrary orders, more likely to listen to you if you pushed back, and more likely to renegotiate the decision. So actual insubordination was rarely necessary, but the principle of thinking for yourself and doing the right thing was very strongly reinforced.

It was also a rule that you should not do things without getting "buy-in" from others who had to implement the decision, who had to provide needed services, or who would be influenced by it. Employees had to be very individualistic and, at the same time, very willing to be team players; hence, the simultaneous feeling that committees were a big drain on time but they could not do without them. To reach a decision and to get buy-in, the individual had to convince others of the validity of his or her idea and be able to defend it against every conceivable argument, which caused the high levels of confrontation and fighting that I observed in groups. However, after an idea had stood up to this level of debate and survived, it could then be moved forward and implemented because everyone was now convinced that it was the right thing to do. This took longer to achieve, but led to more consistent and rapid action. If somewhere down the hierarchy the decision "failed to stick" because someone was not convinced that it was "the right thing to do," that person had to push back, her arguments had to be heard, and either she had to be convinced or the decision had to be renegotiated up the hierarchy.

In asking people about their jobs, I discovered another strong value: each person should figure out what the essence of his or her job is and get very clear about it. Asking the boss what was expected was considered a sign of weakness. If your own job definition was out of line with what the group or department required, you would hear about it soon enough. The role of the boss was to set broad targets, but subordinates were expected to take initiative in figuring out how best to achieve them. This value required a lot of discussion and negotiation, which often led to complaints about time wasting, but, at the same time, everyone defended the value of doing things in this way and continued to defend it even though it created difficulties later in DEC's life.

I also found out that people could fight bitterly in group meetings, yet be very good friends. There was a feeling of being a tight-knit group, a kind of extended family under a strong father figure, Ken Olsen, which led to the norm that fighting does not mean that people dislike or disrespect each other. This norm seemed to extend even to "bad-mouthing" each other: People would call each other "stupid" behind each others' backs or say that someone was a real "turkey" or "jerk," yet they would respect each other in work situations. Olsen often criticized people in public, which made them feel embarrassed, but it was explained to me that this only meant that the person should work on improving his area of operations, not that he was really in disfavor. In fact, people quipped that it was better to have Ken criticize you than not to notice you. Even if someone fell into disfavor, he or she was viewed merely as being in the "penalty box"; stories were told of managers or engineers who had been in this kind of disfavor for long periods of time and then rebounded to become heroes in some other context.

When managers talked about their products, they emphasized quality and elegance. The company was founded by engineers and was dominated by an engineering mentality in that the value of a proposed new product was generally judged by whether the engineers themselves liked it and used it, not by external market surveys or test markets. In fact, customers were talked about in a rather disparaging way, especially those who might not be technically sophisticated enough to appreciate the elegance of the product that had been designed.

Olsen emphasized absolute integrity in designing, manufacturing, and selling. He viewed the company as highly ethical, and he strongly emphasized the work values associated with the Protestant work ethic—honesty, hard work, high standards of personal morality, professionalism, personal responsibility, integrity, and honesty. Especially important was being honest and truthful in their relations with each other and with customers. As this company grew and matured, it put many of these values into formal statements and taught them to new employees. They viewed their culture as a great asset and felt that the culture itself had to be taught to all new employees (Kunda, 1992).

Basic Assumptions: The DEC Paradigm

To understand the implications of these values and to show how they relate to overt behavior, we must seek the underlying assumptions and premises on which this organization was based (see Figures 3.1 and 3.2).

Figure 3.1.   DEC's Cultural Paradigm: Part One.

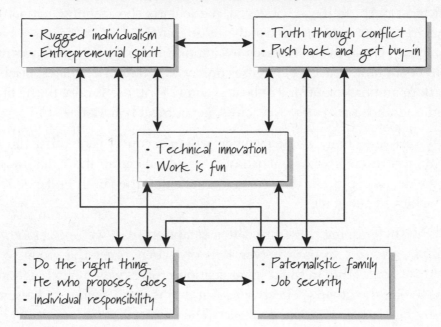

Copyright © E. H. Schein. *DEC Is Dead; Long Live DEC*. Berrett-Koehler, 2003.

The founding group, because of their engineering background, was intensely individualistic and pragmatic in its orientation. They developed a problem-solving and decision-making system that rested on five inter-locking assumptions:

1. The individual is ultimately the source of ideas and entrepreneurial spirit.

2. Individuals are capable of taking responsibility and doing the right thing.

3. No one individual is smart enough to evaluate his or her own ideas, so others should push back and get buy-in. (In effect, the group was say-ing that "truth" cannot be found without debate and that there is no arbitrary way of figuring out what is true unless one subjects every idea to the crucible of debate among strong and intelligent individuals, so individuals must get others to agree before taking action.)

4. The basic work of the company is technological innovation and such work is and always should be "fun."

Without understanding these first four assumptions, we cannot decipher most of the behavior observed, particularly the seeming incongruity between intense individualism and intense commitment to group work and consensus. The fifth interlocking assumption helps to explain how there could be simultaneously (1) intense conflict with authority figures, insubordination, and bad-mouthing of bosses; and (2) intense loyalty to the organization and personal affection across hierarchical boundaries.

5. We are one family whose members will take care of each other (implying that no matter how much of a troublemaker an individual was in the decision process, the person was valued in the family and could not be kicked out of it).

Only by grasping these first five assumptions can we understand, for example, why my initial interventions of trying to get the group to be "nicer" to each other in the communication process were politely ignored. I was seeing the group's "effectiveness" in terms of my values and assumptions of how a "good" group should act. The DEC senior management committee was trying to reach "truth" and make valid decisions in the only way they knew how and by a process that they believed in. The group was merely a means to an end; the real process going on in the group was a basic, deep search for solutions in which they could have confidence because they stood up even after intense debate.

After I shifted my focus to helping them in this search for valid solutions, I figured out what kinds of interventions would be more relevant, and I found that the group accepted them more readily. For example, I began to emphasize agenda setting, time management, clarifying some of the debate, summarizing, consensus testing after the debate was running dry, and a problem-solving process. The interrupting, the emotional conflicts, and the other behavior I observed initially continued, but the group became more effective in its handling of information and in reaching consensus. It was in this context that I gradually developed the philosophy of being a "process consultant" instead of trying to be an expert on how groups should work (Schein, 1969, 1988, 1999a, 2003).

As I learned more about DEC, I also learned that the cultural DNA contained another five key assumptions, shown in Figure 3.2. These five additional assumptions reflected some of the group's beliefs and values pertaining to customers and marketing:

Figure 3.2.   DEC's Cultural Paradigm: Part Two.

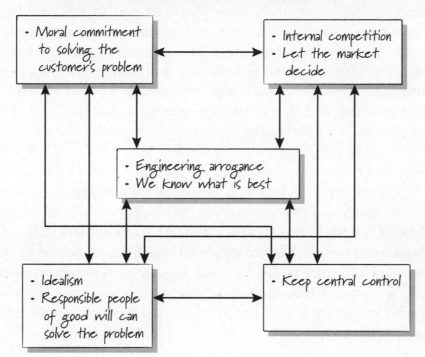

6. The only valid way to sell a product is to find out what the customer's problem is and to solve that problem, even if that means selling less or recommending another company's products.

7. People can and will take responsibility and continue to act responsibly no matter what.

8. The market is the best decision maker if there are several product contenders (internal competition was viewed as desirable throughout DEC's history).

9. Even as the company gets very large and differentiated, it is desirable to keep some central control rather than divisionalizing.

10. DEC engineers "know best" what a good product is, based on whether or not they personally like working with that product.

These ten assumptions can be thought of as the DEC cultural paradigm—its cultural DNA. What is important in showing these interconnections is the fact that single elements of the paradigm could not explain how this organization was able to function. It was only by seeing the *combination* of assumptions—around individual creativity, group conflict as the source of truth, individual responsibility, commitment to each other as a family, commitment to innovation and to solving customer problems, and belief in internal competition and central control—that the observable day-to-day behavior could be explained. It is this level of basic assumptions and their interconnections that defines some of the essence of the culture—the key genes of the cultural DNA.

How general was this paradigm in DEC? That is, if we were to study workers in the plants, salesmen in geographically remote units, engineers in technical enclaves, and so on, would we find the same assumptions operating? One of the interesting aspects of the DEC story is that at least for its first twenty or so years, this paradigm would have been observed in operation across all of its rank levels, functions, and geographies. But, as we will also see later, as DEC grew and evolved, some elements of the DEC culture began to change, and the paradigm no longer fit in some parts of the company.

Ciba-Geigy

The Ciba-Geigy Company in the late 1970s and early 1980s was a Swiss multidivisional, geographically decentralized chemical company with several divisions dealing with pharmaceuticals, agricultural chemicals, industrial chemicals, dyestuffs, and some technically based consumer products. It eventually merged with a former competitor, Sandoz, to become what is today Novartis. I was originally asked to give some talks at their 1979 annual meeting of top executives on the topic of innovation and creativity, and this encounter evolved into a variety of consulting activities that lasted into the mid-1980s.

Artifacts—Encountering Ciba-Geigy

My initial encounter with this company was through a telephone call from its head of management development, Dr. Jurg Leupold, inquiring whether I would be willing to give a talk to their annual meeting in Switzerland.

Ciba-Geigy ran annual meetings of their top forty to fifty executives world-wide and had a tradition of inviting one or two outsiders to the three-day meetings held at a Swiss resort. The purpose was to stimulate the group by having outside lecturers present on topics of interest to the company. Dr. Leupold asked me to give lectures and do some structured exercises to improve the group's understanding of creativity and to increase "innova-tion" and "leadership" in the company. Prior to the annual meeting, I was to visit the company headquarters to be briefed, to meet some other key executives—especially Dr. Sam Koechlin the CEO—and to review the other material that was to be presented at the annual meeting. I got the impression that things were highly organized and carefully planned.

I was "briefed" by further phone contacts and learned that the company was run by a board of directors and an internal executive committee of nine people who were legally accountable as a group for company decisions. The chairman of this executive committee, Sam Koechlin, functioned as the CEO, but the committee made most decisions by consensus.

Each member of the committee had oversight responsibility for a divi-sion, a function, and a geographic area, and these responsibilities rotated from time to time. Both Ciba and Geigy had long histories of growth and had merged in 1970. The merger was considered to be a success, but there were still strong identifications with the original companies, according to many managers. The CEO of Novartis when I asked him in 2006 how the Ciba-Geigy/Sandoz merger went said: "That merger is going fine but I still have Ciba people and Geigy people!"

My first visit to Ciba-Geigy offered a sharp contrast to what I had encountered at DEC. I was immediately struck by the formality as symbol-ized by large gray stone buildings, heavy doors that were always closed, and stiff uniformed guards in the main lobby. This spacious, opulent lobby was the main passageway for employees to enter the inner compound of office buildings and plants. It had high ceilings, large heavy doors, and a few pieces of expensive modern furniture in one corner to serve as a waiting area.

I reacted differently to the Ciba-Geigy and DEC environments. I liked the DEC environment more. In doing a cultural analysis, a person's reac-tions are themselves artifacts of the culture that must be acknowledged and taken into account. It is undesirable to present any cultural analysis with total objectivity because not only would this be impossible, but a person's emotional reactions and biases are also primary data to be analyzed and understood.

Upon entering the Ciba-Geigy lobby, I was asked by the uniformed guard to check in with another guard who sat in a glassed-in office. I had to give my name and state where I was from and whom I was visiting. The guard then asked me to take a seat while he did some telephoning and to wait until an escort could take me to my appointed place. As I sat and waited, I noticed that the guard seemed to know most of the employees who streamed through the lobby or went to elevators and stairs leading from it. I had the distinct feeling that any stranger would have been spotted immediately and would have been asked to report as I had been.

Dr. Leupold's secretary arrived in due course and took me up the elevator and down a long corridor of closed offices. Each office had a tiny nameplate that could be covered over by a hinged metal plate if the occupant wanted to remain anonymous. Above each office was a light bulb, some of which showed red and some green. I asked on a subsequent visit what this meant and was told that if the light was out the person was not in, if it was green it was okay to knock, whereas red meant that the person did not want to be disturbed under any circumstances.

We went around a corner and down another such corridor and did not see another soul during the entire time. When we reached Dr. Leupold's office, the secretary knocked discreetly. When he called to come in, she opened the door, ushered me in, then went to her own office and closed the door. I was offered some tea or coffee, which was brought by the secretary on a large formal tray with china accompanied by a small plate of excellent cookies. I mention that they were "excellent" because it turned out that good food was very much part of Ciba-Geigy's presented identity. Whenever I visited offices in later years in Paris and London, I was always taken to three star restaurants.

Following our meeting, Dr. Leupold took me to the executive dining room in another building, where we again passed guards. This was the equivalent of a first-class restaurant, with a hostess who clearly knew everyone, reserved tables, and provided discreet guidance on the day's specials. Aperitifs and wine were offered with lunch, and the whole meal took almost two hours. I was told that there was a less fancy dining room in still another building and an employee cafeteria as well, but that this dining room clearly had the best food and was the right place for senior management to conduct business and to bring visitors. Whereas in DEC kitchens and food were used as vehicles to get people to interact with each other, in Ciba-Geigy, food, drink, and graciousness had some additional symbolic meaning, possibly having to do with status and rank.

Various senior officers of the company were pointed out to me, and I noticed that whenever anyone greeted another, it was always with their formal titles, usually Dr. This or Dr. That. Observable differences in deference and demeanor made it fairly easy to determine who was superior to whom in the organization. It was also obvious that the tables in the room were assigned to executives on the basis of status and that the hostess knew exactly the relative status of all her guests.

Throughout my consultation, in moving around the company I always felt a hushed atmosphere in the corridors; a slower, more deliberate pace; and much more emphasis on planning, schedules, and punctuality. Whereas in DEC I got the impression of frantic activity to make the most of what time there was, in Ciba-Geigy time was carefully managed to maintain order. If I had an appointment with a manager at 2 P.M., the person I was with just prior to that meeting would start walking down the hall with me at 1:58 so that we would arrive almost exactly on the dot. Only rarely was I kept waiting if I arrived on time, and if I was even a few minutes late, I had the strong sense that I had to apologize and explain.

Ciba-Geigy managers came across as very serious, thoughtful, deliberate, well prepared, formal, and concerned about protocol. I learned later that whereas DEC allocated rank and salary fairly strictly to the actual job being performed by the individual, Ciba-Geigy had a system of managerial ranks based on length of service, overall performance, and the personal background of the individual rather than on the actual job being performed at a given time. Rank and status therefore had a much more permanent quality in Ciba-Geigy, whereas in DEC, fortunes could rise and fall precipitously and frequently with job assignment.

In Ciba-Geigy meetings, I observed much less direct confrontation and much more respect for individual opinion. Meetings were geared to information transmission rather than problem solving. Recommendations made by managers in their specific area of accountability were generally respected, accepted, and implemented. I never observed insubordination, and I got the impression that it would not be tolerated. Rank and status thus clearly had a higher value in Ciba-Geigy than in DEC, whereas personal negotiating skill and the ability to get things done in an ambiguous social environment had a higher value in DEC.

Espoused Beliefs and Values

Beliefs and values tend to be elicited when you ask about observed behavior or other artifacts that strike you as puzzling, anomalous, or inconsistent. If I asked managers in Ciba-Geigy why they always kept their doors closed, they would patiently and somewhat condescendingly explain to me that this was the only way they could get any work done, and they valued work very highly. Meetings were a necessary evil and were useful only for announcing decisions or gathering information. "Real work" was done by thinking things out and that required quiet and concentration. In contrast, in DEC, real work was accomplished by debating things out in meetings!

It was also pointed out to me that discussion among peers was not of great value and that important information would come from the boss. Authority was highly respected, especially authority based on level of education, experience, and rank. The use of titles such as doctor or professor symbolized their respect for the knowledge that education bestowed on people. Much of this had to do with a great respect for the science of chemistry and the contributions of laboratory research to product development.

In Ciba-Geigy, as in DEC, a high value was placed on individual effort and contribution, but in Ciba-Geigy, no one ever went outside the chain of command and did things that would be out of line with what the boss had suggested. In Ciba-Geigy, a high value was placed on product elegance and quality, and, as I discovered later, what might be called product significance. Ciba-Geigy managers felt very proud of the fact that their chemicals and drugs were useful in crop protection, in curing diseases, and in other ways helping to improve the world.

Basic Assumptions—The Ciba-Geigy Company Paradigm

Many of the values that were articulated gave a flavor of this company, but without digging deeper to basic assumptions, I could not fully understand how things worked. For example, the artifact that struck me most as I worked with this organization on the mandate to help them to become more innovative was the anomalous behavior around my memos, previously mentioned in Chapter One. I realized that there was very little lateral communication occurring between units of the organization, so that new ideas developed in one unit never seemed to get outside that unit. If I inquired about cross-divisional meetings, for example, I would get blank stares and questions such as "Why would we do that?" Because the divisions were facing similar problems, it would obviously have been helpful to circulate some of the better ideas that came up in my interviews, supplemented with my own ideas based on my knowledge of what went on in other organizations.

Elaborating on the example provided in Chapter One, I wrote a number of memos along these lines and asked my contact client, Dr. Leupold, the director of management development, to distribute them to those managers he thought could most benefit from the information. Because he reported directly to Sam Koechlin, he seemed like a natural conduit for communicating with those divisional, functional, and geographic managers who needed the information I was gathering. When I would return on a subsequent visit to the company and meet with one of the unit managers, without fail I would discover that he did not have the memo, but if he requested it from Dr. Leupold, it would be sent over almost immediately.

This phenomenon was puzzling and irritating, but its consistency clearly indicated that some strong underlying assumptions were at work here. When I later asked one of my colleagues in the corporate staff unit that delivered training and other development programs to the organization why the information did not circulate freely, he revealed that he had similar problems in that he would develop a helpful intervention in one unit of the organization, but that other units would seek help outside the organization before they would "discover" that he had a solution that was better. The common denominator seemed to be that unsolicited ideas were generally not well received.

We had a long exploratory conversation about this observed behavior and jointly figured out what the explanation was. As previously mentioned, at Ciba-Geigy, when a manager was given a job, that job became the private domain of the individual. Managers felt a strong sense of turf or ownership and made the assumption that each owner of a piece of the organization would be completely in charge and on top of his piece. He would be fully informed and make himself an expert in that area. Therefore, if someone provided some unsolicited information pertaining to the job, this was potentially an invasion of privacy and possibly an insult, as it implied that the manager did not already have this information or idea.

The powerful metaphor that "giving someone unsolicited information was like walking into their home uninvited" came from a number of managers in subsequent interviews. It became clear that only if information was asked for was it acceptable to offer ideas. Someone's superior could provide information, though even that was done only cautiously, but a peer would rarely do so, lest he unwittingly insult the recipient. To provide unsolicited information or ideas could be seen as a challenge to the information base the manager was using, and that might be regarded as an insult, implying that the person challenged had not thought deeply enough about his own problem or was not really on top of his own job.

By not understanding this assumption, I had unwittingly put Dr. Leupold into the impossible position of risking insulting all his colleagues and peers if he circulated my memos as I had asked. Interestingly enough, this kind of assumption is so tacit that even he could not articulate just why he had not followed my instructions. He was clearly uncomfortable and embarrassed about it but had no explanation until we uncovered the assumption about organizational turf and its symbolic meaning.

To further understand this and related behavior, it was necessary to consider some of the other underlying assumptions that this company had evolved (see Figure 3.3). It had grown and achieved much of its success through fundamental discoveries made by a number of basic researchers in the company's central research laboratories. Whereas in DEC truth was discovered through conflict and debate, in Ciba-Geigy truth had come more from the wisdom of the scientist/researcher.

Both companies believed in the individual, but the differing assumptions about the nature of truth led to completely different attitudes toward authority and the role of conflict. In Ciba-Geigy, authority was much more respected, and conflict tended to be avoided. The individual was given areas of freedom by the boss and then was totally respected in those areas. If role occupants were not well enough educated or skilled enough to make

Figure 3.3.   Ciba-Geigy's Cultural Paradigm.

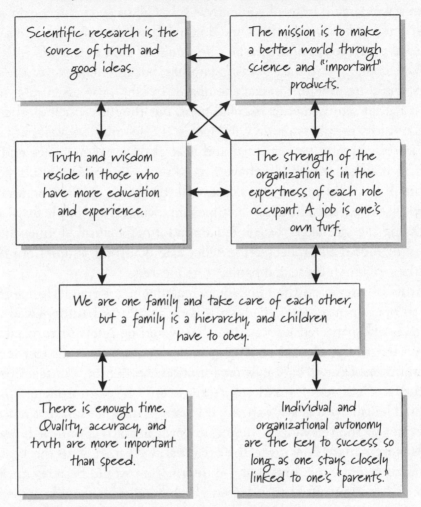

decisions, they were expected to train themselves. If they performed poorly in the meantime, that would be tolerated for quite a while before a decision might be made to replace them. In both companies, there was a "tenure" assumption that once people were accepted, they were likely to remain unless they failed in a major way.

In DEC, conflict was valued and the individual was expected to take initiative and fight for ideas in every arena. In Ciba-Geigy, conflict was suppressed once a decision had been made. In DEC, it was assumed that if a job was not challenging or was not a good match between what the organization needed and what the individual could give, the individual should be moved to a new assignment or would quit anyway. In Ciba-Geigy, the person would be expected to be a good soldier and do the job as best he could, and as long as he was perceived as doing his best he would be kept in the job.

Both companies talked of being families, but the meaning of the word *family* was quite different in each company. In DEC, the essential assumption was that family members could fight, but they loved each other and could not lose membership. In Ciba-Geigy, the assumption was that parental authority should be respected and that children (employees and subordinate managers) should behave according to the rules and obey their parents. If they did so, they would be well treated, taken care of, and supported by the parents. In DEC, lifetime employment was implicit, while in Ciba-Geigy, it was taken for granted and informally affirmed. In each case, the family model also reflected the wider macrocultural assumptions of the countries in which these companies were located.

After I understood the Ciba-Geigy paradigm, I was able to figure out how to operate more effectively as a consultant. As I interviewed more managers and gathered information that would be relevant to what they were trying to do, instead of attempting to circulate memos to the various branches of the Ciba-Geigy organization through my contact client, I found that if I gave information directly, even if it was unsolicited, it was accepted because I was an "expert." If I wanted information to circulate, I sent it out to the relevant parties on my own initiative, or, if I thought it needed to circulate down into the organization, I gave it to the boss and attempted to convince him that the information would be relevant lower down. If I really wanted to intervene by having managers do something different, I could accomplish this best by being an expert and formally recommending it to CEO Sam Koechlin. If he liked the idea, he would then order "the troops" to do it. For example, I had given some lectures on "career anchors" illustrating that different people in the organization built their career around different core values, and that jobs should be described not in terms of responsibilities but in terms of their role networks. Koechlin mandated that the top several layers of the organization should do the career anchor exercise and analyze their role networks (Schein, 1978, 2006).

Other facets of the Ciba-Geigy culture will be discussed in later chapters. For example, their patience and their attitude toward time, and their formality along with their ability to be playful and informal during organizational "time outs" are important in understanding how they were able to get their work done.

Summary and Conclusions

In the preceding case analyses, I have tried to illustrate how organizational culture can be analyzed at several levels: (1) visible artifacts; (2) espoused beliefs, values, rules, and behavioral norms; and (3) tacit, taken-for-granted, basic underlying assumptions. My argument is that unless you dig down to the level of the basic assumptions, you cannot really decipher the artifacts, values, and norms. On the other hand, if you find some of those basic assumptions and explore their interrelationship, you are really getting at the essence of the culture and can then explain a great deal of what goes on. This essence can sometimes be analyzed as a paradigm in that some organizations function by virtue of an interlocking, coordinated set of assumptions. Whereas each one alone might not make sense, the pattern explains the behavior and the success of the organization in overcoming its external and internal challenges.

I have only described certain elements of the culture because these pertained to key goals that the organizations were trying to achieve, so we should not assume that these paradigms describe the whole culture, nor should we assume that we would find the same paradigm operating in every part of the organization. The generality of the assumptions should be investigated and determined empirically.

I discovered these assumptions primarily through observation and exploring with inside informants some of the anomalies that I observed. It is when we do not understand something that we need to pursue vigorously why we do not, and the best way to search is to use our own ignorance and naïveté.

What are some of the lessons to be learned from these cases, and what implications do they have for leadership? The most important lesson for me is the realization that culture is deep, pervasive, complex, patterned, and morally neutral. In both cases, I had to overcome my own cultural prejudices about the right and wrong way to do things, and to learn that culture simply exists. Both companies were successful in their respective technological, political, economic, and broader cultural environments for a long time, but both companies also experienced environmental changes that led to their disappearance as independent economic entities. The role that their cultures played in causing economic problems will be explored in a later chapter.

In both cases, the powerful influence of early leaders and historical circumstance was evident. Cultural assumptions have their roots in early group experience and in the pattern of success and failure experienced by these companies. Their current leaders strongly valued their cultures, were proud of them, and felt it important for members of their organizations to accept the basic assumptions. In both organizations, stories were told of misfits who left because they did not like the way the company operated, or who were not hired in the first place because they either would be disruptive or would not like it there anyway.

In both companies, leaders were struggling with changing environmental demands and faced the issue of whether and how to evolve or change their ways of operating, but this was initially defined as reaffirmation of portions of the existing culture, not as changes in the culture. Though the companies were at different stages in their evolution, they both valued their cultures as important assets and were anxious to preserve and enhance them.

Finally, it is obvious that both companies reflected the national cultures in which they operated and the technologies that underlay their businesses. DEC was a U.S. company of creative electrical engineers evolving a brand new technology; Ciba-Geigy was a Swiss-German company of mostly highly educated chemical engineers working both with very old technologies (dye stuffs) and very new bio-chemical processes (pharmaceuticals). Electrical circuits and chemical processes require very different approaches and time tables for product development, which was pointed out to me many times. An important implication is that culture cannot really be understood without looking at core technologies, the occupations of organization members, and the macrocultural context in which the organizations exist.

4

MACROCULTURES, SUBCULTURES, AND MICROCULTURES

Organizational culture has been the focus of the analysis so far, but as pointed out earlier, both DEC and Ciba-Geigy existed in national and regional macrocultures. To fully understand what goes on *inside* the organization, it is necessary to understand both the organization's *macro context*, because much of what you observe inside simply reflects the national culture, and the interplay of *subcultures* because they often reflect the primary occupational cultures of the organization members.

Much of what goes on inside an organization that has existed for some time can best be understood as a set of interactions of subcultures operating within the larger context of the organizational culture. These subcultures share many of the assumptions of the total organization but also hold assumptions beyond those of the total organization, usually reflecting their functional tasks, the occupations of their members, or their unique experiences. It is important to note that if those subcultures are based on broader occupations such as medicine or engineering, its members bring into the organization assumptions that have a broader, even international, base. Thus, in a large hospital system, the culture is influenced by the subcultures of the doctors, which reflect not only medicine in general but also the different emphasis of medical education in different countries.

Shared assumptions that create subcultures most often form around the functional units of the organization. They are often based on a similarity of educational background in the members, a shared task, and/or a similarity of organizational experience, what we often end up calling "stove pipes" or "silos." We all know that getting cross-functional project teams to work well together is difficult because the members bring their functional cultures into the project and, as a consequence, have difficulty communicating with each other, reaching consensus, and implementing decisions in an effective manner. The difficulties of communication across these boundaries arise not only from the fact that the functional groups have different goals but also from the more fundamental issue that the very meaning of the words they use will differ. The word "marketing" means product development to the engineer, studying customers through market research to the product manager, merchandising to the salesman, and constant change in design to the manufacturing manager (Dougherty, 1990). When they try to work together, they often attribute disagreement to personalities and fail to notice the deeper shared assumptions that color how each function thinks.

Another kind of subculture, less often acknowledged, reflects the common experiences of given levels within a hierarchy. Culture arises through shared experiences of success. If first-line supervisors discover ways of managing their subordinates that are consistently successful, they will gradually build up a set of shared assumptions about how to do their job that can be thought of as the "subculture of first-line supervision." Elders will teach newly promoted supervisors how to perform their roles, and this mentoring will be more powerful than any formal training they might be given. In the same way, middle management and higher levels will develop their own shared assumptions, and, at each level, those assumptions will be taught to newcomers as they get promoted into that level. These hierarchically based subcultures create the communication problems associated with "selling senior management on a new way of doing things," or "getting budget approval for a new piece of equipment," or "getting a personnel requisition through." As each cultural boundary is crossed, the proposal has to be put into the appropriate language for the next higher level and has to reflect the values and assumptions of that higher level (Thomas, 1994). Or, from the point of view of the higher levels, decisions have to be put into a form that lower levels can understand, often resulting in "translations" that actually distort and sometimes even subvert what the higher levels wanted.

Occupational communities also generate cultures that cut across organizations and often become subcultures within organizations (Van Maanen and Barley, 1984; Gladwell, 2008). For example, fishermen around the world develop similar worldviews, as do miners, and the members of any particular industry based on a particular technology. In his popularized account, Gladwell argues persuasively that rice farmers develop a common world view that reflects the difficult requirements of rice farmers just as certain law offices build their practices around the common experiences of their immigrant founders. Shared assumptions derive from common origins, common educational backgrounds, the requirements of a given occupation such as the licenses that have to be obtained to practice, and the shared contact with others in the occupation. I pointed out that DEC was primarily composed of highly trained electrical engineers while Ciba-Geigy had many more chemical engineers and biochemists. Even the various functional cultures that we see in organizations are partly the result of membership in broader cross-organizational occupational communities. Salesmen the world over, accountants, assembly line workers, and, most importantly, engineers, share some basic assumptions about the nature of their work regardless of who their particular employer is at any given time.

We are also increasingly discovering that such similar outlooks across organizations apply to executive managers, particularly CEOs. CEOs face similar kinds of problems across all organizations and in all industries throughout the world. Their connection to the outside world of finance and public relations provides a set of common experiences that shapes their beliefs and values, thus creating yet another subculture. And because executives are likely to have somewhere in their history some common education and indoctrination, they form a common world view, a common set of assumptions about the nature of business and what it takes to run a business successfully. CEOs therefore make up one of the generic subcultures that exist in some form in every organization.

Three Generic Subcultures

In every organization in the public or private sector, three *generic* subcultures have to be identified and managed to minimize destructive conflict. Such conflicts are often misdiagnosed as political interdepartmental fights, power maneuvers, or personality conflicts. What can be missed in that perception is that the different groups may have evolved genuinely different subcultures, that the contributions of each of these subcultures is needed for organizational effectiveness, but that these subcultures can be in conflict with each other. One of the critical functions of leadership is to insure that these subcultures are aligned toward shared organizational goals.

The Operator Subculture

All organizations have some version of what has been called "the line" as opposed to the "the staff," referring to those employees who produce and sell the organization's products or services. I will call these the "operators" to identify the employees who feel they run the place. They will be distinguished from the designers of the work, the "engineers," and from the top executives whose function is to maintain the financial health of the organization. Some of the critical basic assumptions of the operator in all organizations are shown in Exhibit 4.1.

This subculture is the most difficult to describe because it evolves locally in organizations and within operational units. Thus, you can identify an operator subculture in a nuclear plant, in a chemical complex, in an auto manufacturing plant, in the cockpit, and in the office, but it is not clear what elements make this culture broader than the local unit. To get at this issue, we must consider that the operations in different industries reflect the broad technological trends in those industries. At some fundamental level, how someone does things in a given industry reflects the

Exhibit 4.1.   Assumptions of the Operator Subculture.

- The action of any organization is ultimately the action of people. We are the critical resource; we run the place.
- The success of the enterprise therefore depends on our knowledge, skill, learning ability, and commitment.
- The knowledge and skills required are "local" and are based on the organization's core technology and our specific experience.
- No matter how carefully engineered the production process is or how carefully rules and routines are specified, we know that we *will* have to deal with unpredictable contingencies.
- Therefore, we have to have the capacity to learn, to innovate, and to deal with surprises.
- Most operations involve interdependencies between separate elements of the process, so we must be able to work as a collaborative team in which communication, openness, mutual trust, and commitment are highly valued.
- We depend on management to give us the proper resources, training, and support to get our jobs done.

core technologies that created that industry. And as those core technologies themselves evolve, the nature of operations changes. For example, as Zuboff (1988) has persuasively argued, information technology has made manual labor obsolete in many industries and replaced it with conceptual tasks. In a chemical plant, the worker no longer walks around observing, smelling, touching, and manipulating. Instead he or she sits in a control room and infers the conditions in the plant from the various indexes that come up on the computer screen. But what defines this subculture across all of these examples is the sense that these employees have that they really run things, that they are the key to the functioning of the organization, the "front line."

The operator subculture is based on human interaction, and most line units learn that high levels of communication, trust, and teamwork are essential to getting the work done efficiently. Operators also learn that no matter how clearly the rules are specified of what is supposed to be done under different operational conditions, the world is to some degree unpredictable and they must be prepared to use their own innovative skills to deal with it. If the operations are complex as in a nuclear plant, operators learn that they are highly interdependent and that they must work together as a team, especially when unanticipated events have to be dealt with. Rules and hierarchy often get in the way under unpredicted conditions. Operators become highly sensitive to the degree to which the production process is a system of interdependent functions all of which must work together to be efficient and effective. These points apply to all kinds of "production processes" whether we are talking about a sales function, a clerical group, a cockpit, or a service unit.

The operators know that to get the job done effectively, they must adhere to most of the assumptions stated previously, but because conditions are never quite the same as what their training had shown, all operators learn how to deviate from formal procedures, usually to get the job done but sometimes to subvert what they may regard as unreasonable demands from management. One of the most effective variations of this process is to "work to rule," which means to do everything very precisely and slowly, thus making the organization very inefficient. An example that most travelers have experienced is when airline traffic controllers can practically paralyze the system by working strictly to rule.

The general phenomenon of adapting the formal work process to the local situation and then normalizing the new process by teaching it to newcomers has been called "practical drift" and is an important characteristic of all operator subcultures (Snook, 2000). It is the basic reason why sociologists who study how work is actually done in organizations always find sufficient variations from the formally designated procedures to talk of the "informal organization" and to point out that without such innovative behavior on the part of employees, the organization might not be as effective (Hughes, 1958; Dalton, 1959; Van Maanen, 1979b). The cultural assumptions that evolve around how work is actually done are often the most important parts of an organizational culture.

For example, as all observers of production units have learned, employees rarely work to their full capacity except under crisis conditions. More typically, norms develop of "a fair day's work for a fair day's pay," and workers who work harder than this are defined as "rate busters" and are in danger of being ostracized. To fully understand how things work in a total organization, you must, therefore, observe the informal culture, which is the interplay of the various operator subcultures.

The Engineering/Design Subculture

In all organizations, there is a group that represents the basic design elements of the technology underlying the work of the organization, and this group has the knowledge of how that technology is to be used. Within a given organization, they function as a subculture, but what makes this group significant is that their basic assumptions are derived from their occupational community and their education. Though engineer designers work within an organization, their occupational identification is much broader and cuts across nations and industries. In technically based companies, the founders are often engineers in this sense and create an organization that is dominated by these assumptions. DEC was such an organization, and, as we will see later, the domination of the engineering subculture over other business functions is part of the explanation of DEC economic success as well as failure (Schein, 2003; Kunda, 1992). The basic assumptions of the engineering subculture are listed in Exhibit 4.2.

Exhibit 4.2.   Assumptions of the Engineering Subculture. (Global Community)

- The ideal world is one of elegant machines and processes working in perfect precision and harmony without human intervention.
- People are the problem—they make mistakes and therefore should be designed out of the system wherever possible.
- Nature can and should be mastered: "That which is possible should be done" (proactively optimistic).
- Solutions must be based on science and available technology.
- Real work is to solve puzzles and overcome problems.
- Work must be oriented toward useful products and outcomes.

The shared assumption of this subculture are based on common education, work experience, and job requirements. Their education reinforces the view that problems have abstract solutions, and those solutions can, in principle, be implemented in the real world with products and systems that are free of human foibles and errors. Engineers, using this term in the broadest sense, are designers of products and systems that have utility, elegance, permanence, efficiency, safety, and, maybe, as in the case of architecture, even aesthetic appeal, but they are basically designed to require standard responses from their human operators or, ideally, to have no human operators at all.

In the design of complex systems such as jet aircraft or nuclear plants, the engineer prefers a technical routine to insure safety rather than relying on a human team to manage the contingencies that might arise. Engineers recognize the human factor and design for it, but their preference is to make things as automatic as possible because of the basic assumption that it is ultimately humans who make mistakes. Ken Olsen, the founder of DEC, would get furious if someone said there was a "computer error," pointing out that the machine does not make mistakes, only humans do. Safety is built into the designs themselves. I once asked an Egyptian Airlines pilot whether he preferred the Russian or U.S. planes. He answered immediately that he preferred the U.S. planes and gave as his reason that the Russian planes have only one or two back-up systems, while the U.S. planes have three back-up systems. In a similar vein, I overheard two engineers saying to each other during a landing at the Seattle airport that the cockpit crew was totally unnecessary. The plane could easily be flown and landed by computer.

In other words, one of the key themes in the subculture of engineering is the preoccupation with designing humans out of the systems rather than into them. Recall that the San Francisco Bay Transit Authority known as BART has totally automated trains. In this case, it was not the operators but the customers who objected to this degree of automation, forcing management to put human operators onto each train even though they had nothing to do except to reassure people by their presence. Automation and robotics are increasingly popular because of the lower cost and greater reliability of systems that have no humans in them. But, as pointed out earlier, humans are needed when conditions change and innovative responses are needed.

In Thomas's study, the engineers were very disappointed that the operations of the elegant machine they were purchasing would be constrained by the presence of more operators than were needed, by a costly retraining program, and by management-imposed policies that had nothing to do with "real engineering" (Thomas, 1994). In my own research on information technology I found that the engineers fundamentally wanted the operators to adjust to the language and characteristics of the particular computer system that was being implemented and were quite impatient with the "resistance to change" that the operators were exhibiting. From the point of view of the users—the operators—not only was the language arcane, but the systems were often not considered useful for solving the operational problems (Schein, 1992).

I have focused on engineers in technical organizations but their equivalent exists in all organizations. In medicine, it would be the doctors who are developing a new surgical technique; in law offices, the designers of computerized systems for creating necessary documents; in the insurance industry, the actuaries and product designers; and in the financial world, the designers of new and sophisticated financial instruments. Their job is not to do the daily work but to design new products, new structures, and new processes to make the organization more effective.

Both the operators and the engineers often find themselves out of alignment with a third critical culture, the culture of executives.

The Executive Subculture

A third generic subculture that exists in all organizations is the executive subculture based on the fact that top managers in all organizations share a similar environment and similar concerns. Sometimes, this subculture is represented by just the CEO and his or her executive team. The executive worldview is built around the necessity to maintain the financial health of the organization and is fed by the preoccupations of boards, of investors, and of the capital markets. Whatever other preoccupations executives may have, they cannot get away from having to worry about and manage the financial issues of the survival and growth of their organization. In private enterprise, the executives have to worry specifically about profits and return on investments, but financial issues around survival and growth are just as salient in the public and nonprofit enterprise. The essence of this executive subculture is described in Exhibit 4.3.

Exhibit 4.3.   Assumptions of the Executive Subculture. (Global Community)

1. Financial focus
   - Without financial survival and growth, there are no returns to shareholders or to society.
   - Financial survival is equivalent to perpetual war with competitors.
2. Self image: The embattled lone hero
   - The economic environment is perpetually competitive and potentially hostile; "in a war you cannot trust anyone."
   - Therefore, the CEO must be "the lone hero," isolated and alone, yet appearing to be omniscient, in total control, and feeling indispensable.
   - You cannot get reliable data from below because subordinates will tell you what they think you want to hear; therefore, the CEO must trust his or her own judgment more and more (i.e., lack of accurate feedback increases the leader's sense of rightness and omniscience).
   - Organization and management are intrinsically hierarchical; the hierarchy is the measure of status and success and the primary means of maintaining control.
   - Though people are necessary, they are a necessary evil not an intrinsic value; people are a resource like other resources to be acquired and managed, not ends in themselves.
   - The well-oiled machine organization does not need whole people, only the activities they are contracted for.

The basic assumptions of the executive subculture apply particularly to CEOs who have risen through the ranks and have been promoted to their jobs. Founders of organizations or family members who have been appointed to these levels exhibit different kinds of assumptions and often can maintain a broader focus (Schein, 1983). The promoted CEO adopts the exclusively financial point of view because of the nature of the executive career. As managers rise higher and higher in the hierarchy, as their level of responsibility and accountability grows, they not only have to become more preoccupied with financial matters, but they also discover that it becomes harder and harder to observe and influence the basic work of the organization. They discover that they have to manage at a distance, and that discovery inevitably forces them to think in terms of control systems and routines, which become increasingly impersonal. Because accountability is always centralized and flows to the tops of organizations, executives feel an increasing need to know what is going on while recognizing that it is harder and harder to get reliable information. That need for information and control drives them to develop elaborate information systems alongside the control systems and to feel increasingly alone in their position atop the hierarchy.

Paradoxically, throughout their career, managers have to deal with people and surely recognize intellectually that it is people who ultimately make the organization run. First-line supervisors, especially, know very well how dependent they are on people. However, as managers rise in the hierarchy, two factors cause them to become more "impersonal." First, they become increasingly aware that they are no longer managing operators but other managers who think like they do, thus making it not only possible but likely that their thought patterns and worldview will increasingly diverge from the worldview of the operators. Second, as they rise, the units they manage grow larger and larger until it becomes impossible to know everyone personally who works for them. At some point, they recognize that they cannot manage all the people directly and, therefore, have to develop systems, routines, and rules to manage "the organization." People increasingly come to be viewed as "human resources" and are treated as a cost rather than a capital investment.

The executive subculture thus has in common with the engineering subculture a predilection to see people as impersonal resources that generate problems rather than solutions. Or, another way to put this point is to note that in both the executive and engineering subcultures, people and relationships are viewed as means to the end of efficiency and productivity, not as ends in themselves. Both of these subcultures also have in common their occupational base outside the particular organization in which they work. Even if a CEO or engineer has spent his or her entire career inside a given organization, he or she still tends to identify with the occupational reference group outside the organization. For example, when conducting executive programs for CEOs, CEOs will only attend if other CEOs will be there. Similarly, design engineers count on being able to go to professional conferences where they will learn of the latest technologies from their outside professional colleagues.

I have highlighted these three subcultures because they are often working at cross purposes with each other, and we cannot understand the organizational culture if we do not understand how these conflicts are dealt with in the organization. Many problems that are attributed to bureaucracy, environmental factors, or personality conflicts among managers are in fact the result of the lack of alignment between these subcultures. So when we try to understand a given organization, we must consider not only the overall corporate culture but also the identification of subcultures and their alignment with each other.

For example, in DEC, the growth period worked so smoothly because the designers, operators, and executives all came from electrical engineering and found it very easy to run the company from an engineering point of view. As they grew and had to compete on costs with other organizations, it became more important to honor the executive subculture, but because the founder and CEO was still thinking like an engineer, the financial managers within DEC had a very hard time getting their point of view across. Similarly, the sales and marketing organizations had developed subcultures but had relatively little clout with the increasingly strong engineering subculture. One way of understanding DEC's ultimate economic failure is to realize that it was dominated by the engineering subculture to the end; neither the operators nor the executives were ever in control.

Furthermore, conflicts arose between powerful subcultures within the engineering function because of the assumption that internal competition was good, that the market would ultimately decide what products to continue to build, that innovation and growth would absorb the increasing costs of doing "everything," and that everyone should "do the right thing." The DEC culture empowered people, so people who had been successful and had built up powerful groups within DEC were now convinced that they had the answer to DEC's future. As technology became more complex and as costs became more of a factor because of competition, it was no longer possible to support the several projects that powerful groups within engineering advocated, resulting in the reality that all of them were too slow in getting to the market. In effect, DEC had never developed a strong executive subculture and could not, therefore, control the conflict between the warring engineering subcultures.

The subculture situation in Ciba-Geigy was very different because it was a much older more differentiated organization. However, one could clearly see the impact of the engineering and operator subcultures in that they both derived from the occupational culture of chemical engineering. Science and chemistry were sacred cows, which made it much harder for the executive subculture to manage acquisitions if they were financially successful but did not fit the cultural ideals of producing important products. Ciba-Geigy had acquired the American air freshener company Airwick and then made it difficult for Airwick to function. For example, the CEO of Airwick France needed an accounting system that was more responsive than the one Ciba-Geigy was using and was told by the corporate head of accounting that the more ponderous slower corporate system "should be adequate." As we will see later, only the subculture of law began to have significant influence on executive decision making as the organization evolved.

Beyond the three generic subcultures that we have discussed, organizations that have any history and growth will have evolved other subcultures that should be analyzed to understand the dynamics of how things work. For example, in most hospital systems, there are "doctors" and "nurses" subcultures that will be in varying degrees of alignment with each other. In banks, there is a subculture around the lending function and a different one around the investment function. In many production organizations, the maintenance organization develops its own subculture, and in universities, each department develops a subculture based on the subject matter of its teaching and research. Though the tenure requirements might be the same for all faculty, the subcultures show up in the actual criteria used in assessing what kind of work qualifies. In mathematics, it might be one brilliant solution of an old problem; in science, the evolution of a new theory; in engineering, the development of a new practical solution; and in the humanities, the publication of one or more books. Though it might be tempting to think of "academia" as one culture because of some common basic assumptions, the reality is that different universities and different departments generate different cultures.

Microcultures

Microcultures evolve in small groups that share common tasks and histories. Shared assumptions will arise especially in groups whose task requires mutual cooperation because of a high degree of interdependency. Perhaps the best examples are football teams that clearly develop certain styles of playing based on many hours of practice under the tutelage of a coach. As we will see in Chapter Twelve, it does not take very long for common ways of perceiving and feeling to develop in a new group. To think of these as *cultures* is justified by the way in which such groups initially reject outsiders and, if they let them in, indoctrinate them immediately into "how we do things in this group."

With growing technological complexity and globalization, an increasing emphasis is being placed on multicultural groups composed of members from different macrocultures and occupational cultures. This trend is clearest in health care where the operating room, the recovery room, and various allied operations are each microsystems that have to work collaboratively with other microsystems. Within each of these microsystems, there are members of different occupations such as surgeons, nurses, profusionists, anesthesiologists, and medical technicians, sometimes from different nationalities, yet they have to work as a tightly knit team and have to coordinate smoothly with the other microsystems that they connect with. How members of such diverse macro and occupational cultures develop teamwork is a major issue that will be examined specifically in Chapter Twenty-One.

Summary and Conclusions

Organizational cultures exist in a context. They operate in one or more macrocultures, such as ethnic groups and other larger cultural units. You will find that the macrocultures influence the evolution of the organizational culture. As you observe an organization, you will also find some assumptions that characterize the whole organization, called the corporate culture in private organizations, and a set of assumptions that characterize subunits of the organization. These subcultures reflect the functional units, the rank levels in the hierarchy, isolated geographic units, and any other groups that have a shared history. All organizations also operate with three *generic* subcultures that reflect the operations of the organization, the design of the organization, and the executive/financial function of the organization. For organizations to be effective, these subcultures must be in alignment with each other because each is needed for total organizational effectiveness.

As organizations evolve in the global context, there will be more emphasis on multicultural teams that can be considered to be microcultures. How such microcultures are created and how they relate to other microsystems with different microcultures will be an important issue for the future.

Part Two

THE DIMENSIONS OF CULTURE

In Part I, I defined and described culture as a *structural* concept. The formal structure is the same whether we are describing macrocultures, organizational cultures, occupational subcultures, or microcultures in small groups. However, the *content* of culture—what an observer would view as the actual rules, norms, values, and basic assumptions of a given culture—might vary considerably, both in terms of which content dimensions might be most relevant to understanding that culture and in terms of the position along these dimensions. For example, it might be crucial in trying to understand a given organization to understand how it manages *authority relationships* (a basic dimension of the culture) and whether it is more authoritarian or egalitarian in how it operates (the position along that dimension).

Structural analysis tells us that a culture manifests itself at the level of artifacts and espoused values but that its essence lies in the underlying basic assumptions. We still need to specify: *assumptions about what?* As we will see in the next few chapters, many different dimensions have been proposed by anthropologists and organizational theorists. Not only is it important to decide which of these dimensions are broadly relevant to understanding organizations and leadership, but we also have to decide which dimensions best help us to understand the relationship among macrocultures, organizational cultures, and microcultures. We will see that much of the confusion about how to define culture and how to "measure" culture derives from the failure to distinguish whether a given dimension that we are talking about is being applied to nations, ethnic groups, and occupations, or to organizations or small groups.

In deciding which of the many possible dimensions of culture to review, I have chosen the functional perspective because it is possible to analyze organizations historically and to determine to some degree how given cultural assumptions arose. From this perspective, the content of *organizational* cultures reflects the ultimate problems that every new organization faces: dealing with its *external* environment in order to survive and grow (Chapter Five) and managing its *internal* integration (Chapter Six). Understanding an organization in terms of these dimensions is important but not sufficient. As was pointed out in the cases of DEC and Ciba-Geigy, organizations exist in national and occupational macrocultures, and culture at this macro level reflects deeper issues—assumptions about the nature of truth, time, space, human nature, and human relationships. A way of thinking about and describing some of these deeper dimensions is provided in Chapters Seven, Eight, and Nine. Macrocultural assumptions reflecting national cultures and the occupational cultures that are involved in the technology that underlies an organization are always operating in the organization. Understanding that DEC was a quintessentially American computer company created by electrical engineers and that Ciba-Geigy was quintessentially a Swiss-German chemical company created by chemical engineers and chemists is crucial but not sufficient. The particular histories of the companies need to be understood and are often more relevant.

In trying to understand the bewildering variety of different *organizational* cultures, it is tempting to develop typologies that allow us to categorize different organizations into "types." Such typologies have the advantage of simplifying and building higher-order theoretical categories, but they have the disadvantage of being so abstract that they often fail to describe accurately a particular organization. A number of such typologies have been proposed and are reviewed in Chapter Ten. As we will see, they draw on dimensions that come both from the macro and organizational domain. We need to be careful, then, to not misapply typologies that were developed for macrocultures to organizations or vice versa. Much of the confusion about whether or not we can "measure" culture quantitatively derives from the confusion about whether we are measuring a group, an organization, an occupation, or a nation.

Can we "measure" or "decipher" cultural content in organizations? Is there a difference between such deciphering from a researcher, consultant, or leadership point of view? In Chapter Eleven, I will describe a number of available alternatives and argue for what I call a "clinical" view that takes into account and uses what members of the organization are trying to do. The basic perspective of this book is *organizational* and attempts to provide insights to *leaders*. We will concentrate less on the perspective of the research anthropologist or organizational theorist, which implies that the method of deciphering has to be primarily helpful to the *insiders* trying to accomplish organizational goals and to practitioner/consultants trying to help those insiders.

These chapters focus more on the concept of *culture* and less on the concept of *leadership*. Nevertheless, you should remember that it is leadership that has created the particular culture content that the group ends up with. Leaders who create organizations come from macrocultures and particular occupations, so the broader macrocultural dimensions exist within the leader's head and are externalized in the behavior that the leader demands or tolerates. The actual history of the group is a blend of what the leader brings and what the macro context of the group affords as it grows. You, the reader, should therefore become highly conscious of your own assumptions in each of the content areas we will cover because those assumptions will not only determine how you personally decipher an organization but, more importantly, how you lead or attempt to influence the organizations with which you are personally involved. You could distance yourself somewhat from the stories thus far, but as you read on, you will benefit most from asking yourself in each of the chapters what *your own position* is on every dimension we will review. *Discover the layers of culture within yourself.*

5

ASSUMPTIONS ABOUT EXTERNAL ADAPTATION ISSUES

A formal definition of organizational culture can tell us what culture is from a structural point of view, but it does not tell us what the *content* of culture is—what cultural assumptions are about. What kinds of issues do groups face that lead ultimately to cultural assumptions, or, to put it another way, what critical functions does culture perform for the group and ultimately the organization? Why do certain cultural assumptions survive?

The most useful model for identifying the content dimensions of organizational cultures derives from social psychology and group dynamics. All groups and organizations face two archetypical problems: (1) survival in and adaptation to the external environment, and (2) integration of the internal processes to ensure the capacity to continue to survive and adapt. In other words, from an evolutionary perspective, we need to identify the issues that any group faces from the moment of its origin through to its state of maturity and decline. Although it may be difficult—sometimes even impossible—to study cultural *origins* and functions in macrocultures whose histories are lost in antiquity, it is not at all impossible to study these matters in groups, organizations, or occupations whose histories and evolution are known.

The process of culture formation is, in a sense, identical to the process of group formation in that the very essence of "groupness" or group identity—the shared patterns of thought, belief, feelings, and values that result from shared experience and common learning—results in the pattern of shared assumptions that I am calling the "culture" of that group. Without a group, there can be no culture, and without some shared assumptions, some minimal degree of culture, we are really talking only about an aggregate of people, not a "group." So group growth and culture formation can be seen as two sides of the same coin, and both are the result of leadership activities and shared experiences.

Exhibit 5.1.   The Problems of External Adaptation and Survival.

- **Mission and Strategy:** Obtaining a shared understanding of core mission, primary task, manifest functions, and latent functions.
- **Goals:** Developing consensus on goals, as derived from the core mission.
- **Means:** Developing consensus on the means to be used to attain the goals, such as the organization structure, division of labor, reward system, and authority system.
- **Measurement:** Developing consensus on the criteria to be used in measuring how well the group is doing in fulfilling its goals, such as the information and control system.
- **Correction:** Developing consensus on the appropriate remedial or repair strategies to be used if goals are not being met.

This approach to identifying the elements and dimensions of culture is fundamentally different from what an anthropologist might do because we are trying to understand not only existing cultures but also culture formation, evolution, and destruction. This dynamic view also reflects a more functional point of view in that we are trying to understand not only what culture is but also what functions culture serves for a given group, occupation, nation, and so on. The insights that we can draw from group dynamics as to the problems that all groups face provide a useful guideline for identifying the dimensions that will be most useful in understanding organizations. At the same time, inasmuch as groups and organizations are ultimately created by leaders, it is useful to consider what issues leaders face in creating and managing groups. When reduced to their essence, the problems of external adaptation are shown in Exhibit 5.1.

Shared Assumptions About Mission, Strategy, and Goals

Every new group or organization must develop a shared concept of its ultimate survival problem, from which usually is derived its most basic sense of core mission, primary task, or "reason to be." In most *business* organizations, this shared definition revolves around the issue of economic survival and growth, which, in turn, involves the maintenance of good relationships with the major stakeholders of the organization: (1) the investors and stockholders; (2) the suppliers of the materials needed to produce; (3) the managers and employees; (4) the community and government; and, last, but not least, (5) the customers willing to pay for the product or service.

Many studies of organizations have shown that the key to long-range growth and survival is to keep the needs of these constituencies in some kind of balance, and that the mission of the organization, as a set of beliefs about its core competencies and basic functions in society, is usually a reflection of this balance (Donaldson and Lorsch, 1983; Kotter and Heskett, 1992; Porras and Collins, 1994). It has been a mistake to think in terms of a total focus on any one of these constituencies because all of them together make up the environment in which the organization must succeed.

In religious, educational, social, and governmental organizations, the core mission or primary task is clearly different, but the logic that the mission ultimately derives from a balancing of the needs of different stakeholders is the same. Thus, for example, the mission of a university must balance the learning needs of the students (which includes housing, feeding, and often acting as *in loco parentis*), the needs of the faculty to do research and further knowledge, the needs of the community to have a repository for knowledge and skill, the needs of the financial investors to have a viable institution, and, ultimately, even the needs of society to have an institution to facilitate the transition of late adolescents into the labor market and to sort them into skill groups.

Though core missions or primary tasks are usually stated in terms of a single constituency, such as customers, a more useful way to think about ultimate or core mission is to change the question to "What is our function in the larger scheme of things?" or "What justifies our continued existence?" Posing the question this way reveals that most organizations have multiple functions reflecting the multiple stakeholders and that some of these functions are public justifications, while others are "latent" and, in a sense, not spoken of (Merton, 1957). For example, the *manifest* function of a school system is to educate. But a close examination of what goes on in school systems suggests several *latent* functions as well: (1) To keep children (young adults) off the streets and out of the labor market until there is room for them, and they have some relevant skills; (2) to sort and group the next generation into talent and skill categories according to the needs of the society; and (3) to enable the various occupations associated with the school system to survive and maintain their professional autonomy. In examining the manifest and latent functions, the organization's leaders and members will recognize that to survive, the organization must to some degree fulfill all of these functions. Some of the most important shared assumptions concern how to fulfill the latent functions without publicly admitting the existence of those functions.

Core mission thus becomes a complex multifunctional issue, and some of the functions must remain latent to protect the manifest identity of the organization. For a university to announce publicly the babysitting, sorting, and professional autonomy functions would be embarrassing, but these functions often play an important role in determining the activities of the organization and determining key elements of the culture of the organization. In business organizations, the latent functions include, for instance, the provision of jobs in the community where the business is located, the provision of economic resources to that community in the form of goods and raw materials purchased, and the provision of managerial talent to be used in activities other than running the business.

For example, as DEC became a major economic force in New England, the choice of where to build new factories and other organizational units was partly driven by Ken Olsen's perception of what the economic impact would be on the local areas. The analysis of DEC's culture then revealed a set of tacit assumptions about maintaining the economic health of the regions in which it operated. Though Ciba-Geigy would never have publicly admitted it, members of the so-called "Basel Aristocracy" had career advantages that non-Swiss did not have, and one of the latent functions of the business was to sustain those careers.

Overall corporate culture dimensions evolve around these issues, and subculture dimensions show up in the subunits whose interests are involved in the latent functions. The importance of these latent functions may not surface until an organization is forced to contemplate closing or moving. Then subculture conflicts may erupt if the interests of some of these groups become threatened. The commonest example is, of course, how the subculture of labor surfaces when companies find a need to downsize or move.

Mission relates directly to what organizations call "strategy." To fulfill its manifest and latent functions, the organization evolves shared assumptions about its "reason to be" and formulates long-range plans to fulfill those functions. That involves decisions about products and services and reflects what could usefully be called the "identity" of the organization (Hatch and Schultz, 2004). The shared assumptions about "who we are" become an important element of the organization's culture and limits the strategic options available to the organization. Strategy consultants are often frustrated by the fact that their recommendations are not acted upon. They forget that unless those recommendations are consistent with the organization's assumptions about itself, they will not make sense and hence will not be implemented.

For example, at one stage in the evolution of Ciba-Geigy, I heard lengthy debates among top managers on the question of whether Ciba-Geigy should design and produce "any" product, provided it could be sold at a profit, or whether designs and products should be limited to what some senior managers believed to be "sound" or "valuable" products, based on their conception of what their company had originally been built on, and what their unique talents were. The debate focused on whether or not to keep Airwick, which had been acquired in the American subsidiary, to help Ciba-Geigy become more competent in consumer-oriented marketing. Airwick made air fresheners to remove pet or other odors, and at one of the annual meetings of top management, the president of the U.S subsidiary was very proudly displaying some TV ads for a new product called Carpet Fresh. I was sitting next to a senior member of the internal board, a Swiss researcher who had developed several of the company's key chemical products. He was visibly agitated by the TV ads and finally leaned over to me and loudly whispered, "You know, Schein, those things are not even *products*."

In the later debates about whether to sell Airwick (even though it was financially sound and profitable), I finally understood this comment when it was revealed that Ciba-Geigy could not stomach the image of being a company that produced something as seemingly trivial as an air freshener. Thus a major strategic decision was made on the basis of the company's culture, not on marketing or financial grounds. Ciba-Geigy sold Airwick and affirmed the assumption that they should only be in businesses that had a clear scientific base and that dealt with major problems such as disease and starvation.

This issue came up in a different way in General Foods when it had to face the accusation from consumer groups and nutrition experts that some of its products, although they tasted good because of high sugar and artificial flavoring content, had no nutritional value. The accusation raised for the top management not merely an economic question but an identity question: Is this company a "food" company, or a "consumer-oriented edibles" (i.e., anything that tastes good) company, or both, or neither?

At first the company responded by attempting to develop and sell more nutritious products, but it found that customers genuinely preferred the cheaper, less nutritious but better-tasting ones. An advertising campaign to sell "nutrition" did not overcome this customer resistance, nor did lowering the price. A debate ensued in the company about its basic mission beyond economic survival, and, in this debate, the pragmatic market-oriented subculture was able to argue much more successfully. The company discovered that its commitment to nutrition was not fundamental and that its identity rested much more on the assumption that they were in the "consumer-oriented edibles" business. They would make and sell any kind of food that people were willing to pay money for.

In summary, one of the most central elements of any culture is the assumption the members of the organization share about their identity and ultimate mission or functions. These are not necessarily very conscious but can surface if we probe the strategic decisions that the organization makes.

Shared Assumptions About Goals Derived from the Mission

Consensus on the core mission and identity does not automatically guarantee that the key members of the organization will have common goals or that the various subcultures will be appropriately aligned to fulfill the mission. As noted in the previous chapter, the basic subcultures in any organization may, in fact, be unwittingly working at cross-purposes to some elements of the mission. The mission is often understood but not well articulated. To achieve consensus on goals, the group needs a common language and shared assumptions about the basic logistical operations by which it can move from something as abstract or general as a sense of mission to the concrete goals of designing, manufacturing, and selling an actual product or service within specified and agreed-upon cost and time constraints.

For example, in DEC there was a clear consensus on the mission of bringing out a line of computing products that would "win in the market-place," but this consensus did not solve senior management's problem of how to allocate resources among different product development groups, nor did it specify how best to market such products. Mission and strategy can be rather timeless, whereas goals have to be formulated for what to do next year, next month, and tomorrow. Goals concretize the mission and facilitate the decisions on means. In that process, goal formulation also often reveals unresolved issues or lack of subculture consensus around deeper issues.

In DEC, the debate around which products to support and how to support them revealed a deep lack of semantic agreement on how to think about "marketing." For example, one group thought that marketing meant better image advertising in national magazines so that more people would recognize the name of the company; another group was convinced that marketing meant better advertising in technical journals; one group thought it meant developing the next generation of products; while yet another group emphasized merchandizing and sales support as the key elements of marketing.

Senior management often could not define clear goals because of lack of consensus on the role of key functions and how those functions reflected the core mission of the organization. Senior management had to come to agreement on whether it was better to develop the company through being well known in the technical community or through being recognized nationally as a brand name in the minicomputer industry. The deeper shared assumption that came to dominate this debate was derived from the identity that most senior DEC people had as electrical engineers and innovators. As engineers they believed that good products would sell themselves, that their own judgment of "goodness" was sufficient, and that they should not "waste" money on image building.

In Ciba-Geigy there was a clear consensus on the mission to remain in the pharmaceuticals business because it fitted the broad self-concept of senior management and was profitable, but there was considerable disagreement on goals, such as what rate of return should be expected from that division and over what length of time its growth and performance should be measured.

Because operational goals have to be more precise, organizations typically work out their issues of mission and identity in the context of deciding annual or longer-range goals. To really understand cultural assumptions, we must be careful not to confuse these short-run assumptions about goals with assumptions about mission. Ciba-Geigy's concern with being only in businesses that make "science-based, useful products" did not become evident in their discussions about business goals until they hit a strategic issue like whether or not to buy another company. In fact, one way of looking at what we mean by "strategy" is to realize that strategy concerns the evolution of the basic mission, whereas operational goals reflect the short-run tactical survival issues that the organization identifies. Thus, when a company gets into basic strategy discussions, it is usually trying to assess in a more fundamental way the relationship between mission and operational goals.

In summary, goals can be defined at several levels of abstraction and in different time horizons. Is our goal to be profitable at the end of next quarter, or to make ten sales next month, or to call twelve potential customers tomorrow? Only as consensus is reached on such matters, leading to solutions that work repeatedly, can we begin to think of the goals of an organization as potential cultural elements.

Shared Assumptions About Means to Achieve Goals: Structure, Systems, and Processes

Some of the most important and most invisible elements of an organizational culture are the shared basic assumptions about "how things should be done, how the mission is to be achieved, and how goals are to be met." As indicated before, leaders usually impose structure, systems, and processes, which, if successful, become shared parts of the culture. And once processes have become taken for granted, they become the elements of the culture that may be the hardest to change.

The processes a group adopts reflect not only the preferences of the founders and leaders but also the macroculture in which it exists. A striking example occurred in our MIT Sloan Fellows Program where young, high-potential managers who came for a full year master's degree program were given an exercise to *build an organization*. Groups of about fifteen were each made into a "company that was to produce two-line jingles to be put on greeting cards for birthdays and anniversaries." The products were "bought" by the exercise administrators, and the companies were measured on their output. *Without fail* every group immediately chose some executives, a sales manager, a marketing manager, proofreaders, supervisors, and, *finally*, a couple of writers. Only upon much reflection and analysis did it occur to any group that the best way to win was to have fifteen writers. They all automatically fell into the typical hierarchical and functionally differentiated structure that mirrored the national and organizational cultures they came from.

The tendency to fall back on what we already know does facilitate getting consensus quickly on the means by which goals will be met. Such consensus is important because the means to be used have to do with day-to-day behavior and coordinated action. People can have ambiguous goals, but for anything to happen, they must agree on how to structure the organization, and how to design, finance, build, and sell the products or services. From the particular pattern of these agreements will emerge not only the "style" of the organization but also the basic design of tasks, division of labor, reporting and accountability structure, reward and incentive systems, control systems, and information systems.

The skills, technology, and knowledge that a group acquires in its effort to cope with its environment then also become part of its culture if there is consensus on what those skills are and how to use them. For example, in his study of several companies that made the world's best flutes, Cook and Yanow (1993) show that for generations the craftsmen were able to produce flutes that artists would recognize immediately as having been made by a particular company, but neither management nor the craftsmen could describe exactly what they had done to make them so recognizable. It was embedded in the processes of manufacturing and reflected a set of skills that could be passed on for generations through an apprentice system, yet was not formally identifiable.

In evolving the means by which the group will accomplish its goals, many of the internal issues that the group must deal with get partially settled. The external problem of division of labor structures who gets to know whom and who is in authority. The work system of the group defines its boundaries and its rules for membership. The particular beliefs and talents of the founders and leaders of the group determine which functions become dominant as the group evolves. For example, engineers founding companies based on their inventions create very different kinds of internal structures than venture capitalists creating organizations by putting technical and marketing talent under the direction of financially driven or marketing-oriented leaders.

In Ciba-Geigy the founders believed that solutions to problems result from hard thought, scientific research, and careful checking of that research in the marketplace. From the beginning this company had clearly defined research roles and distinguished them sharply from managerial roles. The norm had developed that a person must become an expert in his or her own area, to the point where he or she knows more about that area than anyone else—a norm clearly derived from some of the assumptions of the scientific model on which the company operated. Historically, this link to the culture of science may have accounted, in part, for the assumption that people's areas of expertise were their own property or turf and the feeling that it might be considered insulting to be given advice in that area. The defined turf included the person's subordinates, budget, physical space, and all other resources that were allocated to that person. This level of felt autonomy and the formal relationships that developed among group members then became their means of getting work done. The high degree of reliance on hierarchical authority also derived from the core technology in which Ciba-Geigy was working and from the Swiss German macroculture. Chemistry and chemical engineering are fairly precise hierarchical fields in which being an experienced expert helps to prevent serious accidents or explosions.

In DEC, on the other hand, a norm developed that the only turf someone really owned is his or her accountability for certain tasks and accomplishments. Budget, physical space, subordinates, and other resources were really seen as common organizational property over which an individual had only influence. Others in the organization could try to influence the accountable manager or his or her subordinates, but there were no formal boundaries or "walls." Physical space also was viewed as common territory, and "sharing" of knowledge was highly valued. Whereas in Ciba-Geigy to give ideas to another was considered threatening, in DEC it was considered mandatory to survival. The core technology of electrical engineering and circuit design lent itself much more to experimentation and individual innovation in that mistakes were a waste of time and resources but not physically threatening.

In DEC, lack of consensus on who "owned" what could be a major source of conflict. For example, at one time in DEC's history, there was a lack of consensus on the rules for obtaining key engineering services, such as drafting and the use of the model-building shop. Some engineers believed that work would be done in the order in which it was submitted; others believed that it would be done according to the importance of the work, and they often persuaded the service manager to break into the queue to give their work priority. This aroused great anger on the part of those who were waiting their turn patiently, and, as might be expected, it made the service managers very anxious.

The whole engineering group eventually had to get together to establish a common set of policies, which, interestingly enough, reinforced the existing *ambiguous* pattern and legitimized it. Both engineering and service managers were to do the "sensible" thing, and, if they could not figure out what that was, they were to refer the matter to the next higher level of management for resolution. The policy discussion ended up reinforcing the assumption that because no one is smart enough to have a "formula" for how to do things, people should use their intelligence and common sense at all times. Ambiguity was considered to be a reality that must be lived with and managed "sensibly."

In summary, as cultural assumptions form around the means by which goals are to be accomplished, they will inevitably involve the internal issues of status and identity, thus highlighting the complexity of both the analysis of means and the issues surrounding efforts to change how an organization accomplishes its goals. Consensus on the means to be used creates the behavioral regularities and many of the artifacts that eventually come to be identified as the visible manifestations of the culture. After these regularities and patterns are in place, they become a source of stability for members and are, therefore, strongly adhered to.

Shared Assumptions About Measuring Results and Correction Mechanisms

All groups and organizations need to know how they are doing against their goals and periodically need to check to determine whether they are performing in line with their mission. This process involves three areas in which the group needs to achieve consensus leading to cultural dimensions that later drop out of awareness and become basic assumptions. Consensus must be achieved on what to measure, how to measure it, and what to do when corrections are needed. The cultural elements that form around each of these issues often become the primary focus for what newcomers to the organization will be concerned about because such measurements inevitably become linked to how each employee is doing his or her job.

What to Measure

Once the group is performing, it must have consensus on how to judge its own performance to know what kind of remedial action to take when things do not go as expected. For example, we have noted that early in DEC's history, the evaluation of engineering projects hinged on whether certain key engineers in the company "liked" the product. The company assumed that internal acceptance was an acceptable surrogate for external acceptance. At the same time, if several competing engineering groups each liked what they were designing, the criterion shifted to "letting the market decide." These criteria could work in tandem as long as there were enough resources to support all the projects because DEC was growing at a rapid rate.

At the Wellmade flute company, evaluation was done at each node in the production process, so that by the time an instrument reached the end of the line, it was likely to pass inspection and to be acceptable to the artist. If a craftsman at a given position did not like what he felt or saw or heard, he simply passed the instrument back to the preceding craftsman; the norm was that it would be reworked without resentment. Each person trusted the person in the next position (Cook, personal communication, March 10, 1992).

Cook also found a similar process in a French brandy company. Not only was each step evaluated by an expert, but the ultimate role of "taster"—the person, who makes the final determination of when a batch is ready—could only be held by a male son of the previous taster. In this company, the last taster had no sons. Rather than pass the role on to the eldest daughter, it was passed on to a nephew, on the assumption that female taste preferences were in some fundamental way different from male taste preferences!

I was involved at one point in the 1980s with the exploration and production division management of the U.S. Shell Oil Company. My consulting assignment was to help them do a cultural analysis to develop better "measurements" of the division's performance. As we collectively began to examine the artifacts and espoused beliefs and values of this group, it immediately became apparent that the exploration group and the production group had completely different concepts of how they wanted to be measured.

The exploration group wanted to be measured on finding evidence of oil, which they felt should be determined on a statistical basis over a long period of time because most wells proved to be "dry." In contrast, the production group, which was charged with safely removing oil from an active well, wanted to be measured on a short-term basis in terms of safe and efficient "production." For the exploration group, the risk was in not finding anything over a long period of time; for the production group the risk was of an accident or fire, which could occur at any moment. In the end, both groups wanted to contribute to the financial performance of the company, so both the cost of exploration and the cost of safe production had to be factored in, but neither group wanted to be measured by a general criterion that did not fit its work.

Some companies teach their executives to trust their own judgment as a basis for decisions; others teach them to check with their bosses; still others teach them not to trust results unless they are based on hard data, such as test markets or at least market research; and still others teach them to rely on staff experts. If members of the group hold widely divergent concepts of what to look for and how to evaluate results, they cannot decide when and how to take remedial action.

For example, senior managers within companies often hold different views of how to assess financial performance—debt/equity ratios, return on sales, return on investment, stock price, credit rating, and other indicators could all be used. If senior management cannot agree on which indicator to pay primary attention to, they cannot decide how well they are doing and what corrective action, if any, they need to take.

Debates can occur over whether financial criteria should override criteria such as customer satisfaction, market share, or employee morale. These debates are complicated by potential disagreements on the correct time horizons to use in making evaluations—daily, monthly, quarterly, annually, or what? Even though the information systems may be very precise, such precision does not guarantee consensus on how to evaluate information.

The potential complexity of achieving consensus on measurement criteria was illustrated in an international refugee organization. Field workers measured themselves by the number of refugees processed, but senior management paid more attention to how favorable the attitudes of host governments were because those governments financed the organization through their contributions. Senior management therefore checked every decision that was to be made about refugees with virtually every other department and several layers of management to ensure that the decision would not offend any of the supporting governments. However, this process markedly slowed the decision making and often led to "lowest common denominator" conservative decisions. This, in turn, led to great consternation on the part of field workers, who felt that while management was dawdling to get everyone's approval, they were dealing with crisis situations in the field in which a slowdown might mean death for significant numbers of refugees. They perceived top management to be hopelessly mired in what they considered to be simply bureaucratic tangles, and they did not understand the caution that top management felt it had to exercise toward sponsoring governments.

The lack of agreement across the hierarchy on how to judge success illustrates the importance of subcultures in organizations. Whereas the field workers tended to think of the core mission as helping the survival of refugees, senior management was clearly more concerned with the survival of the total organization, which, in its view, depended on how it related to the United Nations and to the host governments. Senior management had to decide whether to indoctrinate field workers more effectively on what the core organizational survival problem really was or to live with the internal conflict that the lack of consensus seemed to generate. On the other hand, the younger, idealistic field workers could well argue (and did) that to survive as an organization made no sense if the needs of refugees were not met. This organization, then, had conflicting cultural assumptions or conflicting subcultures in that the headquarters and field each had consensus, but there was an absence of a total organizational consensus on mission, goals, and means.

In Ciba-Geigy a comparable subculture issue arose in evaluating the performance of different divisions. The high-performing division heads chose to compare themselves *internally* to the low-performing divisions and were, therefore, complacent and satisfied with their performance. Senior management, on other hand, chose to compare divisions to their *external* competitors in the same product/market space and found that some were underperforming by this criterion. For example, the pharmaceutical division outperformed the other chemical divisions but did poorly relative to other pharmaceutical companies. Yet the corporate assumption that we are "one family" made it hard to convince the pharmaceutical division managers to accept the tougher "external" standards.

Consensus on Means of Measurement

Consensus must be achieved both on the criteria and on the means by which information is to be gathered. For example, in DEC's early years, there developed a very open communication system, built around high levels of acquaintance and trust among the members of the organization. This system was supported by a computerized e-mail network, constant telephone communications, frequent visits, formal and informal surveys and sensing meetings, and two- to three-day committee meetings in settings away from the office. Individual managers developed their own systems of measurement and were trusted to report progress accurately. DEC operated on the powerful shared assumption that information and truth were the lifeblood of the organization, and the company built many formal and informal mechanisms to ensure a high rate of internal communication, such as the rule in the early years that engineer's offices were not to have doors. They were to be easily accessible to each other physically and through the world-wide electronic network.

Ken Olsen "measured" things by walking around, talking to people at all levels of the organization, sensing morale from the climate he encountered as he walked around. The informal measures were much more important initially than formal financial controls, and consensus developed around the assumption that "we will always be open and truthful with each other."

In contrast, in Ciba-Geigy there was a tightly structured reporting system, which involved weekly telephone calls, monthly reports to the financial control organization in headquarters, semi-annual visits to every department by headquarters teams, and formal meetings and seminars at which policy was communicated downward in the organization. In Ciba-Geigy the main assumption appeared to be that information flowed primarily in designated channels, and informal systems were to be avoided because they could be unreliable. Subculture issues came up around the assessment of scientific information, especially about drugs. The company had laboratories both in the United States and in Europe, and information was assumed to be equally valid in both sets of labs. Yet scientists often reported that they did not entirely trust the data from the other organization because they were perceived to be using somewhat different standards.

In summary, the methods an organization decides to use to measure its own activities and accomplishments—the criteria it chooses and the information system it develops to measure itself—become central elements of its culture as consensus develops around these issues. If consensus fails to develop, and strong subcultures form around different assumptions, the organization will find itself in conflicts that can potentially undermine its ability to cope with the external environment.

Shared Assumptions About Remedial and Repair Strategies

The final area of consensus crucial for external adaptation concerns what to do if a change in course is required and how to make that change. If information surfaces that the group is not on target—sales are off, market share is down, profits are down, product introductions are late, key customers complain about product quality, key staff people or managers leave, or the like—by what process is the problem diagnosed and remedied?

For example, the 2009 major recall of Toyota vehicles illustrates how corporate and macrocultural forces interact to create first a propensity to deny that there is a problem because of the implied loss of face, then an effort to minimize the cost to the organization of fixing the problem, then a series of apologies, and finally an acceptance of the full costs of analyzing and fixing what was really wrong in the cars. There was clearly consensus on the need to protect the company's face but evidently lack of consensus on how to remedy the problem in the cars.

Effective remedial action requires consensus on how to gather external information, how to get that information to the right parts of the organization that can act on it, and how to alter the internal production processes to take the new information into account. Organizations can become ineffective if there is lack of consensus on any part of this information gathering and utilization cycle (Schein, 1980). For example, in General Foods, the product managers used market research to determine whether or not the product they were managing was meeting sales and quality goals. At the same time, sales managers who were out in the supermarkets were getting information on how store managers were reacting to different products by giving them better or worse positions on the shelves. It was well established that shelf position was strongly correlated with sales. Sales managers consistently attempted to get this information to the product managers, who refused to consider it relative to their more "scientifically conducted" market research, thus unwittingly undermining their own performance. In the same vein, in the early days at DEC, the person who knew the most about what competitors were doing was the purchasing manager because he had to buy parts from competitor companies. Yet his knowledge was often ignored because engineers trusted their own judgment more than his information.

If information gets to the right place, where it is understood and acted upon, there is still the matter of reaching consensus on what kind of action to take. For example, if a product fails in the marketplace, does the organization fire the product manager, reexamine the marketing strategy, reassess the quality of the research and development process, convene a diagnostic team from many functions to see what can be learned from the failure, or brush the failure under the rug and quietly move people into different jobs?

At DEC, both the diagnosis and the proposed remedy were likely to result from widespread open discussion and debate among members at all levels of the organization, but more weight was consistently given to the technical people over the financial, marketing, or purchasing people. After the discussion and debate, self-corrective action was often taken locally because people now recognized problems about which they could do something. Thus, by the time top management ratified a course of action and announced it, most of the problem had already been dealt with. However, if the discussion led to proposals that violated some of Ken Olsen's assumptions or intuitions, he would step into the debate and attempt to influence thinking. If that did not work, he sometimes empowered different groups to proceed along different paths in order to "play it safe," to stimulate internal competition, and to "let the market decide." Though this process was at times haphazard, it was well understood and consensually agreed to as the way to get things done in the kind of dynamic marketplace that DEC found itself in.

In Ciba-Geigy, remedial action was taken locally, if possible, to minimize the upward delegation of bad news. However, if problems surfaced that were company-wide, top management went through a formal period of diagnosis, often with the help of task forces and other specific processes. After a diagnosis had been made and remedial action decided on, the decision was formally disseminated through systematic meetings, memoranda, phone calls, and other formal means.

In General Foods, one of the most difficult remedial actions was for the product development function to stop working on a product that was not successful. If market test data showed that customers would not buy a particular product, they rationalized that they had tested the wrong population or that a minor change in the product would cure the problem. No matter what the data showed, the development team would rationalize them away and assume that sooner or later the product would sell. Management had to develop tough rules and time limits that, in effect, forced the abandonment of projects over the objections of the development team.

"Corrective" processes are not limited to problem areas. If a company is getting signals of success, it may decide to grow faster, or develop a careful strategy of controlled growth, or take a quick profit and risk staying small. Consensus on these matters becomes crucial to effectiveness, and the kind of consensus achieved is one of the determinants of the "style" of the company. Organizations that have not had periodic survival problems may not have a "style" of responding to such problems. However, organizations that have had survival crises often discovered in their responses to such crises what some of their deeper assumptions really were. In this sense, an important piece of an organization's culture can be genuinely latent. No one really knows what response it will make to a severe crisis, yet the nature of that response will reveal deep elements of the culture.

For example, many organizations about to go out of business have discovered, to their surprise, high levels of motivation and commitment among their employees. One also hears the opposite kinds of stories, often from wartime, of military units that were counting on high levels of commitment only to find individuals losing their will to fight, seeking excuses to get out of combat, and even shooting their own officers in the back. Crisis situations reveal whether worker subcultures have developed around restriction of output and hiding ideas for improvement from management, or whether these subcultures support productivity goals.

After remedial or corrective action has been taken, new information must be gathered to determine whether results have improved or not. Sensing changes in the environment, getting the information to the right place, digesting it, and developing appropriate responses are parts of a perpetual learning cycle that will ultimately characterize how a given organization maintains its effectiveness.

Summary and Conclusions

In this chapter, I have reviewed how cultural assumptions evolve around all aspects of a group's relationship to its external environment. The group's ultimate mission, goals, means used to achieve goals, measurement of its performance, and remedial strategies all require consensus if the group is to perform effectively. If there is conflict between subgroups that form subcultures, such conflict can undermine group performance; however, if the environmental context is changing, such conflict can also be a potential source of adaptation and new learning.

How these external survival issues are worked out strongly influences the internal integration of the group. Ultimately all organizations are *socio-technical* systems in which the manner of external adaptation and the solution of internal integration problems are interdependent and intertwined. Although we are discussing them in serial order for purposes of exposition, in reality, the external and internal processes are occurring at the same time.

The most important conclusion to be derived from this analysis is that culture is a multidimensional, multifaceted phenomenon, not easily reduced to a few major dimensions. Culture ultimately reflects the group's effort to cope and learn; it is the residue of that learning process. Culture thus not only fulfills the function of providing stability, meaning, and predictability in the present but also is the result of functionally effective decisions in the group's past.

The implications for leadership are several. First, the external issues described are usually the formal leader's primary concern in that it is the leader who creates the group and wants it to succeed. Even if the group precedes the leader historically, it will generally put one or more of its members into leadership roles to worry about external boundary management, survival, and growth. Second, it is the successful management of these several functions that is usually the basis on which leaders are assessed. If they cannot create a group that succeeds, they are considered to have failed as leaders. Internal dissent can be forgiven, but if a leader fails in the external functions, he or she is usually abandoned, voted out, or gotten rid of in a more dramatic way. The steps of the coping cycle and the issues groups face thus can be a useful checklist against which to assess leadership competencies and performance.

6

ASSUMPTIONS ABOUT MANAGING
INTERNAL INTEGRATION

A group cannot accomplish tasks, survive, and grow if it cannot manage its internal relationships. Learning how to manage those internal relationships occurs at the same time that the group is accomplishing its tasks, so the focus of this chapter is analytically separate but the activities occur simultaneously in real life. Having said that, the analytic distinction is very important for leadership because the leader, group member, or outside consultant can focus the group's energy and time on either *task dimensions* such as were described in the previous chapter or on *group and interpersonal dimensions* such as will be described in this chapter. This distinction becomes crucial because there are times in a group's evolution where it is necessary to focus more on external task processes and other times to focus more on internal group and interpersonal processes. In fact, it is one of the most important functions of leadership to manage the group's focus and energy appropriately between these two sets of processes.

Because the processes that build and develop the group occur at the same time as the processes of problem solving and task accomplishment, ultimately the culture of the group will reflect both externally and internally oriented processes. These internal processes reflect the major internal issues that any group must deal with, as shown in Exhibit 6.1.

Creating a Common Language
and Conceptual Categories

To function as a group, the individuals who come together must establish a system of communication and a language that permits setting goals and interpreting and managing what is going on. The human organism cannot

---

Exhibit 6.1.   The Problems of Internal Integration.

- **Creating a common language and conceptual categories:** If members cannot communicate with and understand each other, a group is impossible by definition.

- **Defining group boundaries and criteria for inclusion and exclusion:** The group must be able to define itself. Who is in and who is out, and by what criteria is membership determined?

- **Distributing power, authority, and status:** Every group must work out its pecking order, its criteria and rules for how someone gets, maintains, and loses power and authority. Consensus in this area is crucial to help members manage feelings of aggression.

- **Developing norms of trust, intimacy, friendship, and love:** Every group must work out its "rules of the game" for peer relationships, for relationships between the sexes, and for the manner in which openness and intimacy are to be handled in the context of managing the organization's tasks. Consensus in this area is crucial to help members define trust and manage feelings of affection and love.

- **Defining and allocating of rewards and punishments:** Every group must know what its heroic and sinful behaviors are and must achieve consensus on what is a reward and what is a punishment.

- **Explaining the unexplainable:** Every group, like every society, faces unexplainable events that must be given meaning so that members can respond to them and avoid the anxiety of dealing with the unexplainable and uncontrollable.

---

tolerate too much uncertainty or stimulus overload. Categories of meaning that organize perceptions and thought filter out what is unimportant while focusing on what is important. Such categories not only reduce overload and anxiety but also are a necessary precondition for any coordinated action. Language provides those categories.

Two children on a see-saw need some verbal or nonverbal means of signaling when to push and when to relax, or how far back to sit if their weight is different, or how fast to move. Members of a founding group coming together to create a new organization need to learn about each other's semantic space (even if they start with a common basic language, such as English) to determine what they mean by such abstractions as "a good product," of "high quality," produced at "low cost," to get into the "market" "as rapidly as possible." At a more mundane level, the cartoon of the Eskimo mother makes the point well.

If several members of a group are using different category systems, not only will they not agree on what to do, but they also will not even agree

"Little Jack Horner sat in a corner, eating . . . What's a corner?"

Reprinted by permission of J. Whiting.

on their definition of what is real, what is a fact, when something is true or false, what is important, what needs attention, and so on. Most communication breakdowns between people result from their lack of awareness that at the outset, they are making basically different assumptions about meaning categories.

For example, in my role as a consultant to a small family-owned food company, I asked some managers whether they experienced any "conflicts" with subordinates, peers, or superiors in their daily work. Unless I happened to be talking to a particularly disgruntled person, I usually elicited an immediate and flat denial of any conflict whatsoever. This response puzzled me because I had been called in by the president to help figure out what to do about "severe conflicts" that members of the organization were perceiving and experiencing. I finally realized that I was assuming that the word "conflict" was a generally understood term referring to any degree of disagreement between two or more people, and that conflict was a normal human condition that is always present to some degree.

My interviewees, on the other hand, held two quite different assumptions. In their view, (1) the word conflict referred to a severe disagreement that is difficult if not impossible to reconcile (a different semantic interpretation of the word itself), and (2) conflict was "bad" in the sense that a person who has conflicts is not managing well. After I realized that different semantic assumptions were at the root of the communication problem, I could change my inquiry to: "Can you tell me about the things that make it easy or hard for you to get your job done." If any evidence of interpersonal "disagreements" began to surface, I made explicit my own assumption that such disagreements were, in my view, completely normal in organizations. I then often got vivid and detailed stories of severe "conflicts" and, in subsequent discussions, found that I could use the word conflict itself without further misunderstanding or defensiveness. In this example, my clients and I were building a common meaning system for our own work.

In this same organization, I observed in group meetings that the president often got angry with a member who was not contributing actively and began to draw conclusions about the competence of that member. The president assumed (as I learned later by asking about the situation) that the silence meant ignorance, incompetence, or lack of motivation. The silent member, it turned out, was usually ready to make a presentation and was very frustrated because he was never called on to give it. He assumed that he was not supposed to volunteer, and he began to believe that his boss did not value him because he was not called on. If their different assumptions about the meaning of silence were not brought into the open, the danger was that both would validate their own incorrect assumption, thus setting up a classic case of a self-fulfilling prophecy. In this group, the absence of a consensually validated communication system undermined effective action. A total group culture had not yet formed, though various subgroups might already have been operating on shared assumptions, such as "Our boss does not value our contributions."

Critical conceptual categories are usually built into the basic language a group uses. Thus, English speakers learn through English words the major cultural categories of the Anglo-Saxon cultural tradition. For example, the word *management* reflects the proactive, optimistic, pragmatic approach that characterizes the U.S. culture. It is a surprise to many people who speak only English that a comparable word does not exist in other languages, such as German. Even more important, if the word does not exist, the concept also may not exist in the same sense. For example, in German there are words for leadership, leading, and directing; but managing, as English speakers mean it, does not readily translate either as a word or as a concept.

One of the cultural traps that new organizations face is the failure to note that new members come from very different subcultures and need to establish a common meaning system within the common language. When there are new members from other macrocultures, the problem is likely to be recognized immediately, leading founders and leaders to pay closer attention to building a common language and common meanings through activities that can best be thought of as "cultural islands" in which the primary focus is on language and meaning.

In summary, a common language and common conceptual categories are clearly necessary for any kind of consensus to be established and for any communication to occur at all. This common understanding begins with the categories of action, gesture, and speech that are often provided by the person who brought the group together or by the more active members of the group once it is together. Because the members are usually all from the same host culture, a common language is initially available. However, as the group matures, it invests common words with special meanings, and what certain words really mean ultimately becomes one of the deepest layers of that group's culture. From the outsider's point of view that common language is then labeled as "jargon" and becomes difficult to decipher. With growing globalism and occupational complexity, more groups will be multicultural, requiring special efforts on the part of leadership to create cultural islands in which those differences can be explored. More will be said about this in Chapters Twelve and Twenty-One.

Defining Group Boundaries and Identity

For a group to function and develop, one of the most important areas for clear consensus is the perception of who is *in* the new group and who is *not in*, and the criteria by which such decisions are made. New members cannot really function and concentrate on their primary task if they are insecure about their membership, and the group cannot really maintain a good sense of itself if it does not have a way of defining itself and its boundaries.

Initially, the criteria for inclusion are usually set by the leader, founder, or convener, but as the group members interact, those criteria are tested, and a group consensus arises around the criteria that survive the test. In a young company, there is often intense debate over who should be an owner or a partner, who should have stock options, who should be hired for key functions or be an officer, and who should be ejected because he or she does not fit in. In this debate, real personnel decisions are being made, and at the same time, the criteria of inclusion are being forged, tested, and articulated so that they become clear to everyone. Such debate also provides opportunities for testing mission statements, goal clarity, and means clarity, illustrating how several cultural elements are simultaneously being created, tested, articulated, and reinforced.

One way of determining a group's core assumptions is to ask present members what they really look for in new members and to examine carefully the career histories of present members to detect what accounts for their inclusion in the group. For example, when I inquired about DEC's hiring process, the answer was that every potential new member of the technical or managerial staff had to be interviewed by at least five to ten people, and only if that individual was acceptable to the entire set, was he or she offered a job. Interviewers seemed to be looking for intelligence, self-reliance, the ability to articulate clearly, tolerance for ambiguity, and high motivation. But when asked, they usually just said, "We want someone who will fit in."

After DEC hired people, they were provisionally accepted as permanent members. If they failed in an initial job assignment, the assumption was that they were competent but had been put in the wrong job. In other words, once a person was "in," it was difficult to lose that status. In an economic crisis, the company tended to slow down its rate of hiring but was very reluctant to lay off anybody. And when pressures for staff reduction mounted, the organization redefined layoffs as "transitions" in which employees were given a great deal of latitude and choice.

In Ciba-Geigy, prior education was a key criterion for membership. Most of the young technical and managerial staff members came from a scientific background, highlighting the assumption that to succeed in the company, an individual must understand the scientific base on which it was built. Having an advanced degree, such as a doctorate, was a distinct advantage even if the individual was being hired into a marketing or managerial job.

Both DEC and Ciba-Geigy had difficulty hiring and absorbing what they called MBAs, by which they meant all-purpose generalists who do not have a solid technical or scientific background and who might be more concerned with personal ambition than contributing to the technical work of the organization. Behind these perceptions lay the further assumption (in both of these companies) that general management, though necessary, was not the key to success. Scientific and technical know-how was essential. These assumptions had a powerful impact on DEC's later inability to develop in different directions and to divisionalize because there was always a shortage of experienced general managers.

Who is in and who is out applies not only to the initial hiring decision but also continues to have important symbolic meaning as an individual progresses in the group. One of the immediate consequences of defining who is in and who is out is that differential treatment rules begin to be applied. Insiders get special benefits, are trusted more, get higher basic rewards, and most important, get a sense of identity from belonging to a defined organization. Outsiders such as contract workers not only get fewer of the various benefits and rewards but, more important, lose specific identity. They become part of a mass labeled "outsiders," and they are more likely to be stereotyped and treated with indifference or hostility.

Organizations can be thought of, then, as involving three dimensions of career movement: (1) lateral movement from one task or function to another, (2) vertical movement from one rank to another, and (3) inclusionary movement from outsider to insider (Schein, 1978, 2006). Consensus forms around criteria not only for promotion but also for inclusionary movement. As people move farther "in," they become privy to some of the more secret assumptions of the group. They learn the special meanings attached to certain words and the special rituals that define membership—such as the secret fraternity handshake—and they discover that one of the most important bases for status in the group is to be entrusted with group secrets. Such secrets involve historical accounts of how and why some of the things in the past really happened, who is really part of the dominant coalition or insider group, and what some of the latent functions of the organization are. In the senior management at Ciba-Geigy, there was a "Basel aristocracy,"—board members or senior executives, who were in their jobs by virtue of their social position as well as their technical excellence—but you had to be a real insider to know who they were.

As organizations age and become more complex, the problem of defining clear external and inclusionary internal boundaries becomes more complex. More people—such as salespeople, purchasing agents, distributors, franchisees, board members, and consultants—come to occupy boundary-spanning roles. In some industries, economic circumstances have made it necessary for companies to reduce the size of their workforce, causing an increase in the hiring of temporaries or contract workers, who can be laid off more easily if necessary. Cultural assumptions then come into bold relief when certain questions are raised from a policy perspective: What is a "temporary?" For how long can we keep people in that status? To what benefits if any are they entitled? How do we train them quickly in the essentials of the culture? How do we deal with the threat that temporaries pose to more permanent members of the organization (Kunda, 1992; Barley and Kunda, 2001)?

In a complex society, individuals belong to many organizations, so their identity is not tied up exclusively with any one organization. Locating and defining what a given cultural unit is becomes more difficult because within a given organization, there may be many subcultures reflecting other memberships, occupational identities, or macrocultural origins. It was alleged that at one time the sailors in the U.S. Navy who managed the cooking and serving of food were all Filipinos. In any event, the criteria for membership are always one means of determining whether a cultural unit exists in any given group, and seeking consensus on those criteria will always be a preoccupation of any given group in order to differentiate itself from other groups. Wearing special badges or uniforms is, of course, the obvious means of showing identity. A set of communication rules—the meaning of acronyms and special jargon developed within the new culture—is also one of the clearest ways that a group specifies who is "us" and who is "them."

In summary, defining the criteria for deciding who is in and who is out of an organization or any of its subunits is one of the best ways to begin to analyze a culture. Moreover, the very process by which a group makes those judgments and acts on them is a process of culture formation and maintenance that forces some integration of the external survival issues and the internal integration issues.

Distributing Power, Authority, and Status

A critical issue in any new group is how influence, power, and authority will be allocated and what the rules will be for "deference and demeanor" (Goffman, 1967). The process of stratification in human systems is typically not as blatant as the dominance-establishing rituals of animal societies, but it is functionally equivalent in that it concerns the evolution of workable rules for managing aggression and mastery needs. Human societies develop pecking orders just as chickens do, but both the process and the outcome are, of course, far more complex and varied. As we will see in Chapter Twelve, in a *new* group the process of sorting out who will dominate whom and who will influence whom can be very messy and unpredictable. But most organizations start with founders and leaders who have preconceptions about how things should be run and, therefore, impose rules that initially determine how authority is to be obtained and how aggressive behavior is to be managed.

DEC and Ciba-Geigy differed dramatically in their methods of allocating power and channeling aggression. In DEC, power was derived from personal success and building a support network. Formal rank, seniority, and job description had relatively less influence than personal characteristics and track record. Personal characteristics such as the ability to negotiate, to convince, and to be proved right by circumstance were emphasized. The formal system of status was deliberately de-emphasized in favor of an assumption that everyone has a right to participate, to voice an opinion, and to be heard because good ideas can come from anyone. However, because no one was considered smart enough to evaluate the quality of his or her own idea, the individual always had to get buy-in if others were involved in the implementation of that idea, and anyone had a right and obligation to challenge it. Aggression was thus channeled into the daily working routines but directed at ideas, not people. The further assumption, that once in the organization, you were a member of "the family" and could not really lose membership, protected people from feeling personally threatened if their ideas were challenged.

Ciba-Geigy, on the other hand, had a very formal system of allocating power based on personal background, educational credentials, seniority, loyalty, and successful performance of whatever jobs were allocated to the person by higher authority. After a certain number of years, an employee acquired a rank similar to the kind of rank that comes with promotion in military service or the civil service, and this rank was independent of particular job assignments. Status and privileges went with this rank and could not be lost even if the employee was given reduced job responsibilities. The working climate emphasized politeness, formality, and reason. Displays of aggression were taboo, but behind-the-scenes complaining, badmouthing, and politicking were the inevitable consequences of suppressing overt aggression.

Both organizations could be labeled "paternalistic" from some points of view in that they generated strong family feelings and a degree of emotional dependence on leaders or formal authorities. However, the drastic difference in how the rules of power allocation actually worked in these two organizations serves to remind us how vague and potentially unhelpful broad labels such as "autocratic" or "paternalistic" are in characterizing particular organizational cultures. Note once again the tight interrelationship between the external issues of mission and task, on the one hand, and the internal issues of power distribution, on the other hand. The kind of technology and task involved in each organization had a direct effect on the kind of power distribution that eventually arose. The more autocratic assumptions of the science of chemistry and the more egalitarian assumptions of the electrical engineering community in an emerging technology were powerful influences on the culture.

To understand how an authority system works requires sensitivity to the nuances of language, as illustrated by my experience in a meeting at British Petroleum in the 1980s. I was asked by the incumbent chairman to attend the three-day meeting of all of the senior managers from around the world, observe the culture in action, and facilitate a discussion of the culture during the third day. At this meeting, a major structural change was to be announced and discussed. Whereas previously countries had been fairly autonomous in managing all product lines, in the new organization, worldwide business units would be created for each major product line and would be managed from London. This change meant that the country managers would lose a great deal of autonomy and power, while the headquarters and business units would gain power.

Most of the meeting was devoted to the present chairman's efforts to help the country managers accept their new role as more of a "diplomat" locally and less of a business unit manager. They were clearly being disempowered to a considerable degree. My observation was that the chairman described the new rules and handled the ensuing disappointment and obvious resentment in a most gentle and kindly manner, while reaffirming repeatedly the new reality of their positions. It came across as gently giving the disempowered country managers some advice on how their roles might be restructured in the future. When I reported these observations to my client, the incumbent chairman, he burst out laughing and said: "Ed, what you have just witnessed in that meeting was the worst bloodbath we have ever had; I have never seen our chairman more aggressive in putting down people and asserting the new power structure." So much for my "understanding" of the British culture and the culture of this company!

Sociologists have shown very convincingly how manners and morals, politeness, and tact are not "niceties" of social life, but essential rules for how to keep from destroying each other socially (Goffman, 1959, 1967). Our functioning as human beings requires us not only to develop a self-image of who we are but also a degree of self-esteem—a sense that we have enough value to continue to function. The word "face" captures this publicly claimed value, and the rules of the social order are that we should protect each other's faces. If we offend or insult someone by not upholding their claims—laughing at something serious, humiliating or embarrassing the other—it is a loss of face for *both* parties. Not only has one party failed to uphold his or her claims, but the other party has behaved rudely, destructively, and irresponsibly.

Thus the most fundamental rule of the macroculture in all societies is that we must uphold each other's claims because our self-esteem is based on it. When we tell a joke, others laugh no matter how unfunny the joke; when someone breaks wind in public, we pretend not to have noticed no matter how loud the sound. Human society of any sort hinges on the cultural agreements to try to uphold each other's identities and illusions, even if that means lying. We compliment people to make them feel good even if we don't believe it; we teach little children not to say "Look at that fat lady over there," even though an obese person is clearly visible.

One reason why performance appraisal in organizations is emotionally resisted so strongly is that managers know full well they are violating the larger cultural rules and norms when they sit a subordinate down to give him or her "feedback." To put it bluntly, when we tell people what we "really think of them" in an aggressive way, this can be functionally equivalent to social murder. Someone who goes around doing this is viewed as unsafe to have around, and, if the behavior persists, we often declare such a person mentally ill and lock him or her up. In his analysis of mental hospitals, Goffman showed brilliantly how "therapy" was in many cases teaching the patients the rules of polite society so that they could be let free to function in that society without making others too anxious (Goffman, 1961). In more traditional societies, the jester or the fool played the role of telling the truth about what was going on, and this only worked because the role could be discounted and ignored.

To conclude, every group, organization, occupation, and macroculture develops norms around the distribution of influence, authority, and power. If those norms "work" in the sense of providing a system that gets external tasks done and leaves members in the group reasonably free of anxiety, these norms gradually become shared tacit assumptions and critical genetic elements in the cultural DNA.

As the world becomes more interdependent, more organizations, projects, task forces, and joint ventures of various sorts will involve members from different nations, ethnicities and occupations. In the efforts of those groups to develop a working consensus, it will be differences in the deep assumptions about authority that will be most problematic. A special role for leaders will be to create cultural islands in which it will be possible for members to explore these differences to reach both mutual understanding and new rules for how to manage their own authority relationships.

Developing Rules for Relationships

Every new group must decide simultaneously how to deal with authority problems and how to establish workable peer relationships. Whereas authority issues derive ultimately from the necessity to deal with feelings of aggression, peer relationship and intimacy problems derive ultimately from the necessity to deal with feelings of affection, love, and sexuality. Thus, all societies develop clear sex roles, kinship systems, and rules for friendship and sexual conduct that serve to stabilize current relationships while ensuring procreation mechanisms and thereby the survival of the society. The rules that we learn about whether or not we can trust someone are implicit.

The specific issues of sex and procreation are most relevant in the family firm that is specifically concerned about keeping succession in the family. Then who marries whom and which children come into the firm are indeed major issues, and the emerging norms of the organization will reflect the assumptions of the founding family about succession (Beckhard and Dyer, 1983a, 1983b; Dyer, 1986). Recall Cook's finding that the role of chief taster in the French brandy company could only pass to another male, so the succession went to a nephew instead of a daughter.

One of the most salient features of family firms is that certain levels of intimacy and trust appear to be reserved for family members, creating a kind of dual intimacy system in the organization. In Steinbergs, a large Canadian supermarket chain (to be described in greater detail in Chapter Thirteen), the founder hired another person who became virtually a partner in all business affairs, but the founder never allowed this person to own any voting stock. The two were very intimate in all business relations and were close friends, but ownership had a special meaning to the founder and could only be shared with blood relatives.

As Freud pointed out long ago, one of the models we bring to any new group situation is our own family model, the group in which we spent most of our early life. Thus, the rules that we learned from our own parents for dealing with them and with our siblings are often our initial model for dealing with authority and peer relationships in a new group. Because the different members of a new group are likely to have had widely varying experiences in their families of origin, they may start with very different models of what those relationships should be, leading to potential disagreement and conflict over the right way to relate to others in the new group.

In work organizations, the rules governing intimacy cover a broad range of issues—what to call each other, how much personal life to share, how much emotion to display, whom to ask for help and around what issues, how open to be in communicating and whether or not sexual relationships with colleagues are condoned. In most organizations, the rules around intimacy will be linked to the rules around authority in that newcomers learn quickly with whom they can joke and with whom they must be serious, whom they can trust with intimate personal details, and how appropriate it is to develop personal relationships with other employees, especially across status or rank lines. In some cultures and some organizations, nepotism is welcomed because family members can be trusted more; in other cultures and organizations, it is forbidden because family loyalties could interfere with loyalty to the organization and could bring in less competent employees.

The implicit assumptions about relationships within DEC were paradoxical. On the one hand, "pushing back," " doing the right thing," and "getting buy-in" made the environment extremely individualistic and competitive. On the other hand, the repeated shared experience of building consensus before leaping into action created a high degree of personal intimacy. The many off-site meetings that involved roughing it together in the woods for several days at a time brought DEC groups into much more intimate contact, reflecting the family feeling previously referred to.

Teamwork at DEC was strongly espoused, but the meaning of the concept was unique to Digital in that being a good team player meant pushing back even if that disrupted meetings and slowed projects down. This assumption was the opposite of the Hewlett-Packard assumption that being a good team player meant going along with where the group seemed to want to go, not objecting too much. An insightful internal organization consultant told me recently that he had finally achieved some insight into what kind of a team DEC was. He said it was "a track team or a gymnastics team in which you want the total score to be high, but you get that score by a lot of superior individual efforts."

In Ciba-Geigy, relationships were much more aloof and formal, reflecting the macroculture in which Ciba-Geigy was embedded and the personalities of most of the current leaders of the group. However, Ciba-Geigy compensated for the daily formality by annual rituals of informality through a particular event that occurred at each annual management meeting of the top forty or fifty people. One afternoon and evening of the three-day meeting were always devoted to an event that was planned by the meeting organizer but kept secret until the group actually boarded buses. The event always involved some sport at which everyone would be relatively incompetent and would therefore look foolish in everyone else's eyes, for example, shooting an old-style crossbow. Rank and status were thus deliberately equilibrated and a level of kidding and teasing replaced the work-a-day formality. Following the sports event, everyone went to an informal dinner at which humorous speeches were given, laced with more teasing and jibes at each other. With the consumption of much alcohol, people let their hair down and interacted in a way that would never have been possible at work. The secrecy surrounding what would be done each year heightened the emotionality associated with the event and made the ritual comparable to a group of children anticipating what their Christmas gifts would be. One could almost say that in this organization, intimacy was achieved through periodic regression rituals.

Rules regarding relationships interact powerfully with rules regarding task performance in new organizations, especially multicultural ones where the macrocultures may vary. The specific issue is whether the members of the culture believe that they must establish some level of intimacy with colleagues before they can tackle the task effectively or whether they believe that tasks can be done immediately without concern for building relationships first. Stories abound of meetings where the members of one culture (usually the U.S.) wanted to get right to work while members of the other culture first wanted to "get to know each other through various informal activities" (often Asian or Latin cultures). Here again, the leadership role is to become aware of these differences and to create meetings and events where the issue can be confronted and accepted.

In summary, developing rules for how to get along with each other is critical to the functioning of any group and organization. Within a given culture such as the United States, there will be variations among organizations in the degree of intimacy that is considered appropriate on and off the job. But, as in the case of rules about authority relations, if future organizations will be more multicultural in terms of nations, ethnicities, and occupations, the potential for misunderstanding and offending each other will increase dramatically. Exploring these rules in a safe environment, a "cultural island" created for this purpose, will become an essential component of developing organizations.

Allocating Rewards and Punishment

Every group must develop a system of sanctions for obeying or disobeying its norms and rules. There must evolve some consensus on what symbolically and actually is defined as a reward or punishment and on the manner in which it is to be administered. The shared assumptions concerning this issue constitute some of the most important elements of an emerging culture in a new organization. Changes in the reward and punishment system are also one of the quickest and easiest ways to begin to change behavior and, thereby, begin to change some elements of the culture.

In General Foods, the norm developed that a product manager who did his job competently could expect to be moved to a bigger and better product within approximately eighteen months. Managers who did not move every eighteen months began to feel that they were failing. By way of contrast, in the early years of DEC, the assumption developed that the designer of a product should see it through from cradle to grave, so a reward was defined as being allowed to stay with a product through manufacturing and marketing all the way to sales. Being pulled off a project would have been perceived as a punishment.

In General Foods, promotion to a higher rank also correlated with all kinds of perquisites, notably a more spacious office in a better location with better furniture, higher-quality carpeting, and higher-quality art on the walls. All this was drawn from a central supply of these "status resources" very carefully allocated to each rank level. The headquarters building was designed to have movable walls so that office size could be quickly adjusted as promotions and job reassignments required. By contrast, in DEC, if a manager used promotion as an excuse for getting a bigger house or better car, Ken Olsen began to distrust him as being more concerned about personal welfare than company performance.

In Ciba-Geigy, the key short-run rewards were the personal approval of senior management and public recognition in the company newspaper. Longer-range rewards were promotion to a higher rank or movement to a clearly more important job assignment. Length of assignment to a given job could mean that the person was either dead-ended or doing such a good job that he or she was irreplaceable. DEC used bonuses, stock options, and raises as signals of good performance, whereas Ciba-Geigy relied much more heavily on symbolic nonmonetary rewards such as a special privilege to attend a scientific meeting. Salary was tied more to rank and length of service.

Punishments, like rewards, have local meanings in different organizations. In several high-tech companies that have clear espoused values about not laying people off, people can lose the particular task they are working on and become "boat people" or "wander the halls" while looking for another job within the organization. They will be carried on the payroll indefinitely, but it is clear that they have been punished. Often the signals are subtle, but colleagues know when someone is in the "doghouse" or in the "penalty box." Actual loss of bonuses or the failure to get a raise may follow, but the initial punishment is clear enough already. Some organizations develop a "blame culture," which implies that whenever something goes wrong, someone to blame is found and that person's career is damaged.

One dramatic example was revealed in a cultural analysis of Amoco some years before it was acquired by British Petroleum. Amoco's managers and engineers explicitly called it a "blaming culture" in which the norm was that if something went wrong on a project, they had to identify who was responsible as quickly as possible. *Who* was more important than *why*. The person who was "blamed" was not necessarily punished in any overt way, and often was not even told that others considered him or her responsible. Instead, it was noted in the memory of senior managers as a reason to be less trustful of this person, leading to career limitation. People who were not given good assignments or promotions might never find out why. Consequently, employees viewed it as essential to distance themselves as quickly as possible from any project that might fail, lest they be "blamed" for the failure. This belief prevented Amoco from engaging in a joint venture with another company because if a project failed, any Amoco employees on the project felt vulnerable, even if it was clear that the failure was due to people in the other company.

Deciphering when a person has been rewarded and when a person has been punished is one of the most difficult tasks for newcomers in organizations because the signals are so often ambiguous from an outsider's point of view. Being yelled at by the boss may be a reward, while being ignored may be a punishment, and only someone farther along in the understanding of the culture can reassure the yelled-at newcomer that she or he was, in fact, doing well. As noted before, teamwork is usually touted as an important characteristic for promotion, but the definition of what teamwork is can vary all over the map.

What is rewarding or punishing varies with level in the organization. For junior employees, a raise or better assignment is a key reward, while for very senior managers, only a large promotion to a more responsible assignment or progress along the inclusionary dimension counts. Being told company secrets is a major reward, while being frozen out by not being told can be a major punishment that signals ultimate excommunication. Being no longer "in the loop" is a clear signal that the individual has done something wrong.

In summary, the reward and punishment system of an organization along with its assumptions about authority and intimacy forms the critical mass of the culture that determines how people will relate to each other, manage their anxieties, and derive meaning from their daily interactions. How you treat the boss, how you treat each other and how you know whether you are doing things right or not is a kind of rock bottom of the cultural DNA. So here again, as organizations become more multicultural, we will see different systems clashing with each other leading to hurt feelings, offence, impatience, anxiety, and other dysfunctional behaviors until mutual explorations in a cultural island setting produce understanding and new consensus.

Managing the Unmanageable and Explaining the Unexplainable

Every group inevitably faces some issues not under its control, events that are intrinsically mysterious and unpredictable and hence frightening. At the physical level, events such as natural disasters and the weather require explanation. At the biological and social level, events such as birth, growth, puberty, illness, and death require a theory of what is happening and why in order to avoid anxiety and a sense of meaninglessness.

In a macroculture heavily committed to reason and science, there is a tendency to treat everything as explainable; the mysterious is only as yet unexplained. But until science has demystified an event that we cannot control or understand, we need an alternative basis for putting what has happened into a meaningful context. Religious beliefs can provide such a context and can also offer justification for events that might otherwise seem unfair and meaningless. Superstitions explain the unexplainable and provide guidelines for what to do in ambiguous, uncertain, and threatening situations.

Superstitions and myths tend to form around critical events in the organization's history, especially ones that are difficult to explain or justify because they were not under organizational control. Organizations are capable of developing the equivalent of religion and/or ideology on the basis of the manner in which past critical events were managed. Myths and stories develop around the founding of the company, times when the company had particular difficulty surviving or an unusual growth spurt, times when a challenge to core assumptions brought about a fresh articulation of those assumptions, and times of transformation and change.

For example, certain individual contributors and managers at DEC were associated with getting the company out of trouble whenever a severe crisis occurred. Certain processes were viewed almost superstitiously as "the way" to get out of trouble. One such process was to bring together a task force under the leadership of one of these heroic managers and give that task force complete freedom for a period of time to work on the problem. The ideology of "growth" became an automatic solution to various here-and-now problems and the positive feedback from a small number of special customers overrode other kinds of market information. Sometimes consultants are brought into organizations with the same kind of faith that something constructive will happen as a result of the mere presence of the outsider.

In a study of the introduction of computerized tomography into hospital radiology departments, Barley (1984a, 1984b) observed that if the computer went down at an awkward time, such as when a patient was in the middle of a scan, the technicians tried all kinds of remedial measures, including the proverbial kicking of the machine. If the computer resumed operating, as it did occasionally, the technician carefully documented what he or she had just done. When engineering arrived on the scene, it was made very clear to the technicians that what they had done had "no conceivable connection" to the computer's coming back up, yet this "knowledge" was carefully written down in a little notebook *and passed on to new colleagues as part of their training*. In a real sense, this was superstitious behavior, even in a realm in which logical explanation was possible.

Stories and myths not only explain the unexplainable but also affirm the organization's picture of itself, its own theory of how to get things done, and how to handle internal relationships (Hatch and Schultz, 2004; Pettigrew, 1979; Wilkins, 1983). For example, a story widely circulated about Hewlett-Packard is that during a severe recession no one was laid off because management and hourly people alike were willing to work shorter hours for less pay, thus enabling the company to cut its costs without cutting people. The lesson to be derived is the affirmation of strong values around people (Ouchi, 1981). A similar story is told at DEC about the "rehabilitation" of a key engineer who was associated with several important projects, all of which failed. Instead of firing him, the company—reaffirming its core assumption that if someone fails, it is because he or she is mismatched with the job—found an assignment for him in which he could succeed and once again become a hero. Buried in this story is also the assumption that individuals count and any person whom the company has hired is by definition competent.

A story from DEC's early history concerns an engineer who was sent to the West Coast to repair some equipment. He caught the midnight plane but did not have time to pack any clothing. The work took a week, requiring him to buy clothing, which he duly charged to the company. When the accounting department refused to approve the charge, the engineer threatened to quit. Ken Olsen heard about this and severely punished the accounting department, thereby reaffirming the company's dedication to technical values and to its highly motivated technical employees.

Summary and Conclusions

Every group must learn how to become a group. The process is not automatic. In fact, it is complex and multifaceted. Humans, being what they are, must deal with a finite and describable set of issues in any new group situation. At the most basic level, they must develop a common language and category system that clearly define what things mean. Formal languages do not specify with enough precision what *work, teamwork, respect, quality*, and so on mean. Groups must reach consensus on the boundaries of the group, who is in and who is not in. They must develop consensus on how to distribute influence and power so that aggression can be constructively channeled and formal status accurately determined. They must develop rules that define peer relationships and intimacy so that love and affection can be appropriately channeled. Consensus must be achieved on how important relationships are relative to task performance.

Groups must develop clear assumptions about what is a reward and what is a punishment so that group members can decipher how they are doing. And, finally, groups must develop explanations that help members deal with unpredictable and unexplainable events—the functional equivalents of religion and mythology. Stories develop around all of these issues that provide meaning and are sources of affirming the organization's sense of identity.

The assumptions that develop around these internal issues constitute— along with the assumptions about mission, goals, means, results detection, and correction mechanisms—a set of dimensions along which we can analyze and describe a culture. These are not necessarily the only dimensions we could use, but they have the advantage of being tied to a large body of research on groups, and they permit us to begin to get a sense of the dynamics of culture—how cultural assumptions begin and evolve. They also represent a conceptual grid into which we can sort the cultural data that we observe.

Leadership comes into play once again as the original source of ideas or the original behavioral models that are then tested against the internal and external environments. As we will see in Chapter Twelve, such leadership can come from any member, but someone must initiate something before the group can ratify or reject it. A special role for formal leadership will arise as groups become more multicultural in terms of countries, ethnicities, and occupations. Multiculturalism brings in the additional and deeper dimensions of macrocultures that will be examined in the next several chapters.

7

DEEPER CULTURAL ASSUMPTIONS: WHAT IS REALITY AND TRUTH?

As groups and organizations evolve, the assumptions they develop about external adaptation and internal integration reflect deeper assumptions about more abstract general issues around which humans need consensus to have any kind of society at all. If we cannot agree on what is real, how to determine the truth or falsity of something, how to measure time, how space is allocated, what human nature is, and how people should get along with each other, society is not possible in the first place.

Because different societies have evolved different answers to these questions, we have many different cultures in the world, and these broader macrocultures influence how groups and organizations within them will evolve. The most common macrocultures that have been referred to so far are nations, ethnic and religious groups, and occupations. Thus individualistic competitive behavior is taken for granted in a U.S. company, just as teamwork is taken for granted in a Japanese company. Public hugging and kissing might be entirely acceptable in a public area in the United States and entirely unacceptable in a comparable area in Saudi Arabia. Telling the boss exactly what you think might be expected in a German company and quite impossible in a Chinese or Japanese company.

When we examine the formation of groups that are initially multinational, such as cross-national mergers like that of British Petroleum and Amoco or joint ventures between companies from different countries, we see how disagreement on this higher level of abstraction can make group formation and performance extremely difficult. The best way to think about the categories we will review is to see them primarily as characteristics of macrocultures, which influence in a broad way the formation of organizational cultures, subcultures, and microcultures.

Exhibit 7.1.   The Deeper Assumptions of Macrocultures.

- Assumptions about the nature of reality and truth
- Assumptions about the nature of time
- Assumptions about the nature of space
- Assumptions about the nature of human nature, human activity, and human relationships

---

The dimensions to be reviewed are based on concepts originally developed by the sociologist Talcott Parsons (1951) and were evolved into a set of value dimensions by Kluckhohn and Strodtbeck (1961) in order to do their classic comparative study of four cultures in the U.S. Southwest—Anglo, Hispanic, Mormon, and Navajo. To varying degrees, they overlap other dimensions, such as those promoted by Hofstede (2001), Hall (1959, 1966), and Hampden-Turner and Trompenaars (1993, 2000), but I have also elaborated them on the basis of my own experience in different countries. The categories I will review in the next several chapters are shown in Exhibit 7.1.

Shared Assumptions About the Nature of Reality and Truth

A fundamental part of every culture is a set of assumptions about what is real and how to determine or discover what is real. Such assumptions tell members of a group how to determine what is relevant information, how to interpret information, and how to determine when they have enough of it to decide whether or not to act, and what action to take.

For example, as I have already pointed out several times, reality and truth in DEC were defined by debate and by pragmatic criteria of whether things work. If an objective test was impossible or too difficult to construct, the idea was debated to see whether it stood the test of being subjected to severe critical analysis. In Ciba-Geigy, much more emphasis was given to research results from the laboratory and to the opinions of those considered wise and experienced. Both companies existed in broader Western cultures dominated by concepts of science and empirically based knowledge. But the fact that these companies differed greatly from each other shows that even within this broader macrocultural context, different definitions of reality can be distinguished based on the occupational macrocultures of electrical engineering and chemistry as well as the national differences between German Switzerland and the United States.

Levels of Reality

External physical reality refers to those things that can be determined empirically by objective or, in our Western tradition, "scientific" tests. For example, if two people are arguing about whether or not a piece of glass will break, they can hit it with a hammer and find out (Festinger, 1957). If two managers are arguing over which product to introduce, they can agree to define a test market and establish criteria by which to resolve the issue. On the other hand, if two managers are arguing over which of two political campaigns to support, both would have to agree that there are no physical criteria by which to resolve their conflict.

Different cultures have different assumptions about what constitutes external physical reality. For example, many of us would not regard the spirit world or extra-sensory perception as having a physical reality basis, but in other cultures such phenomena might be regarded as very real. Vivid examples of how ambiguous the borderline can be are provided in Castaneda's (1968, 1972) descriptions of his experiences with the Indian shaman Don Juan and in the controversies that surround research on extra-sensory perception. At its core, physical reality is obvious; at its boundaries, it becomes very much a matter of macrocultural consensus, which raises the issue of "social reality."

Social reality refers to those things that members of a group regard as matters of consensus, that are not externally, empirically testable. The nature of human nature—the correct way for humans to relate to nature and to each other, the distribution of power and the entire political process, assumptions about the meaning of life, ideology, religion, group boundaries, and culture itself—are obviously matters of consensus, not empirically determinable. How a group defines itself and the values it chooses to live by obviously cannot be tested in terms of our traditional notions of empirical scientific testing but certainly can be strongly held and shared unanimously. If people believe in something and define it as real, it becomes real for that group.

In the international context, there is no way to test who is right about a territorial conflict or a belief system, as the continuing war in Afghanistan has amply demonstrated. Negotiation becomes very difficult if people hold different assumptions about "reality," leading nations to resort to the use of economic and military power. The bad joke about the naïve diplomat who tells the Arabs and the Israelis to settle their differences in a good Christian manner makes the point well.

One of the reasons why business decisions are often difficult to make and why management is an intrinsically complex activity is the lack of consensus on whether a given decision area belongs in the realm of physical or social reality. For an organization to have coherent action, there must be shared assumptions about which decisions can be empirically resolved and which ones are based on consensual criteria such as "Let the most experienced person decide" or "Let's decide by majority vote." Notice that the consensus must be on the *criteria* and on the *decision process* to be used, not necessarily on the ultimate substance of the decision. For example, in the western democratic tradition, we assume that majority rules, yet there is no empirical basis for that criterion. In fact, for many kinds of decisions, majority rule can be the worst kind of decision rule because it polarizes the debate into the two camps of "winners" and "losers."

Individual reality refers to what you have learned from your own experience and has a quality of absolute truth to you. However, that truth may not be shared by anyone else. When we disagree at this level, it becomes very hard to move forward until we can clearly articulate what our actual experience base is. We must also have some kind of consensus on whose experience we are willing to trust. In a traditional society based on hierarchical authority, if so-called elder statesmen speak, we take their experience as valid and act as if what they say is objectively true. In a pragmatic, individualistic society, on the other hand, the attitude might well be "Prove it to me," and beyond that, what is accepted as proof might be all over the map. Of course, what is defined as physical, social, or individual reality is itself the product of social learning and hence, by definition, a part of a given culture (Van Maanen, 1979b; Michael, 1985).

Reaching consensus is a process of building a shared social reality, which becomes more and more difficult as groups become more multicultural because each member brings his or her individual reality and many cultural rules about what it is okay to share and what must be withheld. As Bushe points out in his book *Clear Leadership* (2009), the cultural rules of the social order require us to make our own interpretations about why others do what they do. We make up stories to explain the behavior of others because it would be rude to keep asking "Why did you do that" or "I don't understand your behavior." To get into better communication requires us to get into situations where such rules can be suspended so that the members of the group can explain their own experience and learn to calibrate the experiences of others. I have called those situations "cultural islands" and have referred to them frequently in the previous chapters. To summarize, when group members come with different concepts of reality, then reaching common ground requires special situations and processes.

High Context and Low Context

A useful distinction can be found in Hall's (1977) differentiation between what he calls high-context and low-context cultures and Maruyama's (1974) contrast between unidirectional and mutual causal cultural paradigms. In the low-context, unidirectional culture, events have clear universal meanings; in the high-context, mutual causality culture, events can be understood only in context, meanings can vary, categories can change, and causality cannot be unambiguously established.

Though this distinction has more meaning when comparing macrocultures, it has utility for organizations as well. For example, DEC was a high-context culture in which the meaning of words and actions depended on who was speaking and under what conditions. Managers knew each other well and always took into account who the actors were. When a senior manager was observed publicly punishing a subordinate for doing something "dumb," this sometimes simply meant that the subordinate should have gotten buy-in from a few more people before going off on his own. When Ken Olsen publicly berated one of his engineers, observers often pointed out that Ken only did that with engineers whom he highly respected and therefore expected perfection from them. Ciba-Geigy, by contrast, was a low-context culture in which messages tended to have the same meaning no matter whom they were coming from. To be labeled "dumb" in Ciba-Geigy would have been a severe negative judgment.

When we refer to language, we often overlook the role of context. We assume that when someone has learned the language of another country, he or she will be able to understand what is going on and take action. But as we know all too well from our own cross-cultural travel experiences, language is embedded in a wider context in which nonverbal cues, tone of voice, body language, and other signals determine the true meaning of what is said. A vivid example from my own experience was the previously cited senior management meeting of the British Petroleum Company at which I thought I observed polite explanations from the chairman, only to be told later that he had never been more brutal than he was at that meeting.

Moralism-Pragmatism

A useful dimension for comparing groups on their approach to reality testing is an adaptation of England's (1975) moralism-pragmatism dimension. In his study of managerial values, England found that managers in different countries tended to be either *pragmatic*, seeking validation in their own experience, or *moralistic*, seeking validation in a general philosophy, moral system, or tradition. For example, he found that Europeans tended to be more moralistic, whereas Americans tended to be more pragmatic. If we apply this dimension to the basic underlying assumptions that a group makes, we can specify different bases for defining what is true, as shown in Exhibit 7.2.

This dimension not only highlights the basis on which truth is determined but also can be related to "uncertainty avoidance," a major dimension found in Hofstede's survey-based cross-national study, and to "tolerance for ambiguity," an important dimension that came out of post-World War II research (Hofstede, 2001; Adorno and others, 1950). Managers and employees in different countries and in different companies vary in the degree to which they share a certain level of comfort with varying degrees of uncertainty and ambiguity. As environments become more turbulent and occupations become more technically complex, the ability of leaders to tolerate uncertainty will become more necessary for survival and learning, suggesting that organizational and national cultures that can embrace uncertainty more easily will be inherently more adaptive (Michael, 1985).

This discussion can be summarized best by showing how it applies to our two cases. DEC had both high consensus that reality was defined by

---

Exhibit 7.2.   Possible Criteria for Determining Truth.

- **Pure dogma, based on tradition and/or religion:** It has always been done this way; it is God's will; it is written in the scriptures.

- **Revealed dogma, wisdom based on trust in the authority of wise men, formal leaders, prophets, or kings:** Our leader wants to do it this way; our consultants have recommended that we do it this way; she has had the most experience, so we should do what she says.

- **Truth derived by a "rational-legal" process, (as when we establish guilt or innocence via a legal process we have agreed to that acknowledges from the outset that there is no absolute truth, only socially determined truth):** We have to take this decision to the marketing committee and do what they decide; the boss will have to decide this one, it is his area of responsibility; we will have to vote on it and go by majority rule; we agreed that this decision belongs to the production department head.

- **Truth as that which survives conflict and debate:** We thrashed it out in three different committees, tested it on the sales force, and the idea is still sound, so we will do it; does anyone see any problems with doing it this way, if not, that's what we'll do.

- **Truth as that which works, the purely pragmatic criterion:** Let's try it out this way and evaluate how we are doing.

- **Truth as established by the scientific method, which becomes, once again, a kind of dogma:** Our research shows that this is the right way to do it; we've done three surveys, and they all show the same thing, so let's act on them.

---

pragmatic criteria and debate and a very high tolerance for ambiguity. In my consultation work with DEC, for instance, I was *never* asked for a recommendation. If I gave one, it was usually overridden immediately by various ideas from the client, which were then debated among the members. In Ciba-Geigy, I was always treated as an authority and asked what I *knew* from my research and other consulting experience and what I would *recommend*. I was treated as a scientist who was bringing *knowledge* to the organization, and I often found that my recommendations were implemented in a very precise manner. If what I recommended conflicted with other cultural elements, for example, when I suggested more lateral communication, the recommendation was dismissed outright. Ciba-Geigy did not tolerate ambiguity well and operated much closer to the moralistic end of the dimension.

What Is "Information"?

How a group tests for reality and makes decisions also involves consensus on what constitutes data, what is information, and what is knowledge.

As information technology has grown, the issue has become sharpened because of debates about the role of computers in providing "information." Information technology "professionals" often hold shared assumptions that differ in substantial ways from the assumptions of senior managers. For example, many company presidents will point out that all you get on a computer screen is "data" and what they really need is *information*, which implies a level of analysis of the data that is typically not available unless a sophisticated decision support system or expert system has been programmed in (Rockart and DeLong, 1988). For a group to be able to make realistic decisions, there must be a degree of consensus on which information items are relevant to the task at hand.

A good example of the inherent ambiguity of abstract words such as *information* was illustrated in Dougherty's (1990) research on new product development teams. She identified five separate "thought worlds" that were represented by the functional specialists who were brought together in product development teams. The team knew that a good decision required having lots of information about the customer, and each member of the team believed that he or she had all the necessary information about customers. But each person knew something different and did not realize it until they attempted to reach a decision.

- Marketers/business planners knew in general whether or not a market existed, the size of the potential market, what price and volume would produce appropriate profit levels, what the market trends were, and so on.
- The field salespeople knew what the potential customers would use the product for, what the users' specific needs were, and how important the product was to customers relative to competitor's products.
- The distribution people knew how the product would be sold, what the merchandising plans were, and how many sales channels there would be.
- The engineers knew just how big the product should be, what its technical specifications should be, where the power plug should go, and so on.
- The manufacturing people knew what the potential volumes were, how many models might be needed, and what the costs of production would be.

Each of these groups, by virtue of its members' occupational background and functional experience, had built up concepts and language that were common to their occupational group but not necessarily understood clearly or valued by the others.

When members of these subcultures were brought together into a product development team, their ability to discover the others' realities was a major determinant of whether or not the product that was developed would succeed in the marketplace. To achieve mutual understanding, the groups had to go beyond the formal meeting processes into a more personal level of dialogue to create opportunities to discover where they agreed and disagreed, and how their information sets differed in content. They had to become a temporary cultural island to become an effective working group.

The question of "what is information" is of especial interest now as encyclopedias are being replaced by network-based sources such as Wikipedia. Pure scientific criteria for truth are being replaced by a process much more akin to how DEC found truth—through proposal, challenge, debate, and ultimately resolution through survival.

Summary and Conclusions

One of the most important categories of culture is the assumption made about how reality, truth, and information are defined. Reality can exist at the physical, group, and individual levels, and the test for what is real will differ according to the level—overt tests, social consensus, or individual experience. Occupations and macrocultures differ in the degree to which they rely on moralistic traditional criteria for truth as contrasted at the other extreme with pragmatic scientific criteria. Groups develop assumptions about information that determine when they feel they have enough information to make a decision, and those assumptions reflect deeper assumptions about the ultimate source of truth. What is a fact, what is information, and what is truth—each depends not only on shared knowledge of formal language but also on context and consensus.

8

DEEPER CULTURAL ASSUMPTIONS: THE NATURE OF TIME AND SPACE

The deep structure of culture not only consists of how we perceive reality and truth but also how we orient ourselves toward our physical and human environment, which involves unconscious and taken-for-granted concepts of time and space.

Assumptions About Time

The perception and experience of time are among the most central aspects of how any group functions. When people differ in their experience of time, tremendous communication and relationship problems typically emerge. Consider how anxious or irritated we get when someone is late, when we feel our time has been wasted, when we feel that we did not get enough "air time" to make our point, when we feel "out of phase" with someone, someone is taking up too much of our time, or when we can never get our subordinate to do things on time or to show up at the right time.

In an analysis of time, Dubinskas (1988, p. 14) points out its central role in human affairs: "Time is a fundamental symbolic category that we use for talking about the orderliness of social life. In a modern organization, just as in an agrarian society, time appears to impose a structure of workdays, calendars, careers, and life cycles that we learn and live in as part of our cultures. This temporal order has an 'already made' character of naturalness to it, a model of the way things are." Or, as Hassard (1999, p. 336) puts it: "While our sense of temporality is founded on the biology of the human organism, it becomes refined and ordered by participation in society and culture."

Time is not a unidimensional, clear construct. It has been analyzed from many perspectives, and a number of these are particularly relevant to group and organizational analysis because of the ubiquitous problems of scheduling, allocation, and coordination.

Basic Time Orientation

Anthropologists have noted that every culture makes assumptions about the nature of time and has a basic orientation toward the past, present, or future (Kluckhohn and Strodtbeck, 1961; Redding and Martyn-Johns, 1979; Hampden-Turner and Trompenaars, 1993). For example, in their study of the various cultures in the U.S. Southwest, Kluckhohn and Strodtbeck noted that some of the Indian tribes lived mostly in the past, the Spanish-Americans were oriented primarily toward the present, and the Anglo-Americans were oriented primarily toward the near future.

Time orientation is a useful way to distinguish some macrocultural national differences. For example, in their cross-cultural study, Hofstede and Bond identified a dimension that contrasted a past/present orientation with a future orientation and found that economic development was correlated with a future orientation (Hofstede and Bond, 1988; Hofstede, 2001). Hampden-Turner and Trompenaars, based on their own survey, found that among Asian countries, Japan is at the extreme of long-range planning while Hong Kong is at the extreme of short-run planning.

At the level of the organization, we can distinguish companies that are primarily oriented to (1) the past, thinking mostly about how things used to be; (2) the present, worrying only how to get the immediate task done; (3) the near future, worrying mostly about quarterly results; and (4) the distant future, investing heavily in research and development or in building market share at the expense of immediate profits.

Cultural assumptions about time influence the role that planning will play in the management process. For example, one high-tech company I have worked with operated by the assumption that "only the present counts." Employees worked extremely hard on the immediate tasks that challenged them, but they had little sense of past history and did not care much about the future. People in the planning department complained that plans were made in a ritualistic way; planning books were filled with things to do, but nothing ever got implemented.

Many organizations live in the past, reflecting on their past glories and successes while ignoring present and future challenges. They make the basic assumption that if things worked in the past, they must be good enough to work in the present and future and do not need to be reexamined. That assumption can indeed be valid if the technology and the environment have remained stable, but it can lead an organization to destruction if new environmental demands and technological changes require changes in how the organization defines its mission, its goals, and the means by which to accomplish them, as the DEC story illustrates (Schein, 2003).

How future oriented an organization should be is the subject of much debate, with many arguing that one of the problems of U.S. companies is that the financial context in which they operate (the stock market) forces a near-future orientation at the expense of longer-range planning. From an anthropological point of view, it is of course not clear what is cause and what is effect. Is the United States, culturally speaking, a near-future-oriented pragmatic society that has therefore created certain economic institutions to reflect our need for quick and constant feedback, or have our economic institutions created the short-run pragmatic orientation? In either case, the important point is that these cultural assumptions about time dominate daily thinking and activity to the point where a U.S. manager may have a hard time even imagining the alternative of a long-range planning process such as is typical in some Japanese industries.

Monochronic and Polychronic Time

Edward Hall, in several very insightful books about national cultures (1959, 1966, 1977), points out that in the United States, most managers view time as monochronic, an infinitely divisible linear ribbon that can be divided into appointments and other compartments but within which only one thing can be done at a time. If more than one thing must be done within, say, an hour, we divide the hour into as many units as we need and then do one thing at a time. When we get disorganized or have a feeling of being overloaded, we are advised to do one thing at a time. Time is viewed as a valuable commodity that can be spent, wasted, killed, or made good use of; but once a unit of time is over, it is gone forever. Hassard (1999) points out that this concept of "linear time" was at the heart of the industrial revolution in the shift to measuring productivity in terms of the time it took to produce something, insertion of time clocks to measure the amount of work done, paying people by the amount of time they work, and emphasizing the metaphor that "time is money."

In contrast, some cultures in southern Europe, Africa, and the Middle East regard time as primarily polychronic, a kind of medium defined more by what is accomplished than by a clock and within which several things can be done simultaneously. Even more extreme is the cyclical concept of time "as phases, rather circular in form. One season follows the next, one life leads into another" as seen in some Asian societies (Sithi-Amnuai, 1968, p. 82). The manager who operates according to this kind of time "holds court" in the sense that she or he deals simultaneously with a number of subordinates, colleagues, and even bosses, keeping each matter in suspension until it is finished.

This distinction is usefully applied by Hampden-Turner and Trompenaars (1993, 2000) to nations and organizations in terms of whether they are more focused on sequential thinking (monochromic clock time) or synchronization of activities (polychronic). They point out, for example, that the Japanese approach to car manufacturing is based on making as many of the sequential activities of a product line as possible into synchronous activities so that at the point where a given part, such as an engine, is inserted, a number of different engines can be ready to fit into the different models that may be coming down the line. Supplies have to arrive "just in time" so that the costs of keeping things in inventory are minimized.

How a culture views time is, of course, related to other cultural themes, such as the importance of relationships in getting a job done. If relationships are thought of as being more important than short-run efficiency, there is likely to be more emphasis on polychronicity. Punctuality or the rapid completion of a task may not be valued as highly as dealing with all the relationship issues that are brought up in relation to the task. Monochronically oriented managers can become very impatient and frustrated in a polychronic culture when their bosses give attention to several subordinates at the same time, or in a more relationship-oriented culture when they must give time to social events before business can be discussed.

Though there is an emphasis on monochronicity in the United States, polychronic time concepts do exist in U.S. organizations, and cyclical time concepts are introduced, especially by workers in monotonous jobs (Bluedorn, 2000). A doctor or dentist, for example, may simultaneously see several patients in adjacent offices, and a supervisor is usually totally available at all times to all of his or her machine operators. Parents and homemakers may simultaneously cook, clean house, and deal with each of several children. In an airport check-in line, an agent will ask whether any of the people in the line are scheduled for an immediate flight and pull them out of the line so as not to hold up the flight departure. When Alpha Power was required by a court order to become environmentally responsible, electrical workers were told that cleaning up an oil spill from the emergency truck was just as important as fixing the hospital generator; in effect, these tasks had be viewed synchronously, not sequentially. Production workers in monotonous jobs creatively introduce new and informal activities to provide breaks with various meanings to give the day a more rhythmic and cyclical form. The use of cell phones while driving has become a major safety issue raising the whole question of when several things can be done at the same time.

Time concepts also define in a subtle way how status is displayed, as illustrated by the frustrating experiences that Americans and northern Europeans have in Latin cultures, where lining up and doing things one at a time are less common. I have stood in line at a small post office in Southern France only to discover that some people barge to the head of the line and actually get service from the clerk. My friends have pointed out to me that in this situation not only does the clerk have a more polychronic view of the world, leading the clerk to respond to those who shout loudest, but that a higher-status person considers it legitimate to break into the line and get service first as a display of status. If others live in the same status system, they do not get offended by being kept waiting. In fact, it was pointed out to me that by staying in line and fulminating, I was displaying a low sense of my own status; otherwise, I would have been up at the head of the line demanding service as well.

Subculture Variations: Planning Time and Development Time

In a study of biotechnology companies, Dubinskas (1988) found that when biologists who had become entrepreneurs worked with managers who came from an economics or business background, subtle misunderstandings would occur over how long things took, how milestones are viewed, and how the future in general is perceived during the planning process. The managers viewed time in a linear, monochronic way, with targets and milestones that were tied to external objective realities such as market opportunities and the stock market. Dubinskas labeled this form of time *planning time*.

In contrast, the biologists seemed to operate from something he called *development time*, best characterized as "things will take as long as they will take," referring to natural biological processes that have their own internal time cycles. To caricature the distinction, a manager might say we need the baby in five months to meet a business target, while the biologist would say, sorry, but it takes at least nine months to make a baby. Planning time seeks closure; open-ended development time can extend far into the future.

A similar kind of contrast can be seen in the time horizons of electrical engineers and chemical engineers. DEC engineers could plan for market windows because circuit design technology permitted immediate testing of a circuit. Researchers at Ciba-Geigy told me that they could never predict how long the development of a new chemical would take because lab results were often not reproducible at the level of the pilot plant or the final manufacturing plant.

Discretionary Time Horizons and Degree of Accuracy

Another dimension of time on which group members need consensus has to do with the size of relevant time units in relation to given tasks (Jaques, 1982, 1989). Do we measure and plan for things annually, quarterly, monthly, daily, hourly, or by the minute? What is considered "accurate" in the realm of time? Does a given task have to be measured in terms of seconds, minutes, or longer units? How long after an appointed time can someone show up and still be considered on time, and how long after the expected time of arrival can a plane land and still be listed as on time? What are the expected timetables for certain events, such as promotions? How much time is it appropriate to spend on a given task, and what is the length of a feedback loop? How long should a task take?

As Lawrence and Lorsch (1967) noted years ago, one of the reasons why sales and research and development (R&D) people have trouble communicating with each other is that they work with totally different time horizons.

For salespeople, the time horizon involves the completion of a sale, which could take minutes, hours, days, or weeks. In general, however, even their longer time horizons were much shorter than those of the research people, for whom a multiyear horizon was normal. In other words, research people would not get closure, in the sense of knowing that they had a good product, until a much longer period of time had elapsed, partly because they operated more in terms of development time, as described earlier.

If we now consider the communication process between the researcher and the salesperson/marketer, when the latter says that she wants a product "soon," and the researcher agrees that the product will be ready "soon," they might be talking about completely different things and not realize it. For example, at DEC, I constantly heard complaints from the sales department that engineering was not getting the products out "on time." If I talked to engineering, I was told that the product was on schedule and doing just fine, which often meant "we are only six months late, which is nothing in a several-year development cycle." Each function got angry at the other. Neither recognized that the judgments being made about what it meant to be "on time" resulted from different assumptions about time units.

DEC and Ciba-Geigy differed in their overall time horizons, probably because of their underlying technologies and markets. The slow deliberateness of the research process at Ciba-Geigy spilled over into the management process. Things were done slowly, deliberately, and thoroughly. If a project was going to take several years, so be it. Time was expressed in spatial terms in a phrase commonly heard around the company: "The first thousand miles don't count." In other words, be patient and persistent; things will eventually work out.

Time horizons differ not only by function and occupation but also by rank. The higher the rank, the longer the time horizon over which a manager has discretion (Jaques, 1982, 1989), or what Bailyn (1985) has called "operational autonomy." This period of time is usually defined as the time between formal reviews of whether or not an individual is doing his or her basic job. Production workers may get reviewed every few minutes or hours, supervisors may get reviewed monthly or annually, and top executives may get reviewed only once every several years, depending upon the nature of their industry. Different norms about time arise, therefore, at different rank levels. Senior managers assume that they must plan in cycles of several years, whereas such an assumption may not make sense to the middle manager or the worker, whose time cycle is daily, weekly, or monthly.

Different assumptions about discretionary periods can cause difficulty in managing. Bailyn (1985) found that senior managers in one large R&D organization believed that their scientists wanted to set their own research goals (they were given *goal* autonomy), but because those scientists were perceived to be undisciplined in their management of budgets and time, they were reviewed frequently (they were not given very much *operational* autonomy). When Bailyn talked to the scientists, she discovered that two of the main reasons why they felt demoralized was that management was "not allowing them to get involved in helping to set goals" (because they were in industry, they wanted to work on relevant problems as specified by management) and that "they were constantly being reviewed and never allowed to get any work done." In other words, the scientists wanted just the opposite of what management was providing—they wanted less goal autonomy and more operational autonomy.

Jaques (1982, 1989) takes the argument about discretionary time horizons even further by noting that managerial competence can be judged by whether or not a given manager is functioning in terms of the time horizons appropriate to the level of his or her job. A production worker thinking in terms of years and a senior manager thinking in terms of hours and days are equally likely to be ineffective in terms of what their jobs demand of them. As an individual moves up the hierarchy into jobs that require longer-range planning, you can assess that individual's potential for promotion partly in terms of his or her ability to take longer-range points of view. When senior managers operate with too short a time horizon, they are likely to overmanage and fail to plan appropriately.

Temporal Symmetry, Pacing, and Entrainment

A subtle but critical aspect of time is the way in which activities are paced. In his study of the introduction of computerized equipment into radiology departments, Barley (1988) discovered that one of the major impacts of the technology was the degree to which the pacing of the activities of the technicians and the radiologists became more or less symmetrical. In the traditional X-ray department, the technicians worked monochronically as far as scheduling patients and making films. But if they needed to consult a radiologist, the technicians became frustrated by the polychronic world of the radiologists. For example, if a technician needed the services of a radiologist to give an injection to a patient, to conduct a fluoroscopy, or to review preliminary films, the technician would often have to wait. The following quotation captures the asymmetry well.

> To locate a radiologist, a technologist often had to search several offices and ask other technologists about the radiologist's last known whereabouts. Even after the tech found a radiologist, there was no guarantee that he would be immediately available. At the time of the tech's arrival, the radiologist could be talking on the telephone, discussing a film with a physician, consulting a colleague, or about to assist with another examination. In each instance, the technologist would have to wait. But even if the technologist successfully engaged the radiologist's attention, he or she still had no firm claim on the radiologist's time. The radiologist could always be diverted by a number of events, including a telephone call, a consultation, or even another technologist with a request that the radiologist deemed more important. (Barley, 1988, p. 145)

When computerized tomography, magnetic resonance, and ultrasound came into the departments, the temporal orders of the two sets of people became more symmetrical because of (1) the greater duration of each test, (2) the technician's greater level of expertise in reading the results, and (3) the degree to which the special procedures involved in the new technologies often required the radiologists and technicians to work side by side throughout. Furthermore, the diagnostic procedures in ultrasound could not be done in the first place unless the technicians knew how to read results as they were forthcoming. The technicians acquired, de facto, more operational autonomy, which gave them more status, as did the reality that because of their greater amount of experience, they often knew better than the radiologist how to read the results. The new technologies created a world in which both technician and radiologist worked in a monochronic manner, making it easier to coordinate their efforts and achieve efficiency for the patient and in the use of the equipment.

Polychronically driven work always has the potential for frustrating the person who is working monochronically, as exemplified in the interaction between an air traffic controller (polychronic) and the pilot of a single aircraft waiting for landing clearance (monochronic). Similar issues arise when patients get frustrated waiting in the emergency room because they are not aware that the physician is treating many patients at once. Because the monochronically driven person typically does not understand the multiple demands being placed on the polychronically driven person, there is a very high potential for misunderstanding and inaccurate attributions such as perceiving the polychronically driven person as lazy or inefficient.

The temporal context within which groups work, involving the pacing of activities, rhythms, and cycles of work activities, are obviously relevant to how groups perform and can be the source of frustration if there is insufficient consensus within and between groups (Bluedorn, 1997, 2000). To prevent dysfunctional conflicts in pacing, some researchers have noted that organizations tend to try to "entrain" interdependent activities. *Entrainment* is a concept taken from the natural sciences and can be defined as "the adjustment of the pace or cycle of one activity to match or synchronize with that of another" (Ancona and Chong, 1996, p. 251).

Summary

There is probably no more important category for cultural analysis than the study of how time is conceived and used in a group or organization. Time management imposes a social order and conveys status and intention. The pacing of events, the rhythms of life, the sequence in which things are done, and the duration of events are all subject to symbolic interpretation. Misinterpretations of what things mean in a temporal context are therefore extremely likely unless group members are operating from the same sets of assumptions.

The main aspects of time, including (1) past, present, near-, or far-future orientation; (2) monochronicity or polychronicity; (3) planning or developmental time; (4) time horizons; and (5) symmetry of temporal activities, can help you begin to understand how you view time and how it is viewed in a given organization. Time is the key to coordination, planning, and the basic organization of daily life, yet is invisible and totally taken for granted. Though time coordination is central to the workings of all social orders, it is usually so taken for granted that it is even difficult to speak about. For example, when we are late or early, we mumble apologies and possibly provide explanations, but rarely do we ask, "When did you expect me?" or "What does it mean to you when I am late?"

Assumptions About the Nature of Space

Our assumptions about the meaning and use of space are among the most subtle aspects of organizational culture because assumptions about space, like those about time, operate outside of awareness and are taken for granted. At the same time, when those assumptions are violated, very strong emotional reactions occur because space comes to have very powerful symbolic meanings, as expressed in the current phrase, "Don't get into my 'space.'" One of the most obvious ways that rank and status are symbolized in organizations is by the location and size of offices.

Hall (1966) points out that in some cultures, if someone is walking in a certain direction, the space ahead is perceived to belong to that person, so that if someone crosses in front of the individual, that person is "violating" the other's space. In other cultures, notably some Asian ones, space is initially defined as communal and shared, allowing for the complex flow of people, bicycles, cars, and animals you may see in a Chinese city street with everyone somehow moving forward, and no one getting killed or trampled. Space, like time, can be analyzed from a number of different points of view.

Distance and Relative Placement

Space has both a physical and a social meaning (Van Maanen, 1979b). For coordinated social action to occur, an individual must share assumptions about the meaning of the placement of physical objects in an environment and also know how to orient himself or herself spatially in relation to other members of the group. A person's placement in relation to others symbolizes status, social distance, and membership. For example, Hall (1966) points out that in the United States, there is high consensus on four kinds of "normal distance" and that within each of these, there is consensus on what it means to be "very near" or "very far."

- **Intimacy distance:** Among those who consider themselves to be intimate with each other, contact and touching are defined as being very near; six to eighteen inches is the range for being far. This is what sociologists call the "ideal sphere" around each of us that defines the space we only allow to be entered by people with whom we feel we have an intimate relationship. If a stranger is that close to us, it makes us uncomfortable or anxious.

- **Personal distance:** Eighteen to thirty inches is being near, two to four feet is being far. This is the range within which we have personal conversations with another individual even if we are in a crowd or at a party. This distance permits a normal or soft tone of voice to be used and is usually accompanied by intense eye contact. The easiest way to appreciate the power of this distance norm is to recall what happens at parties when someone from another culture—in which personal distance is defined as closer than it is in the United States—moves in "too close." We find ourselves backing up, only to discover that the other person is pursuing us, trying to make the distance seem right to him or her. Eventually we feel cornered, and all kinds of irrelevant motives or personality attributes get called into play, when in fact the only thing operating is the fact that in two different cultures, the norm of what is appropriate personal distance varies. When personal distance is violated one often hears the phrase "You're in my face," or "Get out of my face."

- **Social distance:** Four to seven feet is near; seven to twelve feet is far. Social distance defines how we talk to several people at once, as at a dinner party or a seminar; it usually involves some raising of the voice and less personal focus on any given individual. Our eyes will scan the group or be focused on the floor or ceiling. Designers of seminar rooms or tables for committee meetings have to work around these kinds of norms if they are concerned about making the room feel appropriate for the kinds of meetings that are supposed to go on there. The more we want to meet informally and really get to know each other, the more the room has to be scaled down to allow that to happen. If people are to be seated around a table, the size and shape of the table have to be appropriate so that people can feel socially in each other's presence.

- **Public distance:** Twelve to twenty-five feet is near; more than twenty-five feet is far. At this distance the audience is defined as undifferentiated, and we raise our voice even more or use a microphone. Our eyes rove systematically or do not focus on anyone, as when we read a speech to an audience.

Feelings about distance have biological roots. Animals have a clearly defined *flight distance* (the distance that will elicit fleeing if the animal is intruded upon) and critical distance (the distance that will elicit attacking behavior if the animal is intruded upon or "cornered"). Conditions of crowding not only elicit pathological behavior in nonhuman species but also elicit aggression in humans. Hence, most cultures have fairly clear rules about how to define personal and intimate space through the use of a variety of cues to permit what Hall calls "sensory screening," including partitions, walls, sound barriers, and other physical devices. We use eye contact, body position, and other personal devices to signal respect for the privacy of others (Goffman, 1959; Hatch, 1990; Steele, 1973, 1981).

We also learn how to manage what Hall calls *intrusion distance*; that is, how far away to remain from others who are in personal conversation without interrupting the conversation yet making it known that one wants attention when appropriate. In some cultures, including ours, intrusion occurs only when someone interrupts with speech (someone can stand close by without "interrupting"), whereas in other cultures, even entering the visual field of another person constitutes a bid for attention and hence is seen as an interruption. In these cultural settings, the use of physical barriers such as closed offices has an important symbolic meaning—it is the only way to get a feeling of privacy (Hall, 1966).

At the organizational level, we can clearly see that DEC and Ciba-Geigy had different assumptions about space. DEC opted for a completely open office layout, with partitions low enough to permit everyone to see over the tops. At Ciba-Geigy, the offices were arranged along corridors and had heavy doors that were kept shut.

The Symbolism of Space

Organizations develop different norms of who should have how much and what kind of space. They also hold different implicit assumptions about the role of space use in getting work accomplished. In most organizations, the best views and locations are reserved for the highest-status people. Senior executives are typically on the higher floors of buildings and often are allocated special spaces such as private conference rooms and private bathrooms. Sociologists point out that one important function of private bathrooms is to preserve the image of leaders as "super-human" beings who do not have the ordinary needs of those at lower levels (Goffman, 1967). In some organizations, it would not be comfortable for the employee to find himself urinating next to the president of the corporation.

Some organizations use very precise space allocation as a direct status symbol. As was mentioned before, the headquarters building of General Foods was designed with movable walls so that, as product managers were promoted, their office size could be adjusted to reflect their new rank. At the same time, the company had a department that allocated the kind of carpeting, furniture, and wall decorations that went with particular rank levels. In contrast, DEC aggressively tried to reduce status and privileges by not allocating private parking spaces; by reserving the good locations, such as corners, for conference rooms; and by putting higher-status managers in inside offices so that clerical and secretarial employees could work on the outside, next to windows. Whereas in many organizations the way in which the employees can decorate their own workspace is prescribed, DEC employees were left entirely on their own with regard to decoration. In Apple, the norm was even more extreme in that employees were allowed to bring pets or children to work.

Where buildings are located, how they are built, and the kind of architecture involved will vary from one organization to the next and may well reflect deeper values and assumptions held in the larger culture and by the key leaders. Because buildings and the environment around them are highly visible and relatively permanent, organizations attempt to symbolize important values and assumptions through the design. The physical layout not only has this symbolic function but is often used to guide and channel the behavior of members of the organization, thereby becoming a powerful builder and reinforcer of norms (Berg and Kreiner, 1990; Gagliardi, 1990; Steele, 1973, 1981).

For example, DEC reinforced its values of autonomy and empowerment by being highly decentralized geographically but, at the same time, reinforced its value of communication by employing a fleet of helicopters and shuttle buses to transport people around easily among the decentralized units. The value of frugality was reinforced by opting for inexpensive, unobtrusive, low-rise buildings. The interior open-office layout was designed to stimulate high levels of communication and to symbolize efficiency and cost consciousness. In contrast, Ciba-Geigy, with its greater emphasis on work as a private activity, enclosed areas as much as possible, was comfortable with private dining rooms for different levels of executives, and enclosed its buildings in an almost fortress-like manner.

Body Language

One of the more subtle uses of space is how we use gestures, body position, and other physical cues to communicate our sense of what is going on in a given situation and how we relate to the other people in it. On the gross level, those we sit next to, physically avoid, touch, bow to, and so on convey our perceptions of relative status and intimacy. As sociologists have observed, however, there are many more subtle cues that convey our deeper sense of what is going on and our assumptions about the right and proper way to behave in any given situation (Goffman, 1967; Van Maanen, 1979b).

Rituals of deference and demeanor that reinforce hierarchical relationships are played out in the physical and temporal positioning of behavior, as when a subordinate knows just where to stand at a meeting relative to the boss and how to time his or her questions or comments when disagreeing with the boss. The boss, for her part, knows that she must sit at the head of the table in the boardroom and time her remarks to the group appropriately. But only insiders know the full meaning of all these time/space cues, reminding us forcefully that what we observe around spatial arrangements and the behavioral use of time are cultural artifacts, difficult to decipher if we do not have additional data obtained from insiders through interview, observation, and joint inquiry. It would be highly dangerous to use our own cultural lenses to interpret what we observe, as when I misjudged the tone at the British Petroleum meeting mentioned earlier.

Gestures have symbolic meanings in every culture and, therefore, can be easily misunderstood, as was the case of the South African gold mine workers who were viewed as untrustworthy because they did not maintain eye contact with their supervisors. On the other hand, in the United States where eye contact is considered a "good" indicator of attention, I have had difficulty convincing dialogue groups to "talk to the campfire" instead of directly to each other (Schein, 1993a).

Time, Space, and Activity Interaction

Becoming oriented in both time and space is fundamental for an individual in any new situation. Thus far, we have analyzed time and space as separate dimensions, but, in reality, they always interact in complex ways around the activity that is supposed to occur. It is easiest to see this in relation to the basic forms of time. Monochronic time assumptions have specific implications for how space is organized. If someone must have individual appointments and privacy, he or she needs areas in which they can be held, thus requiring either desks that are far enough apart, cubicles, or offices with doors. Because monochronic time is linked with efficiency, the individual also requires a space layout that allows a minimum of wasted time. Thus it must be easy for people to contact each other, distances between important departments must be minimal, and amenities such as toilets and eating areas must be placed in such a way as to save time. In fact, in DEC, the liberal distribution of water coolers, coffee machines, and small kitchens around the organization clearly signaled the importance of continuing to work even as one satisfied bodily needs.

Polychronic time, in contrast, requires spatial arrangements that make it easy for simultaneous events to occur, where privacy is achieved by being near someone and whispering rather than by retreating behind closed doors. Thus, large rooms are built more like amphitheaters to permit a senior person to hold court, or sets of offices or cubicles are built around a central core that permits easy access to everyone. We might also expect more visually open environments such as the office bullpens that permit supervisors to survey the entire department so that they can easily see who might need help or who is not working.

When buildings and offices are designed in terms of certain intended work patterns, both distance and time are usually considered in the physical layout (Allen, 1977; Steele, 1973, 1981, 1986). These design issues get very complex, however, because information and communication technology is increasingly able to shrink time and space in ways that may not have been considered. For example, a group of people in private offices can communicate by telephone, e-mail, fax, and videophone, and even be a virtual team by using conference calls enhanced by various kinds of computer software (Grenier and Metes, 1992; Johansen and others, 1991).

The difficulty of introducing some of these information technologies highlights the interaction of assumptions, in that some managers become conscious of the fact that they need face-to-face interaction to gauge whether or not their message is getting through and how the other person is reacting. At DEC, for example, e-mail was widely used by certain sets of engineers who felt comfortable solving problems with each other by this means even if they did not know each other personally; senior executives, on the other hand, usually insisted on meetings and face-to-face communication.

The introduction of new information technologies such as email or groupware sometimes forces to the surface assumptions that have been taken for granted, thereby revealing cultural elements that may be incongruent with optimal behavior from the technology point of view. Conference calls, for example, might be resisted because participants cannot read body language and facial expressions. E-mail, on the other hand, can facilitate communication because it does not require the sender to "interrupt" the receiver in the way that a phone call would. New cultural norms about time then arise in terms of the expectations that e-mails will be answered within a certain length of time and that everyone will have e-mail service. Status assumptions come to the fore because senior executives consider it demeaning to have to type and, therefore, resist learning to use a desktop computer. Some of those same executives may be driven to the use of new technologies such as "texting" because it is the only way to communicate with their children!

Summary and Conclusions

It is important to recognize that (1) how we conceptualize reality, what concepts and dimensions guide our perception of time, and how we construct and use our physical spatial environment are very much a matter of prior cultural learning, and that (2) in any given new organization, shared assumptions arise only over the course of time and common experience. The analyst of culture must be careful not to project his or her own conceptions of time and space onto groups and must remember that the visible artifacts surrounding these conceptions are easy to misinterpret.

What are the implications of all this for leaders and managers? The most obvious implication has already been stated—they must learn to decipher cultural cues so that the normal flow of work is not interrupted by cultural misunderstandings. More important than this point, however, is the implication that the way in which leaders act out their own assumptions about time and space trains their subordinates and ultimately their entire organization to accept those assumptions. Most leaders are not aware of how much the assumptions they take for granted are passed on in day-to-day behavior by the way they manage the decision-making process, time, and space. If the external context then changes, requiring new kinds of responses, it will not only be difficult for the leader to learn new things, but it will be even more difficult to retrain members of the organization who have become used to the way the leader structured things in the past. How we define reality, time, and space becomes deeply embedded and fundamentally necessary to avoid uncertainty and anxiety. When we examine cultural evolution and change in later chapters, we will have to realize that if the changes require new assumptions about reality, time, and space, we should expect high levels of anxiety and resistance.

9

DEEPER CULTURAL ASSUMPTIONS: HUMAN NATURE, ACTIVITY, AND RELATIONSHIPS

This chapter explores what it means to be human, what a culture's basic assumptions are about the appropriate action for humans to take with respect to their environment, and most important, what a culture's basic assumptions are about the right and proper forms of human relationships. This last category frequently receives all the attention and defines for many people what the word *culture* is all about. However, it is important to recognize that assumptions about human relationships are deeply connected not only to assumptions about human nature and activity but also to assumptions about time, space, and the nature of truth, as discussed in Chapters Seven and Eight.

Assumptions About Human Nature

Every culture has shared assumptions about what it means to be human, what our basic instincts are, and what kinds of behavior are considered inhuman and therefore grounds for ejection from the group. Being human is not just a physical property but also a cultural construction, as we have seen throughout history. Slavery was often justified by defining slaves as "not human." In ethnic and religious conflicts the "other" is often defined as not human. Within the category of those defined as human, we have further variation. In their comparative study, Kluckhohn and Strodtbeck (1961) noted that in some societies humans are seen as basically evil, in others as basically good, and in still others as mixed or neutral, capable of being either good or bad. Closely related are assumptions about how perfectible human nature is. Is our goodness or badness intrinsic so we simply accept what we are, or can we, through hard work, generosity, or faith, overcome our badness and earn our salvation or nirvana? Where a given macroculture ends up in terms of these categories is often related to the religion that dominates that cultural unit, but, as we shall see, this issue is very much at the heart of leadership.

At the organizational level, the basic assumptions about the nature of human nature are often expressed most clearly in how workers and managers are viewed. Within the Western tradition, we have seen an evolution of assumptions about human nature, as follows:

1. Humans as rational-economic actors

2. Humans as social animals with primarily social needs

3. Humans as problem solvers and self-actualizers, with primary needs to be challenged and to use their talents

4. Humans as complex and malleable (Schein, 1965/1980)

Early theories of employee motivation were almost completely dominated by the assumption that the only incentives available to managers are monetary ones because it was assumed that the only essential motivation of employees was economic self-interest. The Hawthorne studies (Roethlisberger and Dickson, 1939; Homans, 1950) launched a new series of "social" assumptions, postulating that employees are motivated by the need to relate well to their peer and membership groups and that such motivation often overrides economic self-interest. The main evidence for these assumptions came from studies of restriction of output, which showed clearly that workers would reduce their take-home pay rather than break the norm of "a fair day's work for a fair day's pay." Furthermore, workers will put pressure on high producers ("rate busters") to work less hard and make less money to preserve the basic norm of a fair day's work.

Subsequent studies of work, particularly on the effects of the assembly line, introduced another set of assumptions: employees are self-actualizers who need challenge and interesting work to provide self-confirmation and valid outlets for the full use of their talents (Argyris, 1964). Motivation theorists, such as Maslow (1954), proposed that there is a hierarchy of human needs, and an individual will not observe the "higher" needs until lower ones are satisfied: If the individual is in a survival mode, economic motives will dominate; if survival needs are met, social needs come to the fore; if social needs are met, self-actualization needs become salient.

McGregor (1960) observed that within this broad framework, an important second layer of assumptions was held by managers vis-à-vis employees. *Ineffective* managers tended to hold an interlocked set of assumptions that McGregor labeled Theory X. Managers who held these assumptions believed that people are lazy and must therefore be motivated with economic incentives and be controlled by constant surveillance. In contrast, *effective* managers held a different set of assumptions that he labeled Theory Y. These managers assumed that people are basically self-motivated and therefore need to be challenged and channeled, not controlled. McGregor and other researchers saw insufficient financial incentives as "demotivators" but observed that adding financial incentives would not increase motivation. Only challenge and use of a person's talents could increase motivation (Herzberg, 1968). Whereas Theory X assumes that employees are intrinsically in conflict with their employing organization, Theory Y assumes that it is possible to design organizations that enable employee needs to be congruent with organizational needs.

Most current theories are built on still another set of assumptions, namely, that human nature is complex and malleable and that we cannot make a universal statement about human nature. Instead, we must be prepared for human variability. Such variability reflects (1) changes in the life cycle in that motives may change and grow as we mature and (2) changes in social conditions in that we are capable of learning new motives as may be required by new situations. Longitudinal studies of people have shown that with work experience, they develop "career anchors" that begin to guide and constrain the career based on self-perceived competencies, motives, and values (Schein, 1978, 1993, 2006). Such variability makes it essential for organizations to develop some consensus on what their own assumptions are because management strategies and practices reflect those assumptions. Both the incentive and control systems in most organizations are built on assumptions about human nature, and if those assumptions are not shared by the managers of the organization, inconsistent practices and confusion will result.

McGregor (1960) also noted that because humans are malleable, they often respond adaptively to the assumptions that are held about them. This is particularly a problem in organizations that are run by managers who share a Theory X set of assumptions because the more that employees are controlled and treated as untrustworthy, the more likely they are to behave in terms of those expectations. The cynical Theory X manager then feels vindicated but fails to note that the employee behavior was learned and does not reflect intrinsic human nature. A more extreme version occurs when senior managers with personality problems create organizational pathology within the organization they manage (Kets de Vries and Miller, 1984, 1987; Goldman, 2008).

DEC was one of the most Theory Y driven organizations I have ever encountered. The core assumption in Ciba-Geigy was more difficult to decipher, but there were strong indications that individuals were viewed ultimately as good soldiers, who would perform responsibly and loyally, and whose loyalty the organization would reward. Individuals were expected to do their best in whatever was asked of them, but loyalty was ultimately assumed to be more important than individual creativity. It seems that in DEC the individual was ultimately more important than the organization and that in Ciba-Geigy the organization was ultimately more important than the individual.

Assumptions About Appropriate Human Activity

Closely connected to assumptions about human nature are shared assumptions about the appropriate way for humans to act in relation to their environment. Several basically different orientations have been identified in cross-cultural studies, and these have direct implications for variations we can see in organizations.

The Doing Orientation

At one extreme, we can identify a *doing* orientation, which correlates closely with (1) the assumption that nature can be controlled and manipulated, (2) a pragmatic orientation toward the nature of reality, and (3) a belief in human perfectibility (Kluckhohn and Strodtbeck, 1961). In other words, it is taken for granted that the proper thing for people to do is to take charge and actively control their environment and their fate.

Doing is the predominant orientation of the United States and is certainly a key assumption of U.S. managers, reflected in the World War II slogan "We can do it" as immortalized in the Rosie the Riveter posters, and in the stock American phrases "getting things done" and "let's do something about it." The notion that "the impossible just takes a little longer" is central to U.S. business ideology. DEC was a prime example of commitment to "doing the right thing"—when there is a difficulty, do something about it, solve the problem, involve other people, get help, but do something; don't let it fester. The doing orientation focuses on the task, on efficiency, and on discovery. Organizations driven by this assumption seek to grow and to dominate the markets they are in.

The Being Orientation

At the other extreme is a *being* orientation, which correlates closely with the assumption that nature is powerful and humanity is subservient to it. This orientation implies a kind of fatalism—because we cannot influence nature, we must become accepting and enjoy what we have. We must focus more on the here and now, on individual enjoyment, and on acceptance of whatever comes. Organizations operating according to this orientation look for a niche in their environment that allows them to survive, and they try to adapt to external realities rather than create markets or dominate some portion of the environment.

The Being-in-Becoming Orientation

A third orientation, which lies between the two extremes of doing and being, is *being-in-becoming*, referring to the idea that the individual must achieve harmony with nature by fully developing his or her own capacities and, thereby, achieve a perfect union with the environment. The focus is on development rather than a static condition. Through detachment, meditation, and control of those things that can be controlled (for instance, feelings and bodily functions), the individual achieves full self-development and self-actualization. The focus is on what the person is and can become rather than what specific thing the person can accomplish. In short, "the being-in-becoming orientation emphasizes that kind of activity which has as its goal the development of all aspects of the self as an integrated whole" (Kluckhohn and Strodtbeck, 1961, p. 17).

The relevance of this dimension can be seen most clearly in organizational attitudes and norms about the expression of emotions. In Essochem, the European subsidiary of the chemical branch of Exxon, senior managers complained that they could not find any competent managers to put on their internal board of directors. In observing their meetings devoted to succession planning and management development, I observed that French and Italian managers were frequently labeled as "too emotional," and this disqualified them from further consideration for higher-level jobs. Apparently, the assumption in this organization was that good management involves being unemotional, an assumption that I later found out was very dominant in the U.S. headquarters organization. This organization's assumptions limited human growth and development and, through limiting its diversity at senior levels, limited the strategic options available.

In contrast, DEC was extreme in the degree to which it allowed and encouraged all forms of self-development, which was later reflected in the degree to which "alumni" of DEC, now working on their own or in other organizations, used the phrase "I grew up in DEC." In Ciba-Geigy, it was clear that each person had to fit in and become part of the organizational fabric and that socialization into the existing mode was therefore more common than self-development.

This assumption becomes central at the organizational level when we compare companies that settle into a routine based on past success or a successful niche and cease to develop as organizations. DEC was a good example of how individuals could develop while the organization did not. It stayed in its niche producing high-quality innovations and became economically dysfunctional. Hewlett/Packard is a good example of a company that was able to develop from instrumentation and medical equipment to computers and eventually to printers and ink. Similarly, Ciba-Geigy in its major turnaround realized that it existed in multiple environments. Its chemical business existed in an environment that had huge "overcapacity," leading to decisions to scale that business way down. On the other hand, the pharmaceutical business had a high potential for growth, and size and the ability to dominate markets mattered. It was this latter assumption that ultimately led to Ciba-Geigy's merging with one of its former competitors,

Sandoz, to become Novartis, a more powerful and more focused pharmaceutical giant. It evolved from a dyestuffs company with a clear niche into a dominant organization with a strong "doing orientation."

Assumptions About the Nature of Human Relationships

At the core of every culture are assumptions about the proper way for individuals to relate to each other to make the group safe, comfortable, and productive. When such assumptions are not widely shared, we speak of anarchy and anomie. Whereas the previous assumption areas deal with the group's relationship to the external environment, this set of assumptions deals more with the nature of the group itself and the kind of internal environment it creates for its members. These basic assumptions will color how the group copes with the various issues that were outlined in Chapter Six and will be further elaborated on in Chapter Twelve.

As humans, there are several fundamental issues around which consensus must form for any organized action to occur. These issues derive from the fact that as humans we have a brain and a set of highly developed cognitive functions, we have emotions that must be managed, and we have intentions or will that must find outlets. Dealing with these issues can best be conceptualized as a set of questions that every member of a new group or organization must resolve in order to be able to focus on the task to be accomplished. Until these questions are answered to some satisfactory degree, the person will be anxious and preoccupied with his or her own personal issues instead of focusing on the group's task.

What Problems Must be Resolved?

- **Identity and Role:** Who am I supposed to be in this group and what will be my role? (Cognitive clarity)

- **Power and Influence:** Will my needs for influence and control be met? (Management of aggression)

- **Needs and Goals:** Will the group's goals allow me to meet my own needs? (Management of intentions and will)

- **Acceptance and Intimacy:** Will I be accepted, respected, and loved in this group? How close will our relationships be? (Management of love)

Chapter Twelve will show how leadership behavior and group interaction enable members to gradually answer these questions and allow the group to move on to task accomplishment. Every group, organization, and society will develop different solutions to each of these problem areas, but some kind of solution must be found for people to get past self-oriented defensive behavior and be able to function in the group and establish a reliable and meaningful social order that provides cognitive clarity, management of aggression and love, and outlets for intentions and will.

In macrocultures, these questions get dealt with in the process of education and socialization into society and occupations. In Chapter Six, I discussed some variations at this level within groups. If we compare macrocultures, it becomes evident that the basic identity of all members is deeply shaped by the rules of the social order around authority and intimacy. Underlying this is an even more fundamental issue of each member's basic connection to the society.

Individualism and Collectivism

Anthropologists observing a wide variety of macrocultures have noted that one major dimension on which nations and ethnic groups differ is the degree to which they regard the ultimate unit of society to be the individual or the group. All societies have to develop a system for encouraging individuality and group loyalty, but they differ in their assumptions about what is ultimately the basic unit (Kluckhohn and Strodtbeck, 1961; Havrylyshyn,1980). Hofstede's (2001) comparative study reinforces this point in identifying individualism-collectivism as one of the dimensions along which countries differ in his surveys. For example, countries such as the United States, Canada, Australia, and the United Kingdom come out as more individualistic, whereas Pakistan, Indonesia, Colombia, Venezuela, Ecuador, and Japan come out as more collectivist.

One way to test this dimension is to ask if group and individual interests differ, which will be sacrificed and which will be protected? In the United States, our Constitution and Bill of Rights ultimately protect the individual, whereas in more collectivist cultures, the individual is expected to sacrifice for the greater good of the group. At the extreme, this assumption has led to the glorification of suicide as in the case of Japanese kamikaze pilots in World War II and terrorist suicide bombers in the current war against terrorism.

In practice, every society and organization must honor both the group and the individual in the sense that neither makes sense without the other. Where cultures differ dramatically, however, is in the degree to which the espoused behavioral norms and values do or do not reflect the deeper assumption. On the surface, both the United States and Australia appear to be individualistic cultures, yet in Australia (and New Zealand), you hear many references to the "tall poppy syndrome" (that is, it is the tall poppy that gets cut off). For example, an American teenager whose parents had relocated in Australia reported that after a brilliant ride on his surfboard, he had to say to his buddies, "Gee, that was a *lucky* one." A person does not take personal credit in an individualistic culture that has strong espoused collectivist values. In contrast, though the United States espouses team-work, it is evident in sports that it is the superstar who is admired and that building teams is seen as pragmatically necessary, not intrinsically desirable.

In terms of the four fundamental questions, individualistic societies define roles in terms of personal accomplishment, license aggression through personal competition, put a high premium on ambition, and define intimacy and love in very personal terms. The more collectivist society defines identity and role more in terms of group membership, licenses aggression primarily toward other groups, puts less value on personal ambition, and funnels love primarily within the group.

Power Distance

All groups and cultures have the issue of how to manage aggression, so it is not surprising that broad surveys of cultures such as Hofstede's identified the dimension of "power distance"—countries vary in the degree to which people in a hierarchical situation perceive a greater or lesser ability to control each other's behavior. People in high power distance countries, such as the Philippines, Mexico, and Venezuela, perceive more inequality between superiors and subordinates than do people in low power distance countries, such as Denmark, Israel, and New Zealand. If we look at the same index by occupation, we find higher power distance among unskilled and semiskilled workers than among professional and managerial workers, as expected.

At the organizational level, assumptions about relationships, of course, reflect the assumptions of the wider culture, but they become elaborated and differentiated. The founder/leader may believe that the only way to run an organization is to assign individual tasks, hold individuals accountable for performance, and minimize group and cooperative work because that would only lead to lowest-common-denominator group solutions or, worse, diffusion of responsibility. Another leader might emphasize cooperation and communication among subordinates as the best means of solving problems and implementing solutions because that would lead to the level of teamwork that task accomplishment requires. These two leaders would develop quite different working styles, which would be reflected ultimately in the organization's processes, reward systems, and control systems.

DEC was very individualistic but reduced the power distance between superiors and subordinates as much as possible, building on the assumption that good ideas can come from anyone at any time. Senior managers were always available and willing to talk to anyone about any issue, constrained only by the practicalities of time and space. A senior manager in R&D left DEC for a bigger and better job, only to return three months later with the following comment: "In the new company I had an idea for a new product and was told that I would have to talk first to my boss, then to the director of R&D, and then to the senior vice president. In Digital, if I have an idea, I go straight to Ken Olsen, and we kick it around. This is the kind of place in which I want to work."

In contrast, Ciba-Geigy was more collectivist and valued hierarchy, formality, and protocol. Individuals did not approach people informally. Meetings and conferences had to be well defined, have a clear purpose accepted by all, and be planned with rank and appropriate deference in mind. During my consulting visits, I saw only people who had specifically requested some of my time to discuss some specific problems that they were concerned about. It would not have been appropriate for me to drop in on people or to strike up conversations beyond the minimal cordialities in the executive dining room.

Basic Characteristics of Role Relationships

Human relationships can also be usefully analyzed with the aid of Parsons's (1951) original "pattern variables." It is these fundamental characteristics of all role relationships that led to the Kluckhohn and Strodtbeck model

(1961) and the currently popular diagnostic model of Hampden-Turner and Trompenaars (2000).

In any relationship between people, we can ask these questions:

1. **Degree of emotionality:** Is the relationship very aloof and "professional," as in a doctor-patient relationship, or very emotionally charged, as in friendship?

2. **Degree of specificity vs. diffuseness:** Is the relationship very specific, dealing only with the exact reason for the relationship, as in a sales-customer relationship, or diffuse, as in most friendships?

3. **Degree of universalism vs. particularism:** Do the participants in the relationship view each other in a very general "universalistic" way based on stereotypes, as in most professional relationships, or do they perceive each other in a very "particularistic" way as whole persons as in a spousal relationship or friendship?

4. **Degree of status ascription vs. achievement:** Are social rewards, such as status and rank, assigned on the basis of what the person is by birth or family membership, or on the basis of what the person has actually accomplished through his or her own effort?

Using these variables, we would say that relationships in DEC were emotionally charged, diffuse, particularistic, and highly achievement oriented; in Ciba-Geigy, they were emotionally aloof, specific, somewhat (though not totally) universalistic, and somewhat mixed on ascription versus achievement. Achievement clearly counted at Ciba-Geigy, but ascriptive criteria such as the right family background, the right level of education, and the right social status also were considered very important. One of the high-potential division managers who was a widower was strongly encouraged to remarry as a prerequisite to being promoted to the internal board of the company. People at Ciba-Geigy were assumed to be ambitious, but the good of the company was taken into account more than it was in DEC, where the assumption seemed to be that if everyone did "the right thing"— that is, made her or his best individual effort—that would turn out to be best for the company as a whole.

These dimensions identify the specific areas where macrocultures differ a great deal, leading to potential communication problems in multicultural groups. Problems of defining business ethics stem from these dimensions in that managers from individualistic countries who believe in universalistic rules and status through achievement find it difficult to work in collectivist countries where emotionally charged diffuse relationships lead to nepotism and requirements for payoffs to get things done. In collectivist countries, the building of relationships necessarily precedes getting down to work, which creates problems for the individualistic competitive manager who believes that getting the job done supercedes all other values. What the task-oriented person does not understand is that from the relationship-oriented person's point of view, the task *cannot* be accomplished *unless a good relationship has been built.* Getting mutual understanding around this issue will become critical as more work will be done in multicultural teams whose members will arrive with very different assumptions about all of these relationship dimensions.

Rules of Interaction—The Joint Effect of Time, Space, and Relationship Assumptions

In Chapter Eight, we saw how intimacy is defined by timing, distance, and position. If we combine those assumptions with assumptions about the appropriate way for people to relate to each other, we have, in effect, the assumption set that specifies what in most cultures make up the basic rules of interaction (Goffman, 1967; Van Maanen, 1979b). What we think of as tact, poise, good manners, and etiquette can be deconstructed into a set of rules that preserve the social order—what Goffman and others have called "face work." In other words, in every human group, the members sooner or later learn that to survive as a group, they must develop rules and norms that make the environment safe for all. Members must learn to preserve each other's face and self-esteem, lest the social environment become dangerous. If I humiliate you, I license you to humiliate me.

The content of these basic rules of interaction differs from culture to culture, but the existence of some set of such rules can be safely predicted for any group that has had some stability and joint history. The function of the social order is to provide meaning to its members, to create psychological safety through the rules of interaction that protect face and self-esteem, and to define personal boundaries and the interactional rules for love and intimacy.

Summary and Conclusions

This chapter has reviewed the deeper cultural dimensions that deal with human nature, human activity, and human relationships. The set of issues and dimensions reviewed constitutes a kind of grid against which to map a given organizational culture, but one should always remember that not all dimensions are equally salient or important in a given culture. Furthermore, the dimensions interact to form a kind of pattern or paradigm, as was shown in Chapter Three for DEC and Ciba-Geigy.

We reviewed the basic assumptions about human nature as being, calculative, social, self-actualizing, or complex; as being positive and malleable (Theory Y); or as negative and fixed (Theory X). We noted that some cultures emphasize doing and conquering, while other cultures emphasize being and accepting one's fate and niche, while still others emphasize being-in-becoming by focusing on self-development as the fundamentally "right" way to be. These dimensions characterize how organizations view their relationship to the environment in which they operate.

We then reviewed basic dimensions that have been used to characterize human relationships. The most fundamental of these is whether the group is primarily individualistic and competitive or collectivist and cooperative. All groups have some form of hierarchy, but a relevant cultural dimension is the degree of distance that is felt between higher-ups and lower-downs in the hierarchy.

In the formation of any society, all members must solve for themselves the problem of identity: who to be in that group, how much influence or control they will have, whether their needs and goals will be met, and how intimate the group will become. In that process, groups learn how to structure a given relationship in terms of the dimensions of how emotionally charged or neutral it should be, how diffuse or specific it should be, how universalistic or particularistic it should be, and how much the value placed on the other person should be based on achievement. A critical dimension is whether building a relationship is considered a priority before work can be done because cultures vary greatly in the relative importance they place on relationship building.

We also noted that in all groups, the assumptions about space, time, and relationships form rules of interaction that create and maintain a social order that manages meaning, aggression, and intimacy. Culture is deep, wide, complex, and multidimensional, so we should avoid the temptation to stereotype organizational phenomena in terms of one or two salient dimensions. Many such typologies have been suggested, as will be examined in the next chapter.

10

CULTURE TYPOLOGIES AND CULTURE SURVEYS

In the previous several chapters, I reviewed a great many dimensions that have been used to characterize cultures. I chose to focus on those that are useful for describing *organizational* cultures in particular. Other dimensions have been proposed, and these are often presented as universal typologies or as *sets* of dimensions that can be presented in combination to give a more complete profile of the organization. Many of the typologies and profiles proposed are based on questionnaires or surveys of members of the organization. We will therefore discuss typologies both as theoretical constructs and as labels derived from factor analyzing a lot of perceptual data. The fact that there are a number of different models built around questionnaires requires us to consider how to evaluate the relative validity and utility of such models. Before reviewing some of those models, we need to understand what role typologies play in trying to understand an abstract concept such as organizational culture and what the advantages and disadvantages are of using them.

Why Typologies and Why Not?

When we observe the "natural" world, what we see, hear, taste, smell, and feel are potentially overwhelming. By itself, "raw experience" does not make sense, but our own cultural upbringing has taught us how to make sense of it through conceptual categories that are embedded in our language. What we experience as an infant is a "blooming, buzzing confusion" that is slowly put into order as we learn to discriminate objects such as chairs and tables, mother and father, light and dark and to associate words with those experienced objects and events.

By the time we are young adults, we have a complete vocabulary and set of conceptual categories that allow us to discriminate and label most of what we experience. We must not forget, however, that these categories and the language that goes with them are *learned within a given culture*, and such learning continues as we move into new cultures such as occupations and organizations. The engineer learns new categories and words, as do the doctor, the lawyer, and the manager. The employee going into DEC and the employee going into Ciba-Geigy learn different things.

New concepts become useful if they (1) help to make sense and provide some order out of the observed phenomena, (2) help to define what may be the underlying structure in the phenomena by building a theory of how things work, which, in turn, (3) enables us to predict to some degree how other phenomena that may not yet have been observed are going to look. However, in the process of building new categories, we inevitably must become more abstract. As we develop such abstractions, it becomes possible to develop models, typologies, and theories of how things work. The advantage of such typologies and the theories they permit us to postulate is that they attempt to order a great variety of different phenomena. The disadvantage and danger is that they are so abstract that they do not reflect adequately the reality of a given set of phenomena being observed. In this sense, typologies can be useful if we are trying to compare many organizations but can be quite useless if we are trying to understand one particular organization.

The typologies and models that we use gradually come to be our view of reality, and this simplifies the daily work of making sense of lived experience. Such simplification is useful in reducing anxiety and conserving mental energy. The danger is that we narrow our attention span and become more mindless with respect to what we are observing. Such narrowing can be very useful if we are dealing with phenomena of little consequence. Labeling restaurants or banks as being "command and control" type organizations is okay if we are just occasional customers. However, if it becomes critical in an economic downturn to decide whether or not to continue to keep our money in the *particular* bank in our neighborhood, the "type" of bank it is may become critical, and we may then need a broader set of dimensions around which to analyze the culture of that particular bank. If we have relied too much on a given typology, we may not have the conceptual tools to analyze our particular bank.

A third issue in using typologies concerns the question of how we arrive at the abstract label. A number of the culture models we will review gather data by asking employees how they *perceive* their organization. The perceptions are then aggregated and combined into a more abstract concept. The concept is often derived from factor analyzing a broad set of questionnaire responses to determine which items hang together and, therefore, suggest a category that hangs together in the employee's perceptions. Those "factors" are then labeled and described in summary fashion. For example, the label "strategic direction and intent" (Denison, 1990) and the culture score on that dimension is based on combining employee ratings of their own organization on the following items:

- There is a long-term purpose and direction.
- Our strategy leads other organizations to change the way they compete in the industry.
- There is a clear mission that gives meaning and direction to our work.
- There is a clear strategy for the future.
- Our strategic direction is unclear to me (reverse scoring).

That final score can be a *reliable* measure of employee perception and a *valid* indicator of the degree to which a given set of employees believes that their organization has a strong or weak strategy, but the question remains whether that score can be a measure of *culture* as defined in this book.

Problems in the Use of Surveys

A number of the typologies we will review depend upon employee surveys that are scored in the manner described so we need to ask what are the problems and issues in the use of surveys as culture measures.

- **Not knowing what to ask.** If we define culture as covering all of the internal and external dimensions that have been reviewed in the past several chapters, we would need a huge survey to cover all of those possible dimensions. What this means for a particular organization is that basically we would not know what questions to put into the survey.

Unless we did some other form of deciphering first, we would not know which dimensions are salient for the organization and part of their deep cultural "DNA" and which dimensions are basically irrelevant. If we used one of the existing surveys, we would not know whether or not we had picked the right one in terms of what was important in that organization. Each survey would claim to analyze "the culture" or important "dimensions of the culture," but there would be no *a priori* way of knowing how to evaluate those claims.

- **Employees may not be motivated to be honest.** Employees are always encouraged to be frank and honest in their answers, usually supplemented by the assurance that their answers will be kept completely confidential. The fact that such assurances need to be given in the first place implies that our original assumption is that employees would not be open if their answers were known. Because culture is a living reality, we ought to use a method that allows people to be open. Too many questions in the surveys require evaluations and judgments that cause employees to be careful in how they answer.

- **Employees may not understand the questions or interpret them differently.** "There is a clear strategy for the future" presumes that the employees have similar definitions of the word "strategy." If we cannot make this assumption, then amalgamating their answers does not make sense. It is therefore very difficult to infer a "shared" concept from individual responses.

- **What is measured may be accurate but superficial.** It is difficult to get at the deeper levels of a culture from paper and pencil perceptions. Culture is an intrinsically shared phenomenon that only manifests itself in interaction, so whatever dimensions are measured by the survey are bound to be superficial.

- **The sample of employees surveyed may not be representative of the key culture carriers.** Most survey administrators assume that if they have done a careful job of sampling and testing their sample against total organizational demographics, that they can validly describe the whole based on the sample. This logic may not work for culture because the driving forces in a culture can be the executive subculture, and, as Martin has pointed out, the culture may be fragmented and differentiated around many subcultures that the survey would have no way of identifying statistically. With qualitative knowledge of the organization based on observation and group interviews, we could identify certain groups and test for survey differences, but we would need the prior knowledge.

- **The profile of dimensions does not reveal their interaction or patterning into a total system.** The survey reports are often presented as profiles or as scores on the spokes of a wheel to give an impression of an integrated measure, but the deep interactions of assumptions about dimensions such as "the nature of truth" and how that was related in DEC to the egalitarian and conflictive style of decision making will not reveal itself.

- **The impact of taking the survey will have unknown consequences some of which may be undesirable or destructive.** Answering questions forces employees to think about categories that may never have occurred to them and to make value judgments in areas that are controversial. Not only are individuals influenced in this way, but if they share value judgments such as discovering that they are each very cynical about the leadership of the organization, negative group attitudes can be built up that will damage the organization's ability to function. Furthermore, expectations are set up in employees that once management gets the results, they will take action to improve areas in which employees voiced complaints. If management does not respond, morale can go down, and management may not know why this happened.

When to Use Surveys

Having identified some of the problems with surveys as measures of a particular organization's culture, there are, nevertheless, times when surveys might be useful and appropriate, as described in the following list.

- **Determining whether particular dimensions of culture are systematically related to some element of performance.** To that end, we want to study a large number of cultures and need a way of comparing them on just those dimensions and on their performance. Doing full ethnographic studies is either impractical or too expensive, so we settle for an operational definition of the abstract dimension we want to measure and design a standardized interview, observational checklist, or survey to get a rating or score on each organization. These scores can then be correlated with various other performance measures across many organizations (Corlett and Pearson, 2003; Denison, 1990; Denison and Mishra, 1995; Cooke and Szumal, 1993).

- **Giving a particular organization a profile of itself to stimulate a deeper analysis of the culture of that organization.** The assumption here is that the scores on the dimensions measured are presented as "how the employees perceive this organization" not as an absolute measure of the culture. These perceptions can then become a stimulus for further work on improving organizational performance. To facilitate such improvement, the surveys ask not only "how you perceive your organization in the present" but also "how would you like your organization to be in the future." In terms of the preceding example, employees might indicate on the Strategic Intent dimension that they have a low score in the present and would like their organization to be higher on this dimension. When using surveys in this way, it is important to follow up the cultural deciphering with other methods and not to assume that the given profile *is* the culture.

- **Comparing organizations to each other on selected dimensions as preparation for mergers, acquisitions, and joint ventures.** This can be useful if we have some idea of the dimensions that need to be compared and if we can assume that the employees will willingly take the survey and answer honestly.

- **Testing whether certain subcultures that we suspect to be present can be objectively differentiated and defined in terms of preselected dimensions that a survey can identify.** If we suspect that the engineering subculture and the operator subculture have different assumptions along the lines described in the "Three Generic Subcultures" section of Chapter Four, we can design a survey to check this out, provided we can get valid samples and assuming that we are getting honest answers.

- **Educating employees about certain important dimensions that management wants to work on.** For example, if the future performance of the organization depends on consensus and commitment to a certain strategy, the survey questions reviewed previously can become a vehicle both for testing present perceptions and for launching change programs around building commitment to the strategy.

In each of these cases, the principle applies that we should think carefully whether or not giving the survey will have possible negative consequences and involve the relevant parties in making the decision on whether or not to go ahead. Having provided this background, we can now look at several typologies that are based on theoretical categories and "measured" with survey data.

Typologies That Focus on Assumptions About Authority and Intimacy

Organizations are ultimately the result of people doing things together for a common purpose. The basic relationship between the individual and the organization can, therefore, be thought of as the most fundamental cultural dimension around which to build a typology because it will provide critical categories for analyzing assumptions about authority and intimacy. One of the most general theories here is Etzioni's (1975) fundamental distinction between three types of organizations that exist in every society:

- **Coercive organizations:** The individual is essentially captive for physical or economic reasons and must, therefore, obey whatever rules are imposed by the authorities. Examples include prisons, military academies and units, mental hospitals, religious training organizations, prisoner of war camps, cults, and so on. The cultures that evolve in such organizations usually generate strong counter-cultures among the participants as defenses against the arbitrary authority.

- **Utilitarian organizations:** The individual provides "a fair day's work for a fair day's pay" and, therefore, abides by whatever rules are essential for the performance of the organization. Examples include business organizations of all sorts. As has been found in most such organizations, they also develop countercultural norms so that employees can protect themselves from exploitation by the authorities.

- **Normative organizations:** The individual contributes his or her commitment and accepts legitimate authority because the goals of the organization are basically the same as the individual's goals. Examples include churches, political parties, voluntary organizations, hospitals, and schools.

Authority in the coercive kind of organization is arbitrary and absolute; in the utilitarian system, the typical business, authority is a negotiated relationship in the sense that the employee is presumed to accept the method by which people in higher ranks have achieved their status. In the normative system, authority is more informal and more subject to personal consent in that the employee or member can exit if he or she is not satisfied with the treatment received.

This typology is important because *type of organization* supercedes many of the macrocultures that exist in the world. For example, in a high power distance culture, we expect the authority system to be coercive, but if it is a business organization, there might be strong pressures toward more negotiated utilitarian kinds of management structures. One of the main problems of globalism is that some of the western utilitarian management styles simply don't work in macrocultures that are more coercive. And to make matters worse, the western managers believe that their authority system is the *correct* one, forgetting that no one culture is more correct than any other culture. In many Asian or Latin countries, businesses cannot be effective unless they are coercive, and the authoritarian structure is accepted by both management and the employees because it fits the larger macrocultural norms.

Assumptions about peer relationships and intimacy are also illuminated by this typology. In the coercive system, close peer relationships develop as a defense against authority, leading to unions and other forms of self-protective groups that develop strong counter-cultures. In the utilitarian system, peer relations evolve around the work group and typically reflect the kind of incentive system that management uses. Because such systems are often built around *task* performance, close relationships are discouraged on the assumption that they might get in the way of clear task focus. In the normative system, relationships evolve naturally around tasks and in support of the organization. In such organizations, more intimate relationships are typically seen as aiding the members in building strong motivation and commitment to the goals of the organization. For this reason, some businesses attempt to be normative organizations by involving employees in the mission of the organization and encouraging more intimate relationships. Professional organizations such as law firms or service organizations that consist of groups of "partners" combine some of the elements of the utilitarian and normative (Jones, 1983; Shrivastava, 1983: Greiner and Poulfelt, 2005).

The value of this typology is that it enables us to differentiate the broad category of utilitarian business organizations from coercive total institutions such as prisons and mental hospitals, and from normative organizations such as schools, hospitals, and nonprofits (Goffman, 1961). The difficulty, however, is that within any given organization, variations of all three authority systems may be operating, which requires us to rely on still other dimensions to capture the uniqueness of a given organization. To deal with variations of authority within an organization, a number of typologies have been proposed that focus specifically on how authority is used and what level of participation is expected in the organization: (1) autocratic, (2) paternalistic, (3) consultative or democratic, (4) participative and power sharing, (5) delegative, and (6) abdicative (which implies delegating not only tasks and responsibilities but power and controls as well) (Bass, 1981, 1985; Harbison and Myers, 1959; Likert, 1967; Vroom and Yetton, 1973).

These organizational typologies deal much more with aggression, power, and control than with love, intimacy, and peer relationships. In that regard, they are always built on underlying assumptions about human nature and activity. Thus a manager who holds the assumptions of Theory X, namely that people cannot be trusted, would automatically go toward the autocratic management style and stay there. On the other hand, the manager who holds the assumptions of Theory Y, namely that people are motivated and want to do their job, would select a management style according to the task requirements and vary his or her behavior. Some tasks require autocratic authority as in carrying out a military mission while others should be totally delegated because the subordinates have all the information (McGregor, 1960; Schein, 1975).

The arguments that managers get into about the "correct" level of participation and use of authority usually reflects the different assumptions they are making about the nature of the subordinates they are dealing with. Looking at participation and involvement as a matter of cultural assumptions makes clear that the debate about whether leaders should be more autocratic or participative is ultimately highly colored by the assumptions of a particular group in a particular context. The search for the universally correct leadership style is doomed to failure because of cultural variation by country, by industry, by occupation, by the particular history of a given organization, and, most importantly, by the actual task to be performed.

Typologies of Corporate Character and Culture

Typologies trying to capture cultural essences in organizations were first introduced by Harrison (1979) and Handy (1978) with four "types" based on their primary focus. Harrison's four types were:

- **Power oriented:** Organizations dominated by charismatic/autocratic founders.
- **Achievement oriented:** Organizations dominated by task results.
- **Role oriented:** Public bureaucracies.
- **Support oriented:** Nonprofit or religious organizations.

Handy saw a connection between types of organizations and what some of the main Greek gods represented:

- **Zeus:** The Club culture.
- **Athena:** The Task culture.
- **Apollo:** The Role culture.
- **Dionysus:** The Existential culture.

Both of these typologies are measured with brief questionnaires and are used to help an organization get some insight into its "essence" (Handy, 1978; Harrison and Stokes, 1992).

The concept of corporate "character" was introduced by Wilkins (1989), who saw it as a component of culture consisting of "Shared Vision," "Motivational Faith" that things would be fair and that abilities would be used, and "Distinctive Skills." In his view, building character was possible by emphasizing programs dealing with each of the components, but he did not build a typology around the dimensions. Building on personality dimensions, Pearson presents a more elaborate model based on the theory of twelve Jungian archetypes—ruler, creator, innocent, sage, explorer, revolutionary, magician, hero, lover, jester, caregiver, and everyperson (Corlett and Pearson, 2003). She measures through a self-report questionnaire how things are done in the organization and then scores the results for the twelve archetypes to determine which are the most salient in the organization. By obtaining self-insight, the organization is presumed to be more able to be effective.

Goffee and Jones (1998) saw character as equivalent to culture and created a typology based on two key dimensions: "solidarity"—the tendency to be like-minded, and "sociability"—the tendency to be friendly to each other. These dimensions are measured with a twenty-three-item self-description questionnaire. They closely resemble and are derivative from the classical group dynamics distinction between *task* variables and *building and maintenance* variables. These two dimensions were used extensively by Blake and Mouton (1964, 1969, 1989) in their "Managerial Grid," which was built on the two dimensions of task and group building, each to be measured on a scale of 1 to 9. A highly sociable, person-oriented organization that cared little for task accomplishment would be rated as 1,9, whereas a highly task-oriented, driven, and insensitive organization would be rated 9,1. Various other combinations were possible, ranging from 1,1 (which is virtually a state of anomie) to 5,5 (a compromise solution) to 9,9, the hero of the model, in which task and personal factors are given equal weight.

Goffee and Jones use these dimensions to identify four types of cultures:

- **Fragmented:** Low on both dimensions.
- **Mercenary:** High on solidarity, low on sociability.
- **Communal:** High on sociability, low on solidarity.
- **Networked:** High on both.

Each type has certain virtues and liabilities that are described, but the typology misses a crucial dimension that has been identified by Ancona (1988) and others: the relationship between the group (organization) and its external environments, which is the boundary management function that must be added to the task and maintenance functions. Without a model of what happens at the boundary, it is not possible to determine which type of culture is effective under different environmental conditions.

Cameron and Quinn (1999, 2006) also developed a four-category typology based on two dimensions, but in their case, the dimensions are more structural—how stable or flexible the organization is and how externally or internally focused it is. These dimensions are seen as perpetually competing values:

- **Hierarchy:** Internal focus and stable; structured, well coordinated.
- **Clan:** Internal focus and flexible; collaborative, friendly, family like.
- **Market:** External focus and stable; competitive, results oriented.
- **Adhocracy:** External focus and flexible; innovative, dynamic, entrepreneurial.

Whereas the Goffee and Jones typology was built on basic dimensions that derived from group dynamics (task versus maintenance), the Cameron and Quinn typology was built on factor analyzing large numbers of indicators of organizational performance and finding that these reduce to two clusters that correlate closely with what cognitive researchers have found to be "archetypical" dimensions as well. Markets, hierarchies, and clans as organizational types had previously been identified by Ouchi (1978, 1981), and markets versus hierarchies were analyzed in detail by economists such as Williamson (1975).

In this typology as in the previous one, we don't know the relative importance of these dimensions within the organization being analyzed, we don't know which typology is the more relevant, and we don't know whether a short questionnaire can validly "type" a culture. On the other hand, the questionnaire focuses on managerial behavior, so it may be a useful diagnostic for determining the kinds of climates that managers set for their subordinates and correlating that with performance. The Cameron and Quinn typology is also based on the theoretical idea that the poles of any given dimension are in conflict with each other and the cultural solution is how to reconcile them. This is the same idea as the Hampden-Turner and Trompenaars model of showing organizations how cultural solutions are always some level of integration of the extremes of the dimension (2000). For example, all cultures have to be *both* collectivist and individualistic; how they solve this dilemma gives them their distinctive flavor.

Examples of Survey-Based Profiles of Cultures

Another approach, best illustrated by Denison (1990), is to identify a number of dimensions of culture that are presumed to be relevant to a given organizational outcome such as performance, growth, innovation, or learning. The survey questions are then focused on just the dimensions considered relevant, and if those dimensions cannot conveniently be measured with a survey, the researcher/consultant can supplement with interviews and observations. This approach worries less about creating a typology and more about measuring key dimensions in many organizations and then relating those to performance. For example, Denison's survey measures the following twelve dimensions under four general headings:

Mission
- Strategic direction and intent
- Goals and objectives
- Vision

Consistency
- Core values
- Agreement
- Coordination and integration

Involvement
- Empowerment
- Team orientation
- Capability development

Adaptability
- Creating change
- Customer focus
- Organizational learning

Scores on each of the twelve dimensions are shown in a circular profile of the group and can be compared to norms based on a large sample of organizations that have been rated as more or less effective. Notice that the categories are quite abstract, so we have to go back to the actual items to discover just what was meant by each dimension.

The Human Synergistics International company developed a similar approach with its "Organizational Culture Inventory" (Cooke and Szumal, 1993). The company's twelve dimensions, also shown as a "circumplex" profile are organized around three basic organizational styles:

Constructive Styles
    Achievement
    Self-actualizing
    Humanistic-encouraging
    Affiliative
Aggressive/Defensive Styles
    Oppositional
    Power
    Competitive
    Perfectionistic
Passive/Defensive Styles
    Avoidance
    Dependent
    Conventional
    Approval

From the point of view of this analysis, the main problem with these diagnostics is that they require an outsider to help interpret the results. If culture is an interactive phenomenon, as I am claiming, then insiders should be able to decipher their own cultural dimensions without needing profiles to tell them what their culture is. It should also be noted that the focus of this widely used survey is "the shared values guiding how members of an organization interact and work." Certainly how workers interact and work is critical, but rather than covering all aspects of this domain, it is probably more important to focus more specifically on issues of authority and intimacy, which can easily be lost in these large surveys.

Examples of Using *A Priori* Criteria for Culture Evaluation

A different kind of approach is illustrated in a German publishing company offering a prize in 2003 to six companies selected from a nominated pool of sixty-three for the following:

> individual models of excellence in developing and living a corporate culture . . . An international working commission composed of experts from academia and the business world developed ten critical dimensions of corporate culture in intense discussion . . . Then a team of researchers from Bertelsman Stiftung and the consulting firm of Booz Allen Hamilton evaluated these companies against the ten dimensions and their related criteria. (Sackman, Bertelsman Stiftung, 2006, p. 43)

The dimensions are shown in Figure 10.1

Figure 10.1.   Corporate Culture and Leadership Behavior as Success Factors: Key Dimensions.

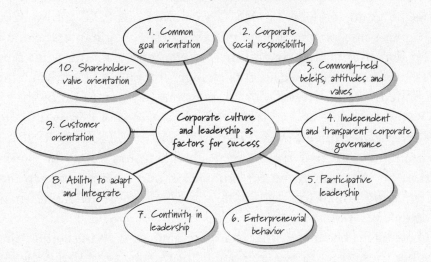

Source: Booz Allen Hamilton 2003; Bertelsmann stiftung 2003 p. 44.

The research team then examined economic performance for the past ten years and publicly available information about the companies to winnow the list down to ten finalists who were then evaluated against the ten criteria. The evaluations were done through company visits and interviews of all levels from board chairs to members of the works council. For each of the ten factors, detailed checklists were developed to enable the evaluation teams to score each company relatively objectively. The detailed findings were then reviewed with the original commission leading to the selection of six companies as outstanding examples of the evolution and use of corporate culture in achieving their excellent performance: The BMW Group, Deutsche Lufthansa, Grundfos, Henkel, Hilti, and Novo Nordisk. Sackman concludes, "the corporate culture that distinguished each of them today [in 2006] has, on the one hand, contributed to their success and, on the other hand, placed them in a strong position as they face challenges to come" (p. 45). What makes this research valuable is the detailed description of the six companies so that the reader can get past the abstractions that the ten dimensions represent and see how things actually worked in each company. Note that the ten criteria involve *both* issues of survival in the external environment and issues of internal integration.

A second example is the detailed analysis of a corporate culture change program conducted in HSBC in Hong Kong (O'Donovan, 2006). I will give some of the change process details in Chapter Seventeen, but for purposes of this chapter, it is relevant to examine what dimensions of culture were used in this change program. O'Donovan started with Schein's hypothesized set of dimensions of what an innovative culture would look like and added several dimensions of her own to create the twenty-three dimensions shown in Figure 10.2 (Schein, 1990). It is important to note that the Xs on each dimension show the optimum position on that dimension for innovation and learning, which means that on some dimensions, a middle position is more desirable than an extreme position.

There have been many other change programs involving culture dimensions, but these recent ones are notable for the degree of detail they have provided on how culture was conceptualized and assessed.

Figure 10.2.   Characteristics of Healthy Culture.

PEOPLE

The Individual's Locus of Control

Externally directed   Internally directed

The Nature of an Individual's Value

Useful to job on hand   Intrinsic to being human

The Power of Mankind

A law unto himself   Subject to universal laws

The Complexity of Human Intelligence

One-demensional   Multi-faceted

The Nature of Corporate Culture

Dull   Intelligent

The Essence of Diversity

Differences in appearance   Differences in thinking

PLACES

The Natural Environment

An externality   The centre of existence

THINGS

The Organization's Central Paradigm

Other   Principle-centred in   Principle-centred in
                             word only   word and spirit

The Nature of Company Values

A meaningless statement   A public relations ploy   A true commitment

Public Image

Manufactured   Authentic

The Nature of the Organization

Inert structures   The inert and the human   An Entity

(Continued)

Figure 10.2.   (Continued)

Core Purpose

Increase shareholder value   Responsible provision of goods & services

Workforce—Organization Relationship

Human resources/tools   Members/citizens

Organization—External Stakeholder Relationship

To be manipulated   To be respected

Organization—Business Environment Relationship

Estranged   Attuned

Bad News and Whistle-blowing

A threat   A learning opportunity

Decision-making

Immoral   Amoral   Moral

Ownership for Learning and Development

Centralized   Localized

Communication

Closed   Open

How Best Results Are Achieved

Self-interest   Self-interest and group interest   Altruism

Speed of Response to Customer Demands

Low   Medium   High

The Service Provider

Front-line workers   Contracted parties   All staff

Emotional Expression

Unacceptable   To be encouraged and managed   To be encouraged

Source: O'Donovan (2006), p. 125–127.

Summary and Conclusions

The value of typologies is that they simplify thinking and provide useful categories for sorting out the complexities we must deal with when we confront organizational realities. They provide categories for thinking and classifying, which is useful. The weakness of culture typologies is that they oversimplify these complexities and may provide us categories that are incorrect in terms of their relevance to what we are trying to understand. They limit our perspective by prematurely focusing us on just a few dimensions, they limit our ability to find complex patterns among a number of dimensions, and they do not reveal what a given group feels intensely about.

Typologies also introduce a bias toward what Martin (2002) calls the "integration perspective" in culture studies—an approach that emphasizes those dimensions on which there is a high degree of consensus. She notes that many organizations are "differentiated" or even "fragmented" to the extent that there is little consensus on any cultural dimensions. An integrated culture is one in which the whole organization shares a single set of assumptions; a differentiated culture is an organization in which powerful subcultures disagree on certain crucial issues, such as labor and management; and a fragmented culture is an organization such as a financial conglomerate that has a great many subcultures and no single overarching set of shared assumptions. Clearly the effort to classify a given organization into a single typological category, such as "clan" or "networked," presumes not only integration around two dimensions but also the assumption that those dimensions can be measured well enough to determine the degree of consensus. Martin's categories are a powerful way to describe organizations that have different kinds of cultural landscapes within them, but they do not require any redefinition of the basic concept of culture as a shared set of assumptions that is taken for granted. It is then an empirical matter whether in a given organization we find various levels of integration, differentiation, and/or fragmentation.

Some typologies attempt to reduce all organizations to a few types, while others rely more on profiling organizations in terms of a number of dimensions that are separately measured by means of employee surveys. We reviewed the pros and cons of using such surveys to "measure" cultures. The main issue is whether individual responses on a survey can get at the deeper levels of shared tacit assumptions that may only reveal themselves in actual interaction. What surveys measure may be valid, but it may not get at cultural essence.

Several examples were cited of developing dimensions for the specific purpose of identifying ones that correlate with organizational performance and showing in two cases how the assessment of the culture involved multiple methods, including site visits, observation, and interview. In the next chapter, we will pick up this theme by tackling the question of how to decipher organizational cultures.

11

DECIPHERING ORGANIZATIONAL CULTURES

Organizational culture can be studied in a variety of ways. The method should be determined by the purpose. Just deciphering a culture for curiosity is as vague as just assessing personality or character in an individual. Assessment makes more sense when there is some problem to be illuminated or some specific purpose for which we need information. And, as we will see, how we perform the assessment and what tools we use very much depend on our purpose. If you think about all of the cultural dimensions that have just been reviewed in the past five chapters, you will realize that deciphering a culture to the level of its basic assumptions can be a formidable task.

This chapter describes what you might want to do if you have a general or research interest in deciphering a culture. Chapter Eighteen describes a particular way that change agents assess culture in the context of a specific change program.

Why Decipher Culture?

There are several quite different reasons for wanting to decipher or assess an organizational culture. At one extreme is pure academic research where the researcher is trying to present a picture of a culture to fellow researchers and other interested parties to develop theory or test some hypothesis. This covers most anthropologists who go to live in a culture to get an insider's view and then present the culture in written form for others to get a sense of what goes on there (for example, Dalton, 1959; Kunda, 1992; Van Maanen, 1973).

At the other extreme is the student's need to assess the culture of an organization to decide whether or not to work there, or the need of an employee or manager to understand his or her organization better in order to improve it. In between is the consultant's and change agent's need to decipher the culture to facilitate some change program that the organization has launched to solve a business problem. What differs greatly in these cases is the focus and level of depth involved in the deciphering and who needs to know the results. At the end of this chapter, we will also discuss the ethical issues and risks involved in each of these approaches.

Deciphering from the Outside

It is not only the ethnographer or researcher who needs to decipher an organization's culture. The job applicant, the customer, and the journalist all have the need from time to time to figure out what goes on inside a particular organization. They do not need to know the totality of a given culture, but they need to know some of its essences in relation to their goal. The commonest version of this need is the graduate wanting to know whether or not to go to work in a particular organization. Exhibit 11.1 shows the major activities that might be involved in such deciphering.

The essential point is not to get too involved with the *content* of the culture until you have experienced it at the artifact level. That means visiting the public aspects, taking tours, asking to see inside areas, and reading whatever literature the organization makes available. The first cut at thinking about content areas should come out of the things that puzzle you. Why are the offices laid out the way they are, why is it so quiet or noisy, why are

Exhibit 11.1. How to Decipher an Organization from the Outside.

1. Visit and observe.
2. Identify artifacts and processes that puzzle you.
3. Ask insiders why things are done that way.
4. Identify espoused values that appeal to you, and ask how they are implemented in the organization.
5. Look for inconsistencies, and ask about them.
6. Figure out from all you have heard what deeper assumptions actually determine the behavior you observe.

there no pictures on the walls, and so on? Your personal needs and interests should guide this process, not some formal checklist. To give yourself some content focus, try to observe how the insiders behave toward each other in terms of the critical issues of authority and intimacy.

You will have met some insiders in the process—recruiters, customer representatives, tour guides, friends who work there or friendly strangers with whom you can strike up a conversation. When you interact with insiders, the culture will reveal itself in the way that the insiders deal with you. Culture is best revealed through interaction. Ask insiders about the things you have observed that puzzle you. To your surprise, they may be puzzled as well because insiders do not necessarily know why their culture works the way it does. But being jointly puzzled begins to give you some insight into the layers of the culture, and you can ask the same question of other insiders some of whom may be more insightful as to what is going on. If you have read all about the organization and have heard its claims about its goals and values, look for evidence that they are or are not being met, and ask insiders how those goals and values are met. If you discover inconsistencies, ask about those. Whenever you hear a generalization or an abstraction such as "we are a team here," ask for some specific behavioral examples.

This process of deciphering cannot be standardized because organizations differ greatly in what they allow the outsider to see. Instead you have to think like the anthropologist, lean heavily on observation, and then follow up with various kinds of inquiry. The reason for focusing on things that puzzle you is that it keeps the inquiry pure. If you start with trying to verify your assumptions or stereotypes of the organization, you will be perceived as threatening and will elicit inaccurate defensive information. If you display genuine puzzlement, you will elicit efforts on the part of insiders to help you understand. In that regard, the best form of inquiry may be to reveal something that puzzles you and then say, "Help me to understand why the following things are happening...."

Deciphering in a Researcher Role

If you are a researcher trying to decipher what is going on in relation to a particular research question, your first issue is getting entry. In the process of contacting the organization, negotiating what you need and what you offer them in return, you will go through all of the preceding steps with the insiders whom you have already met. You will acquire a great deal of superficial but potentially relevant cultural knowledge. Depending on your research goals, you then have to decide what additional information to gather to get a deeper understanding of the culture.

You must realize that gathering valid data from a complex human system is intrinsically difficult, involves a variety of choices and options, and is always an intervention into the life of the organization.

The most obvious difficulty in gathering valid cultural data is the well-known phenomenon that when human "subjects" are involved in research, there is a tendency for the subjects either to resist and hide data that they feel defensive about or to exaggerate to impress the researcher or to get cathartic relief—"Finally someone is interested enough in us to listen to our story." The need for such "cathartic relief" derives from the fact that even the best of organizations generate "toxins"—frustrations with the boss, tensions over missed targets, destructive competition with peers, scarce resources, exhaustion from overwork, and so on (Frost, 2003; Goldman, 2008).

In the process of trying to understand how the organization really works, you may find yourself listening to tales of woe from anxious or frustrated employees who have no other outlet. To get any kind of accurate picture of what is going on in the organization, you must find a method that encourages the insiders to "tell it like it is" rather than trying to impress you, hide data, or blow off steam.

If you have made any kind of contact with the organization, even if it is only getting permission to observe silently, the human system has been perturbed in unknown ways. The employees being observed may view you as a spy or as an opportunity for catharsis, as noted earlier. Motives will be attributed to management as to why you are there. You may be seen as a nuisance, a disturbance, or an audience to whom to play. But you have no way of knowing which of the many possible reactions you are eliciting and whether or not they are desirable either from a data gathering or ethical point of view. For this reason, you should examine carefully the broad range of data gathering interventions available and choose carefully which method to use.

The many possible ways of gathering data are shown in Table 11.1. They differ along two dimensions—how involved the researcher becomes

Table 11.1.   Categories of Research on Organizations.

Levels of Subject Involvement	Levels of Researcher Involvement	
	Low to Medium; Quantitative	*High; Qualitative*
Minimal	Demographics: Measurement of "distal variables"	Ethnography: Participant observation; content analysis of stories, myths, rituals, symbols, other artifacts
Partial	Experimentation, questionnaires, ratings, objective tests, scales	Educational interventions, projective tests; assessment centers; interviews
Maximal	Total quality tools such as statistical quality control; action research, contract research	Clinical research; process consultation, organization development

with the organization being studied and how involved the members of the organization become in the data gathering process.

Some cultural artifacts can be gathered by purely demographic methods or by observation at a distance, such as photographing buildings, observing action in the organization without getting involved, entering the organization incognito, and so on. As was pointed out in Chapter Two, the problem with this method is that the data may be clear but undecipherable. I could see all the fighting in DEC from a distance, but I had no idea what it meant.

If you want to understand more of what is going on, you must get more involved through becoming a participant observer/ethnographer, but you do not, in this role, want the subjects to become too directly involved lest you unwittingly change the very phenomena you are trying to study. To minimize the inevitable biases that result from your own involvement, you may use insiders as "informants" to help clarify what you observe or to decipher the data you are gathering, still limiting the organization's involvement as much as possible.

The middle row of Table 11.1 depicts data gathering methods that involve the members of the organization to a greater degree. If you still want to minimize your own outsider involvement, you try to rely on "objective" measurements such as experiments or questionnaires. Experiments are usually not possible for ethical reasons, but surveys and questionnaires are often used, with the limitations that were discussed in detail in the previous chapter. If you recognize that the interpretation of cultural data may require interaction with the subjects, you could use semistructured interviews, projective tests, or standardized assessment situations, but these methods again raise the ethical issues of whether you are intervening in their system beyond what they might have agreed to.

In an interview, you can ask broad questions such as the following:

- What was it like to come to work in this organization?
- What did you notice most as being important to getting along?
- How do bosses communicate their expectations?

The main problem with this approach is that it is very time consuming, and it may be hard to put data from different individuals together into a coherent picture because each person may see things differently even though he or she uses the same words.

The important point to remember is that after you have described the organization by abstracting "scores" from individual survey or interview responses, you have only a superficial understanding of the cultural dynamics that may be operating. That level of understanding may be enough to compare many organizations but can be quite useless if you are trying to understand a particular organization in any kind of depth. For example, DEC, HP, and Apple would have looked very similar on culture surveys as being very decentralized, innovative, employee centered, constructive, and self-actualizing, yet were quite different at the level of basic assumptions. In DEC, you fought everything out and were personally responsible to "do the right thing;" in HP, you had to publicly be nice but develop competitive and political skills to get things done; and in Apple, you were in a project, not a company, and you were free to "do your own thing."

Even more important, the three companies had very different strategies, which were also embedded in their cultures but would have been hard to measure. DEC was creating a new concept of computing with its evolution of the minicomputer. HP was an instrumentation company that went into computing and ended up with major subcultures that eventually split into Agilent and HP. Apple wanted to evolve a simpler model of computing for school kids and a "fun" model of computing for "yuppies" and shunned marketing to government and big business early in its life. These cultural differences in strategy can be seen in HP and Apple today in their different product sets and marketing styles but would only have been observed in the group interactions of senior executives. Ciba-Geigy's obsession with science and technology only surfaced from their reaction to Airwick.

The dilemma for you, then, is how to get access to groups where the deeper cultural assumptions reveal themselves. The answer is that you must somehow motivate the organization to want to reveal itself to you because it has something to gain. That brings us to the bottom row of Table 11.1 and the concepts of *action research* and *clinical research*. Action research is generally thought of as a process where the members of the organization being studied become involved in the gathering of data and, especially, in the interpretation of what is found. If the motivation for the project is to help the researcher gather valid data, the action research label is appropriate. However, if the project was initiated by the organization to solve a problem, we move to the lower-right corner of the table into what I have called "clinical research or inquiry" (Schein, 1987a, 2001, 2008).

Clinical Research: Deciphering in a Consultant/Helper Role. In the bottom-right cell of Table 11.1 is the methodology that I believe is most appropriate to cultural deciphering if you want to get to the deeper levels and the cultural pattern. This level of analysis can be achieved if the organization needs some kind of help from you and if you are trying to help the organization understand itself better to make changes. Your deeper insight into the culture is then a byproduct of your helping.

Most of the information I have provided so far about cultural assumptions in different kinds of organizations was gathered as a byproduct of my consulting with those organizations. The critical distinguishing feature of this inquiry model is that the data come *voluntarily* from the members of the organization because either they initiated the process and have something to gain by revealing themselves to you, the outsider, or, if you initiated the project, they feel they have something to gain from cooperating with you. In other words, no matter how the contact was initiated, the best cultural data will surface if the members of the organization feel they are getting some help from you.

If you are an ethnographer/researcher, you must analyze carefully what you may genuinely have to offer the organization and work toward a psychological contract in which the organization benefits in some way or, in effect, becomes a client. This way of thinking requires you to recognize from the outset that your presence will be an intervention in the organization and that the goal should be how to make that intervention useful to the organization.

Ethnographers tell stories of how they were not "accepted" until they became helpful to the members of the organization in some way, by either doing a job that needed to be done or contributing in some other way (Van Maanen, 1979a; Barley, 1988; Kunda, 1992). The contribution can be entirely symbolic and unrelated to the work of the group being studied. For example, Kunda reports that in his work in a DEC engineering group, he was "permitted" to study the group, but they were quite aloof, which made it hard to inquire about what certain rituals and events in the group meant. However, Kunda was a very good soccer player and was asked to join the lunchtime games. He made a goal for his team one day and from that day forward, he reports, his relationship to the group changed completely. He was suddenly "in" and "of" the group, and that made it possible to ask about many issues that had previously been off limits.

Barley (1988), in his study of the introduction of computerized tomography into a hospital radiology department, offered himself as a working member of the team and was accepted to the extent that he actually contributed in various ways to getting the work done. The important point is to approach the organization with the intention of helping, not just gathering data.

Alternatively, a consultant may be invited into the organization to help with some problem that has been presented that initially has no relationship to culture. In the process of working on the problem, the consultant will discover culturally relevant information, particularly if the process consultation model is used, with its emphasis on inquiry and helping the organization to help itself (Schein, 1999a, 2009a).

If you are in the helper role, you are licensed to ask all kinds of questions that can lead directly into cultural analysis, and, thereby, allow the development of a research focus as well. Both you and the "client" become fully involved in the problem-solving process, and, therefore, the search for relevant data becomes a *joint* responsibility. It is then in the client's interest to say what is really going on instead of succumbing to the potential biases of hiding, exaggerating, and blowing off steam. Furthermore, you again have the license to follow up, to ask further questions, and even to confront the respondent if you feel he or she is holding back.

In this clinical helping role, you are not limited to the data that surface around the client's specific issues. There will usually be many opportunities to hang around and observe what else is going on, allowing you to combine some of the best elements of the clinical and the participant observer ethnographic models. In fact, the ethnographic model when the ethnographer comes to be seen as a helper and the helper model as just described converge and become one and the same.

How Valid Are Clinically Gathered Data?   How can you judge the "validity" of the data gathered by this clinical model? The validity issue has two components: (1) factual accuracy based on whatever contemporary or historical data you can gather, and (2) interpretative accuracy in terms of you representing cultural phenomena in a way that communicates what members of the culture really mean, rather than projecting into the data your own interpretations (Van Maanen, 1988). To fully understand cultural phenomena thus requires at least a combination of history and clinical research, as some anthropologists have argued persuasively (Sahlins, 1985).

Factual accuracy can be checked by the usual methods of triangulation, multiple sources, and replication. Interpretative accuracy is more difficult, but three criteria can be applied. First, if the cultural analysis is "valid," an independent observer going into the same organization should be able to see the same phenomena and interpret them the same way. Second, if the analysis is valid, you should be able to predict the presence of other phenomena and anticipate how the organization will handle future issues. In other words, *predictability* and *replication* become the key validity criteria. Third, the members of the organization should feel comfortable that what you have depicted makes sense to them and helps them to understand themselves.

The clinical model makes explicit two fundamental assumptions: (1) it is not possible to study a human system without intervening in it, and

(2) we can only fully understand a human system by *trying* to change it (Lewin, 1947). This conclusion may seem paradoxical in that we presumably want to understand a system as it exists in the present. This is not only impossible because our very presence is an intervention that produces unknown changes, but if we attempt to make *helpful changes*, we will enable the system to reveal both its goals and its defensive routines, essential parts of its culture. For this process to work, the intervention goals must be jointly shared by the outsider and insider. If the consultant tries to change the organization in terms of his or her own goals, the risk of defensiveness and withholding of data rises dramatically. If the consultant is helping the organization to make some changes that it wants, the probability rises that organization members will reveal what is really going on. A more detailed analysis of how such a managed change process works is provided in Chapter Eighteen.

Ethical Issues in Deciphering Culture

Deciphering culture has some inherent risks that both the insider and the outsider should assess before proceeding. The risks differ, depending on the purpose of the analysis, and they are often subtle and unknown. Therefore, the desire to go ahead and the organization's permission to do so may not be enough to warrant proceeding. The outside professional, whether consultant or ethnographer, must make a separate assessment and sometimes limit his or her own interventions to protect the organization.

Risks of an Analysis for Research Purposes

An organization can be made vulnerable by having its culture revealed to outsiders. The obvious solution is always to disguise the organization in published accounts, but if the intent is to communicate accurately to outsiders, the data are much more meaningful if the organization and the people are identified. Naming the organizations, as I have done in most of the examples used in this book, makes it possible to gain a deeper understanding of cultural phenomena and also makes it possible for others to check for accuracy and replicate the findings.

On the other hand, if a correct analysis of an organization's culture becomes known to outsiders because it either is published or is simply discussed among interested parties, the organization or some of its members may be put at a disadvantage because data that would ordinarily remain private now may become public. For various reasons, the members of the organization may not want their culture laid bare for others' viewing. If the information is inaccurate, potential employees, customers, suppliers, and any other categories of outsiders who deal with the organization may be adversely influenced.

Cases used in business schools are rarely disguised, even though they often include revealing details about an organization's culture. If the organization fully understands what it is revealing and if the information is accurate, no harm is done. But if the case reveals material that the organization is not aware of, such publication can produce undesirable insight or tension on the part of members and can create undesirable impressions on the part of outsiders. If the information is not accurate, then both insiders and outsiders may get wrong impressions and may base decisions on incorrect information.

For example, when I was teaching at the Centre d'Etudes Industrielle in Geneva in the early 1980s, they were using a case about DEC that was outdated and gave an entirely incorrect impression of what was going on in DEC, yet students were influenced by this case in terms of whether or not they would apply for jobs at DEC. Furthermore, most cases are only a slice through the organization at a particular time and do not consider historical evolution. The case material about DEC may have been accurate at one point in time but was presented as a general picture.

Researchers often attempt to avoid this danger by providing their analysis to the members of the organization before it is published. This step has the advantage of also testing, to some degree, the validity of the information. However, it does not overcome the risk that the members of the organization who "clear" the data for publication might not be aware of how the analysis might make others in the organization more vulnerable. Nor does it overcome the risk that the members of the organization who review the material may want to play it safe and forbid the publication of anything that names the organization. *The ultimate ethical responsibility therefore falls to the researcher.* Whenever a researcher publishes information about an individual or organization, he or she must think carefully about the potential consequences. Where I have named organizations in this book, I have either been given permission or have decided that the material can no longer harm organizations or individuals.

Risks of an Internal Analysis

If an organization is to understand its own strengths and weaknesses, if it wants to learn from its own experience and make informed strategic choices based on realistic assessments of external and internal factors, it must at some point study and understand its own culture (Bartunek & Louis, 1996; Coghlan & Brannick, 2005). This process is not without its problems, risks, and potential costs, however. Basically, two kinds of risks must be assessed: (1) The analysis of the culture could be incorrect, and/or (2) the organization might not be ready to receive feedback about its culture.

If decisions are made on the basis of incorrect assumptions about the culture, serious harm could be done to the organization. Such errors are most likely to occur if culture is defined at too superficial a level—if espoused values or data based on questionnaires are taken to be an accurate representation of the underlying assumptions without conducting group and individual interviews that specifically dig for deeper assumptions and patterns. This is the major risk in the use of typologies and surveys.

The second risk is that the analysis may be correct, but insiders other than those who made the analysis may not be prepared to digest what has been learned about them. If culture functions in part as a set of defense mechanisms to help avoid anxiety and to provide positive direction, self-esteem, and pride, then an individual's reluctance to accept certain cultural truth about himself or herself is a normal human reaction. Psychotherapists and counselors constantly must deal with resistance or denial on the part of patients and clients. Similarly, unless an organization's personnel recognize a real need to change and unless they feel psychologically safe enough to examine data about the organization, they will not be able to hear the cultural truths that inquiry may have revealed, or, worse, they may lose self-esteem because some of their myths or ideals about themselves may be destroyed by the analysis.

Another risk is that some members will achieve instant insight and automatically and thoughtlessly attempt to produce changes in the culture that (1) some other members of the organization may not want, (2) some other members may not be prepared for and therefore may not be able to implement, and/or (3) may not solve the problem.

Therefore, the culture analyst should make the client system fully aware that there are consequences to having elements of culture laid bare, so to speak. Consultants are often called in by insiders to reveal what some insiders know but feel they cannot say for various reasons. The risk in agreeing to do this is that the organization may not like to hear the consultant's analysis of its culture. For example, I was asked in 1979 to present my analysis of the Ciba-Geigy culture to its top management at the annual meeting. I had been asked to observe and interview people to get a sense of the key assumptions forming the paradigm that was presented in Chapter Three. From my point of view, I had clear data, and I attempted to be objective and neutral in my analysis, knowing that my clients valued scientific objectivity. I had discussed my analysis with several key insiders, and they concurred that the data were accurate and would be useful for the top fifty executives to hear. At one point during my presentation, I likened certain aspects of Ciba-Geigy's culture to a military model. Several members of the executive committee who were themselves former military men and who loved the Swiss Army suddenly took offense at what they viewed to be a derogatory depiction of the army (though I believed I had been neutral in my statements). Their perception that I misunderstood and had challenged one of their values led to an unproductive argument about the validity of the cultural description, a polarization into two factions, and to my being discredited as a consultant in the eyes of one of the factions.

There are several possible lessons here. The most obvious one is that the outsider should never lecture insiders on their own culture because the outsider cannot know where the sensitivities will lie and cannot overcome his or her own subtle biases. Perhaps if I had stated each of my points carefully as hypotheses or questions for them to react to, I might have avoided this trap. Second, I learned that my analysis plunged the group members into an internal debate that they were not prepared for and that had multiple unanticipated consequences. The people who objected to my analogy revealed some of their own biases at the meeting in ways they might not have intended, and comments made later suggested that some people were shocked because so-and-so had revealed himself to be a such-and-such kind of person.

The analogy itself, likening aspects of the organization's functioning to the military, unleashed feelings that had more to do with the Swiss-German macroculture in which Ciba-Geigy operated, and it introduced a whole set of irrelevant feelings and issues. Many people in the group were made very uncomfortable by the insight that they were indeed operating like the military because they had either forgotten this aspect or had illusions about it. My comments stripped away those illusions.

Third—and perhaps this is the most important lesson—giving feedback to an individual is different from giving feedback to a group because the group very likely is not homogeneous in its reactions. My "lecture" on the culture was well received by some members of the group, who went out of their way to assure me that my depiction was totally accurate. Obviously, this segment of the group was not threatened by what I had to say. But with others I lost credibility, and with still others I created enough of a threat to unleash defensiveness, plunging the group into an uncomfortable new agenda that then had to be managed.

The point is that I had been doing what they requested me to do, yet it had unanticipated consequences that I, as a culture researcher, should have anticipated and controlled for. At the minimum, I should have forewarned my clients that if I gave this lecture, it might unleash a variety of group feelings—and were we prepared for this?

Professional Obligations of the Culture Analyst

If the foregoing risks are real, then who should worry about them? Is it enough to say to an organization that we will study your culture and let you know what we find and that nothing will be published without your permission? If we are dealing with surface manifestations, artifacts, and publicly espoused values, then the guideline of letting members clear the material seems sufficient. However, if we are dealing with the deeper levels of the culture, the basic assumptions and the patterns among them, then the insiders clearly may not know what they are getting into, and the obligation shifts to the outsider as a professional, to make the client genuinely aware of what the consequences might be of a cultural analysis. The principle of informed consent does not sufficiently protect the client or research subject if he or she cannot initially appreciate what will be revealed.

The analyst of a culture undertakes a professional obligation to understand fully what the potential consequences of an investigation are. Such consequences should be carefully spelled out before the relationship reaches a level at which there is an implied psychological contract that the outsider will give feedback to the insiders on what has been discovered about the culture, either for inside purposes of gaining insight or for clearing what may eventually be published. For all of these reasons, deciphering and reporting on a culture works best and is psychologically safest when the organization is motivated to make changes that may involve the culture.

As should be evident by now, there is no simple formula for gathering cultural data. Artifacts can be directly observed; espoused values are revealed through the questions the researcher/consultant asks of whoever is available and through the organization's published materials; and shared tacit assumptions have to be inferred from a variety of observations and further inquiry around inconsistencies and puzzlements. Because culture is a shared group phenomenon, the best way to gather systematic data is to bring representative groups of ten to fifteen people together and ask them to discuss artifacts, values, and the assumptions behind them. A detailed way to do this is described in Chapter Eighteen when the process is used to help the organization solve problems.

If the researcher is simply trying to gather information for his or her own purposes and if problems of reliability and validity can afford to be ignored, then the various culture content categories described in the previous chapters are perfectly adequate guidelines for what to ask about. The actual questions around each of the content areas should be constructed by the researcher in terms of the goals of the research, bearing in mind that culture is broad and deep. To capture a whole culture is probably impossible, so the researcher must have some more specific goal in mind before a set of questions for the groups can be designed.

Summary and Conclusions

There are many ways of deciphering or "assessing" cultural dimensions, which can be categorized in terms of the degree to which the researcher is directly involved with the organization and the degree to which organization members become directly involved in the research process. For purposes of academic research or theory building, it is important to learn what is really going on, which requires real entry into and involvement with the organization beyond what questionnaires, surveys, or even individual interviews can provide. The researcher must create a relationship with the organization that permits him or her to become a researcher/consultant to ensure that reliable and valid data will be forthcoming because it is in the organization's own interest to provide data.

If the consultant is helping leaders to manage a change process, he or she may design a culture assessment process and may learn some things about the culture, but it is only essential that the *insiders* come to understand their own culture. I have been in many situations where insiders achieved clarity about essential elements of their culture while I went away from the project not really understanding their culture at all, *and this was okay*. In either case, the deeper cultural data will only reveal themselves if the researcher/consultant establishes a helping relationship with the organization, such that the organization members feel they have something to gain by revealing what they really think and feel to the researcher. Such a "clinical inquiry" relationship is the minimum requirement for getting valid cultural data, but the outsider researcher can go beyond helping the organization and gather additional data relevant to his or her research purpose.

A relatively detailed description of the kind that I provided in Chapter Three for DEC and Ciba-Geigy requires long periods of observation and experience inside the organization. And, as I pointed out, my deciphering of these cultures was not my initial aim. I was there as a process consultant to help with a variety of problems that were not even defined initially as culture problems. Formal assessment was not required; it became a more informal process in the various task forces working on specific change problems.

The process of deciphering a culture for purposes of an insider or for purposes of describing that culture to outsiders, each has a set of associated risks and potential costs. These risks are internal in the sense that the members of the organization may not want to know or may not be able to handle the insights into their own culture, and they are external in that the members of the organization may not be aware of the manner in which they become vulnerable once information about their culture is made available to others.

In our effort to define a culture, we may discover that no single set of assumptions has formed as a deep-down paradigm for operating, or that the subgroups of an organization have different paradigms, which that may or may not conflict with each other. Furthermore, culture is perpetually evolving; the cultural researcher must therefore be willing to do perpetual searching and revising. To present "data" about that organization to either an insider or an outsider is inherently risky.

Even if we begin to have an intuitive understanding of an organization's culture, we may find it extraordinarily difficult to write down that understanding in such a way that the essence of the culture can be communicated to someone else. We have so few examples in our literature that it is hard even to point to models of how it should be done (Barley, 1984a, b; Van Maanen, 1988; Kunda, 1992; Weeks, 2004). But when we see the essence of a culture—the paradigm by which people operate—we are struck by how powerful our insight into that organization now is, and we can see instantly why certain things work the way they do, why certain proposals are never bought, why change is so difficult, why certain people leave, and so on. It is the search for and the occasional finding of this central insight that makes it all worthwhile. Suddenly we understand an organization; suddenly we see what makes it tick. This level of insight is worth working for, even if in the end, we can share it only with colleagues.

The implication for leaders is "be careful." Cultural analysis can be very helpful if you know what you are doing and why. By this I mean that there must be some valid purpose to a cultural analysis. If it is done for its own sake, the risks of either wasting time or doing harm increase. However, the potential for insight and constructive action is tremendous if you work with a responsible outsider to analyze and decipher your culture in the service of legitimate organizational ends. A specific process for working with culture for purposes of such organizational development is described in Chapter Eighteen.

Part Three

THE LEADERSHIP ROLE IN BUILDING, EMBEDDING, AND EVOLVING CULTURE

Part II focused on the content of culture and the process of deciphering cultural assumptions. The primary focus was on culture. We now shift the focus to leadership, especially the role that leadership plays in creating and embedding culture in a group. As I have argued throughout, the unique function of leadership that distinguishes it from management and administration is this concern for culture. Leadership begins the culture creation process and, as we will see, must also manage and sometimes change culture.

To fully understand the relationship of leadership to culture, we have to take a developmental view of organizational growth. The role of leadership in beginning the formation of culture in a learning group is covered in Chapter Twelve. How founders of organizations begin the process of culture formation in an organizational culture is covered in Chapter Thirteen. We then examine in Chapter Fourteen how leaders of a young and successful organization can systematically embed their own assumptions in the daily workings of the organization, thereby creating and maintaining a stable culture. The growth and evolution of the organization into subunits is described and the growth of subcultures is noted in Chapter Fifteen.

As organizations grow and evolve, so do their cultures. In Chapter Sixteen, I will describe ten different "mechanisms" or "processes" that cause cultures to change, and I will point out the role that leadership can and should play in using these processes to influence cultural evolution to their purposes. All of these are "natural processes" that should be distinguished from what I am calling "managed change," the process by which leaders set out to solve specific organizational problems that may or may not involve cultural elements. In Part IV, the focus shifts to what leaders can do to manage cultural change and to deal with the increasing problems of multiculturalism.

12

HOW CULTURE EMERGES
IN NEW GROUPS

The rules of the social order that dominate our day-to-day interactions are the bedrock of culture. We learn those rules as we are socialized into our family and acculturated into our nation and ethnic group. How those rules were created in the first place is difficult to decipher in cultures that have existed for some time, but it is possible to observe this process of creation in new groups and organizations. The best way to demystify the concept of culture is first of all to become aware of culture *creation* in our own experience, to perceive how something comes to be shared and taken for granted, and to observe this particularly in the groups that we enter and belong to. We bring culture with us from our past experience, but we are constantly reinforcing that culture or building new elements as we encounter new people and new experiences.

The strength and stability of culture derives from the fact that it is group based—that the individual will hold on to certain basic assumptions to ratify his or her membership in the group. If someone asks us to change our way of thinking or perceiving, and that way is based on what we have learned in a group that we belong to or identify with, we will resist the change because we do not want to deviate from our group even if privately we think that the group is wrong. This process of trying to be accepted by our membership and reference groups is unconscious and, by virtue of that fact, very powerful. But how does a group develop a common way of thinking in the first place?

To examine how this aspect of culture actually begins, how a group learns to deal with its external and internal environment and develops assumptions that then get passed on to new members, we need to analyze group situations in which such events are actually observable. Fortunately such groups are created from time to time in various kinds of human relations training workshops where strangers come together for purposes of learning about group dynamics and leadership. When the National Training Laboratories first evolved such group dynamics workshops at Bethel, Maine in the late 1940s, it was not accidental that they labeled Bethel as a "cultural island" to highlight the fact that the participants would be encouraged to suspend some of their learned rules of the existing social order to learn how norms and rules emerge in the microcultures of the learning groups (Bradford, Gibb, & Benne, 1964; Schein & Bennis, 1965; Schein, 1999a, 1999b).

In making a detailed analysis of small groups, I am not implying that group phenomena can be automatically treated as models for organizational phenomena. Organizations bring in additional levels of complexity and new phenomena that are not visible in the small group. But all organizations started as small groups and continue to function in part through various small groups within them. So the understanding of culture formation in small groups is, in fact, necessary to understanding how culture may evolve in the large organization through small-group subcultures and through the interplay of small groups within the organization.

Group Formation Through Originating and Marker Events

All groups start with some kind of "originating event": (1) An environmental accident (for instance, a sudden threat that occurs in a random crowd and requires a common response), (2) a decision by an "originator" to bring a group of people together for some purpose, or (3) an advertised event or common experience that attracts a number of individuals. Human relations training groups start in the third mode—a number of people come together voluntarily to participate in a one- or two-week workshop for the advertised purpose of learning more about themselves, groups, and leadership (Bradford, Gibb, & Benne, 1964; Schein & Bennis, 1965; Schein, 1993a). The workshops are typically held in a geographically remote, isolated location and require full, round-the-clock participation—hence "cultural islands."

The staff of the workshop, usually one "trainer" per ten to fifteen participants, has typically met for several days to plan the basic structure of lectures, group meetings, focused "exercises" designed to bring out certain points about leadership and group behavior, and free time. The staff members start out with their own assumptions, values, and behavior patterns in initiating the groups and therefore will bias the culture that is eventually formed. But culture formation really occurs in the T (training) group, the key component of every workshop. The T group consists of ten to fifteen strangers who will meet for four to eight hours every day with one or two staff members. Because such groups typically develop distinct microcultures within a matter of days, what goes on in these groups is crucial to an understanding of culture formation.

When the group first comes together, the most fundamental issue facing it as a whole is "What are we really here for? What is our task?" At the same time, each individual is facing basic social survival issues such as "Will I be included in this group?" "Will I have a role to play?" "Will my needs to influence others be met?" "Will we reach a level of intimacy that meets my needs?" These are in the microcosm the central issues of identity, authority, and intimacy that were discussed in Chapters Six and Nine on culture content.

As the group gathers in its appointed space, the participants begin to display their own coping style for dealing with new and ambiguous situations. Some will silently await events; some will form immediate alliances with others; and some will begin to assert themselves by telling anyone who cares to listen that they know how to deal with this kind of situation. Statements about the goal of "learning about ourselves" have been spelled out in the training literature, in the workshop brochure, in the initial introductory lecture to the entire workshop, and again by the staff member who launches the group. Some people may even have had prior experiences with similar groups, but initially everyone is acutely aware of how ambiguous the words of the staff member are when he or she says: "This is the first meeting of our T group. Our goal is to provide for ourselves a climate in which we can all learn. There is no one correct way to do this. We will have to get to know each other, find out what our individual needs and goals are, and build our group to enable us to fulfill those goals and needs. My role as staff member will be to help this process along in any way that I can, but I will not be the formal leader of the group, and I have no answers as to the right way to proceed. There is no formal agenda. So let's begin." The staff member then falls silent.

How Individual Intentions Become Group Consequences

The general model for understanding the formation of "groupness" and culture is to observe closely how in the formative stages individuals initiate various actions, but what happens immediately *after* an initial act is a *group* response. If person A makes a suggestion, and person B disagrees, it may appear to be just two members of the group arguing, but the emotional reality is that the other members are witnesses and make their own collective choice on whether to enter the conversation or not. Only two people have spoken, but *the group* has acted and is *aware* of having acted as a group.

Return now to our training group's earliest moments. In the silence that follows the staff member's introduction, each person experiences feelings of anxiety in the face of this ambiguous agenda and power vacuum. Even if that silence is only a few seconds long, it is usually a key "marker event" that almost everyone remembers vividly at a later time. Even though all the members usually come from the same macroculture and share the same formal language, everyone is aware that this group is a unique combination of personalities and that those personalities are initially unknown. What makes the initial silence a marker event is that every person is aware of his or her own emotional response to the sudden silence. Group members can recall clearly at a later time how they felt when the typical crutches of the formal agenda, leadership structure, and procedural rules were deliberately removed as part of the training design. This novel situation heightens members' awareness of how much they typically depend on the structures and rules of the social order. The group is deliberately thrown onto its own resources to allow members to observe their own feelings and reactions as they cope with this initially "norm-less" and "rule-less" situation.

Each member brings to this new situation a wealth of prior learning in the form of assumptions, expectations, and patterns of coping, but, as the group gets started by someone's making a suggestion or revealing a feeling, it immediately becomes apparent that there is little consensus within the group on how to proceed, and that the group cannot become a copy of any other group. Thus, even though individual members bring prior cultural learning to the new situation, by definition this particular group starts out with no culture of its own. Goals, means, working procedures, measurements, and rules of interaction all have to be forged out of new common experience. A sense of mission—what the group is ultimately all about—develops only as members begin genuinely to understand each other's needs, goals, talents, and values, and as they begin to integrate these into a shared mission and define their own authority and intimacy system.

How does group formation now proceed? Often, the very first thing said by any person in the group will become the next marker event if it succeeds in reducing some of the tension. For example, one of the more active members often will initiate with a suggestion of how to get started: "Why don't we go around the group and each introduce ourselves?" or "Let's each say what we are here for" or "I feel pretty tense right now, does anyone else feel the same way?" or "Ed, can you give us some suggestion on how best to get started?" and so on.

The silence is broken, there is a huge sigh of relief, and the group becomes aware through this joint sensing of relief that it is sharing something unique to itself. No other group in the world will have this particular pattern of initial tension and manner of resolving the initial silence. Members also become aware of something that is easy to forget—that a person cannot, in an interpersonal situation, "not" communicate. Everything that happens has potential meaning and consequences for the group.

If that initial suggestion fits the mood of the group or at least of some other members who are ready to speak up, it will be picked up and may become the beginning of a pattern. If it does not fit the mood, it will elicit disagreement, counter-suggestions, or some other response that will make members aware that they cannot easily agree. Whatever the response, however, the crucial event of group formation has taken place when the group, including the staff member, has participated in a shared emotional reaction. What makes the event *shared* is the fact that all members have been witnesses to the same behavior on the part of one of their members and have observed the responses together. After the meeting, they can refer to the event, and people will remember it. This initial sharing is what defines, at an emotional level, that "we are now a group; we have been launched."

The most fundamental act of culture formation, the defining of crude group boundaries, has occurred with this shared emotional response. Everyone who has shared the response is now, by definition, in the group at some level, and anyone who has not shared the experience is initially not in the group. This feeling of being in or out of the group is quite concrete, in that any person who did not attend and witness the event cannot know what happened or how people reacted. A new member who arrives one hour late will already feel the presence of a group and will want to know "what has gone on so far." And the group will already feel that the newcomer is a "stranger" who "has to be brought on board." Members will remember at a later time "how painful it was to get started" and will tell stories of what happened in the first meeting.

Thus, in any new group situation—whether we are talking about a new company, a task force, a committee, or a team—though the initial behavior of founders, leaders, and other initiators is individually motivated and reflects their own particular assumptions and intentions, as the individuals in the group begin to do things together and share experiences around such individually motivated acts, "groupness" arises.

Building Meaning Through Sharing Perceptions and Articulating Feeling

Initially, this groupness is only an emotional substrate that permits the defining of who is in and who is not. For the group to begin to *understand* its sense of groupness, someone must articulate what the experience has been and what it means. Such articulation is again an individual act, motivated by individual intentions to lead, or to be a prophet, or whatever, but the consequences are *group* consequences if the articulation "works," if things are stated in a way that makes sense and helps group members to understand what has happened and why they are feeling the way they are. For example, to break the silence a member might say "We all seem to be pretty tense right now," or "I guess we won't get much help from the staff member," or "I don't know how the rest of you feel, but I feel the need to get going, so here's a suggestion...." Such statements help to make some sense of the situation and are, therefore, crucial components of what we call "leadership" and can be understood as acts of culture creation if the process imparts meaning to an important shared emotional experience and provides some relief from the anxiety of meaninglessness. Some of the deepest and most potent shared experiences occur within the first few hours of group life, so the deepest levels of consensus on who we are, what our mission is, and how we will work are formed very early in the group's history.

Leadership as Timely Intervention

To help this process of understanding and articulation, the staff member or some group member will choose moments when something vivid has happened and ask the group to reflect and name what they saw or felt. For example, to break the silence one member says, "Let's go around the table and introduce ourselves..." The silence continues. Another member then says, "I would like the staff member to tell us how to proceed. . . . " More silence. A third member then says, "Ed isn't going to tell us anything, we have to figure this thing out ourselves. . . . " More silence. A fourth member then says, "My name is Peter Jones and I would like to learn more about how I relate to other people." Peter looks around expectantly for response but nothing happens. Ed, the staff member, might then say, "What is happening here? Can we quickly review what has just happened in the last few minutes and talk about what we see going on and how we feel about it."

Various members then come in to tell what they observed and how they felt about it. One of the members may point out that the staff member's refusal to be the authority figure has created a power struggle in terms of whose suggestion will get the group going. The silences after the various member suggestions were a kind of decision to resist, *not to go along with what a member had suggested.* By recognizing this resistance, the group members are learning one of the most powerful lessons of how social systems work. *Collectively not acting* on what a member proposes is a powerful *group* decision, a kind of decision that is very common and that received a colloquial name in the workshops—a "plop." In other words, a suggestion to act was made, and it plopped. Plops mean that the group was not willing to grant a level of authority to a given member to tell the group what to do.

At the same time, if the staff member's suggestion to examine what has just happened gets the group going, the group has also learned something very important about leadership—that one can lead by focusing on *the process* of what is going on instead of making content suggestions. Such "process analysis" enables the members to speak about their perceptions and feelings in a nonevaluative context and with the sense that everyone's perceptions and feelings have an equal social value. An individual can have different perceptions and feelings but cannot tell another member that their experiences were wrong or less valuable. In such process analysis, the group is creating cultural neutrality and making it possible to actually observe in a nonevaluative way the different cultural norms members bring to the group from their prior cultural experience. It is this kind of exploratory conversation that makes the workshop a "cultural island." The T-group is creating a new culture by beginning to understand and act on what members learn about each other's cultures that they brought with them into the group.

The mission of the group begins to be understood in terms of a shared insight that the learning occurs through a process of shared reflection on whatever action has taken place. But the issues of authority and intimacy don't go away. The underlying assumptions that members bring to the group around authority and intimacy issues have to be confronted and dealt with if the group is to make any progress toward being able to work on a task together. You can think of this process of group formation in terms of stages as shown in Table 12.1.

Stage 1: Dealing with Assumptions About Authority

Initially, each member of a new group is struggling with the personal issues of inclusion, identity, authority, and intimacy, and the group is not really a group but a collection of individual members, each focused on how to make the situation safe and personally rewarding. Even as they learn how to learn in the T-group, they are much more preoccupied with their own feelings than with the problem of the group as a group and, most likely, they are operating on the *unconscious* assumption that "the leader [staff member] knows what we are supposed to do." Therefore, the best way to achieve safety is to remain dependent on the staff member and try to find out what the group is supposed to do and do it. This group stage, with its associated feelings and moods, is, in my experience, similar to what Bion (1959) described in his work as the "dependence assumption" and what

Table 12.1.   Stages of Group Evolution.

Stage	Dominant Assumption	Socioemotional Focus
1. Group formation	*Dependence:* "The leader knows what we should do."	*Self-Orientation:* Emotional focus on issues of (a) inclusion, (b) power and influence, (c) acceptance and intimacy, and (d) identity and role.
2. Group Building	*Fusion:* "We are a great group; we all like each other."	*Group as Idealized Object:* Emotional focus on harmony, conformity, and search for intimacy. Member differences are not valued.
3. Group Work	*Work:* "We can perform effectively because we know and accept each other."	*Group Mission and Tasks:* Emotional focus on accomplishment, teamwork, and maintaining the group in good working order. Member differences are valued.
4. Group Maturity	*Maturity:* "We know who we are, what we want, and how to get it. We have been successful, so we must be right."	*Group Survival and Comfort:* Emotional focus on preserving the group and its culture. Creativity and member differences are seen as threat.

other theories note as the first issue the group has to deal with (Bennis & Shepard, 1956).

The evidence for the operation of this assumption is the behavior in the early minutes and hours of the group's life. First of all, much of the initial behavior of group members is, in fact, directed to the staff member in the form of questions, requests for explanations and for suggestions about how to proceed, and constant checking for approval. Even if the behavior is not directed to the staff member, group members constantly look at him or her, pay extra attention if the staff member does speak, and in other non-verbal ways indicate their preoccupation with the staff member's reaction.

Members may share the assumption of being dependent on the staff member yet react very differently. These differences can best be understood in terms of what they have learned in their prior macrocultural experience, starting in the family. One way to deal with authority is to suppress one's aggression, accept dependence, and seek guidance. If the staff member makes a suggestion, members who cope in this way will automatically accept it and attempt to do what is asked of them. Others have learned that the way to deal with authority is to resist it. They also will seek to find out what the leader wants, but their motive is to find out in order to resist rather than to comply—to be "counter dependent." Still others will attempt to find other members to share their feelings of dependence and, in effect, set up a subgroup within the larger group.

The mixture of tendencies in the personalities of group members is, of course, not initially predictable, nor is any given person inflexible. The range of possible variations in response to the initial leadership/authority vacuum is thus immense in a ten- to fifteen-person group. The early interaction can best be described as a mutual testing out—testing of the staff member to see how much guidance will be offered, and testing by members of other members to see who can influence whom and who will control whom—a process not unlike establishing a pecking order in the barnyard.

Several members will emerge as competitors for leadership and influence. If any one of these members suggests something or makes a point, one of the others will contradict it or try to go off in a different direction. This aggressive competition among the "sturdy battlers" keeps the group from achieving any real consensus early in its life, and one paradox of group formation is that there is no way to short-circuit this early power struggle. If it is swept under the rug by strong authoritarian leadership or formal procedures, it will surface later around the task issues that the group is trying to address and will be potentially damaging to task performance. Interpersonal competition becomes one of many "covert processes" that the group will have to deal with (Marshak, 2006).

From the point of view of the staff member, confirmation that this process is indeed going on comes from the frequent experience of trying to give the group guidance and finding that some members leap at the help, while others almost blindly resist it. If frustration is high, one or the other extreme mode may build up in the group as a whole, what Bion labeled "fight or flight." The group may collectively attack the staff member, aggressively deny his suggestions, and punish him for his or her silence, or the group may suddenly go off on its own, led by a group member, with the implicit or explicit statement "We need to get away from the disappointing leader and do it on our own."

Building New Norms Around Authority

In its early life, the group cannot easily find consensus on what to do, so it bounces from one suggestion to another and becomes increasingly more frustrated and discouraged at its inability to act. And this frustration keeps the shared emotional assumption of dependency alive. The group continues to act as if the leader knows what to do. In the meantime, members are, of course, beginning to be able to calibrate each other, the staff member, and the total situation. As the group learns to analyze its own processes, a common language slowly gets established; and, as shared learning experiences accumulate, more of a sense of groupness arises at the emotional level, providing some reassurance to all that they are being included. Inclusion anxieties are slowly reduced.

This sense of groupness arises through successive dealings with marker events that arouse strong feelings and then are dealt with definitively. The group may not be consciously aware of this process of norm building, however, unless attention is drawn to it in process analysis periods. For example, within the first few minutes, a member may speak up strongly for a given course of action. Joe suggests that the way to proceed is to take turns introducing ourselves and stating why we are in the group. This suggestion requires some behavioral response from other members; therefore, no matter what the group does, it will be setting some kind of precedent for how to deal with future suggestions that are "controlling"—that require behavior from *others*.

What are the options at this point? One common response in groups is to act as if the suggestion had not even been made at all. There is a moment of silence, followed by another member's comment irrelevant to the suggestion. This is the "plop"—a group decision by nonaction. The member who made the suggestion may feel ignored. At the same time, *a group norm has been established.* The group has, in effect, said that *members need not respond to every suggestion, that it is permissible to ignore someone.* A second common response is for another person to immediately agree or disagree overtly with the suggestion. This response begins to build a different norm—that a person *should respond to suggestions in some way.* If there has been agreement, the response may also begin to build an alliance; if there has been disagreement, it may begin a fight that will force others to take sides.

A third possibility is for another member to make a "process" comment, such as "I wonder if we should collect some other suggestions before we decide what to do?" or "How do the rest of you feel about Joe's suggestion?" Again, a norm is being established—that *a person does not have to plunge into action but can consider alternatives.* A fourth possibility is to plunge ahead into action. The suggestion is made to introduce ourselves, and the next person to speak launches into an introduction. This response not only gets the group moving but may set two precedents: (1) that *suggestions should be responded to,* and (2) that *Joe is the one who can get us moving.* The implication of this last response is that Joe may feel empowered and be more likely to make a suggestion the next time the group is floundering. Note that this process happens very fast, often in a few seconds, so the important group consequences are not noticed until a process analysis period reconstructs them. As Joe becomes more of a leader, some group members may scratch their heads and wonder, how did Joe get anointed into this position. They don't remember the early group events that de facto anointed him.

Norms are thus formed when an individual takes a position, and the rest of the group deals with that position by either letting it stand (by remaining silent), by actively approving it, by "processing" it, or by rejecting it. Three sets of consequences are always observed: (1) the personal consequences for the member who made the suggestion (he may gain or lose influence, disclose himself to others, develop a friend or enemy, and so on); (2) the interpersonal consequences for those members immediately involved in the interplay; and (3) the normative consequences for the group as a whole. So here again we have the situation in which an individual has to act, but the subsequent shared reaction turns the event into a group product. It is the joint witnessing of the event and the reaction that makes it a group product.

The early life of the group is filled with thousands of such events and the responses to them. At the cognitive level, they deal with the effort to define working procedures to fulfill the primary task—to learn. Prior assumptions about how to learn will operate initially to bias the group's effort, and limits will be set by the staff member in the form of calling attention to the consequences of behavior considered clearly detrimental to learning—behavior such as failure to attend meetings, frequent interruptions, personally hostile attacks, and the like. At the emotional level, such events deal with the problem of authority and influence. The most critical of such events are ones that overtly test or challenge the staff member's authority. Thus, we note that the group pays special attention to the responses that occur immediately after someone has directed a comment, question, or challenge to the staff member.

We also note anomalous behavior that can be explained only if we assume that an authority issue is being worked out. For example, the group actively seeks leadership by requesting that some member should help the group to get moving, but then systematically ignores or punishes anyone who attempts to lead. We can understand this behavior if we remember that feelings toward authority are always ambivalent and that the anger felt toward the staff member for not leading the group cannot be expressed directly if the individual feels dependent on the staff member. The negative feelings are split off and projected onto a "bad leader," thus preserving the illusion that the staff member is the "good leader." Acts of insubordination or outbursts of anger at the staff member may be severely punished by other group members, even though those members have themselves been critical of the staff member.

How, then, does a group learn what is "reality"? How does it develop workable and accurate assumptions about how to deal with influence and authority? How does it normalize its relationship to the staff member, the formal authority who is presumed to know what to do and yet does not do it?

Reality Test and Catharsis

Though members begin to feel they know each other better, the group continues to be frustrated by its inability to act in a consensual manner because the unconscious dependence assumption is still operating, and members are still working out their influence relationships with each other. The event that moves the group forward at such times, often many hours into the group's life, is an insightful comment by a member who is less conflicted about the authority issue and, therefore, able to perceive and articulate what is really going on. In other words, while those members who are most conflicted about authority are struggling in the dependent and counter-dependent mode, some members find that they care less about this issue, are able psychologically to detach themselves from it, and come to recognize the reality that for this particular group at this time in its history, the staff member *does not* and *cannot*, in fact, know what to do.

The less conflicted members may intervene in any of a number of ways that expose this reality: (1) by offering a direct interpretation—"Maybe we are hung up in this group because we expect the staff member to be able to tell us what to do, and he doesn't know what to do"; (2) by offering a direct challenge—"I think the staff member doesn't know what to do, so we better figure it out ourselves"; (3) by offering a direct suggestion for an alternative agenda—"I think we should focus on how we feel about this group right now, instead of trying to figure out what to do"; or (4) by making a process suggestion or observation—"I notice that we ask the leader for suggestions but then don't do what he suggests" or "I wonder why we are fighting so much among ourselves in this group" or "I think it is interesting that every time Joe makes a suggestion, Mary challenges him or makes a counter-suggestion."

If the timing is right, in the sense that many members are "ready" to hear what may be going on because they have all observed the process for a period of time, there will be a strong cathartic reaction when the assumption-lifting intervention is made. The group members will suddenly realize that they have been focusing heavily on the staff member and that, indeed, that person is not all-knowing and all-seeing and, therefore, probably does not, in fact, know what the group should do. With this insight comes the feeling of responsibility: "We are all in this together, and we each have to contribute to the group's agenda." *The magical leader has been killed, and the group begins to seek realistic leadership from whoever can provide it.*

Leadership comes to be seen as a shared set of activities rather than a single person's trait, and a sense of ownership of group outcomes arises. Some work groups never achieve this state, remaining dependent on whatever formal authority is available and projecting magically onto it; but in the training/learning situation in the cultural island in which the social order is somewhat suspended, the emphasis on process analysis makes it very likely that the issue will be brought to the surface and dealt with.

A comparable process occurs in formally constituted groups, but it is less visible. The group founder or chairperson does have real intentions and plans, but the group initially tends to attribute far more complete and detailed knowledge to the leader than is warranted by reality. Thus, early in the life of a company, the entrepreneur is viewed much more magically as the source of all wisdom, and only gradually is it discovered that he or she is only human and that the organization can function only if other members begin to feel responsible for group outcomes as well. But all this may occur implicitly and without very visible marker events. If such events occur, they will most likely be in the form of challenges of the leader or outright insubordination. How the group and the leader then handle the emotionally threatening event determines, to a large extent, the norms around authority that will become operative in the future (as exemplified in the next chapter).

The "insight" that the leader is not omniscient or omnipotent gives members a sense of relief not to be struggling any longer with the staff members. They are likely to develop a feeling of euphoria that they have been able to deal with the tough issue of authority and leadership. There is a sense of joy in recognizing that everyone in the group has a role and can make a leadership contribution, and this, in turn, strengthens the group's sense of itself.

At this point, the group often takes some joint action, as if to prove to itself that it can do something, and gets a further sense of euphoria from being successful at it. Such action is often externally directed—winning a competition with another group or tackling a difficult task under time pressure and completing it. Whatever the task, the end result is a feeling of "We are a great group" and possibly, at a deeper level, even the feeling of "We are a better group than any of the others." It is this state of affairs that leads to the unconscious assumption of "fusion" and brings to the fore the intimacy issue.

Stage 2: Building Norms Around Intimacy

As the group solves the problem of authority, begins to share leadership, and accomplishes some tasks successfully, it begins to operate in terms of another unconscious assumptions that *we are the best group, and we all like each other*. Turquet (1973) used the term *fusion* to reflect a strong emotional need to feel merged with the group and to deny internal differences.

If this assumption is operating, at the overt behavior level, we observe a marked absence of interpersonal conflict, a tendency to bend over backward to be nice to each other, emotional expressions of affection, a mood of euphoria, and a group solidarity in the face of any challenge. Symptoms of conflict or lack of harmony are ignored or actively denied. Hostility is suppressed or punished severely if it occurs. An image of solidarity must be presented at all costs.

Different members of the group will vary in their need to attain and maintain a high level of intimacy, and those who care most, the "over-personals" will become the most active guardians of the group harmony image and will suppress the "counter-personals" who are made anxious by the implied level of intimacy. In particular, some members will resolve conflicts about intimacy by seeking it and by attempting to maintain harmony at all costs. But other group members, those who resolve their conflict about intimacy by avoiding it, will rock the boat and challenge the harmony image because the harmony makes them anxious. They will complain that the group is wasting time, is being too "cozy," and is ignoring conflicts that are visible. But their complaints will be ignored or actively put down if the need to prove group harmony is strong.

The staff member is now "one of the regulars" and is labeled as "no different from the rest of us," which is, of course, just as unrealistic as the assumption that the staff member is omniscient and omnipotent. At this stage, interventions that may be disturbing to the group are simply ignored or laughed off.

The strength of the fusion assumption will be a function of the individual needs of group members and the actual experience of the group. The more the group feels itself to be in a hostile environment or vulnerable to destruction, the more it may cling to the assumption as a way of claiming strength. Or, to put it the other way, only when the group feels reasonably secure can it give up the false solidarity that the fusion assumption claims. Such security comes gradually from increasing experience, success with tasks, and tests of strength against other groups.

The group moods of "fight" or "flight" are likely to arise around the fusion assumption because both fight and flight involve solidarity and joint action. Thus, if the authority issue arises again, the group may at this point turn collectively against the staff member or may deliberately run away from its real task of learning about itself by rationalizing that it has overcome all of its problems already, that there is nothing more to learn. Or the group may project its negative feelings onto someone outside the group— the administration of the workshop or some other group—and fight or flee from that outside enemy.

What Bion (1959) called *pairing* is also common at this stage because the need for love and intimacy that is operating can easily be projected onto those members who display such feelings overtly. By projecting the fate of the group into the "pair," by hoping for a magic solution through what the pair will produce, the group can maintain its sense of solidarity. All these responses preserve the assumption that "we are a great group, we like each other, and we can do great things together."

Many organizations get stuck at this level of group evolution, developing an adequate authority system and a capacity to defend themselves against external threat but never growing internally to a point of differentiation of roles and clarification of personal relationships.

Reality Test and Catharsis

The fusion assumption will not be given up until some marker event brings its falsity into consciousness. There are four group events that have the potential for revealing the assumption: (1) Disagreements and conflicts will occur in the attempts to take joint action, (2) noticeable avoidance of confrontation, (3) overt denial of the fact that some members may not like each other, and (4) eruptions of negative feelings toward other members. The actual marker event that tests the reality of the fusion assumption is most likely to come from those group members who are least conflicted about intimacy issues and who, therefore, are most likely to have insight into what is happening. For example, on one of the many occasions when a "counter-personal" member challenges the solidarity of the group, one of the less conflicted members may support the challenge by providing incontrovertible examples indicating that group members actually do not seem to get along all that well. This introduction of data that cannot be denied will pierce the illusion and thus force the recognition of the assumption.

Realistic norms about intimacy will evolve around incidents that involve aggression and affection. For example, if member A strongly attacks member B, it is *what the rest of the group does immediately after the attack that will create a norm.* The group may immediately move on to another topic or someone may actually say, "We should not attack each other," and the group may send signals of approval. The norm *we should not attack each other in this group* begins to form. Or the group may join in the attack leading to the norm that *attacking members is okay in this group.* Similarly if one member expresses a higher degree of intimacy by saying to another member something like, "I really like you and want to get to know you much better," what others do immediately after that will determine whether the group moves toward more intimate revelations or sets the norm that *we don't get into very personal stuff in this group.*

At some point in this exploration, members will realize that not only is liking and disliking each other highly variable within the group but, even more important, *liking each other is not the learning goal of this group.* Instead, members realize that they need to *accept each other enough to enable learning and joint task performance.* Liking and personally more intimate relationships may occur, especially outside the group meetings, but within the group, they only need to be intimate enough to enable the group to fulfill its mission of learning. A crucial learning is that a person can *accept* and work with another person without having to *like* him or her.

I have frequently observed similar events in more formally constituted groups. A work group in a growing company erupts into a hostile confrontation between two members. The manner in which the group handles the ensuing tense silence builds a norm for future expressions of feeling. If the group or the leader punishes either or both combatants, norms get built that feelings should be kept in check; if the group or leader encourages resolution, norms get built that hostility is okay and that feelings can be expressed, as was consistently the case in DEC. The moments when these norm-building activities occur are often very brief and easy to miss if one is not alert to them. But it is at those moments that culture begins to form, and the eventual assumptions about what is appropriate and right will reflect a long series of such incidents and the reactions to them.

The T-groups differed greatly in the degree of intimacy that evolved in them just as they differed in the kind of influence and authority system they evolved. Such differences reflected both the personalities of staff members and participants, and the actual experiences of the groups in their efforts to learn. But all groups developed fairly stable norms that collectively could be labeled microcultures. The evidence for this conclusion was the observed differences in how the groups dealt with tasks that the workshop required them to perform and in how it felt when visiting a group.

Which Norms Survive? The Role of Experience and Learning

How are norms reinforced and built up into the assumptions that eventually come to be taken for granted? The two basic mechanisms of learning involved are (1) positive *problem solving* to cope with external survival issues, and (2) *anxiety avoidance* to cope with internal integration issues. For example, if a group challenges its formal leader and begins to build norms that support more widely shared leadership and higher levels of member involvement, it is an empirical matter whether or not this way of working is effective in solving real-world problems. In the T-group, members decide whether or not they feel that such norms are enabling them to fulfill their primary task of learning. In formal work groups, it is a matter of actual experience whether or not the work gets done better with a given set of norms that have evolved.

If the group fails repeatedly or is chronically uncomfortable, sooner or later someone will propose that a new leadership process be found or that the original leader be reinstated in a more powerful role, and the group will find itself experimenting again with new behaviors that lead to new norms of how to work with authority. It then again must test against reality how successful it is. The norms that produce the greatest success will survive. As they continue to work, they gradually turn into assumptions about how things really are and should be. As new norms form around authority, there is also an immediate test of whether the members of the group are more or less comfortable as a result of the new way of working. Do the new norms enable them to avoid the anxiety inherent in the initially unstable or uncertain situation? If the leader is challenged, gives up some authority, and shares power with the group, some group members, depending on their own pattern of needs and prior experiences, may feel less comfortable than before. In some groups, a greater comfort level might be achieved by norms that, in effect, reassert the authority of the leader and make members more dependent on the leader and less intimate with each other. The needs of the leader will also play a role in this process, so the ultimate resolution—what makes everyone most comfortable—will be a set of norms that meets the many internal needs as well as the external experiences. Because so many variables are involved, the resultant group culture will usually be a unique and distinctive one.

The stability of the assumptions that evolve out of a group's experience will reflect whether or not the learning has been primarily the result of success or the avoidance of failure. If a group has learned primarily through positive successes, the mentality will be "Why change something that has been successful?" However, if what the group does ceases to be successful, that will be visible and will be a potential stimulus to change and new learning. If a group has learned something in order to avoid pain or failure, the mentality will be "We must avoid what has hurt us in the past," which will prevent trying out new things and thus discovering that they may not any longer be hurtful. Assumptions about what to avoid are, therefore, more stable than assumptions based on success. At the personal level, we know this from how phobias work in our own experience.

Stage 3: Group Work and Functional Familiarity

If the group deals successfully with the fusion assumption, it usually achieves an emotional state that can best be characterized as *mutual acceptance*. The group will have had enough experience so that members not only know what to expect of each other—what we can think of as "functional familiarity"—but also will have had the chance to learn that they can coexist and work together even if they do not all like each other. The emotional shift from maintaining the illusion of mutual liking to a state of mutual acceptance and functional familiarity is important in that it frees up emotional energy for work. Being dominated by either the dependence or the fusion assumption ties up emotional energy because of the denial and defensiveness required to avoid confronting the disconfirming realities. Therefore, if a group is to work effectively, it must reach a level of emotional maturity at which reality-testing norms prevail.

At this stage, a new implicit assumption arises, the work assumption—"We know each other well enough, both in a positive and negative light, that we can work well together and accomplish our external goals." The group now exerts less pressure to conform and builds norms that encourage some measure of individuality and personal growth, on the assumption that the group ultimately will benefit if all members grow and become stronger. Many groups never get to this stage, leading to the erroneous generalization that all groups require a high degree of solidarity and conformity. In my own experience, high conformity pressures are symptomatic of unresolved issues in the group, and the best way to get past them is to help the group to a more mature stage of mutual acceptance, using individual differences as a resource instead of a liability.

Groups always have some kind of task, even if that task is to provide learning to its members, so the need to work, to fulfill the task, is always psychologically present. But the ability to *focus* on the task is a function of the degree to which group members can reduce and avoid their own anxieties. Such anxieties are intrinsically highest when the group is very young and has not yet had a chance to build up cultural assumptions to control the anxiety. Therefore, the emotional energy available for work is lowest in the early stages of group formation, a crucial point for leaders to understand so that they do not force task pressures prematurely, that is, before the members have worked out their authority and intimacy issues. On the other hand, the quickest way for the group to lose its ability to work productively is to question some of its cultural assumptions because such a threat re-arouses the primary anxieties that the cultural solutions dealt with in the first place.

Stage 4: Group Maturity

Only a few remarks will be made about this final group stage because it will receive much more focus in later chapters. If a group works successfully, it will inevitable reinforce its assumptions about itself and its environment, thus strengthening whatever culture it has developed. Because culture is a learned set of responses, culture will be as strong as the group's learning history has made it. The more the group has shared emotionally intense experiences, the stronger the culture of that group will be.

Given these forces, a group or organization inevitably will begin to develop the assumption that it knows who it is, what its role in the world is, how to accomplish its mission, and how to conduct its affairs. If the culture that develops works, it will ultimately be taken for granted as the only correct way for group members to see the world. Conformity pressures arise once again and that produces the dangers inherent in "group think," the avoidance of exploration of ideas and actions that may be counter-cultural. The inevitable dilemma for the group, then, is how to avoid becoming so stable in its approach to its environment that it loses its ability to adapt, innovate, and grow.

Summary and Conclusions

To understand organizational or occupational cultures, it is necessary to understand cultural origins. In this chapter, I have reviewed how this happens in a learning group by examining the stages of group growth and development based on social psychological concepts and what we know about group dynamics. By examining in detail the interactions of members, it is possible to reconstruct how norms of behavior arise through what members do or do not do when critical incidents occur. The basic socio-psychological forces that operate in all of us are the raw material around which a group organizes itself both to accomplish its task and to create for itself a viable and comfortable organization. Thus every group must solve the problems of member identity, common goals, mechanisms of influence, and how to manage both aggression and love through norms around authority and intimacy. Norms that work gradually become cultural assumptions. This process is most visible in the learning groups, but the same issues of group growth arise in regular work groups. How these processes of culture formation work out in organizations will be examined next.

13

HOW FOUNDERS/LEADERS CREATE ORGANIZATIONAL CULTURES

One of the most mysterious aspects of organizational culture is how two companies with similar external environments, working in similar technologies on similar tasks and with founders of similar origins, come to have entirely different ways of operating over the years? In Chapter Twelve, I analyze this process in terms of the spontaneous events that occur in an unstructured group. In this chapter, we further analyze this process, considering what happens when a formal leader builds a group and launches an organization.

Culture Beginnings Through Founder/Leader Actions

Cultures basically spring from three sources: (1) the beliefs, values, and assumptions of founders of organizations; (2) the learning experiences of group members as their organization evolves; and (3) new beliefs, values, and assumptions brought in by new members and new leaders.

Though each of these mechanisms plays a crucial role, by far the most important for cultural beginnings is the impact of founders. Founders not only choose the basic mission and the environmental context in which the new group will operate, but they choose the group members and thereby shape the kinds of responses that the group will make in its efforts to succeed in its environment and to integrate itself.

Few organizations form accidentally or spontaneously. They are usually created by one or more individuals who perceive that the coordinated and concerted action of a number of people can accomplish something that individual action cannot. Social movements or new religions begin with prophets, messiahs, or other kinds of charismatic leaders. Political groups are initiated by leaders who sell new visions and new solutions to problems.

Firms are created by entrepreneurs who have a vision of how the concerted effort of the right group of people can create a new good or service in the marketplace.

Founders usually have a major impact on how the group initially defines and solves its external adaptation and internal integration problems. Because they had the original idea, they will typically have their own notion, based on their own cultural history and personality, of how to fulfill the idea. Founders not only have a high level of self-confidence and determination, but they typically have strong assumptions about the nature of the world, the role that organizations play in that world, the nature of human nature and relationships, how truth is arrived at, and how to manage time and space (Schein, 1978, 1983, 2006). They will, therefore, be quite comfortable in imposing those views on their partners and employees as the fledgling organization fights for survival, and they will cling to them until such time as they become unworkable or the group fails and breaks up (Donaldson & Lorsch, 1983).

The examples we will look at here illustrate several different kinds of culture evolution. Steinbergs created a strong culture around external adaptation, but the founder's own conflicts created internal turmoil that eventually undermined the company's performance. Smithfield is an example of a serial entrepreneur who avoided imposing himself on his organization and therefore let cultures develop as a function of various leaders below him. The DEC story built around Ken Olsen's personality illustrates how to create a very strong culture that is suited to growth and innovation but becomes dysfunctional when their market matures, yet is so strong that it survives while the company as an economic entity does not. Though I have less personal experience with IBM, HP, and Apple, I will illustrate how thinking about cultural origins can illuminate some of the differences we see in these companies today.

Sam Steinberg

Sam Steinberg was an immigrant whose parents had started a corner grocery store in Montreal. His parents, particularly his mother, taught him some basic attitudes toward customers and helped him form the vision that he could succeed in building a successful enterprise. He assumed from the beginning that if he did things right, he would succeed and could build a major organization that would bring him and his family a fortune. Ultimately, he built a large chain of supermarkets, department stores, and related businesses that became for many decades the dominant force in its market area.

Sam Steinberg was the major ideological force in his company throughout its history and continued to impose his assumptions on the company until his death in his late seventies. He assumed that his primary mission was to supply a high-quality, reliable product to customers in clean, attractive surroundings and that his customers' needs were the primary consideration in all major decisions. There are many stories about how Sam Steinberg, as a young man operating the corner grocery store with his wife, gave customers credit and thus displayed trust in them. He always took products back if there was the slightest complaint, and he kept his store absolutely spotless to inspire customer confidence in his products. Each of these attitudes later became a major policy in his chain of stores and was taught and reinforced by close personal supervision.

Sam Steinberg believed that only personal examples and close supervision would ensure adequate performance by subordinates. He would show up at his stores unexpectedly, inspect even minor details, and then—by personal example, by stories of how other stores were solving the problems identified, by articulating rules, and by exhortation—would "teach" the staff what they should be doing. He often lost his temper and berated subordinates who did not follow the rules or principles he had laid down. Sam Steinberg expected his store managers to be highly visible, to be very much on top of their own jobs, to supervise closely in the same way he did, to set a good example and to teach subordinates the "right way" to do things.

Most of the founding group in this company consisted of Sam Steinberg's three brothers, but one "lieutenant" who was not a family member was recruited early and became, in addition to the founder, the main leader and culture carrier. He shared the founder's basic assumptions about "visible management" and set up formal systems to ensure that those principles became the basis for operating realities. After Sam Steinberg's death, this man became the CEO and continued to perpetuate those same management practices.

Sam Steinberg assumed that you could win in the marketplace only by being highly innovative and technically in the forefront. He always encouraged his managers to try new approaches, brought in a variety of consultants who advocated new approaches to human resource management, started selection and development programs through assessment centers long before other companies tried this approach, and traveled to conventions and other businesses where new technological innovations were displayed. This passion for innovation resulted in Steinbergs being one of the first companies in the supermarket industry to introduce the bar code technology and one of the first to use assessment centers in selecting store managers. Steinberg was always willing to experiment to improve the business. His view of truth and reality was that you had to find them wherever you could; therefore, you must be open to your environment and never take it for granted that you have all the answers. If things worked, Sam Steinberg encouraged their adoption; if they did not, he ordered them to be dropped. He trusted only those managers who operated by assumptions similar to his own, and he clearly had favorites to whom he delegated more authority.

Power and authority in this organization remained very centralized, in that everyone knew that Sam Steinberg or his chief lieutenant could and would override decisions made by division or other unit managers without consultation and often in a very peremptory fashion. The ultimate source of power, the voting shares of stock, were owned entirely by Sam Steinberg and his wife, so that after his death, his wife was in total control of the company.

Though he was interested in developing good managers throughout the organization, he never shared ownership through granting stock options. He paid his key managers very well, but his assumption was that ownership was strictly a family matter, to the point that he was not even willing to share stock with his chief lieutenant, close friend, and virtual co-builder of the company.

Sam Steinberg introduced several members of his own family into the firm and gave them key managerial positions. As the firm diversified, family members were made heads of divisions, often with relatively little management experience. If a family member performed poorly, he would be bolstered by having a good manager introduced under him. If the operation then improved, the family member would likely be given the credit. If things continued badly, the family member would be moved out, but with various face-saving excuses. Though he wanted open communication and a high level of trust among all members of the organization, he never realized that his own assumptions about the role of the family and the correct way to manage were, to a large degree, in conflict with each other. He did not perceive his own conflicts and inconsistencies and hence could not understand why some of his best young managers failed to respond to his competitive incentives and even left the company. He thought he was adequately motivating them and could not see that for some of them, the political climate, the absence of stock options, and the arbitrary rewarding of family members made their own career progress too uncertain. Sam Steinberg was perplexed and angry about much of this, blaming the young managers while holding onto his own assumptions and conflicts.

Several points should be noted about the description given thus far. By definition, something can become part of the culture only if it works in the sense of making the organization successful and reducing the anxiety of the members. Steinberg's assumptions about how things should be done were congruent with the kind of environment in which he operated, so he and the founding group received strong reinforcement for those assumptions.

Following Sam Steinberg's death, the company experienced a long period of cultural turmoil because of the vacuum created by both his absence and the retirement of several other key culture carriers, but the basic philosophy of how to run stores was thoroughly embedded and was carried on by Steinberg's chief lieutenant. When he retired, a period of instability set in marked by the discovery that some of the managers who had been developed under Sam Steinberg were not as strong and capable as had been assumed. None of Sam Steinberg's daughters or their spouses were able to take over the business decisively, so various other family members continued to run the company. None of them had Sam Steinberg's business skills, so an outside person was brought in to run the company. This person predictably failed because he could not adapt to the culture and to the family. After two more failures with CEOs drawn from other companies, the family turned to a manager who had originally been with the company and had subsequently made a fortune outside the company in various real estate enterprises. This manager stabilized the business because he had more credibility by virtue of his prior history and his knowledge of how to handle family members. Under his leadership, some of the original assumptions began to evolve in new directions. Eventually, the family decided to sell the company, and this manager and one of Sam Steinberg's cousins started a company of their own, which ended up competing with Steinbergs.

One clear lesson from this example is that a culture does not survive if the main culture carriers depart and if the bulk of the members of the organization are experiencing some degree of conflict because of a mixed message that emanates from the leaders during the growth period. Steinbergs had a strong culture, but Sam Steinberg's own conflicts became embedded in that culture, creating conflict and ultimately lack of stability.

Fred Smithfield Enterprises

Smithfield built a chain of financial service organizations using sophisticated financial analysis techniques in an area of the country where insurance companies, mutual funds, and banks were only beginning to use such techniques. He was the conceptualizer and salesman, but once he had the idea for a new kind of service organization, he got others to invest in, build, and manage it.

Smithfield believed that he should put only a very small amount of his own money into each enterprise because if he could not convince others to put up money, maybe there was something wrong with the idea. He made the initial assumption that he did not know enough about the market to gamble with his own money, and he reinforced this assumption publicly by telling a story about the one enterprise in which he had failed. He had opened a retail store in a Midwestern city to sell ocean fish because he loved it. He assumed that others felt as he did, trusted his own judgment about what the market would want, and failed. Had he tried to get many others to invest in the enterprise, he would have learned that his own tastes were not necessarily a good predictor of what others would want.

Because Smithfield saw himself as a creative conceptualizer but not as a manager, he not only kept his financial investment minimal but also did not get very personally involved with his enterprises. After he put together the package, he found people whom he could trust to manage the new organization. These were usually people like himself who were fairly open in their approach to business and not too concerned with imposing their own assumptions about how things should be done.

We can infer that Smithfield's assumptions about concrete goals, the best means to achieve them, how to measure results, and how to repair things when they were going wrong were essentially pragmatic. Whereas Sam Steinberg had a strong need to be involved in everything, Smithfield seemed to lose interest after the new organization was on its feet and functioning. His theory seemed to be to have a clear concept of the basic mission, test it by selling it to the investors, bring in good people who understand what the mission is, and then leave them alone to implement and run the organization, using only financial criteria as ultimate performance measures.

If Smithfield had assumptions about how an organization should be run internally, he kept them to himself. The cultures that each of his enterprises developed therefore had more to do with the assumptions of the people he brought in to manage them. As it turned out, those assumptions varied a good deal. And if we analyze Smithfield Enterprises as a total organization, we would find little evidence of a corporate culture because there was no group that had a shared history and shared learning experiences. But each of the separate enterprises would have a culture that derived from the beliefs, values, and assumptions of their Smithfield-appointed managers.

This brief case illustrates that there is nothing automatic about founders imposing themselves on their organizations. It depends on their personal needs to externalize their various assumptions. For Smithfield, the ultimate personal validation lay in having each of his enterprises become financially successful and in his ability to continue to form creative new ones. His creative needs were such that after a decade or so of founding financial service organizations, he turned his attention to real estate ventures, then became a lobbyist on behalf of an environmental organization, tried his hand at politics for a while, and then went back into business, first with an oil company and later with a diamond mining company. Eventually, he became interested in teaching, and ended up at a Midwestern business school developing a curriculum on entrepreneurship!

Ken Olsen/DEC

The culture of DEC has been described in detail in Chapter Three. In this section, I want to focus more specifically on how DEC's founder, Ken

Olsen, created a management system that led eventually to the culture I described in that chapter. Olsen developed his beliefs, attitudes, and values in a strong Protestant family and at MIT, where he worked on Whirlwind, the first interactive computer. He and a colleague founded DEC in the mid-1950s because they believed they could build small interactive computers for which there would eventually be a very large market. They were able to convince General Doriot, then head of American Research and Development Corp., to make an initial investment because of their own credibility and the clarity of their basic vision of the company's core mission. After some years, the two founders discovered that they did not share a vision of how to build an organization, so Olsen became the CEO.

Olsen's assumptions about the nature of the world and how a person discovers truth and solves problems were very strong at this stage of DEC's growth and were reflected in his management style. He believed that good ideas could come from anyone regardless of rank or background, but that neither he nor any other individual was smart enough to determine whether a given idea was correct. Olsen felt that open discussion and debate in a group was the only way to test ideas and that no one should take action until the idea had survived the crucible of an active debate. An individual might have intuitions, but he or she should not act on them until they had been tested in the intellectual marketplace. Hence, Olsen set up a number of committees and internal boards to ensure that all ideas were discussed and debated before they were acted on.

Olsen bolstered his assumptions with a story that he told frequently to justify his thrusting issues onto groups. He said that he would often refuse to make a decision because, "I'm not that smart; if I really knew what to do I would say so. But when I get into a group of smart people and listen to them debate the idea, I get smart very fast." For Ken Olsen, groups were a kind of extension of his own intelligence, and he often used them to think out loud and get his own ideas straight in his head.

Olsen also believed that ideas cannot be implemented well if people do not fully support them and that the best way to get support is to let people debate the issues and convince themselves. He often told the story, "I remember making a decision once; I was walking down that road and turned around, only to discover that there was no one else there." Therefore, on any important decision, Olsen insisted on a wide debate, with many group meetings to test the idea and sell it down the organization and laterally. Only when it appeared that everyone wanted to do it and fully understood it would he "ratify" it. He even delayed important decisions if others were not on board, though he was personally already convinced of the course of action to take. He said that he did not want to be out there leading all by himself and run the risk that the troops were not committed and might disown the decision if it did not work out.

Olsen's theory was that a person must be given clear and simple individual responsibility and then be measured strictly on that area of responsibility. Groups could help to make decisions and obtain commitment, but they could not under any circumstances be responsible or accountable. The intellectual testing of ideas, which he encouraged among individuals in group settings, was extended to organizational units if it was not clear which products or markets should be pursued. He was willing to create overlapping product and market units and to let them compete with each other—not realizing, however, that such internal competition eventually undermined openness of communication and made it more difficult for groups to negotiate decisions.

Recognizing that circumstances might change the outcome of even the best-laid plans, Olsen expected his managers to renegotiate those plans as soon as they observed a deviation. Thus, for example, if an annual budget had been set at a certain level, and the responsible manager noticed after six months that he would overrun it, he was expected to get the situation under control according to the original assumptions or to come back to senior management to renegotiate. It was absolutely unacceptable either not to know what was happening or to let it happen without informing senior management and renegotiating.

Olsen believed completely in open communications and the ability of people to reach reasonable decisions and make appropriate compromises if they openly confronted the problems and issues, figured out what they wanted to do, and were willing to argue for their solution and honor any commitments they made. He assumed that people have "constructive intent," a rational loyalty to organizational goals, and shared commitments. Withholding information, playing power games, competitively trying to win out over another member of the organization on a personal level, blaming others for your own failures, undermining or sabotaging decisions you have agreed to, and going off on your own without getting others' agreement were all defined as sins and brought public censure.

This "model" of how to run an organization to maximize individual creativity and decision quality worked very successfully in that the company experienced dramatic growth for more than thirty years and had exceptionally high morale. However, as the company grew larger, people found that they had less time to negotiate with each other and did not know each other as well personally, making these processes more frustrating. Some of the paradoxes and inconsistencies among the various assumptions came to the surface. For example, to encourage individuals to think for themselves and do what they believed to be the best course for DEC, even if it meant insubordination, clearly ran counter to the dictum to honor their commitments and support decisions that have been made. In practice, the rule of honoring commitments was superseded by the rule of doing only what the person believes is right, which meant that sometimes group decisions would not stick.

DEC had increasing difficulty in imposing any kind of discipline on its organizational processes. If a given manager decided that for organizational reasons a more disciplined autocratic approach was necessary, he or she ran the risk of Olsen's displeasure because freedom was being taken away from subordinates and that would undermine their entrepreneurial spirit. Olsen felt he was giving his immediate subordinates great freedom, so why would they take it away from the levels below them? At the same time, Olsen recognized that at certain levels of the organization, discipline was essential to getting anything done; the difficulty was in deciding just which areas required discipline and which areas required freedom.

When the company was small and everyone knew everyone else, when "functional familiarity" was high, there was always time to renegotiate, and basic consensus and trust were high enough to ensure that if time pressure forced people to make their own decisions and to be insubordinate, others would, after the fact, mostly agree with the decisions that had been made locally. In other words, if initial decisions made at higher levels did not stick, this did not bother anyone—until the organization became larger and more complex. What was initially a highly adaptive system ideally suited for innovation began to be regarded by more and more members of the organization as disorganized, chaotic, and ill adapted to a more mature commodity market.

The company thrived on intelligent, assertive, individualistic people who were willing and able to argue for and sell their ideas. The hiring practices of the company reflected this bias in that each new applicant had to be approved by a large number of interviewers. So over the course of its first decade, the organization tended to hire and keep only those kinds of people who fit the assumptions and were willing to live in the system even though it might at times be frustrating. The people who were comfortable in this environment and enjoyed the excitement of building a successful organization found themselves increasingly feeling like members of a family, and they were emotionally treated as such. Strong bonds of mutual support grew up at an interpersonal level, and Ken Olsen functioned symbolically as a brilliant, demanding, but supportive and charismatic father figure.

Ken Olsen is an example of an entrepreneur with a clear set of assumptions about how things should be, both at the level of how to relate externally to the environment and how to arrange things internally in the organization. His willingness to be open about his theory and his rewarding and punishing behavior in support of it led both to the selection of others who shared the theory and to strong socialization practices that reinforced and perpetuated it. Consequently, the founder's assumptions were reflected in how the organization operated well into the 1990s. DEC's economic collapse and eventual sale to Compaq in the late 1990s also illustrates how a set of assumptions that works under one set of circumstances may become dysfunctional under other sets of circumstances.

Wozniak and Jobs in Apple, Watson in IBM, and Packard and Hewlett in HP

I know less about the details of the founding of these companies, but taking a cultural perspective and analyzing cultures from the point of view of what we do know about the founders produces some immediate insights into the cultures of these companies. This kind of analysis also helps us understand why three companies in similar technologies ended up with very different cultures. Apple was founded by Steve Jobs and Steve Wozniak, both engineers, with the intention of creating products for children in the education market and products that would be fun and easy to use by "yuppies."

Their base was clearly technical, as in the case of DEC, and this showed up in the aggressively individualistic "do your own thing" mentality that I encountered there. When Apple attempted to become more market oriented by bringing in John Scully from PepsiCo, the company grew, but many insiders felt that the technical community within Apple never accepted this marketing-oriented executive. Scully fired Jobs who then started a second company; however, it is significant that Apple eventually returned to its roots in bringing back Steve Jobs. If you observe the direction of Apple in 2009–2010), you can see a return to its roots of creating products that are easy to use and fun, such as the I-Touch phone, the I-Pod for music, and the I-Chat camera for videoconferencing. The attractive design of products and the proliferation of user-friendly stores to display them suggests that Apple now has very much a marketing orientation, but that this orientation had to be combined with its technical skills, something that perhaps only Steve Jobs could do.

Many people point out that IBM did much better in bringing in an outside marketing executive, Lou Gerstner, in its efforts to revitalize its business in the 1990s. Why might this have worked better than Scully in Apple? The insight that cultural analysis provides is that IBM was not founded by a technical entrepreneur and never built an engineering-based organization in the first place. Tom Watson was a sales/marketing manager who left National Cash Register Company to found IBM (Watson & Petre, 1990). He thought like a salesman/marketer throughout his career, and his son Tom Watson, Jr. had the same kind of marketing mentality. Building a clear image with the public became an IBM hallmark, symbolized by its insistence on blue suits and white shirts, for all its salespeople. Watson, Jr. clearly had the wisdom to become strong technically, but the deeper cultural assumptions were always derived more from sales and marketing. Is it any surprise, then, that an outstanding marketing executive would be accepted as an outsider to help the company regain its competitive edge and that he would succeed, not by really changing the culture but reinvigorating it (Gerstner, 2002)?

What of HP? Dave Packard and Bill Hewlett both came out of Stanford with the intention of building a technical business, initially in measurement and instrumentation technology (Packard, 1995). Computers were only brought in later as adjuncts to this core technology, which led to the discovery that the kinds of people working in these technologies were different from each other, and to some degree incompatible, leading ultimately to the splitting off of Agilent to pursue the original technology while HP evolved computers, printers, and various other related products.

HP's growth and success reflected an effective division of labor between Hewlett, who was primarily a technical leader, and Packard, who was more of a business leader. Their ability to collaborate well with each other was undoubtedly one basis for "teamwork" becoming such a central value in the "HP Way." What we know of Packard's managerial style contrasts strongly with Ken Olsen's, in that HP formed divisions early on in its history and put much more public emphasis on teamwork and consensus, even as individual competition remained as the deeper covert assumption. HP became much more dogmatic about standardizing processes throughout the company and was much more formal and deliberate than DEC, which made the computer types at HP uncomfortable.

HP's and DEC's views of teamwork illustrate the importance of defining abstractions such as "teamwork" very carefully in any cultural analysis. Whereas teamwork in HP was defined as coming to agreement and not fighting too hard for your own point of view if the consensus was headed in a different direction, teamwork in DEC was defined as fighting for your own point of view until you either convinced others or truly changed your own mind.

Subsequent to the splitting off of Agilent, the most significant event in the HP story is the introduction of an outsider, Carly Fiorina, as CEO. It appears that her strategy for making HP a successful global player in a variety of computer-related markets was to *evolve* the HP culture by the mega merger with Compaq, acquiring in that process a large segment of DEC employees who had remained at Compaq. The computer market had become commoditized so becoming an efficient, low-cost producer of commodities such as printers and ink became strategically advantageous but required the abandonment of some of the original values of the HP Way. We can speculate that Fiorina was brought in as an outsider to start the change process but that her replacement after some years by homegrown executives reflected a desire to keep parts of the HP culture even as some elements evolved.

Summary and Conclusions

The several cases presented in this chapter illustrate how organizations begin to create cultures through the actions of founders who operate as strong leaders. It is important to recognize that even in mature companies, we can trace many of their assumptions to the beliefs and values of founders and early leaders. The special role that these leaders play is to propose the initial answers to the questions that the young group has about how to operate internally and externally. The group cannot test potential solutions if nothing is proposed. After a leader has activated the group, it can determine whether its actions solve the problems of working effectively in its environment and create a stable internal system. Other solutions can then be proposed by strong group members, and the cultural learning process becomes broadened. Nevertheless, we cannot overlook the tremendous importance of leadership at the very beginning of any group process.

I am not suggesting that leaders consciously set out to teach their new group certain ways of perceiving, thinking, and feeling (though some leaders probably do precisely that). Rather, it is in the nature of entrepreneurial thinking to have strong ideas about what to do and how to do it. Founders of groups tend to have well-articulated theories of their own about how groups should work, and they tend to select as colleagues and subordinates others who they sense will think like them. Both founders and the new group members will be anxious in the process of group formation and will look for solutions. The leader's proposal, therefore, will always receive special attention in this phase of group formation.

Early group life also will tend toward intolerance of ambiguity and dissent. In the early life of any new organization, we can see many examples of how partners or cofounders who do not think alike end up in conflicts that result in some people leaving, thus creating a more homogeneous climate for those who remain. If the original founders do not have proposals to solve the problems that make the group anxious, other strong members will step in, and leaders other than the founders will emerge. I did not observe this in the cases reviewed in this chapter, but I have seen it happen in many other organizations. The important point to recognize is that the anxiety of group formation is typically so high and covers so many areas of group functioning that leadership is highly sought by group members. If the founder does not succeed in reducing the group's anxiety, other leaders will be empowered by the group.

Because founder leaders tend to have strong theories of how to do things, their theories get tested early. If their assumptions are wrong, the group fails early in its history. If their assumptions are correct, they create a powerful organization whose culture comes to reflect their original assumptions. If the environment changes, and those assumptions come to be dysfunctional, the organization must find a way to change some of its culture—a process that is exceptionally difficult if the founder is still in control of the organization. Such change is difficult particularly because over time the founder leaders have multiple opportunities to *embed* their assumptions in the various routines of the organization. How this process occurs is detailed in Chapter Fourteen.

14

HOW LEADERS EMBED AND
TRANSMIT CULTURE

In Chapter Thirteen, we saw how founders of organizations start the culture formation process by imposing their own assumptions on a new group. In this chapter, we will explore the many mechanisms that leaders have available to them to reinforce the adoption of their own beliefs, values, and assumptions as the group gradually evolves into an organization. As the organization succeeds in accomplishing its primary task, the leader's assumptions become shared and part of the culture of the organization. New members now experience these cultural assumptions as a given, no longer as something to be discussed—"this is the way we do things around here." From the point of view of the leader, whether in the role of a parent, teacher, or boss, what are the mechanisms available to ensure that new members will get the message?

How Leaders Embed Their Beliefs, Values, and Assumptions

The simplest explanation of how leaders get their message across is that they do it through "charisma"—that mysterious ability to capture the subordinates' attention and to communicate major assumptions and values in a vivid and clear manner (Bennis and Nanus, 1985; Conger, 1989; Leavitt, 1986). Charisma is an important mechanism of culture creation, but it is not, from the organization's or society's point of view, a reliable mechanism of embedding or socialization because leaders who have it are rare, and their impact is hard to predict. Historians can look back and say that certain people had charisma or had a great vision. It is not always clear at the time, however, how they transmitted the vision. On the other hand, leaders of organizations without charisma have many ways of getting their message across, and it is these other ways that will be the focus of this chapter. Exhibit 14.1 shows twelve embedding mechanisms divided into primary and secondary to highlight the difference between the most powerful daily behavioral things that leaders do and the more formal mechanisms that come to support and reinforce the primary messages.

Primary Embedding Mechanisms

The six primary embedding mechanisms shown in Exhibit 14.1 are the major "tools" that leaders have available to them to teach their organizations how to perceive, think, feel, and behave based on their own conscious and unconscious convictions. They are discussed in sequence, but they operate simultaneously. They are visible artifacts of the emerging culture that directly create what would typically be called the "climate" of the organization (Schneider, 1990; Ashkanasy, Wilderom, and Peterson, 2000).

Exhibit 14.1. Embedding Mechanisms.

Primary Embedding Mechanisms
- What leaders pay attention to, measure, and control on a regular basis
- How leaders react to critical incidents and organizational crises
- How leaders allocate resources
- Deliberate role modeling, teaching, and coaching
- How leaders allocate rewards and status
- How leaders recruit, select, promote, and excommunicate

Secondary Articulation and Reinforcement Mechanisms
- Organizational design and structure
- Organizational systems and procedures
- Rites and rituals of the organization
- Design of physical space, facades, and buildings
- Stories about important events and people
- Formal statements of organizational philosophy, creeds, and charters

What Leaders Pay Attention To, Measure, and Control. The most powerful mechanisms that founders, leaders, managers, and parents have available for communicating what they believe in or care about is what they systematically pay attention to. This can mean anything from what they notice and comment on to what they measure, control, reward, and in other ways deal with systematically. Even casual remarks and questions that are *consistently* geared to a certain area can be as potent as formal control mechanisms and measurements.

If leaders are aware of this process, then being systematic in paying attention to certain things becomes a powerful way of communicating a message, especially if leaders are totally consistent in their own behavior. On the other hand, if leaders are not aware of the power of this process, or they are inconsistent in what they pay attention to, subordinates and colleagues will spend inordinate time and energy trying to decipher what a leader's behavior really reflects and will even project motives onto the leader where none may exist. This mechanism is well captured by the phrase "you get what you settle for."

It is the consistency that is important, not the intensity of the attention. To illustrate, at a recent conference on safety in industrial organizations, the speaker from Alcoa pointed out that one of their former CEOs, Paul McNeill, wanted to get across to workers how important safety was and did this by insisting that the first item on *every* meeting agenda was to be a discussion of safety issues. In Alpha Power, supervisors start every job with a discussion of the safety issues they might encounter as part of the job briefing. The organization has many safety programs, and senior managers announce the importance of safety, but the message really gets across in the questions they ask on a daily basis.

Douglas McGregor (1960) tells of a company that wanted him to help install a management development program. The president hoped that McGregor would propose exactly what to do and how to do it. Instead, McGregor asked the president whether he really cared about identifying and developing managers. On being assured that he did, McGregor proposed that the president should build his concern into the reward system and set up a consistent way of monitoring progress; in other words, he should start to pay attention to it. The president agreed and announced to his subordinates that henceforth 50 percent of each senior manager's annual bonus would be contingent on what he had done to develop his own immediate subordinates during the past year. He added that he himself had no specific program in mind, but that in each quarter, he would ask each senior manager what had been done. You might think that the bonus was the primary incentive for the senior managers to launch programs, but far more important was the fact that they had to report regularly on what they were doing. The senior managers launched a whole series of different activities, many of them pulled together from work that was already going on piecemeal in the organization. A coherent program was forged over a two-year period and has continued to serve this company well. The president continued his quarterly questions and once a year evaluated how much each manager had done for development. He never imposed any program, but by paying consistent attention to management development and by rewarding progress, he clearly signaled to the organization that he considered management development to be important.

At the other extreme, some DEC managers illustrated how inconsistent and shifting attention causes subordinates to pay less and less attention to what senior management wants, thereby empowering the employee by default. For example, a brilliant manager in one technical group would launch an important initiative and demand total support, but two weeks later, he would launch a new initiative without indicating whether or not people were supposed to drop the old one. As subordinates two and three levels down observed this seemingly erratic behavior, they began to rely more and more on their own judgment of what they should actually be doing.

Some of the most important signals of what founders and leaders care about are sent during meetings and in other activities devoted to planning and budgeting, which is one reason why planning and budgeting are such important managerial processes. In questioning subordinates systematically on certain issues, leaders can transmit their own view of how to look at problems. The ultimate content of the plan may not be as important as the learning that goes on during the planning process.

For example, in his manner of planning, Smithfield (see Chapter Thirteen) made it clear to all his subordinates that he wanted them to be autonomous, completely responsible for their own operation, but financially accountable. He got this message across by focusing only on financial results. In contrast, both Sam Steinberg and Ken Olsen asked detailed questions about virtually everything during a planning process. Steinberg's obsession with store cleanliness was clearly signaled by the fact that he always commented on it, always noticed deviations from his standards, and always asked what was being done to ensure it in the future. Olsen's assumption that a good manager is always in control of his own situation was clearly evident in his questions about future plans and his anger when plans did not reveal detailed knowledge of product or market issues.

Emotional Outbursts. An even more powerful signal than regular questions is a visible emotional reaction—especially when leaders feel that one of their important values or assumptions is being violated. Emotional outbursts are not necessarily very overt because many managers believe that they should not allow their emotions to become too involved in the decision-making process. But subordinates generally know when their bosses are upset, and many leaders do allow themselves to get overtly angry and use those feelings as messages.

Subordinates find their bosses' emotional outbursts painful and try to avoid them. In the process, they gradually come to condition their behavior to what they perceive the leader to want, and if, over time, that behavior produces desired results, they adopt the leader's assumptions. For example, Olsen's concern that line managers stay on top of their jobs was originally signaled most clearly in an incident at an executive committee meeting when the company was still very young. A newly hired chief financial officer (CFO) was asked to make his report on the state of the business. He had analyzed the three major product lines and brought his analysis to the meeting. He distributed the information and then pointed out that one product line in particular was in financial difficulty because of falling sales, excessive inventories, and rapidly rising manufacturing costs. It became evident in the meeting that the vice president (VP) in charge of the product line had not seen the CFO's figures and was somewhat embarrassed by what was being revealed.

As the report progressed, the tension in the room rose because everyone sensed that a real confrontation was about to develop between the CFO and the VP. The CFO finished, and all eyes turned toward the VP. The VP said that he had not seen the figures and wished he had had a chance to look at them; because he had not seen them, however, he had no immediate answers to give. At this point, Olsen blew up, but to the surprise of the whole group he blew up not at the CFO but at the VP. Several members of the group later revealed that they had expected Olsen to blow up at the CFO for his obvious grandstanding in bringing in figures that were new to everyone. However, no one had expected Olsen to turn his wrath on the product line VP for not being prepared to deal with the CFO's arguments and information. Protests that the VP had not seen the data fell on deaf ears. He was told that if he were running his business properly he would have known everything the CFO knew, and he certainly should have had answers for what should now be done.

Suddenly everyone realized that there was a powerful message in Olsen's outburst. He clearly expected and assumed that a product-line VP would always be totally on top of his own business and would never put himself in the position of being embarrassed by financial data. The fact that the VP did not have his own numbers was a worse sin than being in trouble. The fact that he could not respond to the troublesome figures was also a worse sin than being in trouble. The Olsen blowup at the line manager was a far clearer message than any amount of rhetoric about delegation, accountability, and the like would have been.

If a manager continued to display ignorance or lack of control of his own situation, Olsen would continue to get angry at him and accuse him of incompetence. If the manager attempted to defend himself by noting that his situation either was the result of actions on the part of others over whom he had no control or resulted from prior agreements made by Olsen himself, he would be told emotionally that he should have brought the issue up right away to force a rethinking of the situation and a renegotiation of the prior decision. In other words, Olsen made it very clear, by the kinds of things to which he reacted emotionally, that poor performance could be excused but not being on top of one's own situation and not informing others of what was going on could never be excused.

Olsen's deep assumption about the importance of always telling the truth was signaled most clearly on the occasion of another executive committee meeting, when it was discovered that the company had excess inventory because each product line, in the process of protecting itself, had exaggerated its orders to manufacturing by a small percentage. The accumulation of these small percentages across all the product lines produced a massive excess inventory, which the manufacturing department disclaimed because it had only produced what the product lines had ordered. At the meeting in which this situation was reviewed, Olsen said that he had rarely been as angry as he was then because the product-line managers had *lied*. He stated flatly that if he ever caught a manager exaggerating orders again, it would be grounds for instant dismissal no matter what the reasons. The suggestion that manufacturing could compensate for the sales exaggerations was dismissed out of hand because that would compound the problem. The prospect of one function lying while the other function tried to figure out how to compensate for it totally violated Olsen's assumptions about how an effective business should be run.

Both Steinberg and Olsen shared the assumption that meeting the customer's needs was one of the most important ways of ensuring business success, and their most emotional reactions consistently occurred whenever they learned that a customer had not been well treated. In this area, the official messages, as embodied in company creeds and the formal reward system, were completely consistent with the implicit messages that could be inferred from founder reactions. In Sam Steinberg's case, the needs of the customer were even put ahead of the needs of the family, and one way that a family member could get in trouble was by mistreating a customer.

Inferences from What Leaders Do Not Pay Attention To. Other powerful signals that subordinates interpret for evidence of the leader's assumptions are what leaders do *not* react to. For example, in DEC, managers were frequently in actual trouble with cost overruns, delayed schedules, and imperfect products, but such troubles rarely caused comment if the manager had displayed evidenced that he or she was in control of the situation. Trouble was assumed to be a normal condition of doing business; only failure to cope and regain control was unacceptable. DEC's product design departments frequently had excess personnel, very high budgets, and lax management with regard to cost controls, but none of this occasioned much comment. Subordinates correctly interpreted this to mean that it was far more important to come up with a good product than to control costs.

Inconsistency and Conflict. If leaders send inconsistent signals in what they do or do not pay attention to, this creates emotional problems for subordinates, as was shown in the Steinberg case. Sam Steinberg valued high performance but accepted poor performance from family members, causing many competent nonfamily members to leave. Ken Olsen wanted to empower people, but he also signaled that he wanted to maintain "paternal" centralized control. Once some of the empowered engineering managers developed enough confidence in their own decision-making abilities, they were forced into a kind of pathological insubordination—agreeing with Olsen during the meeting but then telling me as we were walking down the hall after the meeting that "Ken no longer is on top of the market or the technology, so we will do something different from what he wants." A young engineer coming into DEC would also find an organizational inconsistency in that the clear concern for customers coexisted with an implicit arrogance toward certain classes of customers because the engineers often assumed that they knew better what the customer would like in the way of product design. Olsen implicitly reinforced this attitude by not reacting in a corrective way when engineers displayed such arrogance.

The fact that leaders may be unaware of their own conflicts or emotional issues and, therefore, may be sending mutually contradictory messages leads to varying degrees of culture conflict and organizational pathology (Kets de Vries and Miller, 1987; Frost, 2003; Goldman, 2008). Both Steinbergs and DEC were eventually weakened by their leaders' unconscious conflicts between a stated philosophy of delegation and decentralization and a powerful need to retain tight centralized control. Both intervened frequently on very detailed issues and felt free to go around the hierarchy. Subordinates will tolerate and accommodate contradictory messages because, in a sense, founders, owners, and others at higher levels are always granted the right to be inconsistent or, in any case, are too powerful to be confronted. The emerging culture will then reflect not only the leader's assumptions but also the complex internal accommodations created by subordinates to run the organization in spite of or around the leader. The group, sometimes acting on the assumption that the leader is a creative genius who has idiosyncrasies, may develop compensatory mechanisms, such as buffering layers of managers, to protect the organization from the dysfunctional aspects of the leader's behavior. In those cases, the culture may become a defense mechanism against the anxieties unleashed by inconsistent leader behavior. In other cases, the organization's style of operating will reflect the very biases and unconscious conflicts that the founder experiences, thus causing some scholars to call such organizations "neurotic" (Kets de Vries and Miller, 1984, 1987). At the extreme, subordinates or the board of directors may have to find ways to move the founder out altogether, as has happened in a number of first-generation companies.

In summary, what leaders consistently pay attention to, reward, control, and react to emotionally communicates most clearly what their own priorities, goals, and assumptions are. If they pay attention to too many things or if their pattern of attention is inconsistent, subordinates will use other signals or their own experience to decide what is really important, leading to a much more diverse set of assumptions and many more subcultures.

Leader Reactions to Critical Incidents and Organizational Crises. When an organization faces a crisis, the manner in which leaders and others deal with it reveals important underlying assumptions and creates new norms, values, and working procedures. Crises are especially significant in culture creation and transmission because the heightened emotional involvement during such periods increases the intensity of learning. Crises heighten anxiety, and the need to reduce anxiety is a powerful motivator of new learning. If people share intense emotional experiences and collectively learn how to reduce anxiety, they are more likely to remember what they have learned and to ritually repeat that behavior to avoid anxiety.

For example, a company almost went bankrupt because it over-engineered its products and made them too expensive. The company survived by hitting the market with a lower quality, less expensive product. Some years later, the market required a more expensive, higher quality product, but this company was not able to produce such a product because it could not overcome its anxiety based on memories of almost going under with the more expensive high-quality product.

What is defined as a crisis is, of course, partly a matter of perception. There may or may not be actual dangers in the external environment, and what is considered to be dangerous is itself often a reflection of the culture. For purposes of this analysis, a crisis is what is perceived to be a crisis and what is defined as a crisis by founders and leaders. Crises that arise around the major external survival issues are the most potent in revealing the deep assumptions of the leaders.

A story told about Tom Watson, Jr., highlights his concern for people and for management development. A young executive had made some bad decisions that cost the company several million dollars. He was summoned to Watson's office, fully expecting to be dismissed. As he entered the office, the young executive said, "I suppose after that set of mistakes you will be wanting to fire me." Watson was said to have replied, "Not at all, young man, we have just spent a couple of million dollars educating you."

Innumerable organizations have faced the crisis of shrinking sales, excess inventories, technological obsolescence, and the subsequent necessity of laying off employees to cut costs. How leaders deal with such crises reveals some of their assumptions about the importance of people and their view of human nature. Ouchi (1981) cites several dramatic examples in which U.S. companies faced with layoffs decided instead to go to short workweeks or to have all employees and managers take cuts in pay to manage the cost reduction without people reduction. We have seen many examples of this sort in the economic crisis of 2009.

The DEC assumption that "we are a family who will take care of each other" came out most clearly during periods of crisis. When the company was doing well, Olsen often had emotional outbursts reflecting his concern that people were getting complacent. When the company was in difficulty, however, Olsen never punished anyone or displayed anger; instead, he became the strong and supportive father figure, pointing out to both the external world and the employees that things were not as bad as they seemed, that the company had great strengths that would ensure future success, and that people should not worry about layoffs because things would be controlled by slowing down hiring.

On the other hand, Steinberg displayed his lack of concern for his own young managers by being punitive under crisis conditions, sometimes impulsively firing people only to have to try to rehire them later because he realized how important they were to the operation of the company. This gradually created an organization built on distrust and low commitment, leading good people to leave when a better opportunity came along.

Crises around issues of internal integration can also reveal and embed leader assumptions. I have found that a good time to observe an organization very closely is when acts of insubordination take place. So much of an organization's culture is tied up with hierarchy, authority, power, and influence that the mechanisms of conflict resolution have to be constantly worked out and consensually validated. No better opportunity exists for leaders to send signals about their own assumptions about human nature and relationships than when they themselves are challenged.

For example, Olsen clearly and repeatedly revealed his assumption that he did not feel that he knew best through his tolerant and even encouraging behavior when subordinates argued with him or disobeyed him. He signaled that he was truly depending on his subordinates to know what was best and that they should be insubordinate if they felt they were right. In contrast, a bank president with whom I have worked, publicly insisted that he wanted his subordinates to think for themselves, but his behavior belied his overt claim. During an important meeting of the whole staff, one of these subordinates, in attempting to assert himself, made some silly errors in a presentation. The president laughed at him and ridiculed him. Though the president later apologized and said he did not mean it, the damage had been done. All the other subordinates who witnessed the incident interpreted the outburst to mean that the president was not really serious about delegating to them and having them be more assertive. He was still sitting in judgment on them and was still operating on the assumption that he knew best.

How Leaders Allocate Resources. How budgets are created in an organization reveals leader assumptions and beliefs. For example, a leader who is personally averse to being in debt will bias the budget-planning process by rejecting plans that lean too heavily on borrowing and favoring the retention of as much cash as possible, thus undermining potentially good investments. As Donaldson and Lorsch (1983) show in their study of top-management decision making, leader beliefs about the distinctive competence of their organization, acceptable levels of financial crisis, and the degree to which the organization must be financially self-sufficient strongly influence their choices of goals, the means to accomplish them, and the management processes to be used. Such beliefs not only function as criteria by which decisions are made but are constraints on decision making in that they limit the perception of alternatives.

Olsen's budgeting and resource allocation processes clearly revealed his belief in the entrepreneurial bottom-up system. He always resisted letting senior managers set targets, formulate strategies, or set goals, preferring instead to stimulate the engineers and managers below him to come up with proposals, business plans, and budgets that he and other senior executives would approve if they made sense. He was convinced that people would give their best efforts and maximum commitment only to projects and programs that they themselves had invented, sold, and were accountable for.

This system created problems as the DEC organization grew and found itself increasingly operating in a competitive environment in which costs had to be controlled. In its early days, the company could afford to invest in all kinds of projects whether they made sense or not. In the late 1980s, one of the biggest issues was how to choose among projects that sounded equally good when there were insufficient resources to fund them all. The effort to fund everything resulted in several key projects being delayed and this became one of the factors in DEC's ultimate failure as a business (Schein, 2003).

Deliberate Role Modeling, Teaching, and Coaching. Founders and new leaders of organizations generally seem to know that their own visible behavior has great value for communicating assumptions and values to other members, especially newcomers. Olsen and some other senior executives made videotapes that outlined their explicit philosophy, and these tapes were shown to new members of the organization as part of their initial training. However, there is a difference between the messages delivered by videos or from staged settings, such as when a leader gives a welcoming speech to newcomers, and the messages received when that leader is observed informally. The informal messages are the more powerful teaching and coaching mechanism.

Sam Steinberg, for example, demonstrated his need to be involved in everything at a detailed level by his frequent visits to stores and the minute inspections he made once he got there. When he went on vacation, he called the office every day at a set time and asked detailed questions about all aspects of the business. This behavior persisted into his semiretirement, when he would call every day from his retirement home thousands of miles away. Through his questions, his lectures, and his demonstration of personal concern for details, he hoped to show other managers what it meant to be highly visible and on top of one's job. Through his unwavering loyalty to family members, Steinberg also trained people in how to think about family members and the rights of owners. Olsen made an explicit attempt to downplay status and hierarchy in DEC by driving a small car, dressing informally, and spending many hours wandering among the employees at all levels, getting to know them personally.

An example of more explicit coaching occurred in Steinbergs when the Steinberg family brought back a former manager as the CEO after several other CEOs had failed. One of the first things this CEO did as the new president was to display at a large meeting his own particular method of analyzing the performance of the company and planning its future. He said explicitly to the group: "Now that's an example of the kind of good planning and management I want in this organization." He then ordered his key executives to prepare long-range plans in the format, which he had just displayed. He then coached their presentations, commented on each one, corrected the approach where he felt it had missed the point, and gave them new deadlines for accomplishing their goals as spelled out in the plans. Privately, he told an observer of this meeting that the organization had done virtually no planning for decades and that he hoped to institute formal strategic planning as a way of reducing the massive deficits that the organization had been experiencing. From his point of view, he had to change the entire mentality of his subordinates, which he felt required him to instruct, model, correct, and coach.

How Leaders Allocate Rewards and Status. Members of any organization learn from their own experience with promotions, from performance appraisals, and from discussions with the boss what the organization values and what the organization punishes. Both the nature of the behavior rewarded and punished and the nature of the rewards and punishments themselves carry the messages. Leaders can quickly get across their own priorities, values, and assumptions by consistently linking rewards and punishments to the behavior they are concerned with.

I am referring here to the actual practices—what really happens—not what is espoused, published, or preached. For example, product managers in General Foods were each expected to develop a successful marketing program for their specific product and then were rewarded by being moved to a better product after about eighteen months. Because the results of a marketing program could not possibly be known in eighteen months, what was really rewarded was the performance of the product manager in creating a "good" marketing program—as measured by the ability to sell it to the senior managers who approved it—not by the ultimate performance of the product in the marketplace.

The implicit assumption was that only senior managers could be trusted to evaluate a marketing program accurately; therefore, even if a product manager was technically accountable for his product, it was, in fact, senior management that took the real responsibility for launching expensive marketing programs. What junior managers learned from this was how to develop programs that had the right characteristics and style from senior management's point of view. If junior-level managers developed the illusion that they really had independence in making marketing decisions, they had only to look at the relative insignificance of the actual rewards given to successful managers—they received a better product to manage, they might get a slightly better office, and they received a good raise—but they still had to present their marketing programs to senior management for review, and the preparations for and dry runs of such presentations took four to five months of every year even for very senior product managers. An organization that seemingly delegated a great deal of power to its product managers was, in fact, limiting their autonomy very sharply and systematically training them to think like senior managers.

To reiterate the basic point, if the founders or leaders are trying to ensure that their values and assumptions will be learned, they must create a reward, promotion, and status system that is consistent with those assumptions. Although the message initially gets across in the daily behavior of the leader, it is judged in the long run by whether the important rewards such as promotion are allocated consistently with that daily behavior.

The safety program in Alpha Power is a good example of the potential tension between espoused and actual rewards. The entire organization is geared to rewarding safe behavior on the job, and employees are encouraged to call time outs if they observe something unsafe. An expert is then brought in to make a judgment. Of course this takes time and reduces productivity, but safety is paramount. The employee and the supervisory level are rewarded for safe behavior, but the middle managers feel that their careers hinge more on how productive they are. This leaves the supervisors in an ambiguous and mixed incentive situation. They want to ensure safety, but they are also highly aware that their bosses while espousing safety will reward them for reliability and productivity.

Most organizations espouse a variety of values, some of which are intrinsically contradictory, so new employees must figure out for themselves what is really rewarded—customer satisfaction, productivity, safety, minimizing costs, or maximizing returns to the investors. Only by observing actual promotions and performance reviews can newcomers figure out what the underlying assumptions are by which the organization works.

How Leaders Select, Promote, and Excommunicate. One of the subtlest yet most potent ways through which leader assumptions get embedded and perpetuated is the process of selecting new members. For example, Olsen assumed that the best way to build an organization was to hire very smart, articulate, tough, independent people and then give them lots of responsibility and autonomy. Ciba-Geigy, on the other hand, hired very well educated, smart people who would fit into the more structured culture that had evolved over a century.

This cultural embedding mechanism is subtle because in most organizations it operates unconsciously. Founders and leaders tend to find attractive those candidates who resemble present members in style, assumptions, values, and beliefs. They are perceived to be the best people to hire and are assigned characteristics that will justify their being hired. Unless someone outside the organization is explicitly involved in the hiring, there is no way of knowing how much the current implicit assumptions are dominating recruiters' perceptions of the candidates.

If organizations use search firms in hiring, an interesting question arises as to how much the search firm will understand some of the implicit criteria that may be operating. Because they operate outside the cultural context of the employing organization, do they implicitly reproduce or change the culture, and are they aware of their power in this regard? Basic assumptions are further reinforced through who does or does not get promoted, who is retired early, and who is, in effect, excommunicated by being fired or given a job that is clearly perceived to be less important, even if at a higher level (being "kicked upstairs"). In DEC, any employee who was not bright enough or articulate enough to play the idea-debating game and to stand up for his own ideas soon became walled off and eventually was forced out through a process of benign but consistent neglect. In Ciba-Geigy, a similar kind of isolation occurred if an employee was not concerned about the company, the products, and/or senior management. Neither company fired people except for dishonesty or immoral behavior, but in both companies such isolation became the equivalent of excommunication.

Primary Embedding Mechanisms: Some Concluding Observations

These embedding mechanisms all interact and tend to reinforce each other if the leader's own beliefs, values, and assumptions are consistent. By breaking out these categories, I am trying to show the many different ways by which leaders can and do communicate their assumptions. Most newcomers to an organization have a wealth of data available to them to decipher the leader's real assumptions. Much of the socialization process is, therefore, embedded in the organization's normal working routines. It is not necessary for newcomers to attend special training or indoctrination sessions to learn important cultural assumptions. They become quite evident through the daily behavior of the leaders.

Secondary Articulation and Reinforcement Mechanisms

In a young organization, design, structure, architecture, rituals, stories, and formal statements are cultural reinforcers, not culture creators. Once an organization has matured and stabilized, these same mechanisms come to be constraints on future leaders. But in a growing organization, these six mechanisms are secondary because they work only if they are consistent with the primary mechanisms discussed previously. When they are consistent, they begin to build organizational ideologies and thus to formalize much of what is informally learned at the outset. If they are inconsistent, they will either be ignored or will be a source of internal conflict.

All these secondary mechanisms can be thought of as cultural artifacts that are highly visible but may be difficult to interpret without insider knowledge obtained from observing leaders' actual behaviors. When an organization is in its developmental phase, the driving and controlling assumptions will always be manifested first and most clearly in what the leaders demonstrate through their own behavior, not in what is written down or inferred from visible designs, procedures, rituals, stories, and published philosophies. However, as we will see later, these secondary mechanisms can become very strong in perpetuating the assumptions even when new leaders in a mature organization would prefer to change them.

Organizational Design and Structure

As I have observed executive groups in action, particularly first-generation groups led by their founder, I have noticed that the design of the organization—how product lines, market areas, functional responsibilities, and so on are divided up—elicits high degrees of passion but not too much clear logic. The requirements of the primary task—how to organize to survive in the external environment—seem to get mixed up with powerful assumptions about internal relationships and with theories of how to get things done that derive more from the founder's background than from current analysis. If it is a family business, the structure must make room for key family members or trusted colleagues, cofounders, and friends. Even in publicly held companies, the organization's design is often built around the talents of the individual managers rather than the external task requirements.

Founders often have strong theories about how to organize for maximum effectiveness. Some assume that only they can ultimately determine what is correct; therefore, they build a tight hierarchy and highly centralized controls. Others assume that the strength of their organization is in their people and therefore build a highly decentralized organization that pushes authority down as low as possible. Still others, like Olsen, believe that their strength is in negotiated solutions, so they hire strong people but then create a structure that forces such people to negotiate their solutions with each other—creating, in the process, a matrix organization. Some leaders believe in minimizing interdependence to free each unit of the organization; others believe in creating checks and balances so that no one unit can ever function autonomously.

Beliefs also vary about how stable a given structure should be, with some leaders seeking a solution and sticking with it, while others, like Olsen, were perpetually redesigning their organization in a search for solutions that better fit the perceived problems of the ever-changing external conditions. The initial design of the organization and the periodic reorganizations that companies go through thus provide ample opportunities for the founders and leaders to embed their deeply held assumptions about the task, the means to accomplish it, the nature of people, and the right kinds of relationships to foster among people. Some leaders are able to articulate why they have designed their organization the way they have; others appear to be rationalizing and are not really consciously aware of the assumptions they are making, even though such assumptions can sometimes be inferred from the results. In any case, the organization's structure and design can be used to reinforce leader assumptions but rarely does it provide an accurate initial basis for embedding them because structure can usually be interpreted by the employees in a number of different ways.

Organizational Systems and Procedures

The most visible parts of life in any organization are the daily, weekly, monthly, quarterly, and annual cycles of routines, procedures, reports, forms, and other recurrent tasks that have to be performed. The origins of such routines are often not known to participants or, sometimes, even to senior management. But their existence lends structure and predictability to an otherwise vague and ambiguous organizational world. The systems and procedures thus serve a function similar to the formal structure in that they make life predictable and thereby reduce ambiguity and anxiety. Though employees often complain of stifling bureaucracy, they need some recurrent processes to avoid the anxiety of an uncertain and unpredictable world.

Given that group members seek this kind of stability and anxiety reduction, founders and leaders have the opportunity to reinforce their assumptions by building systems and routines around them. For example, Olsen reinforced his belief that truth is reached through debate by creating many different kinds of committees and attending their meetings. Steinberg reinforced his belief in absolute authority by creating review processes in which he would listen briefly and then issue peremptory orders. Ciba-Geigy reinforced its assumptions about truth deriving from science by creating formal research studies before making important decisions. Alpha Power reinforced its assumptions about the inherent danger of delivering electricity, gas, and steam by writing hundreds of procedures for how to do things and providing constant training and monitoring to ensure compliance.

Systems and procedures can formalize the process of "paying attention" and thus reinforce the message that the leader really cares about certain things. This is why the president who wanted management development programs helped his cause immensely by formalizing his quarterly reviews of what each subordinate had done. Formal budgeting or planning routines are often adhered to less to produce plans and budgets and more to provide a vehicle to remind subordinates what to pay attention to.

If founders or leaders do not design systems and procedures as reinforcement mechanisms, they open the door to historically evolved inconsistencies in the culture or weaken their own message from the outset. Thus, a strong CEO who believes, as Olsen did, that line managers should be in full control of their own operation must ensure that the organization's financial control procedures are consistent with that belief. If he allows a strong centralized corporate financial organization to evolve and if he pays attention to the data generated by this organization, he is sending a signal inconsistent with the assumption that managers should control their own finances. Then one subculture may evolve in the line organization and a different subculture in the corporate finance organization. If those groups end up fighting each other, it will be the direct result of the initial inconsistency in design logic, not the result of the personalities or the competitive drives of the managers of those functions.

Rites and Rituals of the Organization

Some students of culture view the special organizational processes of rites and rituals as central to deciphering as well as communicating cultural assumptions (Deal and Kennedy, 1982, 1999; Trice and Beyer, 1984, 1985). Rites and rituals are symbolic ways to formalize certain assumptions and are, therefore, important artifacts to observe. However, their lessons are not always easy to decipher, so I do not consider them to be primary embedding mechanisms. Instead, they might be considered important reinforcers of key cultural assumptions if those assumptions are made clear by the primary embedding mechanisms.

In DEC, for example, the monthly "Woods meetings" devoted to important long-range strategic issues were always held off-site in highly informal surroundings that strongly encouraged informality, status equality, and dialogue. The meetings usually lasted two or more days and involved some joint physical activity such as a hike or a mountain climb. Olsen strongly believed that people would learn to trust each other and be more open with each other if they did enjoyable things together in an informal setting. As the company grew, various functional groups adopted this style of meeting as well, to the point where periodic off-site meetings became corporate rituals with their own various names, locales, and informal procedures.

In Ciba-Geigy, the annual meeting always involved the surprise athletic event that no one was good at and that would therefore equalize status. The participants would let their hair down, try their best, fail, and be laughed at in a good-humored fashion. It was as if the group were trying to say to itself, "We are serious scientists and business people, but we also know how to play." During the play, informal messages that would not be allowed in the formal work world could be conveyed, thus compensating somewhat for the strict hierarchy.

In Alpha Power, the values of teamwork, especially in environmental, health and safety activities, were symbolized by monthly "Way we work" special lunches attended by three or four teams that had been nominated for outstanding achievements and senior management. Each team was asked to tell the entire group what they had accomplished and how they had done it. Group photographs then published in the house organ served as additional reward and publicity. In addition the company had all kinds of prizes for safety performance.

You can find examples of ritualized activities and formalized ritual events in most organizations, but they typically reveal only very small portions of the range of assumptions that make up the culture of an organization. Therein lies the danger of putting too much emphasis on the study of rituals. You can perhaps decipher one piece of the culture correctly, but you may have no basis for determining what else is going on and how important the ritualized activities are in the larger scheme of things.

Design of Physical Space, Facades, and Buildings

Physical design encompasses all the visible features of the organization that clients, customers, vendors, new employees, and visitors encounter. The messages that can be inferred from the physical environment, as in the case of structure and procedures, potentially reinforce the leader's messages, but only if they are managed to accomplish this (Steele, 1973, 1986; Gagliardi, 1990). If they are not explicitly managed, they may reflect the assumptions of architects, the organization's planning and facilities managers in the organization, local norms in the community, or other subcultural assumptions. Often the architecture also reflects macroculture assumptions in that buildings have to fit the style of the community in which they exist.

DEC chose to locate itself initially in an old woolen mill to emphasize frugality and simplicity. What the visitor experienced visually in this organization was an accurate reflection of deeply held assumptions, and one indicator of this depth was that the effects were reproduced in the offices of this organization all over the world.

Ciba-Geigy strongly valued individual expertise and autonomy. But because of its assumption that the holder of a given job becomes the ultimate expert on the area covered by that job, it physically symbolized turf by giving people privacy. In both companies, physical arrangements were not incidental or accidental physical artifacts. They reflected the basic assumptions of how work gets done, how relationships should be managed, and how to arrive at truth.

Stories About Important Events and People

As a group develops and accumulates a history, some of this history becomes embodied in stories about events and leadership behavior (Allan, Fairtlough and Heinzen, 2002; Martin and Powers, 1983; Neuhauser, 1993; Wilkins, 1983). Thus, the story—whether it is in the form of a parable, legend, or even myth—reinforces assumptions and teaches assumptions to newcomers. However, because the message to be found in the story is often highly distilled or even ambiguous, this form of communication is somewhat unreliable. Leaders cannot always control what will be said about them in stories, though they can certainly reinforce stories that they feel good about and perhaps can even launch stories that carry desired messages. Leaders can make themselves highly visible to increase the likelihood that stories will be told about them, but sometimes attempts to manage the message in this manner backfire because the story may reveal inconsistencies and conflicts in the leader.

Efforts to decipher culture from collecting stories encounter the same problem as the deciphering of rituals—unless we know other facts about the leaders, we cannot always correctly infer what the point of the story is. If we understand the culture, then stories can be used to enhance that understanding and make it concrete, but it is dangerous to try to achieve that understanding in the first place from stories alone.

For example, two stories told about Ken Olsen state that when he first saw the IBM PC he said, "Who would ever want a computer in their home?" and, on another occasion, "I would fire the engineer who designed that piece of junk." These stories send strong messages about Olsen's prejudices, but it turns out that only one of the stories is correctly interpreted. Olsen did think the PC was less elegant than what he would have wanted to produce, but his remark about computers in the home was in the context of computers *controlling* everything in the home. This remark was made at a time when fears of computers taking over all functions in our lives was very real, as viewers of the film *2001: A Space Odyssey* will recall. Olsen welcomed computers in his home as work and play stations but not as mechanisms for organizing and controlling daily activities. Unfortunately, the story was often told to show that Olsen did not accurately perceive the growing use of home computers, the opposite of what he believed and encouraged.

Formal Statements of Philosophy, Creeds, and Charters

The final mechanism of articulation and reinforcement to be mentioned is the formal statement—the attempt by the founders or leaders to state explicitly what their values or assumptions are. These statements typically highlight only a small portion of the assumption set that operates in the group and, most likely, will highlight only those aspects of the leader's philosophy or ideology that lend themselves to public articulation. Such public statements have a value for the leader as a way of emphasizing special things to be attended to in the organization, as values around which to rally the troops, and as reminders of fundamental assumptions not to be forgotten. However, formal statements cannot be viewed as a way of defining the organization's culture. At best they cover a small, publicly relevant segment of the culture—those aspects that leaders find useful to publish as an ideology or focus for the organization. What I have called *espoused values* as the middle level of cultural definition is reflected in this category.

Summary and Conclusions

The purpose of this chapter is to examine how leaders embed the assumptions that they hold and thereby create the conditions for culture formation and evolution. Six of the mechanisms discussed are powerful primary means by which founders or leaders are able to embed their own assumptions in the ongoing daily life of their organizations. Through what they pay attention to and reward, through the ways in which they allocate resources, through their role modeling, through the manner in which they deal with critical incidents, and through the criteria they use for recruitment, selection, promotion, and excommunication, leaders communicate both explicitly and implicitly the assumptions they actually hold. If they are conflicted, the conflicts and inconsistencies are also communicated and become a part of the culture or become the basis for subcultures and countercultures.

Less powerful, more ambiguous, and more difficult to control are the messages embedded in the organization's structure, its procedures and routines, its rituals, its physical layout, its stories and legends, and its formal statements about itself. These six secondary mechanisms can provide powerful reinforcement of the primary messages if the leader is able to control them. The important point to grasp is that all these mechanisms do communicate culture content to newcomers. Leaders do not have a choice about whether or not to communicate. They only have a choice about how much to manage what they communicate.

At the organization's early growth stage, the secondary mechanisms of structure, procedures, rituals, and formally espoused values are only supportive, but as the organization matures and stabilizes they will become primary maintenance mechanisms—what we ultimately call institutionalization or bureaucratization. The more effective they are in making the organization successful, the more they become the filters or criteria for the selection of new leaders. As a result, the likelihood of new leaders becoming cultural change agents declines as the organization matures. The socialization process then begins to reflect what has worked in the past, not what may be the primary agenda of the current leadership of today. The dynamics of the "midlife" organization are, therefore, quite different from those of the young and emerging organization, as will be shown in the following chapters.

Though the leadership examples in this chapter come primarily from founders, any manager can begin to focus on these mechanisms when attempting to teach subordinates some new ways of perceiving, thinking, and feeling. The manager must recognize that all of the primary mechanisms must be used, and all of them must be consistent with each other. Many change programs fail because the leader who wants the change fails to use the entire set of mechanisms described. To put it positively, when a manager decides to change the assumptions of a work group by using all of these mechanisms, that manager is becoming a leader.

15

THE CHANGING ROLE OF LEADERSHIP IN ORGANIZATIONAL "MIDLIFE"

If an organization is successful in fulfilling its mission, it will mature and probably grow. Founders will age or die and be replaced by leaders who have been promoted within the organization or have been brought in from the outside. Ownership by founders or founding families will evolve into public ownership and governance by boards of directors. The decision whether or not to retain private ownership or "go public" may appear to be a financial decision, but it has enormous cultural consequences. With private ownership, the leaders can continue to enforce their own values and assumptions through all of the mechanisms cited in the previous chapter. After governance has shifted to a CEO and a board of directors, the leadership role becomes more diffuse and transient because CEOs and board members usually have limited terms of office and are more accountable to stockholders.

Growth and aging means that treasured values will be eroded if new CEOs don't adhere to them, but, on other hand, the organization will probably become more diverse, which makes it possible to make necessary changes in its goals and means, and, if necessary, to change elements of the culture. Founders may be blind to these issues and may, therefore, have to be made aware of them by their own managements or outside board members if such are in the picture.

With growth will come differentiation into various subgroups, which will, over time, evolve their own cultures. The environmental context within which the organization and these various subgroups operate will evolve, requiring new responses from the organization. Leadership, especially at the level of the "executive culture" (see Chapter Four), can influence the nature of this differentiation in important ways. But the criteria that executives use to evolve their organization are usually related to finance, marketing, technology, and products. Often overlooked are the *cultural* implications of different ways of differentiating the organization.

The culture of the organization that has been built on past success may become, to varying degrees, dysfunctional, requiring what the leader comes to perceive as a need for "culture change." The way in which growth is managed can facilitate or hinder such change. All of these organizational "midlife" phenomena produce new culture dynamics that require a very different kind of leadership behavior if the organization is to continue to survive.

Differentiation and the Growth of Subcultures

All organizations undergo a process of differentiation as they age and grow. This is variously called division of labor, functionalization, divisionalization, or diversification. The common element, however, is that as the number of people, customers, goods, and services increases, it becomes less and less efficient for the founder to coordinate everything. If the organization is successful, it inevitably creates smaller units that begin the process of culture formation on their own with their own leaders. The major bases on which such differentiation occurs are as follows:

- Functional/occupational differentiation
- Geographical decentralization
- Differentiation by product, market, or technology
- Divisionalization
- Differentiation by hierarchical level

Functional/Occupational Differentiation

The forces creating functional subcultures derive from the technology and occupational culture of the function. The production department hires people trained in manufacturing and engineering, the finance department hires economics and finance types, the sales department hires sales types, research and development hires technical specialists, and so on. Even though these newcomers to the organization will be socialized into the corporate culture, they will bring with them other cultural assumptions derived from their education and from association with their occupational community (Van Maanen and Barley, 1984). Such differences arise initially from personality differences that cause people to choose different occupations and from the subsequent education and socialization into an occupation (Holland, 1985; Schein, 1971, 1978, 1987c; Van Maanen and Schein, 1979).

The cultures of different occupations, in the sense of the shared assumptions that members of that occupation hold, will differ because of the core technology that is involved in that occupation. Thus engineers, doctors, lawyers, accountants, and so on will differ from each other in their basic beliefs, values, and tacit assumptions because they are doing fundamentally different things, have been trained differently, and have acquired a certain identity in practicing their occupation. Therefore, in each functional area, we find a blend of the founder assumptions and the assumptions associated with that functional/occupational group.

For example, a powerful occupational subculture based on technology is information technology (IT), built around the core occupation. The IT professional subculture is a prime example of what I labeled in Chapter Four an "engineering culture," dedicated primarily to improvement and innovation. For example, IT assumes the following:

- Information can be packaged into bits and transmitted electronically.
- More information is always better than less.
- The more quantifiable information is, the better.
- Information can be captured and frozen in time on the computer screen, and so on; hence, a paperless office is possible and desirable.
- Technology leads and people should adapt.
- People can and should learn the language and methods of IT.
- Management will give up hierarchy if IT provides better coordination mechanisms.
- The more fully connected an organization is, the better it will perform.
- People will use information responsibly and appropriately.
- Paper can be replaced by electronically stored information.
- Anything that can be standardized, routinized, and made people-proof should be instituted.

By way of contrast, both the operator culture and the executive culture might hold contrary assumptions. For example, operators and/or executives often assume the following:

- Information relevant to operations must include face-to-face human contact to be accurately understood.

- Information must be extracted from raw data and will be meaningful only in a particular context that is itself perpetually changing.

- Meaning derives only from complex patterns.

- The costs associated with speed may not be worth it.

- Too much connectivity produces information overload.

- The more information you have, the more you need; sometimes having less information is better.

- Certain kinds of information, such as personal feedback in a performance appraisal, should not be quantitative and should not be computerized.

- Not everything should be "paperless"; the ability to see and manipulate paper is intrinsic to many kinds of tasks.

- Technology should adapt to people and be user friendly.

- Hierarchy is intrinsic to human systems and a necessary coordination mechanism, no matter how efficient networked communications are.

- Control of information is a necessary management tool and the only way of maintaining power and status.

- Standardization can inhibit innovation in a dynamic environment.

Note that in many ways these assumption sets are in direct conflict with each other, which explains why IT implementations are often so strongly resisted by employees. If the IT subculture and operator subculture are not recognized as cultures that must be aligned, the organization will flounder. On the other hand, if a CEO understands the different assumptions of these subcultures, he or she can create a cultural island in which operator employees and IT professionals can work together to decide how best to implement a new system.

With organizational growth and continued success, functional subcultures become stable and well articulated. Organizations acknowledge this most clearly when they develop rotational programs for the training and development of future leaders. When a young manager is rotated through sales, marketing, finance, and production, she or he is learning not only the technical skills in each of these functions but also the point of view, perspective, and underlying assumptions of that subculture. Such deeper understanding is thought to be necessary to doing a good job as a general manager later in the career.

In some cases, the communication barriers between functional subcultures become so powerful and chronic that organizations have had to invent new boundary-spanning functions or processes. The clearest case example is "production engineering," a function whose major purpose is to smooth the transition of a product from engineering into production. Engineering often designs things that cannot be built or are too expensive to build while production perceives engineering to be unrealistic, lacking in cost consciousness, and too concerned with product elegance instead of the practicalities of how to build the product. Executive leaders must recognize these as *subcultural* issues that need to be managed. The subcultures of sales/marketing and R&D are often so out of line with each other that organizations have learned to create task forces or project teams that bring all the functions together in the initial product development process.

In summary, functional subcultures bring into the organization the diversity that is associated with the occupational communities and technologies that underlie the functions. This diversity creates the basic problem of general management, in that the leader now has to bring into alignment organizational members who have genuinely different points of view based on their education and experience in the organization. If these problems are anticipated, the leader can either avoid organizing by function, or bring the different functions together in dialogues that stimulate mutual understanding of each other's taken-for-granted assumptions. To facilitate such communication across subcultural boundaries requires cultural humility from the leader and the ability not only to perceive subcultural differences but also to respect them.

Geographical Differentiation

As the organization grows geographically, it becomes necessary to create local units for the following reasons:

- Customers in different regions require different goods and services.
- Local labor costs are lower in some geographical areas.

- It is necessary to get closer to where raw materials, sources of energy, or suppliers are located.

- If products are to be sold in a local market, they must be produced in that market area as well.

With geographical differentiation, the question inevitably arises of whether the corporate culture can be strong enough to assert itself in the different regions. If the corporate leadership feels strongly about perpetuating and extending its core assumptions, it sends senior managers from the home country into the regions; or, if it selects local managers, it puts them through an intensive socialization process. For example, I remember meeting in Singapore an Australian who had just been named head of Hewlett-Packard's local plant there. Though he had been hired in Australia and was to spend most of his career in Singapore, he was a dedicated HPer. When I asked him why, he explained that shortly after being hired, he had been flown to California, where he had immediately been met by Mr. Packard himself and then spent six hours with all the top managers. In the following two weeks, he was given a thorough indoctrination in the "HP Way" and was encouraged to visit headquarters often. What impressed him most was senior management's willingness to spend time with him to really get to know and perpetuate the central values embodied in the HP Way.

In DEC, the senior managers responsible for large regions and countries were based in those countries, but they spent two to three days of every month in meetings with Olsen and other senior managers at headquarters, so the basic assumptions under which DEC operated were constantly reinforced, even though most of the employees were locals.

I was once invited to address a group of Ciba-Geigy managers at the U.S. subsidiary to tell them about the Ciba-Geigy culture as I had experienced it in the Basel headquarters. I had had no contact with the U.S. subsidiary group up to that time. After I described the cultural paradigm to them as I saw it (as outlined in Chapter Three), there was a real sense of shock in the audience, articulated by one manager who said, "My God, you're describing us!" He was particularly shocked because he had believed that the Ciba-Geigy's U.S. group, by virtue of the fact that most of the

THE CHANGING ROLE OF LEADERSHIP   265

members were American, would be very different. Clearly, however, the corporate culture had asserted itself across national boundaries.

On the other hand, the local macroculture inevitably shapes the geographic subculture as well. You find a different blend of assumptions in each geographical area, reflecting the local national culture but also the business conditions, customer requirements, and the like. The process of local influence becomes most salient where business ethics are involved, as when giving money to suppliers or local government officials is defined in one country as a bribe or kickback and is deemed illegal and unethical, while in another country the same activity is not only legal but considered an essential and normal part of doing business.

Geographic variations can operate in basic functions such as R&D. For example, I am familiar with several European pharmaceutical companies that operate in the United States. In each case, the U.S. subsidiary mirrors many of the basic assumptions of the European parent (even if it has an American president), but its day-to-day practices in research and in clinical testing reflect the requirements of the U.S. Food and Drug Administration and the U.S. medical establishment. The U.S. pharmaceutical researchers were saying that the Europeans were much less thorough in their testing of compounds, not because their research was inferior but because many European countries did not require the same amount of testing before a drug was approved. Over time, these different testing methods become habits and become embedded, leading to real conflict between the research organizations in Europe and the United States. In Ciba-Geigy, I encountered a situation in which the U.S. research and development group in one division totally mistrusted the research conducted in the headquarters labs and felt that it had to repeat everything, at enormous cost, to determine whether the results were usable in the U.S. market.

As organizations mature, the geographical units may take over more and more of the functions. Instead of being just local sales or production units, they may evolve into integrated divisions, including even engineering and R&D. In those divisions, you then see the additional subcultural difficulty of alignment across functional boundaries where the home functional culture is geographically distant. For example, DEC's various European divisions, typically organized by country, found that the customers in different countries wanted different versions of the basic products, leading to the question of where the engineering for the local needs should be done. On the one hand, it was very important to maintain common engineering standards worldwide, but, on the other hand, those common standards made the product less attractive in a given geographical region. Engineering units that were placed in various countries then found themselves in conflict with local marketing and sales units about maintaining standards and in conflict with their home engineering department over the need to deviate from standards.

Differentiation by Product, Market, or Technology

As organizations mature, they typically differentiate themselves in terms of the basic technologies they employ, the products this leads to, and/or the types of customers they ultimately deal with. Founders and promoted leaders in older companies must recognize and decide at what point it is desirable to differentiate products, markets, or technologies, knowing that this will create a whole new set of cultural alignment problems down the line. For example, the Ciba-Geigy Company started out as a dyestuffs company, but its research on chemical compounds led it into pharmaceuticals, agricultural chemicals, and industrial chemicals. Though the core culture was based on chemistry, as described previously, subcultural differences clearly reflected the different product sets.

The forces that created such subcultural differences were of two kinds. First, different kinds of people with different educational and occupational origins were attracted into the different businesses; second, the interaction with the customer required a different mindset and led to different kinds of shared experiences. I remember at one point suggesting a marketing program that would cut across the divisions and was told: "Professor Schein, do you really think an educated salesman who deals all day with doctors and hospital administrators has anything in common with an ex-farm boy slogging around in manure talking farmers into buying the newest pesticide?"

One of the most innovative and culturally evolutionary steps Ciba-Geigy took in its efforts to become more of a marketing-based organization was to promote a manager who had grown up in the agricultural division to head of the U.S. pharmaceutical division. It happened that this man was such a good manager and such a good marketer that he overcame the stereotypes based on where he had grown up in the business. Although he was ultimately successful, he had a tough time winning the respect of the pharmaceutical managers when he first took over.

Alpha Power delivers primarily electricity to its city, but it also has a gas unit and a steam unit that use different technologies in delivering their service. In addition, the company has geographical regions within its urban environment leading to a large number of suborganizations that have developed their own subcultures. These are labeled as "silos" in the organization and are viewed as problematic for total corporate safety and environmental programs because local conditions often require modifications of the programs.

Contact with customers is also a very powerful force in creating local subcultures that can appropriately interact with the customer's culture. A vivid example was provided by Northrop, a large aerospace company that prided itself on its egalitarianism, high trust, and participative approach to its employees. An analysis of the company's artifacts revealed that the headquarters organization based in Los Angeles was very hierarchical; even the architecture and office layout of the headquarters building strongly reflected hierarchy and status. The managers themselves felt this to be anomalous, but upon reflection they realized that they had built such a headquarters organization to make their primary customers, representatives of the U.S. Defense Department, feel comfortable. They pointed out that the Pentagon is highly structured in terms of hierarchy and that customer teams on their visits to Northrop were only comfortable if they felt they were talking to managers of a status equivalent to or higher than themselves. To make this visible, the company introduced all kinds of status symbols, such as graded office sizes, office amenities, office locations in the building, private dining rooms, and reserved parking spaces.

A trivial but amusing example of the same phenomenon occurred in DEC, when a young employee who ordinarily drove vans to deliver mail or parts internally was assigned to drive board members and other outsiders with high status to special meetings. On one such an occasion, he was allowed to drive the one fancy company car, and he dressed for the event by putting on a black pinstriped suit! The visitor could well draw the wrong conclusion about the DEC culture based on this one observation.

Divisionalization

As organizations grow and develop different markets, they often "divisionalize" in the sense of decentralizing most of the functions into product, market, or geographical units. This process has the advantage of bringing all the functions closer together around a given technology, product set, or customer set, allowing for more alignment among the subcultures. To run an integrated division requires a strong general manager, and that manager is likely to want a fair amount of autonomy in the running of his or her division. As that division develops its own history, it will begin to develop a divisional subculture that reflects its particular technology and market environment, even if it is geographically close to the parent company.

Strong divisional subcultures will not be a problem to the parent organization unless the parent wants to implement certain common practices and management processes. Two examples from my own experience highlight this issue. In the first case, I was asked to work with the senior management of the Swedish government-owned conglomerate of organizations to help headquarters decide whether or not it should work toward developing a "common culture." This conglomerate included ship building, mining, and, at the other extreme, consumer products such as Ramlosa bottled water. We spent two days examining all of the pros and cons and finally decided that the only two activities that required a common perspective were financial controls and human resource development. In the financial area, the headquarters staff had relatively little difficulty establishing common practices, but in the human resource area, they ran into real difficulty.

From the point of view of headquarters, it was essential to develop a cadre of future general managers, requiring that divisions allow their high-potential young managers to be rotated across different divisions and headquarters functional units. But the division subcultures differed markedly in their assumptions about how to develop managers. One division considered it essential that all of its people be promoted from within because of their knowledge of the business, so its members rejected out of hand the idea of cross-divisional rotation of any sort. In another division, cost pressures were so severe that the idea of giving up a high-potential manager to a development program was unthinkable. A third division's norm was that an individual rose by staying in functional "stovepipes" so managers were rarely evaluated for their generalist potential. When the development program called for that division to accept a manager from another division in a rotational developmental move, it rejected the candidate outright as not knowing enough about the division's business to be acceptable at any level. The divisional subcultures won out, and the development program was largely abandoned.

In the other case, a similar phenomenon occurred in relation to the introduction of information technology. Interviews of a large number of CEOs in different industries revealed that one of the biggest problems in multidivisional organizations was trying to introduce an e-mail system across all the divisions. Each division had developed its own system and was highly committed to it. When the corporate IT department proposed a common system, it encountered strong resistance, and when it actually imposed a common system, it encountered subversion and refusal to use the system. Several CEOs commented that information technology was the single hardest thing to get implemented across autonomous divisions.

One of the significant facts about DEC's evolution is that it did create product lines, but never divisions, which allowed functions such as sales and engineering to remain very dominant. In contrast, HP divisionalized very early in its history. Many managers within DEC speculated that the failure to divisionalize was one of the major reasons for DEC's ultimate economic difficulties.

With globalization, a growing problem will be the imposition of common human resource processes. The assumptions of the parent organization may be that everyone should be treated the same way with respect to pay and benefits, but the realities in other macrocultures may make that impossible. In the United States, we believe that people should be paid for their skills regardless of formal rank or family connections (status is gained through achievement); but many other countries consider it appropriate to hire and pay family members regardless of level of achievement. U.S. companies give out bonuses and stock options while many non-U.S. companies stick to very strict salary guidelines.

A dramatic example of misunderstanding at the macrocultural level concerned performance appraisal. In the 1970s, HP had an international human resource manager who imposed on the entire organization a feedback process that required a boss to tell a subordinate to his or her face how to improve performance. I heard her announce to a meeting of international managers in a University of Hawaii executive development program that the program was now in place worldwide. That evening I happened to have dinner with some of the participants, including several Japanese managers from HP. When I asked them how they implemented the program, they said emphatically that "of course we would not tell our subordinate negative things to his face, we have other ways of getting a message across." Yet they had signed off that they were now using the corporate system.

Differentiation by Hierarchical Level

As the number of people in the organization increases, it becomes increasingly difficult to coordinate their activities. One of the simplest and most universal mechanisms that all groups, organizations, and societies use to deal with this problem is to create additional layers in the hierarchy so that the span of control of any given manager remains reasonable. Of course, what is defined as reasonable will itself vary from five to fifty; nevertheless, it is clear that every organization, if it is successful and grows, will sooner or later differentiate itself into more and more levels.

The interaction and shared experience among the members of a given level provides an opportunity for the formation of common assumptions—a *subculture based on rank or status* (Oshry, 2007). The strength of such shared assumptions will be a function of the relative amount of interaction and the intensity of the shared experience that the members of that level have with each other as contrasted with members of other levels.

For example, the executive subculture that I described in Chapter Four has been shown in a study by Donaldson and Lorsch (1983), to make all decisions through a "dominant belief system" that translated all the needs of their major constituencies—the capital markets from which they must borrow, the labor markets from which they must obtain their employees, the suppliers, and most important, the customers—into financial terms. Executives had complex mental equations by which they made their decisions. There was clearly an executive culture that revolved around finance. Middle management has been identified as a subculture because they have neither the power nor the autonomy and so must learn how to live in this ambiguous authority environment. Similarly, first line supervisors have often been identified as a distinct subculture because they are identified both with the rank-and-file and management.

The subculture at each level of the organization will, over time, structurally reflect the major issues and tasks that must be confronted at that level. Thus all first-line supervisors will develop assumptions about human nature and how to manage employees, but whether they develop idealistic assumptions or cynical assumptions will depend more on the industry and actual company experience. Similarly, all sales managers will develop assumptions about human motivation on the basis of their experience in managing salespeople, but whether they come to believe in salary plus commission, pure commission, bonus systems, or individual or team reward systems will again depend upon the industry and the company.

Summary and Conclusions

Organizational success usually produces the need to grow, and, with growth and aging, organizations need to differentiate themselves into functional, geographic, product, market, or hierarchical units. One of the critical functions of leadership in this process is to recognize the *cultural* consequences of different ways of differentiating. New subgroups will eventually share enough experience to create subcultures based on occupational, national, and uniquely historical experiences. After such differentiation has taken place, the leader's task is to find ways of coordinating, aligning, and/or integrating the different subcultures.

Leaders should not be surprised when they find that different functions seem to be talking completely different languages, when geographically isolated managers do not interpret headquarters memos accurately, or when the concerns of senior management about costs and productivity are not shared by employees. Building an effective organization is ultimately a matter of meshing the different subcultures by encouraging the evolution of common goals, common language, and common procedures for solving problems.

It is essential that leaders recognize that such cultural alignment requires not only cultural humility on the leader's part, but skills in bringing different subcultures together into the kind of dialogue that will maintain mutual respect and create coordinated action. As we will see in later chapters, this will increasingly require the design of cultural islands in which multicultural issues deriving from difference in macrocultures can be confronted and sorted out.

16

WHAT LEADERS NEED TO KNOW ABOUT HOW CULTURE CHANGES

This chapter deals with the *natural* processes by which culture evolves and changes as organizations grow and age. Leaders need to understand these processes to be able to steer them. The emphasis here is on *evolution*; in later chapters, we will look at *managed change*, which leaders may need to initiate if the evolutionary process is too slow or going in the wrong direction.

The way in which culture can and does change depends on the stage at which the organization finds itself. Table 16.1 shows these stages and identifies the particular change mechanisms that are most relevant at each stage. These mechanisms are cumulative in the sense that at a later stage, all the prior change mechanisms are still operating, but additional ones become relevant.

Table 16.1.   Culture Change Mechanisms.

Organizational Stage	Change Mechanism
Founding and early growth	1. Incremental change through general and specific evolution 2. Insight 3. Promotion of hybrids within the culture
Midlife	4. Systematic promotion from selected subcultures 5. Technological seduction 6. Infusion of outsiders
Maturity and decline	7. Scandal and explosion of myths 8. Turnarounds 9. Mergers and acquisitions 10. Destruction and rebirth

Founding and Early Growth

In the first stage—the founding and early growth of a new organization—the main cultural thrust comes from the founders and their assumptions. The cultural paradigm that becomes embedded, if the organization succeeds in fulfilling its primary task and survives, can then be viewed as that organization's distinctive competence, the basis for member identity, and the psychosocial "glue" that holds the organization together. The emphasis in this early stage is on differentiating the organization from the environment and from other organizations; the organization makes its culture explicit, integrates it as much as possible, and teaches it firmly to newcomers (and/or selects them for initial compatibility).

The distinctive competencies in young companies are usually biased toward certain business functions reflecting the occupational biases of the founders. At DEC, the bias was clearly in favor of engineering and manufacturing. Not only was it difficult for the other functions to acquire status and prestige, but also professionals in those functions, such as professional marketers, were often told by managers who had been with the company from its origin that "marketers never know what they are talking about." At Ciba-Geigy, a similar bias persisted for science and research, even though the company was much older. Because R&D was historically the basis of Ciba-Geigy's success, science was defined as the distinctive competence, even though more and more managers were admitting overtly that the future hinged more on marketing, tight financial controls, and efficient operations.

The implications for change at this stage are clear. The culture in young and successfully growing companies is likely to be strongly adhered to because (1) the primary culture creators are still present, (2) the culture helps the organization define itself and make its way into a potentially hostile environment, and (3) many elements of the culture have been learned as defenses against anxiety as the organization struggles to build and maintain itself.

It is therefore likely that proposals to deliberately change the culture from either inside or outside will be totally ignored or strongly resisted. Instead, dominant members or coalitions will attempt to preserve and enhance the culture. The only force that might influence such a situation would be an external crisis of survival in the form of a sharp drop in growth rate, loss of sales or profit, a major product failure, the loss of some key people, or some other event that cannot be ignored. If such a crisis occurs, the founder may be discredited, and a new senior manager may be brought into the picture. If the founding organization itself stays intact, so will the culture. How then does culture change in the early growth phase of an organization?

Incremental Change Through General and Specific Evolution

If the organization is not under too much external stress and if the founder or founding family is around for a long time, the culture evolves in small increments by continuing to assimilate what works best over the years. Such evolution involves two basic processes: general evolution and specific evolution (Sahlins and Service, 1960).

General Evolution. General evolution toward the next stage of development involves diversification, growing complexity, higher levels of differentiation and integration, and creative syntheses into new and more complex forms. The growth of subcultures, diversification into other macrocultures, the gradual aging and retirement of the founding group, going from private to public ownership, and merging with or acquiring other companies all create the need for new structures, new systems of governance, and new cultural alignments. Though there are a number of models that have been proposed for such evolution, it has been my experience that we still need to see many more cases before any of these models can really be validated (Adizes, 1990; Aldrich, and Ruef, 2006; Chandler, 1962; Gersick, 1991; Greiner, 1972; Tushman and Anderson, 1986).

The general principle of this evolutionary process is that the overall corporate culture will adapt to changes in its external environment and internal structure. Basic assumptions may be retained, but the form in which they appear may change, creating new behavior patterns that ultimately change the character of the basic assumptions. For example, in DEC, the assumptions that a person must find "truth through debate" and always "do the right thing" was behaviorally expressed through the intense debate in which members of the executive committee used their individual logical power to test any given idea or proposed course of action. The emphasis was on reason and logic. With growth, each of the members of the executive committee and/or their successors became leaders of large groups and developed feelings of responsibility for the welfare of these groups. In the meetings of the executive committee, the arguments were as spirited as ever, but I noticed that *reason and logic had evolved to varying degrees into protecting one's group.* Whereas in the early DEC culture individuals were able to stay logical in their debate, as DEC became a large conglomerate of powerful groups, those same individuals argued increasingly from their positions as representatives and defenders of their projects and groups. "Doing the right thing" and "truth through debate" was still espoused but had evolved into more of a political process based on a new assumption of "protect your turf." This is "general" evolution because it is an inevitable consequence of growth and differentiation.

Specific Evolution. Specific evolution involves the adaptation of specific parts of the organization to their particular environments and the impact of the subsequent cultural diversity on the core culture. This is the mechanism that causes organizations in different industries to develop different industry cultures and causes subgroups to develop different subcultures. Thus, a high-technology company will develop highly refined R&D skills, whereas a consumer products company in foods or cosmetics will develop highly refined marketing skills. In each case, such differences will come to reflect important underlying assumptions about the nature of the world and the actual growth experience of the organization. In addition, because the different parts of the organization exist in different environments, each of those parts will evolve to adapt to its particular environment, as discussed in the previous chapter.

As subgroups differentiate and subcultures develop, the opportunity for more major culture change will arise later, but in this early stage, those differences will only be tolerated and efforts will be made to minimize them. For example, it was clear that the service organization at DEC was run more autocratically, but this was tolerated because everyone recognized that a service organization required more discipline if the customers were to get timely and efficient service. The higher-order principle of "do the right thing" justified all kinds of managerial variations in the various functions.

Self-Guided Evolution Through Insight

If we think of culture as, in part, a learned defense mechanism to avoid uncertainty and anxiety, then we should be able to help the organization assess for itself the strengths and weaknesses of its culture and to help it modify cultural assumptions if that becomes necessary for survival and effective functioning. Members of the organization can collectively achieve insight if they collectively examine their culture and redefine some of the cognitive elements. Such redefinition involves either changing some of the priorities within the core set of assumptions or abandoning one assumption that is a barrier by subordinating it to a higher-order assumption.

For example, Ciba-Geigy had held the assumption that "we never lay people off," yet faced the necessity of major shrinking in some of its divisions. It then managed the layoffs by doing them according to the higher order assumption of "we take good care of our people and treat them well." They provided opportunities for retraining, generous severance packages for early retirement, part-time work, good career counseling, and anything else that would make employees who lost their jobs feel that they were still valued human beings.

It should be noted, however, that this occurred in a mature midlife organization, and the same process may not be feasible in a young and growing organization because in the growth process, culture is clung to as part of the evolving of an identity. DEC had strong pressures to lay people off as the market conditions changed and cost pressures mounted, but the company clung to the assumption that once you were hired, you were a member of the family and could not be let go. The higher order assumption of "growth will take care of it" dominated the thinking.

Many of the interventions that occurred over the years at DEC produced cultural insight. For example, at an annual meeting where the company's poor performance was being discussed, a depressive mood overtook senior management and was articulated as "We could do better if only Ken Olsen or someone would decide on a direction and tell us which way to go." A number of us familiar with the culture heard this as a wish for a magic solution, not as a realistic request. I was scheduled to give a short presentation on the company's culture at this meeting and used the opportunity to raise the following question: "Given the history of this company and the kinds of managers and people that you are, if Ken Olsen marched in here right now and told everyone in what direction he wanted you to go, do you think you would do it?" There was a long silence, followed gradually by a few knowing smiles and ultimately by a more realistic discussion. In effect, the group recognized, reaffirmed, and strengthened its assumptions about individual responsibility and autonomy but also recognized that its wish for marching orders was really a wish for more discipline in the organization and that this discipline could be achieved among the senior managers by more negotiation and tighter coordination at their own level.

DEC managers realized that their culture was an important motivator and integrative force, so they created the "boot camps" to help newcomers gain insight and published many internal documents in which the culture was explicitly articulated and touted as a strength. They also recognized that cultural assumptions and the norms that they created could be used as a powerful control mechanism (Kunda, 1992; O'Reilly and Chatman, 1996).

With insight, new norms can be evolved that are still consistent with deeper assumptions. Sometimes it is enough to recognize how they operate so that their consequences can be realistically assessed. If they are considered too costly, an individual can engage in compensatory behavior. For example, DEC's commitment to checking all decisions laterally (getting buy-in) before moving ahead was a defense against the anxiety of not knowing whether a given decision was correct. As the company grew, the costs of such a defense mounted because it not only took longer and longer to make a decision but also the process of checking with others who had not grown up in the company, with whom one was not functionally familiar, often could not resolve issues.

The options then were to (1) give up the mechanism, which was difficult to do unless some way was found to contain the anxiety that would be unleashed in the short run (for example, finding a strong leader who would absorb the anxiety), (2) design compensatory mechanisms (for example, having less frequent but longer meetings, classifying decisions, and seeking consensus only on certain ones, or finding ways to speed up meetings), or (3) break the company down into smaller units in which the consensual process could work because people could remain functionally familiar with each other and build efficient consensual processes. In DEC's evolution, all of these mechanisms were discussed and tried from time to time, but breaking up into smaller units was not ever implemented sufficiently to avoid the dysfunctional intergroup negotiations that arose.

Managed Evolution Through Hybrids

The preceding two mechanisms serve to preserve and enhance the culture as it exists, but changes in the environment often create disequilibria that force more transformational change—change that challenges some of the deeper assumptions of the cultural paradigm. How can a young organization highly committed to its identity make such changes? One mechanism of gradual and incremental change is the *systematic promotion of insiders whose own assumptions are better adapted to the new external realities.* Because they are insiders, they accept much of the cultural core and have credibility. But, because of their personalities, their life experiences, or the subculture in which their career developed, they hold assumptions that are to varying degrees different from the basic paradigm and thus can move the organization gradually into new ways of thinking and acting. When such managers are put into key positions, they often elicit the feeling from others: "We don't like what this person is doing in the way of changing the place, but at least he or she is one of us."

For this mechanism to work, some of the most senior leaders of the company must first have insight into what needs to change and what in their culture is missing or is inhibiting the change. They can obtain such insight by engaging in formal cultural assessment activities, by stimulating their board members and consultants to raise questions, or through educational programs at which they meet other leaders. What all of these activities have in common is to get the leader to step partially outside his or her culture to be able to look at it more objectively. If leaders then recognize the need for change, they can begin to select "hybrids" for key jobs by locating insiders who have a bias toward the new assumptions that they want to introduce or enhance.

For example, at one stage in its history, DEC found itself increasingly losing the ability to coordinate the efforts of large numbers of units. Olsen and other senior managers knew that a proposal to bring an outsider into a key position would be rejected, so they gradually filled several of the key management positions with managers who had grown up in manufacturing and in field service, where more discipline and centralization had been the norm. These managers operated within the culture but gradually imposed more centralization and discipline. In the end, this approach did not work because DEC's cultural paradigm was strong enough that it overrode their efforts, but it was clearly the correct strategy at that time in DEC's history. Several of these hybrid managers left the company in frustration as they found their efforts repeatedly thwarted.

Similarly, when Ciba-Geigy recognized the need to become more marketing oriented, it began to appoint to more senior positions managers who had grown up in the pharmaceutical division, in which the importance of marketing had been recognized earlier. The process worked to make Ciba-Geigy both more marketing oriented and more strategically focused on pharmaceuticals, ultimately resulting in the merger with Sandoz to create Novartis.

Filling key positions with people who have the beliefs, values, and assumptions that are viewed by senior leaders as the necessary ones for the future growth and survival of the organization is, in fact, the commonest evolutionary culture change mechanism that I have observed across all types of organizations. What makes this a powerful mechanism is that a promoted insider, even if he or she is to some degree a cultural deviant, understands the culture well enough to know how to make the necessary changes. Outsiders who are brought into organizations may have the values and assumptions that are needed, but they almost always lack the cultural insight that would enable them to figure out how to implement the desired changes.

Transition to Midlife: Problems of Succession

Organizational midlife can be defined structurally as the stage at which founder owners have relinquished the control of the organization to promoted or appointed general managers. They may still be owners and remain on the board, but operational control is in the hands of a *second* generation of general managers. This stage can occur slowly or rapidly and can happen when the organization is very small or very large, so it is best to think of it structurally rather than temporally. Many start-up companies such as Smithfield Enterprises (see Chapter Thirteen) reach midlife very quickly while an organization such as IBM only reached it when Tom Watson, Jr. relinquished the reins. The Ford Motor Co. is perhaps still in the transition phase in that a family member is still the chair of the board.

The succession from founders and owning families to midlife under general managers often involves many stages and processes. The first and often most critical of these processes is the relinquishing of the CEO role by the founder. Even if the new CEO is the founder's son or daughter or another trusted family member, it is in the nature of founders and entrepreneurs to have difficulty giving up what they have created (Dyer, 1986, 1989; Schein, 1978; Watson, 1990). During the transition phase, conflicts over which elements of the culture employees like or do not like become surrogates for what they do or do not like about the founder because most of the culture is likely to be a reflection of the founder's personality. Battles develop between "conservatives" who like the founding culture and "liberals" or "radicals" who want to change the culture, partly because they want to enhance their own power position. The danger in this situation is that feelings about the founder are projected onto the culture, and, in the effort to displace the founder, much of the culture comes under challenge. If members of the organization forget that the culture is a set of learned solutions that have produced success, comfort, and identity, they may try to change the very things they value and need.

Often missing in this stage is an understanding of what the organizational culture is and what it is doing for the organization, regardless of how it came to be. Succession processes must therefore be designed to enhance those parts of the culture that provide identity, distinctive competence, and protection from anxiety. Such a process can probably be managed only from within, because an outsider could not possibly understand the subtleties of the cultural issues and the emotional relationships between founders and employees. But it may require an outsider to stimulate this inner process, usually a board member or a consultant hired by the board.

The preparation for succession is psychologically difficult, both for the founder and for potential successors because entrepreneurs typically like to maintain high levels of control. They may officially be grooming successors, but unconsciously they may be preventing powerful and competent people from functioning in those roles. Or they may designate successors but prevent them from having enough responsibility to learn how to do the job—the "Prince Albert" syndrome, remembering that Queen Victoria did not permit her son many opportunities to practice being king. This pattern is particularly likely to operate with a father-to-son transition as was the case in IBM (Watson and Petre, 1990).

When senior management or the founder confronts the criteria for a successor, some cultural issues are forced into the open. It is now clear that much of the culture has become an attribute and property of the organization, even though it may have started out as the property of the founder. It is said that in Kodak "the ghost of George Eastman still walks the halls." If the founder or the founder's family remains dominant in the organization, we may expect little culture change but a great deal of effort to clarify, integrate, maintain, and evolve the culture, primarily because it is identified with the founder. For example, David Packard turned over the management of HP to a promoted general manager, but at one stage in its evolution when Packard saw decisions being made that violated some of his own values, he stepped back into the picture and brought in a different CEO who reinforced those values.

When the founder or founding family finally relinquishes control, an opportunity arises to change the direction of the cultural evolution if the successor is the right kind of hybrid: representing what is needed for the organization to survive, yet seen as acceptable "because he is one of us" and therefore also a conserver of the valued parts of the old culture. At Steinbergs, after several outsiders had failed as CEOs, someone was found who had been with the company earlier and was therefore perceived by the family to "understand the company" even though he brought in many new assumptions about how to run the business. After several outside CEOs, Apple brought back Steve Jobs who had run another company and presumably learned some valuable things to bring back to the organization he founded.

During the growth period, culture is an essential glue; at midlife, the most important elements of the culture have become embedded in the structure and major processes of the organization. Hence, consciousness of the culture and the deliberate attempt to build, integrate, or conserve the culture have become less important. The culture that the organization has acquired during its early years now comes to be taken for granted. The only elements that are likely to be conscious are the credos, dominant espoused values, company slogans, written charters, and other public pronouncements of what the company wants to be and claims to stand for—its philosophy and ideology.

At this stage, it is more difficult to decipher the culture and make people aware of it because it is so embedded in routines. It may even be counterproductive to make people aware of the culture, unless there is some crisis or problem to be solved. Managers view culture discussions as boring and irrelevant, especially if the company is large and well established. On the other hand, geographical expansions, mergers and acquisitions, and introductions of new technologies require a careful self-assessment to determine whether the new cultural elements that will have to be dealt with are, in fact, compatible.

If this succession transition occurs when the company has grown and aged, strong forces toward cultural diffusion will operate because powerful subcultures will have developed and because a highly integrated culture is difficult to maintain in a large, differentiated, geographically dispersed organization. Furthermore, it is not clear whether or not all the cultural units of an organization should be uniform and integrated. Several conglomerates I have worked with have spent a good deal of time wrestling with the question of whether to attempt to preserve or, in some cases, build a common culture, as the Swedish government example showed in the previous chapter.

A number of change mechanisms come into play in connection with these transition processes. They may be launched by the outgoing founder/owner or by the new CEO or occur spontaneously. In midlife organizations, these mechanisms will operate *in addition* to the ones previously mentioned.

Culture Change Through Systematic Promotion from Selected Subcultures

The strength of the midlife organization is in the *diversity* of its subcultures. Leaders can therefore evolve midlife organizations culturally by assessing the strengths and weaknesses of different subcultures and then biasing the corporate culture toward one of those subcultures by systematically promoting people from that subculture into key power positions. This is an extension of the previously mentioned use of hybrids but has a more potent effect in midlife because preservation of the corporate culture is not as big an issue as it was in the young and growing organization. Also, the midlife organization is led by general managers who are not as emotionally embedded in the original culture and are therefore better able to assess needed future directions.

Whereas the diversity of subcultures is a threat to the young organization, in midlife it can be a distinct advantage if the environment is changing. *Diversity increases adaptive capacity.* The only disadvantage to this change mechanism is that it is very slow. If the pace of culture change needs to be increased because of crisis conditions, systematic planned change projects of the kind that will be described in the next chapters must be launched.

Culture Change Through Technological Seduction

One of the less obvious but more important ways in which the leaders of midlife organizations change cultural assumptions is through the subtle, cumulative, and sometimes unintended consequences of new technology that they introduce deliberately or take advantage of. At one extreme, we can observe the *gradual* evolutionary diffusion of a technological innovation such as the automobile as it displaces not only the horse and buggy but also, eventually, many of the assumptions and rituals that accompanied the old technology. The infusion of information technology today is probably comparable. At the other extreme, technological seduction involves the deliberate, managed introduction of specific new technologies to change member *behavior*, which will, in turn, require them to reexamine their present assumptions and adopt new values, beliefs, and assumptions.

The espoused reason for the introduction of new technologies is almost always that it will increase efficiency and productivity, but sometimes the goal is to reduce what the leader perceives to be too much cultural diversity by deliberately introducing a seemingly neutral or progressive technology that has the effect of getting people to think and behave in common terms. Sometimes the goal is to force assumptions out into the open in a neutral and ostensibly nonthreatening way. Sometimes the technology is physical, such as the introduction of robots into an assembly line or the automation of a chemical or nuclear plant, and sometimes it is a socio-technical process, such as the introduction of a formal total quality program or the introduction of a new information technology process that requires standard behavior from everyone.

Many companies have used educational interventions to introduce a new *social* technology as part of an organization development program, with the avowed purpose of creating some common concepts and language in a situation where they perceive a lack of shared assumptions; for example, Blake's Managerial Grid (Blake and Mouton, 1969; Blake, Mouton and McCanse, 1989). The most recent and increasingly popular versions of this type of intervention are "Systems Dynamics" and "The Learning Organization" as presented in Senge's *The Fifth Discipline* (1990, 2006), and Total Quality Management, as presented in a variety of books and programs (for example, Ciampa, 1992; Womack, Jones, and Roos, 2007). The assumption underlying this strategy is that a new common language and concepts in a given cultural area, such as "how people relate to subordinates" or "how people define reality in terms of their mental models," will gradually force organization members to adopt a common frame of reference that will eventually lead to common assumptions. As the organization builds up experience and resolves crises successfully, new shared assumptions gradually come into being.

The growing practice of introducing personal computers and related information technology tools to several layers of management as a vehicle for networking the organization, the mandatory attendance at training courses, the introduction of expert systems to facilitate decision making, and the use of various kinds of groupware to facilitate meetings across time and space barriers all clearly constitute another version of technological seduction, though perhaps unintended by the original architects (Gerstein, 1987; Grenier and Metes, 1992; Johansen and others, 1991; Savage, 1990; Schein, 1992).

In high hazard organizations such as Alpha Power, the introduction of cell phones for all operators has not only made field operations more efficient but has changed relations between supervisors and front-line employees. In the chemical industry, Zuboff (1984) showed how the automation of the control room displaced many workers who could not switch from using observation, smell, and other hands-on techniques for control to monitoring data on a computer screen. Barley's (1988) study of the introduction of CT scanners into hospitals showed how relations between technicians and radiologists were fundamentally altered.

An unusual example of technological seduction was provided by a manager who took over a British transportation company that had grown up with a royal charter 100 years earlier and had developed strong traditions around its blue trucks with the royal coat of arms painted on their sides (Lewis, 1988). The company was losing money because it was not aggressively seeking new concepts of how to sell transportation. After observing the company for a few months, the newly appointed CEO abruptly and without giving reasons ordered that the entire fleet of trucks be painted solid white. Needless to say, there was consternation. Delegations urging the president to reconsider, protestations about loss of identity, predictions of total economic disaster, and other forms of resistance arose. All of these were patiently listened to, but the president simply reiterated that he wanted it done, and soon. He eroded the resistance by making the request nonnegotiable.

After the trucks were painted white, the drivers suddenly noticed that customers were curious about what they had done and inquired what they would now put on the trucks in the way of new logos. These questions got the employees at all levels thinking about what business they were in and initiated the market-oriented focus that the president had been trying to establish in the first place. Rightly or wrongly, he assumed that he could not get this broader focus just by requesting it. He had to seduce the employees into a situation in which they had no choice but to rethink their identity.

Beyond these intra-organizational processes, we have to acknowledge that the broader IT revolution is at least as powerful as the introduction of the automobile in creating sweeping world-wide changes even in the concept of "organization" and "occupational community." As Tyrell puts it in his summary of these impacts:

> . . . the development and deployment of rapid interactive communications technologies (especially . . . the Internet, intranets, EDI, and the World Wide Web) has produced new environments that give many people unprecedented access to specialized communities of interest." (In Ashkanasy, Wilderhorn, and Peterson, 2000, p. 96)

If the boundaries of organizations and occupational communities become fluid, the whole question arises of how culture can form and operate in a group of people who interact only electronically. Some of the most fundamental aspects of culture deal with how people manage their interactions, so in the electronic age, new forms of social contract will have to evolve to deal with authority and intimacy issues.

For example, many professional service firms now consist of a very small headquarters organization and a vast network of the relevant experts (lawyers, consultant, doctors) who are "on call" but are not employees of the organization except on a contract basis. As various employment contracts change, the concept of what is a "career" changes as well, leading to further cultural evolution in the macrocultural domain.

Culture Change Through Infusion of Outsiders

Shared assumptions can be changed by changing the composition of the dominant groups or coalitions in an organization—what Kleiner in his research has identified as "the group who really matters" (2003). The most potent version of this change mechanism occurs when a board of directors brings in a new CEO from outside the organization, or when a new CEO is brought in as a result of an acquisition, merger, or leveraged buyout. The new CEO usually brings in some of his or her own people and gets rid of people who are perceived to represent the old and increasingly ineffective way of doing things. In effect, this destroys the group or hierarchical subculture that was the originator of the corporate culture and starts a process of new culture formation. If there are strong functional, geographic, or divisional subcultures, the new leaders usually have to replace the leaders of those units as well.

Dyer (1986, 1989) has examined this change mechanism in several organizations and found that it follows certain patterns:

1. The organization develops a sense of crisis because of declining performance or some kind of failure in the marketplace, and concludes it needs new leadership.

2. Simultaneously, there is a weakening of "pattern maintenance" in the sense that procedures, beliefs, and symbols that support the old culture break down.

3. A new leader with new assumptions is brought in from the outside to deal with the crisis.

4. Conflict develops between the proponents of the old assumptions and the new leadership.

5. If the crisis is eased and the new leader is given the credit, he or she wins out in the conflict, and the new assumptions begin to be embedded and reinforced by a new set of pattern maintenance activities.

Employees may feel "We don't like the new approach, but we can't argue with the fact that it made us profitable once again, so maybe we have to try the new ways." Members who continue to cling to the old ways are either forced out or leave voluntarily because they no longer feel comfortable with where the organization is headed and how it does things. The new leader can fail in three ways—improvement does not occur, the new leader is not given credit for the improvement that does occur, or the new leader's assumptions threaten too much of the core of the culture that is still embodied in the founder's traditions. If any of these three conditions apply, the new leader will be discredited and forced out as happened with Scully at Apple (it is said that he never got the respect of the technical community within Apple, yet that was Apple's core, no pun intended).

This situation occurs frequently when an outsider is brought into young companies in which the founders or owning families are still powerful. In those situations, the probability is high that the new leader will violate the owners' assumptions and be forced out by them.

Culture change is sometimes stimulated by systematically bringing outsiders into jobs below the top management level and allowing them gradually to educate and reshape top management's thinking. This is most likely to happen when those outsiders take over subgroups, reshape the cultures of those subgroups, become highly successful, and thereby create a new model of how the organization can work. Probably the most common version of this process is to bring in a strong outsider or an innovative insider to manage one of the more autonomous divisions of a multidivisional organization. If that division becomes successful, it not only generates a new model for others to identify with, but it also creates a cadre of managers who can be promoted into more senior positions and thereby influence the main part of the organization.

For example, the Saturn division of General Motors and the NUMMI (New United Motor Manufacturing Inc.) plant—a joint venture of GM and Toyota—were deliberately given freedom to develop new assumptions about how to involve employees in the design and productions of cars and thus learn some new assumptions about how to handle human relationships in a manufacturing plant context. GM also acquired EDS (Electronic Data Systems) as a technological stimulus to organizational change. Each of these units was successful with different cultures and thus could become a model for the parent organization to change, but as things have turned out, an innovative subculture within the larger culture does not guarantee that the larger culture will reexamine or change its culture. The innovative subculture helps in disconfirming some of the core assumptions, but again, unless there is sufficient anxiety or sense of crisis, the top management culture may remain impervious to the very innovations they have created. As of this writing, GM is closing down Saturn and NUMMI in spite of its need to make major changes.

Organizational Maturity and Potential Decline

Continued success creates two organizational phenomena that make culture change more difficult: (1) Many basic assumptions become more strongly held, and (2) organizations develop espoused values and ideals about themselves that are increasingly out of line with the actual assumptions by which they operate. If the internal and external environments remain stable, strongly held assumptions could be an advantage. However, if there is a change in the environment, some of those shared assumptions can become a liability, precisely because of their strength.

If an organization has had a long history of success based on certain assumptions about itself and the environment, it is unlikely to want to challenge or reexamine those assumptions. Even if the assumptions are brought to consciousness, the members of the organization are likely to want to hold on to them because they justify the past and are the source of their pride and self-esteem. Such assumptions now operate as filters that make it difficult for key managers to understand alternative strategies for survival and renewal. For example, DEC understood very well that the computer market had shifted toward commodities that could be built cheaply and efficiently by using components from other organizations, but to take this path would have required both a whole different approach to manufacturing and the abandonment of the company's commitment to the fun and excitement of technical innovation. It was easier to rationalize that continued growth and innovation would solve the cost problems.

As an organization matures, it also develops a positive ideology and a set of myths about how it operates. The organization develops a self-image, an organizational "face" so to speak, that will be built around the best things they do. Organizations, like individuals, have a need for self-esteem and pride so it is not unusual for them to begin to claim to be what they *aspire* to be, while their actual practices are more responsive to the realities of getting their primary task accomplished. Espoused values therefore come to be, to varying degrees, out of line with the actual assumptions that have evolved out of successful daily practices and with some of the assumptions that evolve in the various subcultures.

For example, an organization's espoused values may be that it takes individual needs into consideration in making geographical moves; yet its basic assumption may be that "employees are resources to be managed like any other resource," and "anyone who refuses an assignment is disloyal and should be taken off the promotional list." An organization's espoused value may be that when it introduces new products, it uses rational decision-making techniques based on market research; yet its basic assumption may be that "if our engineers like it, it must be good," as was the assumption within DEC. An organization may espouse the value of teamwork, but all of its practices may be strongly individualistic and competitive as was the case in the computer division of HP. An organization may espouse concern for the safety of its employees, but its practices may be driven by assumptions that they must keep costs down to remain competitive, leading to the subtle encouragement of unsafe practices as was the case in BP leading up to the Texas City explosion. If, in the history of the organization, nothing happens to expose these incongruities, myths may grow up that support the espoused values, thus even building up reputations that are out of line with reality. The most common example in the 1990s was the myth in many companies that they would never lay anybody off, and, in 2009, the myth that the banks, the financial companies, and the auto companies could survive the consequences of the housing bubble bursting.

It is the growing strength of culture and the illusion that the espoused values are actually how the organization operates that makes culture change so difficult in a mature company. Most executives will say that nothing short of a "burning platform," some major crisis, will motivate a real assessment and change process.

Culture Change Through Scandal and Explosion of Myths

Where incongruities exist between espoused values and basic assumptions, scandal and myth explosion become primary mechanisms of culture change. Nothing will change until the consequences of the actual operating assumptions create a public and visible scandal that cannot be hidden, avoided, or denied. One of the most powerful triggers to change of this sort occurs when an organization experiences a disastrous accident, such as the near-meltdown at Three Mile Island, the losses of the Challenger and Columbia space shuttles, the Bhopal chemical explosion, the Texas City refinery explosion in BP, or the Alpha Power Company explosion that led to the accusation that the company had denied the existence of asbestos, which was blown into the neighborhood. Alpha Power was brought up on criminal charges and was ordered by the court to improve environmental management leading to a major culture change program.

In all of these cases, it is usually discovered that the assumptions by which the organization was operating had drifted toward what was practical to get the job done, and those practices came to be in varying degrees different from what the official ideology claimed (Snook, 2000; Gerstein, 2008). Often there have been employee complaints identifying such practices but because they are out of line with what the organization wants to believe about itself, they are ignored or denied, sometimes leading to the punishment of the employees who brought up the information. When an employee feels strongly enough to "blow the whistle," a scandal may result, and practices then may finally be reexamined.

Whistle blowing may be to go to the newspapers to expose a practice that is labeled as scandalous or the scandal may result from a tragic event.

For example, a company that prided itself on a career system that gave managers real choices in overseas assignments had to face the reality that one of their key overseas executives committed suicide and stated in his suicide note that he had been pressured into this assignment in spite of his personal and family objections. At the espoused values level, they had idealized their system. The scandal exposed the shared tacit assumption by which they operated: that people were expected to go where senior executives wanted them to go. The recognition of this discrepancy then led to a whole program of revamping the career assignment system to bring espoused values and assumptions more into line with each other.

In a different kind of example, a product development group operated by the espoused theory that its decisions were based on research and careful market analysis, but in fact one manager dominated all decisions and operated from pure intuition. Eventually, one of the products he had insisted on failed in such a dramatic way that a reconstruction of why it had been introduced had to be made public. The manager's role in the process was revealed by unhappy subordinates and was labeled as scandalous. He was moved out of his job, and a more formal process of product introduction was immediately mandated.

Public scandals force senior executives to examine norms and practices and assumptions that were taken for granted and operated out of awareness. Disasters and scandals do not automatically cause culture change, but they are a powerful disconfirming force that cannot be denied and that start, therefore, some kind of public self-assessment and change program. In the United States, this kind of public reexamination started with respect to the occupational culture of finance through the public scandals involving Enron and various other organizations that have evolved questionable financial practices. Government oversight practices are now being reviewed in the wake of the Bernie Madoff scandal, and even some of the more fundamental assumptions of the capitalist system of free enterprise are being reexamined because of the deep recession of 2009. These reexaminations lead to new practices, but they do not automatically create new cultures because the new practices may not result in greater external success or internal comfort. Scandals create the conditions for new practices and values to come into play but they become new cultural elements only if they produce better results.

Culture Change Through Turnarounds

After a scandal or crisis has brought basic assumptions into consciou and been assessed as dysfunctional, the basic choices are between some kind of "turnaround," a more rapid transformation of parts of the culture to permit the organization to become adaptive once again, or destruction of the organization and its culture through a process of total reorganization via a merger, acquisition, or bankruptcy proceedings. In either case, strong new change managers or "transformational leaders" are likely to be needed to unfreeze the organization and launch the change programs (Kotter and Heskett, 1992; Tichy and Devanna, 1987).

Turnaround as a mechanism of cultural change is actually a combination of many of the preceding mechanisms, fashioned into a single program by a strong leader or team of change agents. In turnaround situations, the replacement of key people with internal hybrids and/or outsiders combined with major changes in technology become central elements of the change process, as we will see in the next chapters on managed change.

Turnarounds usually require the involvement of all organization members, so that the dysfunctional elements of the present culture become clearly visible to everyone. The process of developing new assumptions involves defining new values and goals through teaching, coaching, changing the structure and processes where necessary; consistently paying attention to and rewarding evidence of learning the new ways; creating new slogans, stories, myths, and rituals; and in other ways *coercing* people into adopting new behaviors. All the other mechanisms described earlier come into play, but it is the willingness to coerce that is the key to turnarounds.

Two fundamentally different leadership models have been promulgated for managing turnarounds—or, as they have come to be more popularly known, "transformations." In the strong vision model, the leader has a clear vision of where the organization should end up, specifies the means by which to get there, and consistently rewards efforts to move in that direction (Tichy and Devanna, 1987; Bennis and Nanus, 1985; Leavitt, 1986). This model works well if the future is reasonably predictable and if a visionary leader is available. If neither of these conditions can be met, organizations can use the fuzzy vision model, whereby the new leader states forcefully that the present is intolerable and that performance must improve within a certain time frame but then relies on the organization to develop new visions of how to actually get there (Pava, 1983). The "We need to change" message is presented forcefully, repeatedly, and to all levels of the organization, but it is supplemented by the message "and we need your help." As various proposals for solutions are generated throughout the organization, the leader selects and reinforces the ones that seem to make the most sense.

This model is obviously more applicable in situations in which the turnaround manager comes from the outside and therefore does not initially know what the organization is capable of. It is also more applicable when the future continues to appear turbulent, in that this model begins to train the organization to become conscious of how to change its own assumptions as part of a continuous adaptive process. Turnarounds usually have to be supplemented with longer-range organization development programs to aid in new learning and to help embed new assumptions. Embedding new assumptions in a mature organization is much more difficult than in a young and growing organization because all of the organization structures and processes have to be rethought and, perhaps, rebuilt.

Culture Change Through Mergers and Acquisitions

When one organization acquires another organization or when two organizations are merged, there is inevitable culture clash because it is unlikely that two organizations will have the same cultures. The leadership role is then to figure out how best to manage this clash. The two cultures can be left alone to continue to evolve in their own way. A more likely scenario is that one culture will dominate and gradually either convert or excommunicate the members of the other culture. A third alternative is to blend the two cultures by selecting elements of both cultures for the new organization, either by letting new learning processes occur or by deliberately selecting elements of each culture for each of the major organizational processes (Schein, 2009b).

For example, in the merger of HP with Compaq, though many felt that it was really an acquisition that would lead to domination by HP, in fact the merger implementation teams examined each business process in both organizations, chose the one that looked better, and imposed it immediately on everyone. Elements of both cultures were imported by this means, which accomplished the goal of eliminating those elements that the HP leadership felt had become dysfunctional in the HP culture.

As organizations become more global, we will see many other forms of culture mixing as in joint ventures of various sorts. How these new multicultural entities stimulate culture change will be taken up in Chapter Twenty-One.

Culture Change Through Destruction and Rebirth

Little is known or understood about this process, so little will be said about it here. Suffice it to say that a culture or at least some key elements of a culture can be destroyed by removing the key culture carriers. Some turnaround managers simply fire the top one or two echelons of the organization and bring in new people with new assumptions. To a considerable degree, this happened when Ken Olsen was fired and Robert Palmer, a strong hybrid who had been brought into DEC many years earlier from the semiconductor industry, took over and began to replace key executives with outsiders. People who left DEC at this point all agreed that Palmer was destroying the culture.

When a company is acquired, a similar process can take place in that the acquiring company can impose its culture by replacing all of the key people in the acquisition with its own people. A third version of such destruction often occurs through bankruptcy proceedings. During such proceedings, a board can bring in entirely new executives, decertify a union, reorganize functions, bring in new technologies, and in other ways force real transformation. A new organization then begins to function and begins to build its own new culture. This process is traumatic and therefore not typically used as a deliberate strategy, but it may be relevant if economic survival is at stake. In the recession of 2009, many financial organizations and auto companies went through such destructive proceedings, but it is not always predictable in what form "rebirth" will occur. Historical research on past transformations in industry shows that sometimes even with crises only small changes occur, while at other times, changes are truly transformational (Tushman and Anderson, 1986; Gersick, 1991).

Summary and Conclusions

I have described various mechanisms and processes by which culture changes. As was noted, different functions are served by culture at different organizational stages, and the change issues are therefore different at those stages. In the formative stage of an organization, the culture tends to be a positive growth force, which needs to be elaborated, developed, and articulated. In organizational midlife, the culture becomes diverse, in that many subcultures have formed. Deciding which elements need to be changed or preserved then becomes one of the tougher strategic issues that leaders face, but at this time leaders also have more options to change assumptions by differentially rewarding different subcultures. In the maturity and decline stage, the culture often becomes partly dysfunctional and can only be changed through more drastic processes such as scandals and turnarounds.

Culture evolves through the entry into the organization of people with new assumptions and from the different experiences of different parts of the organization. Organizations differentiate themselves over time into many subcultures, and each of these subcultures evolves as it adapts to its unique environment. Leaders have the power to enhance diversity and encourage subculture formation, or they can, through selection and promotion, reduce diversity and thus manipulate the direction in which a given organization evolves culturally. The more turbulent the environment, the more important it is for the organization to maximize diversity.

Cultural change in organizational midlife is primarily a matter of deliberately taking advantage of the diversity that the growth of subcultures makes possible. Unless the organization is in real difficulty, there will be enough time to use systematic promotion of hybrids and technological seduction as the main evolutionary mechanisms. If leaders want to speed up this process, they have to "manage" culture change more deliberately, a process that will be examined in the next several chapters.

Part Four

HOW LEADERS CAN MANAGE CULTURE CHANGE

In Part IV, we turn to the difficult question of how to change culture when the normal evolutionary processes are not working or are too slow. Chapter Seventeen provides a general model of "managed change" that needs to be understood by leaders when they function as "change agents" whether or not culture change is the primary issue. Then in Chapter Eighteen, I lay out a focused process of culture assessment that should be used in the context of change programs. In Chapter Nineteen, I describe a number of cases that illustrate culture assessment and its role in change programs, including a detailed analysis of the Ciba-Geigy major change effort.

17

A CONCEPTUAL MODEL FOR MANAGED CULTURE CHANGE

In Chapter Sixteen, I reviewed all the ways in which culture can and does change, noting how leaders can influence these processes. However, many of the mechanisms described are either too slow or cannot be conveniently implemented. Subcultural diversity may not be sufficient, outsiders with the right new assumptions may not be available, and creating scandals or introducing new technology may not be practical. How then does a leader systematically set out to change how an organization operates, recognizing that such change may involve varying degrees of culture change?

In this chapter, I will describe a model of planned, managed change and discuss the various principles that have to be taken into account if the changes involve culture. It is my experience that culture change is rarely the primary change goal even though it is announced as such. Instead, change occurs when leaders perceive some problems that need fixing or identify some new goals that need to be achieved. Whether these changes will involve culture change remains to be seen. In the context of such *organizational* changes, culture change may become involved, but the leader must first understand the *general* processes of organizational change before managed *culture* change as such becomes relevant.

The Psycho-Social Dynamics of Organizational Change

The fundamental assumptions underlying *any* change in a human system are derived originally from Kurt Lewin (1947). I have elaborated and refined his basic model in my studies of coercive persuasion, professional education, group dynamics training, and management development (Schein, 1961a,

---

Exhibit 17.1.   The Stages of Learning/Change.

Stage 1 Unfreezing: Creating the Motivation to Change

- Disconfirmation
- Creation of survival anxiety or guilt
- Creation of psychological safety to overcome learning anxiety

Stage 2 Learning New Concepts, New Meanings for Old Concepts, and New Standards for Judgment

- Imitation of and identification with role models
- Scanning for solutions and trial-and-error learning

Stage 3 Internalizing New Concepts, Meanings, and Standards

- Incorporation into self-concept and identity
- Incorporation into ongoing relationships

1961b, 1964, 1972; Schein and Bennis, 1965). This elaborated model is shown in Exhibit 17.1

All human systems attempt to maintain equilibrium and to maximize their autonomy vis-à-vis their environment. Coping, growth, and survival all involve maintaining the integrity of the system in the face of a changing environment that is constantly causing varying degrees of disequilibrium. The function of cognitive structures such as concepts, beliefs, attitudes, values, and assumptions is to organize the mass of environmental stimuli, to make sense of them, and to provide, thereby, a sense of predictability and meaning to the individual members (Weick, 1995; Weick and Sutcliffe, 2001). The set of shared assumptions that develop over time in groups and organizations serves this stabilizing and meaning-providing function. The evolution of culture is therefore one of the ways in which a group or organization preserves its integrity and autonomy, differentiates itself from the environment and other groups, and provides itself an identity.

Unfreezing/Disconfirmation

If any part of the core cognitive structure is to change in more than minor incremental ways, the system must first experience enough disequilibrium to force a coping process that goes beyond just reinforcing the assumptions that are already in place. Lewin called the creation of such disequilibrium *unfreezing*, or creating a motivation to change. Unfreezing, as I have subsequently analyzed it, is composed of three very different processes, each of which must be present to a certain degree for the system to develop any motivation to change: (1) enough disconfirming data to cause serious discomfort and disequilibrium; (2) the connection of the disconfirming data to important goals and ideals, causing anxiety and/or guilt; and (3) enough psychological safety, in the sense of being able to see a possibility of solving the problem and learning something new without loss of identity or integrity (Schein, 1980, 2009b).

Transformative change implies that the person or group that is the target of change must *unlearn* something as well as learning something new. Most of the difficulties of such change have to do with the unlearning because what we have learned has become embedded in various routines and may have become part of our personal and group identity. The key to understanding "resistance to change" is to recognize that some behavior that has become dysfunctional for us may, nevertheless, be difficult to give up and replace because it serves other positive functions. Psychotherapists call this "secondary gain" as an explanation of why we sometimes continue to live with our neurotic behavior.

Disconfirmation is any information that shows the organization that some of its goals are not being met or that some of its processes are not accomplishing what they are supposed to: sales are off, customer complaints are up, products with quality problems are returned more frequently, managers and employees are quitting in greater numbers than usual, employees are sick or absent more and more, and so on. Disconfirming information can be economic, political, social, or personal—as when a charismatic leader chides a group for not living up to its own ideals and thereby induces guilt. Scandals or embarrassing leaks of information are often the most powerful kind of disconfirmation. However, the information is usually only symptomatic. It does not automatically tell the organization what the underlying problem might be, but it creates disequilibrium in pointing out that something is wrong somewhere. It makes members of the organization uncomfortable and anxious—a state that we can think of as *survival anxiety* in that it implies that unless we change, something bad will happen to the individual, the group, and/or the organization.

Survival anxiety does not, by itself, automatically produce a motivation to change because members of the organization can deny the validity of the information or rationalize that it is irrelevant. For example, if employee turnover suddenly increases, leaders or organization members can say, "It is only the bad people who are leaving, the ones we don't want anyway." Or if sales are down, it is possible to say, "This is only a reflection of a minor recession."

What makes this level of denial and repression likely is the fact that the prospect of learning new ways of perceiving, thinking, feeling, and behaving also creates anxiety—what we can think of as *learning anxiety*, a feeling that "I cannot learn new behaviors or adopt new attitudes without losing a feeling of self-esteem or group membership." *The reduction of this learning anxiety is the third and most important component of unfreezing—the creation of psychological safety.* The learner must come to feel that the new way of being is possible and achievable, and that the learning process itself will not be too anxiety provoking or demeaning.

For example, in the case of Amoco, the new reward and control system required engineers to change their self-image from being members of an organization to being self-employed consultants who now had to sell their services. The Amoco engineers simply could not imagine how they could function as freelance consultants; they had no skills along those lines. In the case of the Alpha Power Company, the electrical workers had to change their self-image from being employees who heroically kept power and heat on to being responsible stewards of the environment, preventing and cleaning up spills produced by their trucks or transformers. The new rules required them to report incidents that might be embarrassing to their group, and even to report on each other if they observed environmentally irresponsible behavior in fellow workers. But they were in a panic because they did not know how to diagnose environmentally dangerous conditions—how to determine, for example, whether a spill required a simple mop-up or was full of dangerous chemicals such as PCBs, or whether a basement was merely dusty or was filled with asbestos dust.

Sometimes disconfirming data have existed for a long time but because of a lack of psychological safety, the organization has avoided anxiety or guilt by denying the data's relevance, validity, or even its existence. It is our capacity both as individuals and as organizations to deny or even repress disconfirming data that makes whistle blowing or scandals such powerful change motivators. The failure to pay attention to disconfirming data occurs at two levels—leaders who are in a position to act deny or repress the data for personal psychological reasons, and/or the information is available in various parts of the organization but is suppressed in various ways. In the analysis of accidents, it is routinely found that some employees had observed various hazards and did not report them, were not listened to, or were actually encouraged to suppress their observations (Gerstein, 2008; Perin, 2005). The organizational dynamic is to deny information because to accept it would compromise the ability to achieve other values or goals, or would damage the self-esteem or face of the organization itself.

Survival Anxiety Versus Learning Anxiety

If the disconfirming data "get through" the learners' denial and defensiveness, they will recognize the need to change, the need to give up some old habits and ways of thinking, and the need to learn some new habits and ways of thinking. However, this produces learning anxiety. The interaction of these two anxieties creates the complex dynamics of change.

The easiest way to illustrate this dynamic is in terms of learning a new stroke in tennis or golf. The process starts with disconfirmation—you are not beating some of the people you are used to beating, or your aspirations for a better score or a better-looking game are not met, so you feel the need to improve your game. But, as you contemplate the actual process of unlearning your old stroke and developing a new stroke, you realize that you may not be able to do it, or you may be temporarily incompetent during the learning process. These feelings are "learning anxiety." Similar feelings arise in the cultural area when the new learning involves becoming computer competent; changing your supervisory style; transforming competitive relationships into teamwork and collaboration; changing from a high-quality, high-cost strategy into becoming the low-cost producer; moving from engineering domination and product orientation to a marketing and customer orientation; learning to work in nonhierarchical diffuse networks; and so on.

It is important to understand that learning anxiety can be based on one or more *valid* reasons:

- **Fear of loss of power or position:** The fear that with new learning, we will have less power or status than we had before.

- **Fear of temporary incompetence:** During the learning process, we will be unable to feel competent because we have given up the old way and have not yet mastered the new way. The best examples come from the efforts to learn to use computers.

- **Fear of punishment for incompetence:** If it takes a long time to learn the new way of thinking and doing things, we fear that we will be punished for lack of productivity. In the computer arena, there are some striking cases in which employees never learned the new system sufficiently to take advantage of its potential because they felt they had to remain productive and thus spent insufficient time on the new learning.

- **Fear of loss of personal identity:** We may not want to be the kind of people that the new way of working would require us to be. For example, in the early days of the break-up of the Bell System, many old-time employees left because they could not accept the identity of being a member of a hard-driving, cost-conscious organization that "would take phones away from consumers who could not afford them." Some electrical workers in Alpha Power resigned or retired because they could not stand the self-image of being environmental stewards.

- **Fear of loss of group membership:** The shared assumptions that make up a culture also identify who is in and who is out of the group. If by developing new ways of thinking or new behavior, we will become a deviant in our group, we may be rejected or even ostracized. This fear is perhaps the most difficult to overcome because it requires the whole group to change its ways of thinking and its norms of inclusion and exclusion.

One or more of these forces lead to what we end up calling *resistance to change*. It is usually glibly attributed to "human nature," but as I have tried to indicate, it is actually a rational response to many situations that require people to change. As long as learning anxiety remains high, an individual will be motivated to resist the validity of the disconfirming data or will invent various excuses why he or she cannot really engage in a transformative learning process right now. These responses come in the following stages (Coghlan, 1996):

1. **Denial:** Convincing ourselves that the disconfirming data are not valid, are temporary, don't really count, reflect someone just crying "wolf," and so on.

2. **Scapegoating, passing the buck, dodging:** Convincing ourselves that the cause is in some other department, that the data do not apply to us, and that others need to change first.

3. **Maneuvering, bargaining:** Wanting special compensation for the effort to make the change; wanting to be convinced that it is in our own interest, and will be of long-range benefit.

Given all of these bases of resistance to change, how then does the change leader create the conditions for transformative change? Two principles come into play:

- **Principle 1:** Survival anxiety or guilt must be greater than learning anxiety.
- **Principle 2:** Learning anxiety must be reduced rather than increasing survival anxiety.

From the change leader's point of view, it might seem obvious that the way to motivate learning is simply to increase the survival anxiety or guilt. The problem with that approach is that greater threat or guilt may simply increase defensiveness to avoid the threat or pain of the learning process. And that logic leads to the key insight about transformative change embodied in Principle 2: The change leader must *reduce learning anxiety* by increasing the learner's sense of psychological safety—the third component of unfreezing.

How to Create Psychological Safety

Creating psychological safety for organizational members who are undergoing transformational learning involves eight activities that must be carried on almost simultaneously. They are listed chronologically, but the change leader must be prepared to implement all of them.

1. **A compelling positive vision:** The targets of change must believe that the organization will be better off if they learn the new way of thinking and working. Such a vision must be articulated and widely held by

senior management and must spell out in clear *behavioral* terms what "the new way of working" will be. It must also be recognized that this new way of working is nonnegotiable.

2. **Formal training:** If the new way of working requires new knowledge and skill, members must be provided with the necessary formal and informal training. For example, if the new way of working requires teamwork, then formal training on team building and maintenance must be provided. As we will see, this will be especially relevant in multicultural groups.

3. **Involvement of the learner:** If the formal training is to take hold, the learners must have a sense that they can manage their own informal learning process. Each learner will learn in a slightly different way, so it is essential to involve learners in designing their own optimal learning process. The *goals* of learning are nonnegotiable, but the *method* of learning can be highly individualized.

4. **Informal training of relevant "family" groups, and teams:** Because cultural assumptions are embedded in groups, informal training and practice must be provided to whole groups so that new norms and new assumptions can be jointly built. Learners should not feel like deviants if they decide to engage in the new learning.

5. **Practice fields, coaches, and feedback:** Learners cannot learn something fundamentally new if they don't have the time, the resources, the coaching, and valid feedback on how they are doing. Practice fields are particularly important so that learners can make mistakes without disrupting the organization.

6. **Positive role models:** The new way of thinking and behaving may be so different from what learners are used to that they may need to be able to see what it looks like before they can imagine themselves doing it. They must be able to see the new behavior and attitudes in others with whom they can identify.

7. **Support groups in which learning problems can be aired and discussed:** Learners need to be able to talk about their frustrations and difficulties in learning with others who are experiencing similar difficulties

so that they can support each other and jointly learn new ways of dealing with the difficulties.

8. **Systems and structures that are consistent with the new way of thinking and working:** For example, if the goal of the change program is to learn how to be more of a team player, the reward system must be group oriented, the discipline system must punish individually aggressive selfish behavior, and the organizational structures must make it possible to work as a team.

Most transformational change programs fail because they do not create the eight conditions outlined here. And when we consider the difficulty of achieving all eight conditions and the energy and resources that have to be expended to achieve them, it is small wonder that changes are often short-lived or never get going at all. On the other hand, when an organization sets out to really transform itself by creating psychological safety, real and significant changes can be achieved.

When and how does culture become involved? The disconfirming data are only symptoms, which should trigger some diagnostic work, focusing on the underlying problem or issue that needs to be addressed. Before we even start to think about culture, we need to (1) have a clear definition of the operational problem or issue that started the change process, and to (2) formulate specific new behavioral goals. It is in this analysis that we may first encounter the need for some culture assessment to determine to what degree cultural elements are involved in the problem situation. At this point, an assessment of the kind I will describe in the next chapter first becomes relevant. It should not be undertaken, however, until some effort has been made to identify what changes are going to be made, what the "new way of working" will be to fix the problem, and how difficult and anxiety-provoking the learning of the "new way" will be (Coutu, 2002; Schein, 2009b).

After the desired changes have been made behaviorally specific, it is now relevant to ask: "How will the existing culture help us or hinder us?" Some form of cultural assessment now becomes relevant and will be described in detail in the next chapter. The remainder of this chapter must now examine how change actually takes place.

Cognitive Restructuring

After an organization has been unfrozen, the change process proceeds along a number of different lines that reflect either new learning, through trial and error based on *scanning* the environment broadly, or imitation of role models, based on psychological *identification* with the role model. The Amoco change initiative to redefine the roles of the engineers falls into the scanning model in that engineers had to figure out for themselves how to make the transition to the consulting role. Alpha's program of environmental responsibility was primarily a case of teaching employees how to follow procedures based on extensive training, which is based more on identification with role models. In either case, the essence of the new learning is some "cognitive redefinition" of some of the core concepts in the assumption set. For example, when companies which assume that they are lifetime employers who never lay anyone off are faced with the economic necessity to reduce payroll costs, they cognitively redefine layoffs as "transitions" or "early retirements," make the transition packages very generous, provide long periods of time during which the employees can seek alternative employment, offer extensive counseling, provide outplacement services, and so on, all to preserve the assumption that "we treat our people fairly and well." This process is more than rationalization. It is a genuine cognitive redefinition on the part of the senior management of the organization and is viewed ultimately as "restructuring."

Most change processes emphasize the need for behavior change. Such change is important in laying the groundwork for cognitive redefinition, but behavior change alone will not last unless it is accompanied by cognitive redefinition. For example, the Alpha environmental program began with the enforcement of rules but eventually became internalized as employees cognitively redefined their job/role and their identity. Some engineers at Amoco were able to redefine their self-image quickly and become comfortable with the new job structure.

Behavior change can be coerced at the beginning of a change program, but it will not last after the coercive force is lifted unless cognitive redefinition has preceded or accompanied it. Some change theories (for example, Festinger, 1957) argue that if behavior change is coerced for a long enough period of time, cognitive structures will adapt to rationalize the behavior change that is occurring. The evidence for this is not clear, however, as recent developments in former Communist countries reveal. People living under communism did not automatically become Communists even though they were coerced for fifty years or more.

Learning New Concepts and New Meanings for Old Concepts

If someone has been trained to think in a certain way and has been a member of a group that has also thought that way, how can that person imagine changing to a new way of thinking? As pointed out earlier, if you were an engineer in Amoco, you would have been a member of a division working as an expert technical resource with a clear career line and a single boss. In the new structure of a centralized engineering group "selling its services for set fees," you were now asked to think of yourself as a member of a consulting organization selling its services to customers who could purchase those services elsewhere if they did not like your deal. For you to make such a transformation would required you to develop several new concepts— "freelance consultant," "selling services for a fee," and "competing with outsiders who could underbid you." In addition, you would have to learn a new meaning for the concept of what it meant to be an "engineer" and what it meant to be an "employee of Amoco." You would have to learn a new reward system—that you would now be paid and promoted based on your ability to bring in work. You would have to learn to see yourself as much as a salesman as an engineer. You would have to define your career in different terms and learn to work for lots of different bosses.

Along with new concepts would come new standards of evaluation. Whereas in the former structure you were evaluated largely on the quality of your work, now you had to estimate more accurately just how many days a given job would take, what quality level could be achieved in that time, and what it would cost if you tried for the higher-quality standard you were used to. This might require a whole new set of skills of how to make estimates and create accurate budgets.

If standards do not shift, problems do not get solved. The computer designers at DEC who tried to develop products competitive with the IBM PC never changed their standards for evaluating what a customer expected.

They over-designed the products, building in far too many bells and whistles, which made them too expensive.

Imitation and Identification Versus Scanning and Trial-and-Error Learning

As I stated at the outset of this section, there are basically two mechanisms by which we learn new concepts, new meanings for old concepts, and new standards of evaluation—either we learn through imitating a role model and psychologically identifying with that person, or we keep inventing our own solutions until something works. The leader as change manager has a choice as to which mechanism to encourage. Imitation and identification work best when (1) it is clear what the new way of working is to be, and when (2) the concepts to be taught are themselves clear. For example, the leader can "walk the talk" in the sense of making himself or herself a role model of the new behavior that is expected. As part of a training program, the leader can provide role models through case materials, films, role-plays, or simulations. Learners who have acquired the new concepts can be brought in to encourage others to get to know how they did it. This mechanism is also the most efficient, but has the risk that what the learner learns does not integrate well into his or her personality or is not acceptable to the groups he or she belongs to. This means that the new learning may not be internalized, and the learner will revert to prior behavior after the coercive pressure to perform is no longer there.

If the change leader wants us to learn things that really fit into our personality, then we must learn to scan our environment and develop our own solutions. For example, Amoco could have developed a training program for how to be a consultant, built around engineers who had made the shift successfully. However, senior management felt that such a shift was so personal that they decided merely to create the structure and the incentives but to let individual engineers figure out for themselves how they wanted to manage the new kinds of relationships. In some cases, this meant people leaving the organization. But those engineers who learned from their own experience how to be consultants genuinely evolved to a new kind of career that they integrated into their total lives.

The general principle here is that the leader as change manager must be clear about the ultimate goals—the new way of working that is to be achieved—but that does not necessarily imply that everyone will get to that goal in the same way. Involvement of the learner does not imply that the learner has a choice about the ultimate goals, but it does imply that he or she has a choice of the means to get there.

Refreezing

The final step in any given change process is *refreezing*, by which Lewin meant that the new learning will not stabilize until it is reinforced by actual results. The Alpha employees discovered that not only could they deal with environmental hazards but that it was satisfying and worthwhile to do so, hence they internalized the attitude that a clean and safe environment was in everyone's interest even if it meant slowing jobs down when a hazard was encountered. If the change leaders have correctly diagnosed what behavior is needed to fix the problems that launched the change program, then the new behavior will produce better results and be confirmed.

If it turns out that the new behavior does not produce better results, this information will be perceived as disconfirming information and will launch a new change process. Human systems are, therefore, potentially in perpetual flux, and the more dynamic the environment becomes, the more that may require an almost perpetual change and learning process.

Principles in Regard to Culture Change

When an organization encounters disconfirming information and launches a change program, it is not clear at the outset whether culture change will be involved and how the culture will aid or hinder the change program. To clarify these issues, a culture assessment process of the kind described in the next chapter becomes appropriate. However, it is generally better to be very clear about the change goals before launching the culture assessment.

- **Principle 3:** The change goal must be defined concretely in terms of the specific problem you are trying to fix, not as "culture change."

For example, in the Alpha Power Company case, the court said that the company had to become more environmentally responsible and more open in its reporting. The change goal was to get employees (1) to become more aware of environmental hazards, (2) to report them immediately to the appropriate agencies, (3) to learn how to clean up the hazardous conditions, and (4) to learn how to prevent spills and other hazards from occurring in the first place. Whether or not the "culture" needed to be changed was not known when the change program was launched. Only as specific goals were identified could the change leaders determine whether or not cultural elements would aid or hinder the change. In fact, it turned out that large portions of the culture could be used positively to change some specific elements in the culture that did have to be changed. The fact that the entire workforce could be trained immediately in how to identify hazards and what to do about them was a reflection of the highly structured, technical, autocratic Alpha culture. The bulk of the existing culture was used to change some peripheral cultural elements.

One of the biggest mistakes that leaders make when they undertake change initiatives is to be vague about their change goals and to assume that "culture change" would be needed. When someone asks me to help him or her with a "culture change program," my most important initial question is "What do you mean? Can you explain your goals without using the word 'culture'?"

- **Principle 4:** Old cultural elements can be destroyed by eliminating the people who "carry" those elements, but new cultural elements can only be learned if the new behavior leads to success and satisfaction.

Once a culture exists, once an organization has had some period of success and stability, the culture cannot be changed directly unless the group itself is dismantled. A leader can impose new ways of doing things, can articulate new goals and means, and can change reward and control systems, but none of those changes will produce *culture* change unless the new way of doing things actually works better and provides the members a new set of shared experiences that eventually lead to culture change.

- **Principle 5:** Culture change is always transformative change that requires a period of unlearning that is psychologically painful.

Many kinds of changes that leaders impose on their organizations require only new learning and therefore will not be resisted. These are usually new behaviors that make it easier to do what we want to do anyway, such as learning a new software program to make our work on the computer more efficient. However, once we are adults and once our organizations have developed routines and processes that we have become used to, we may find that new proposed ways of doing things look like they will be hard to learn or will make us feel inadequate in various ways. We may feel comfortable with our present software and may feel that to learn a new system is not worth the effort. The change leader therefore needs a model of change that includes "unlearning" as a legitimate stage and that can deal with transformations, not just enhancements.

Summary and Conclusions

Culture change inevitably involves unlearning as well as relearning and is, therefore, by definition, transformative. This chapter describes a general change model that acknowledges from the outset the difficulty of launching any transformative change because of the anxiety associated with new learning. The change process starts with disconfirmation, which produces survival anxiety or guilt—the feeling that we must change—but the learning anxiety associated with having to change our competencies, our role or power position, our identity elements, and possibly our group membership causes denial and resistance to change. The only way to overcome such resistance is to reduce the learning anxiety by making the learner feel "psychologically safe." The conditions for creating psychological safety were described. If new learning occurs, it usually reflects "cognitive redefinition," which consists of learning new concepts, learning new meanings for old concepts, and adopting new standards of evaluation. Such new learning occurs either through identification with role models or through trial-and-error learning based on scanning the environment.

The change goals should initially be focused on the concrete problems to be fixed; and only when those goals are clear is it appropriate to do a culture assessment to determine how the culture will aid or hinder the change process. How such a culture assessment would be done is the topic of the next chapter.

18

CULTURE ASSESSMENT AS PART OF MANAGED ORGANIZATIONAL CHANGE

Chapters Sixteen and Seventeen described the various ways in which cultures evolve and change. Many of those changes are stimulated by leadership behavior such as promoting people with certain kinds of values and beliefs. When those kinds of activities are too slow, as when an organization is facing the need for rapid change, executive leaders turn to a managed change process, using the change model described in the previous chapter and the processes that are elaborated in my book, *Corporate Culture Survival Guide, 2d Ed.* (2009b). As was pointed out, culture will become implicated in such changes and sometimes becomes the direct target of change. It becomes necessary, then, to have a way of *assessing culture rapidly* so that the change leaders can determine how cultural elements will help them, will hinder them, or will become change targets in their own right.

Rapid Deciphering—A Multistep Group Process

The process that I will describe is designed to give the leaders of a change process a *rapid* way of deciphering elements of their own culture so that they can assess its relevance to their change program. I have often been asked to design a survey or do an interview program in this context and have always argued that this is neither necessary nor desirable. The group interview process described next is both faster and more valid because an interactive process gets to shared assumptions more quickly. This process is most useful in the context of a change program in which the *change goals have already been made explicit* so that the culture can be assessed as a potential aid or hindrance to the change program (Schein, 2009b). Without the change focus, this process can seem boring and pointless.

If I am asked to do a culture assessment, I always ask, "Why do you want to do this?" "What problem are you trying to solve?" "What do you mean by *culture*, and why do you think a culture assessment would be useful." The answers typically reveal some change agenda that the client has, and it is important to get the client to specify clearly what that change agenda is. After the client has identified in concrete terms what the desired "new way of working" is, the culture assessment can then be done rapidly (Schein, 2009b).

The essence of the assessment process is to bring together one or more representative groups in the organization, provide them a model of how to think about organizational culture and subcultures, and then ask them to identify the main artifacts, the espoused values, and the shared tacit assumptions, with an outsider playing the role of facilitator, documenter, and, when necessary, gadfly and question asker. A member of the organization in a leader role can be the facilitator, as long as it is not his or her own department and as long as he or she has an understanding of how culture works. This kind of assessment is based on several key assumptions:

- Culture is a set of *shared* assumptions; hence, obtaining the initial data in a *group* setting is more appropriate and valid than conducting individual interviews.

- The contextual meaning of cultural assumptions can only be fully understood by members of the culture; hence, creating a vehicle for *their understanding* is more important than for the researcher or consultant to obtain that understanding.

- Not all parts of a culture are relevant to any given issue the organization may be facing; hence, attempting to study an entire culture in all of its facets is not only impractical but also usually inappropriate.

- Insiders are capable of understanding and making explicit the shared tacit assumptions that make up the culture, but they need outsider help in this process. The helper/consultant should therefore operate primarily from a process-consulting model and should avoid, as much as possible, becoming an expert on the content of any given group's culture (Schein, 1999a, 2009a).

- Some cultural assumptions will be perceived as *helping* the organization to achieve its change goals or resolving its current issues, while others will be perceived as *constraints or barriers*; hence it is important for the group members to have a process that allows them to sort cultural assumptions into both of these categories.

- Changes in organizational practices to solve the problems that initiated the culture assessment can usually be achieved by building on existing assumptions; that is, the culture-deciphering process often reveals that new practices not only can be derived from the existing culture, but *should* be.

- If *changes in the culture* are discovered to be necessary, those changes will rarely involve the entire culture; it will almost always be a matter of changing one or two assumptions. Only rarely does the basic paradigm have to change, but if it does, the organization faces a multiyear major change process.

Step One: Obtaining Leadership Commitment

Deciphering cultural assumptions and evaluating their relevance to some organizational change program must be viewed as a major intervention in the organization's life and, therefore, must only be undertaken with the full understanding and consent of the formal leaders of the organization. This means not only probing why the leaders in an organization want to do this assessment but also fully describing the process and its potential consequences to obtain their full commitment to the group meetings that will be involved.

Step Two: Selecting Groups for Self-Assessment

The next step is for the facilitator to work with the formal leaders to determine how best to select some groups representative of the corporate culture. The criteria for selection usually depend on the concrete nature of the problem to be solved. Groups can either be homogeneous with respect to a given department or rank level or made deliberately heterogeneous by selecting diagonal slices from the organization. The group can be as small as three and as large as thirty. If important subcultures are believed to be operating, the process can be repeated with several different groups or samples of members can be brought in from different groups in order to test, in the meetings, whether the assumed differences exist.

The composition of the group is further determined by the client leaders' perceptions of the level of trust and openness in the organization, especially in regard to deciding whether senior people who might inhibit the discussion should be present. On the one hand, it is desirable to have a fairly open discussion, which might mean not mixing rank levels. On the other hand, it is critical to determine the extent to which the assumptions that eventually come out in the group meetings are shared across hierarchical levels, which argues for mixed rank groups. Because the level of trust and openness across various boundaries is itself a cultural characteristic, it is best to start with a heterogeneous group and let the group experience the extent to which certain areas of communication are or are not inhibited by the presence of others. Because authority relationships and level of intimacy are primary cultural dimensions, the process of group selection *with insiders* will itself reveal some important elements of the culture. The consultant/facilitator should use his or her interactions with members of the client system as diagnostic data throughout this planning process.

After groups have been chosen, the formal leader should inform the groups of the purpose of the meetings, review his or her conversations with the facilitator, and explain the basis on which people were chosen to attend. Just being summoned to a meeting to do a culture assessment is too vague. The participants must know what change problems are being worked on, and they must become aware that the leaders are committed to the assessment process. The leader should emphasize that openness and candor are needed, and that culture is not good or bad.

Step Three: Selecting an Appropriate Setting for the Group Self-Assessment

The group meeting should stimulate perceptions, thoughts, and feelings that are ordinarily implicit. The room in which the meeting is to be held must therefore be comfortable, allow people to sit in a circular format, and permit the hanging of many sheets of flip chart paper on which cultural elements will be written. In addition there should be available a set of breakout rooms in which subgroups can meet, especially if the basic group is larger than fifteen or so participants.

Step Four: Explaining the Purpose of the Group Meeting (15 mins.)

The meeting should start with a statement of the purpose of the meeting by someone from the organization who is perceived to be in a leadership or authority role, so that openness of response is encouraged. The organizational change problem should be clearly stated and written down, allowing for questions and discussion. The purpose of this step is not only to be clear as to *why* this meeting is being held but also to begin to get the group involved in the process.

The insider then introduces the process consultant as the "facilitator who will help us to conduct an assessment of how our organization's culture will help or constrain us in solving the problem or resolving the issue we have identified." The process consultant can be an outsider, a member of the organization who is part of a staff group devoted to providing internal consulting services, or even a leader from another department *if* he or she is familiar with how culture works and is familiar with this group process.

Step Five: A Short Lecture on How to Think About Culture (15 mins.)

It is essential for the group to understand that culture manifests itself at the level of artifacts and espoused values, but that the goal is to try to decipher the shared tacit assumptions that lie at a lower level of consciousness. The consultant should, therefore, present the three-level model of assumptions, espoused values, and basic assumptions shown in Chapter Two, and ensure that everyone understands that culture is a learned set of assumptions based on a group's shared history. It is important for the group to understand that what they are about to assess is a product of *their own history* and that the culture's stability rests on the organization's *past success.*

Step Six: Eliciting Descriptions of the Artifacts (60 mins.)

The process consultant then tells the group that they are going to start by describing the culture through its *artifacts.* A useful way to begin is to find out who has joined the group most recently and ask that person what it felt like to enter the organization and what she or he noticed most upon entering it. Everything mentioned is written down on a flip chart, and as the pages are filled, they are torn off and hung on the wall so that everything remains visible.

If group members are active in supplying information, the facilitator can stay relatively quiet, but if the group needs priming, the facilitator should suggest categories such as dress codes, desired modes of behavior in addressing the boss, the physical layout of the workplace, how time and space are used, what kinds of emotions someone would notice, how people get rewarded and punished, how someone gets ahead in the organization, how decisions are made, how conflicts and disagreements are handled, how work and family life are balanced, and so forth. The facilitator can use the categories reviewed in Chapters Five and Six to ensure that many different area of how things are done in the organization get discussed, but it is important *not* to give out such a list before a spontaneous group discussion has occurred because it may bias the group's perception of what is important. The consultant does not know initially what areas of the culture are especially salient and relevant and so should not bias the process of deciphering by providing a checklist. Noting later what areas do *not* come out spontaneously can itself be an indicator of cultural characteristics that are important but difficult to talk about.

This process should continue for about one hour or until the group clearly runs dry, and it should produce a long list of artifacts covering all sorts of areas of the group's life. Being visually surrounded by the description of their own artifacts is a necessary condition for the group to begin to stimulate its own deeper layers of thinking about what assumptions its members share.

Step Seven: Identifying Espoused Values (15-30 mins.)

The question that elicits artifacts is "*What* is going on here?" By contrast, the question that elicits espoused values is "*Why* are you doing what you are doing?" It is often the case that values will already have been mentioned during the discussion of artifacts so these should be written down on different pages. To elicit further values, I pick an area of artifacts that is clearly of interest to the group and ask people to articulate the reasons why they do what they do. For example, if they have said that the place is very informal and that there are few status symbols, I ask why. This usually elicits value statements such as "We value problem solving more than formal authority" or "We think that a lot of communication is a good thing" or even "We don't believe that bosses should have more rights than subordinates."

As values or beliefs are stated, I check for consensus; if there appears to be consensus, I write down the values or beliefs on the new chart pad. If members disagree, I explore why by asking whether this is a matter of different subgroups having different values or there is genuine lack of consensus, in which case the item goes on the list with a question mark to remind us to revisit it. I encourage the group to look at all the artifacts they have identified and to figure out as best they can what values seem to be implied. If I see some obvious values that they have not named, I will suggest them as possibilities—but in a spirit of *joint* inquiry, *not* as an expert conducting a content analysis of their data. After we have a list of values to look at, we are ready to push on to underlying assumptions.

Step Eight: Identifying Shared Underlying Assumptions (15–30 mins.)

The key to getting at the underlying assumptions is to check whether the espoused values that have been identified really explain all of the artifacts or whether things that have been described as going on have clearly *not* been explained or are in actual conflict with some of the values articulated. For example, the members of a group from Apple Computer conducted some cultural assessments in the 1980s for the purpose of identifying how their rate of growth would impact their organizational structure and needs for physical expansion. On the list of artifacts, they noted that they spend a great deal of time in planning and in documenting the plans, but that the plans usually got overridden by the needs of a here-and-now crisis. They had put *planning* on their list of espoused values and felt genuinely puzzled and ashamed that they followed through so little on the plans they had made. This raised the whole issue of how time was perceived, and, after some discussion, the group members agreed that they operated from a deeper shared assumption that could best be stated as "Only the present counts." Once they stated the assumption in this form, they immediately saw on their own artifact list other items that confirmed this and thought of several new artifacts that further reinforced their orientation toward and preoccupation with the immediate present.

The same group identified many different informal activities that members engaged in, including parties at the end of workdays, celebrations when products were launched, birthday parties for employees, joint travel to recreational areas such as ski resorts, and so on. The *value* they espoused was that they liked being with each other. But as we pondered the data, it became clear that a deeper *assumption* was involved, namely, "Business can and should be more than making money; it can and should be fun as well." Once this assumption was articulated, it immediately led the group to realize that a further assumption was operating: "Business not only should be more than just making money; it can and should be socially significant."

The latter assumption reminded the group members of a whole other set of artifacts concerning the value they put on their products, why they liked some products better than others, why they valued some of their engineers more than others, how their founders had articulated their original values, and so on. A whole new issue was raised about the pros and cons of selling to the government and to the defense industries versus continuing to focus on the education sector.

Once assumptions are made conscious, this usually triggers a whole new set of insights and begins to make sense of a whole range of things that previously had not made sense. Sometimes assumptions reconcile what the group may have perceived as value conflicts. For example, in doing this exercise, a group of human resource professionals at an insurance company identified as an important value "becoming more innovative and taking more risks as the environment changes," but the members could not reconcile this goal with the fact that very little actual innovation was taking place. In pushing deeper to the assumption level, they realized that throughout its history, the company had operated on two very central assumptions about human behavior: (1) People work best when they are given clear rules to cover all situations (among the artifacts the group had listed was a "mile-long shelf of procedure manuals"), and (2) people like immediate feedback and will not obey rules unless rule violation is immediately punished. Once the group stated these tacit assumptions, they realized that those assumptions were driving their behavior far more than the espoused value of innovation and risk taking. Not only was there no real positive incentive for innovating, in fact, it was risky because any false steps would immediately be punished. Another example was the previously cited case of the engineering group at HP that discovered that the espoused values of "teamwork" and "being nice to each other" were overruled by the tacit assumption that individualistic competitive behavior was the way to get things done and get ahead.

As assumptions surface, the facilitator should test for consensus and then write them down on a separate list. This list becomes important as the visible articulation of the cultural essences that have been identified. This phase of the exercise is finished when the group and the facilitator feel that they have identified most of the critical assumption areas, and participants are now clear on what an assumption is.

Step Nine: Identifying Cultural Aids and Hindrances (30-60 mins.)

If the group is small enough (fifteen to twenty), it should take this next step together. If the group is larger than twenty, it is best to divide it into two or three subgroups. The task for subgroups depends in part on what the presenting problems were, whether or not subcultures were identified in the large group exercise, and how much time is available. For example, if there was evidence in the large group meeting that there are functional, geographical, occupational, or hierarchical subcultures, the facilitator may want to send off subgroups that reflect those presumed differences and have each subgroup further explore its own assumption set. Or, if the facilitator finds that there is reasonable consensus in the large group on the assumptions identified, he or she can compose the subgroups randomly, by business unit, or by any other criterion that makes sense given the larger problem or issue that is being addressed.

In any case, the next task is to categorize the assumptions according to whether they will *aid or hinder the change process* that is being pursued. The group needs to review what the "new way of working" is and how the assumptions identified will help or hinder in getting there. It is very important to require the participants to look at assumptions from this dual point of view because of a tendency to see culture only as a constraint and thus put too much emphasis on the assumptions that will hinder. In fact, successful organizational change probably arises more from identifying assumptions that will aid than from changing assumptions that will hinder, but groups initially have a harder time seeing how the culture can be a source of positive help.

Step Ten: Decisions on Next Steps (30 mins.)

The purpose of this step is to reach some kind of consensus on what the important shared assumptions are and their implications for what the organization wants to do next. If there have been subgroups meeting, the process starts when the subgroups report their own separate analyses to the full group. If there is a high degree of consensus, the facilitator can go straight into a discussion of implications and next steps. More likely there will be some variations, and possibly disagreements, which will require some further inquiry and analysis by the total group with the help of the facilitator.

For example, the group may agree that there are strong subculture differences that must be taken into account. Or some of the assumptions may have to be reexamined to determine whether they reflect an even deeper level that would resolve disagreements. Or the group may come to recognize that for various reasons, it does not have many shared assumptions. In each case, the role of the facilitator is to raise questions, force clarification, test perceptions, and in other ways help the group achieve as clear a picture as possible of the assumption set that is driving the group's day-to-day perceptions, feelings, thoughts, and ultimately, behavior.

Once there is some consensus on what the shared assumptions are, the discussion proceeds to the implications of what has been identified. One of the biggest insights at this point comes from seeing how some of the assumptions will aid them, creating the possibility that their energy should go into strengthening those positive assumptions instead of worrying about overcoming the constraining ones. If, however, real constraints are identified, the group discussion then has to shift to an analysis of how culture can be managed and what it would take to overcome the identified constraints. At this point a brief further lecture on the material described in Chapters Sixteen and Seventeen may be needed to review some of the culture change mechanisms that are implied, and a new set of groups may be formed to develop a culture change strategy. Typically, this requires, at a minimum, an additional half-day with possibly new groups.

The process described so far can be done in a day or even less. It is not necessary to think of culture assessment as a slow, time-consuming process. It is not only more efficient to work in groups instead of doing individual interviews or surveys but, more importantly, the data are likely to be more valid because the deeper elements of culture only surface interactively and, having been produced in a group context, their validity can be tested immediately. Culture is a group phenomenon best assessed in a group context.

But there is an important possible limitation that has to be considered from a researcher's point of view—the results of the assessment may be completely clear to the insiders and still puzzling to the outsider. If the goal is to help the organization, this is okay. The outsider does not need to fully understand the culture. If, on the other hand, the researcher wants enough clarity to be able to represent the culture to others, additional observational data and group meetings are likely to be necessary.

What If Culture Elements Need to Change?

In my experience, the assessment process usually reveals that most of the culture will aid the change process. However, there may well be *elements* of the culture that are a barrier and require their own change program. For example, when the Alpha Power employees were required to identify and fix environmental hazards, this was recognized as a culture *change* in that it required employees to develop a different self-image and a different understanding of what their basic job was.

If the new required behavior involves changing the *norms of a subgroup* over which management may have only limited control, then a longer-range change process using a variety of tools may be necessary. For example, in Alpha Power, the ultimate goal of having employees monitor each other and *report on each other* if safety or environmental hazards are discovered runs into the deep assumption in the union subculture that "peers will not rat on each other." The goal in the company is ultimately to be able to rely on all employees to take full responsibility in this area and not to cover up dangerous behavior by fellow employees. That has resulted in a long-range change program built around involvement of the union and changes in both the reward and discipline system. Such a program where elements of subcultures need to change can take years and a variety of intensive efforts.

Consequently just announcing "a culture change" is meaningless until the change leadership has specified what the new behavior is to be and has differentiated those cultural elements that are under their direct behavioral control from those that require changes in the behavior of members of subcultures.

How these processes work themselves out in organizations is highly variable, as the next chapter will show. Subcultures are discovered, macrocultural assumptions affect what is defined as a crisis or business problem, culture assessments reveal that culture need not change at all if certain other business processes are fixed, and culture change goals are defined that may take years to accomplish successfully. Rather than make generalizations about this variety of issues, in the next chapter I will provide several short cases and one long case where I was involved and, therefore, knew what was really happening. Published cases are hard to decipher because I cannot know how much the author and/or consultant is using definitions similar to mine in telling the story. For example, Gerstner in his analysis of IBM's turnaround is widely credited with having achieved a major culture change in IBM, yet when you read his account carefully, it appears to be a case of getting IBM management to realize that they needed to get back to their roots, their effective sales/marketing culture (Gerstner, 2002). They had gone off course and become complacent, but their culture was viewed as a strength. So as you read the cases in the next chapter, be alert to the fact that *organizational change* is often no culture change at all or, at best, a change only in some elements of the culture.

Summary and Conclusions

The assessment process described and illustrated reflects a number of conclusions:

- Culture *can* be assessed by means of various individual and group interview processes, with group interviews being by far the better method in terms of both validity and efficiency. Such assessments can be usefully made by insiders in as little as a half-day.

- A culture assessment is of little value unless it is tied to some organizational problem or issue. In other words, assessing a culture for its own sake is not only too vast an undertaking but also can be viewed as boring and useless. On the other hand, when the organization has a purpose, a new strategy, a problem to be solved, or a change agenda, then to determine how the culture impacts the issue is not only useful but in most cases necessary. The issue should be related to the organization's effectiveness and should be stated in as concrete a way as possible. We cannot say that the culture itself is an issue or problem. The culture impacts how the organization performs, and the initial focus should always be on where the performance needs to be improved.

- The assessment process should first identify cultural assumptions, and then assess them in terms of whether they are a strength or a constraint on what the organization is trying to do. In most organizational change efforts, it is much easier to draw on the strengths of the culture than to overcome the constraints by changing the culture.

- In any cultural assessment process, we should be sensitive to the presence of subcultures and be prepared to do separate assessments of them to determine their relevance to what the organization is trying to do.

- For a culture assessment to be valuable, it must get to the assumptions level. If the client system does not get to assumptions, it cannot explain the discrepancies that almost always surface between the espoused values and the observed behavioral artifacts.

It should be noted that the ten-step group process described here is extremely fast. Within a few hours, a group can get a good approximation of what some of its major assumptions are. The facilitator may not understand the culture, but unless he or she is a researcher, it does not matter as long as the group can move forward on its change agenda. If it is important for the outsider/researcher to be able to describe the culture in more detailed terms, then additional observations, participant observation, and more group assessments need to be made until a complete picture emerges.

In the next chapter, I will provide several illustrations of the role of culture in organizational change processes and show where the assessment process aided the overall change program.

19

ILLUSTRATIONS OF ORGANIZATIONAL CULTURE CHANGES

The organizational examples that follow illustrate different aspects of managed culture change beginning with a case that did not require an assessment of the kind described in the previous chapter but highlights how behavior change can launch culture change. Later examples show how variations of the ten-step process fit into different kinds of organization change programs. The case of Ciba-Geigy, which closes the chapter, illustrates all the stages of change described in Chapter Seventeen and also raises the question of just what we mean when we say culture has changed.

Illustration 1. Beta Service Company—Rapid Change Through Behavior Modification

This case illustrates that behavior can be changed by leaders and, thereby, can launch an immediate culture change process. Two years ago, the head of organization development of Beta, a large urban utility, called to ask if I would do a culture assessment because the CEO and his Chief Operating Officer (COO) wanted to "change their culture." When I inquired what she meant, it was reported that "the culture was very old, rigid, bureaucratic, and, therefore, very inefficient." We agreed that I needed more information and that the best way to proceed would be to have the CEO, COO, and Head of Organization Development (OD) visit me to figure out the appropriate next steps.

We met at my house for a half-day session that began with asking them what they meant when they said their culture was "rigid." Both the CEO and COO complained that there were too many meetings, that there were too many processes that were designed long ago and were no longer relevant, and that subordinates were too rigid in their behavior. In general, it took too long to get anything done. I asked for concrete examples to learn more about what was really bothering them and to identify the business problem that was really motivating them to do any kind of change program.

The COO jumped into the conversation with the following tale:

"I'll give you an example. We have this regular staff meeting of fifteen senior managers that meets in a large room at headquarters. *Everyone always sits in the same chairs.* Just yesterday I attended the meeting and there were just five people there and they sat in the same seats all around this big room so that we had to shout at each other. It was ridiculous, what were they thinking, but that's just what is bothering me, this rigid behavior."

The CEO nodded and communicated that he concurred that this was a great example of the rigid culture. What happened next was quite revealing. I said to the COO:

"Well, when you were sitting there, feeling uncomfortable, what did you do?"

"I didn't do anything."

"Why not? Why did you tolerate this behavior if it made you uncomfortable?"

What was on my mind at this point was that the COO was the boss and chair of this committee and had the power to intervene directly. If he objected or made a suggestion to change things, the signal would go out to the rest of the organization that he wanted some changes.

Both the CEO and COO broke into a smile of insight. It suddenly dawned on them that by *not* acting they were perpetuating the very thing they were complaining about. They suddenly produced a whole stream of examples of rigidities that they could influence directly by mandating a new process and by demonstrating *changes in their own behavior.* The COO realized that he could have asked the five people to move to the front of the room, changed the meeting format, and announced new ways that he wanted things done.

Our meeting shifted immediately into a process-solving mode with all four of us thinking of ways that the CEO and COO could change their behavior, and how the head of OD could monitor their behavior, and provide feedback and suggestions on other innovations. The half-day meeting ended with a series of specific changes that they would make. In a telephone call several weeks later, I learned that all kinds of "culture changes" were occurring as a result of the changed behavior of the CEO and COO. Two years have passed, and when I met the CEO recently he affirmed that great changes were taking place and that "the new culture was working much better."

Lessons Learned

What leaders describe as cultures may not be embedded so deeply as to be impervious to being changed by new behaviors on the part of the leaders. It is therefore very important for the change consultant to identify the actual behaviors that the client wants to change. The assessment process can, as in this case, be quite informal and occur in the very first meeting with the client.

Illustration 2. MA-COM—Revising a Change Agenda as a Result of Cultural Insight

Culture assessment done for one purpose can reveal cultural elements that were not anticipated yet explain much of the observed behavior of the organization and its leaders. In this case, once the deeper and unanticipated elements of the culture were identified, the change agenda was revised toward a better solution.

A newly appointed CEO of MA-COM, a high-tech company that consisted of ten or more divisions, asked me to help him figure out how the organization could develop a "common culture." He felt that its history of decentralized autonomous divisions was now dysfunctional and that the company should work toward a common set of values and assumptions. The CEO, the director of human resources, and I were the planning group to decide how to approach the problem. We reached the conclusion that all of the division directors, all of the heads of corporate staff units, and various other individuals who were considered to be relevant to the discussion would be invited to an all-day meeting whose purpose was to identify the elements of a common culture for the future. Thirty people attended the meeting.

We began with the CEO stating his goals and why he had asked the group to come together. He introduced me as the person who would stage-manage the day, but made it clear that we were working on his agenda. I then gave a thirty-minute lecture on how to think about culture and launched into the assessment process described in the previous chapter by asking some of the less-senior people in the group to share what it was like to enter this company. As people brought out various artifacts and norms, I wrote them down on flip charts and hung up the filled pages around the room. It appeared clear that there were powerful divisional subcultures, but it was also clear that there were many common artifacts across the group. My role, in addition to writing things down, was to ask for clarification or elaboration as seemed appropriate to me.

As we worked into our second and third hours, some central value conflicts began to emerge. The various divisional units really favored the traditional assumption that high degrees of decentralization and divisional autonomy were the right way to run the overall business, but at the same time, they longed for strong centralized leadership and a set of core values that they could rally around as a total company. My role at this point was to help the group confront this conflict and to try to understand both its roots and its consequences. We broke at lunchtime and instructed randomly selected subgroups of seven to eight members to continue the analysis of values and assumptions for a couple of hours after lunch, and then met at around three o'clock for a final two-hour analysis and wrap-up session.

To start off the final session, each group gave a brief report of the assumptions that it felt aided and those it felt hindered achievement of a common corporate culture. In these presentations, the same divisional-versus-corporate conflict kept emerging, so when the reports were done, I encouraged the group to dig into this a little more. Because some mention had been made of strong founders, I asked the group to talk further about how the divisions had been acquired. This discussion led to a major insight. It turned out that almost every division had been acquired with its founder still in place; the corporate headquarters policy of granting autonomy to divisions had encouraged those founders to stay on as CEOs even though they had given up ownership.

Most of the managers in the room had grown up under those strong leaders and had enjoyed that period of their history very much. Now, however, all the founders had retired, left, or died, and the divisions were led by general managers who did not have the same charisma the founders had. What the group longed for was the *sense of unity and security* they each had had in their respective divisions under their founders. They did not, in fact, want a strong *corporate* culture and leadership because the businesses of the divisions were really quite different. What they wanted was stronger leadership at the *divisional* level but the same degree of divisional autonomy that they had always had. They realized that their desire for a stronger corporate culture was misplaced.

These insights, based on historical reconstruction, led to a very different set of proposals for the future. The group, with the blessing of corporate leadership, agreed that they only needed a few common corporate policies in areas such as public relations, human resources, and research and development. They did not need common values or assumptions, though if such developed naturally over time that would be fine. On the other hand, they wanted stronger leadership at the divisional level and a development program that would maximize their chances to obtain such leadership. Finally, they wanted to strongly reaffirm the value of divisional autonomy to enable them to do the best possible job in each of their various businesses.

Lessons Learned

This case illustrates the following important points about deciphering culture and managing cultural assumptions:

- A senior management group with the help of an outside facilitator is able to decipher key assumptions that pertain to a particular business problem—in this case, whether or not to push for a more centralized common set of values and assumptions.

- The cultural analysis can reveal several assumptions that were centrally related to the business problem, as judged by the participants. However, other elements of the culture that were clearly revealed in the artifacts were judged to be not relevant. Inasmuch as every culture includes assumptions about virtually everything, it is important to have an assessment technique that permits individuals to set priorities and to discover what aspects of a culture are relevant.

- The resolution of the business problem did not require any culture change. In fact, the group reaffirmed one of its most central cultural assumptions. In this context, the group did, however, define some new priorities for future action—to develop common policies and practices in certain business areas and to develop stronger divisional leaders. Often what is needed is a *change in business practices within the context of the given culture*, not necessarily a change in culture.

Illustration 3. U.S. Army Corps of Engineers–Reassessing Mission

This case example illustrates the culture-deciphering process in a different type of organization. As part of a long-range strategy-planning process, I was asked in 1986 to conduct an analysis of the culture of the U.S. Army Corps of Engineers because of concerns that their mission was changing, and they were uncertain what future sources of funding would be. In attendance were the twenty-five or so senior managers, both military and civilian, with the specific purpose of analyzing their culture to (1) remain adaptive in a rapidly changing environment, (2) conserve those elements of the culture that are a source of strength and pride, and (3) manage the evolution of the organization realistically. The managers knew that the Corps's fundamental mission had changed over the past several decades and that the survival of the organization hinged on getting an accurate self-assessment of its strengths and weaknesses.

We followed the ten-step assessment procedure, and the discussion developed the following themes, stated as either key values or assumptions, depending on how the group itself experienced that element:

- Our mission is to solve problems of river control, dams, bridges, and so forth pragmatically, not aesthetically, but our responsiveness to our environment leads to aesthetic concerns within the context of any given project.
- We always respond to crisis and are organized to do so.
- We are conservative and protect our turf but value some adventurism.
- We are decentralized and expect decisions to be made in the field but control the field tightly through the role of the district engineer.
- We are numbers driven and always operate in terms of cost/benefit analyses, partly because quality is hard to measure.

- We minimize risk because we must not fail; hence things are over-designed, and we use only safe, well-established technologies.
- We exercise professional integrity and say no when we should.
- We try to minimize public criticism.
- We are responsive to externalities but attempt to maintain our independence and professional integrity.
- We are often an instrument of foreign policy through our non-U.S. projects.

The group identified as its major problem that the traditional mission of flood control was largely accomplished, and, with changing patterns in Congress, it was not easy to tell what kinds of projects would continue to justify the budget. Financial pressures were seen to cause more projects to be cost-shared with local authorities, requiring degrees of collaboration that the Corps was not sure it could handle. The culture discussion provided useful perspectives on what was ahead but did not provide clues as to the specific strategy to pursue in the future.

Lessons Learned

This case, like the others, illustrates that we can get a group to decipher major elements of its culture and that this can be a useful exercise in clarifying what is strategically possible. It is also evident once again that a culture assessment need not lead to culture change even though that might have been an initial goal.

Illustration 4. Apple Computer–Culture Assessment as Part of a Long-Range Planning Process

Apple Computer decided in 1991 to conduct a cultural analysis as part of a long-range planning exercise focused on human resource issues. How big would the company be in five years, what kind of people would it need, and where should it locate itself geographically under different size scenarios? A ten-person working group, consisting of several line managers and several members of the human resource function, was assigned the task of figuring out how Apple's culture would influence growth and what impact it might have on the kinds of people who would be attracted to it in the future. The vice president for human resources knew of my work on culture and asked me to be a consultant to this working group. He functioned as its chairman.

The original plan was to sort out various planning tasks and delegate these to other committees for more detailed work because the presentation to the company meeting was six months off. One of these other groups was charged with analyzing the impact of Apple's culture on future growth. My role was to help organize the study, teach the group how best to study culture, and consult with the culture subcommittee down the line.

The first meeting of the group was scheduled for a full day and involved the planning of several different kinds of activities, of which the culture study was just one. When it came to deciding how to study the Apple culture, I had twenty minutes in which to describe the model of artifacts, espoused values, and basic underlying assumptions. I also described in general terms how I had used the model with other organizations to help them decipher their culture. The group was intrigued enough to accept my next suggestion, which was to try the ten-step process in this group. The group agreed, so after the twenty-minute lecture, we launched directly into uncovering artifacts and values. It was easy for the group to mix the analysis of assumptions, values, and artifacts, so we ended up rather quickly with a provisional set of tacit assumptions backed by various kinds of data that the group generated. These were written down in draft form on flip charts, which I organized into a more ordered set of what we ended up calling Apple's "governing assumptions":

1. We are not in the business for the business alone but for some higher purpose—to change society and the world, create something lasting, solve important problems, have fun.

One of Apple's major products was designed to help children learn. Another major product was designed to make computing easier and more fun. Apple engaged in many rituals designed to be fun, for example, after-hours parties, playfulness at work, and magic shows at executive-training events. The group felt that only what is fun and what is unique gets the big rewards.

It was alleged that many people at Apple would object if the company went after the broad business market and if it sold products to selected groups who would misuse the product (for example, the Department of Defense).

2. Task accomplishment is more important than the process used or the relationships formed.

The group listed several versions of this assumption:

- When you fail at Apple, you are alone and abandoned; you become a "boat person."
- Seniority, loyalty, and past experience don't count relative to present task achievements.
- When you trip, no one picks you up.
- Out of sight, out of mind; you are only as good as your latest hit; relationships formed at work do not last.
- People are so intent on their mission that they don't have time for you or to form relationships.
- Bonding occurs only around tasks and is temporary.
- Groups are security blankets.
- Apple is a club or a community, not a family.

3. The individual has the right and obligation to be a total person.

This showed up as the following assumptions:

- Individuals are powerful, can be self-sufficient, and can create their own destiny.
- A group of individuals motivated by a shared dream can do great things.
- People have an inherent desire to be their best and will go for it.
- Apple neither expects company loyalty from individuals nor expects to guarantee employment security to individuals.
- Individuals have the right to be fully themselves at work, to express their own personality and uniqueness, to be different.
- There is no dress code and no restriction on how personal space is decorated.

- Children or pets can be brought to work.
- Individuals have the right to have fun, to play, to be whimsical.
- Individuals have the right to be materialistic, to make lots of money, and to drive fancy cars no matter what their formal status.

4. Only the present counts.

This assumption was discussed earlier, but it had some other ramifications, expressed as norms and artifacts:

- Apple has no sense of history or concern for the future.
- Seize the moment; the early bird gets the worm.
- Apple is not a lifetime employer.
- Longer-range plans and tasks get discussed but not done.
- People do not build long-range, cross-functional relationships.
- Nomadic existence inside Apple is normal; people don't have offices, only "campsites" and "tents."
- The physical environment is constantly rearranged.
- It is easier to fix things than to plan for perfection; flexibility is our greatest skill.
- People are forgotten quickly if they leave a project or the company.
- "We learn by doing."

These governing assumptions and the supporting data were passed on to the subcommittee dealing with the Apple culture, where they were tested and refined with further interviews. Interestingly enough, after several more months of work, no substantial changes had been made to the list, suggesting that a group can get at the essentials of its culture very rapidly.

Lessons Learned

This case illustrates the following important points:

- If a motivated insider group is provided with a process for deciphering its culture, members can rather quickly come up with some of their most central governing assumptions. I revisited Apple several years after this event and was shown a recent report on the company's culture.

The same set of assumptions was written down in this report as still being the essence of the culture, though the various assumptions were stated in somewhat different order and with some additional comments about areas that needed to change. I have no current data on the Apple culture, but their range of products and the way their stores are run suggests that the earlier description is still valid, especially with one of its founders returning as CEO.

- Stating these governing assumptions allowed the company managers to assess where their strategy might run into cultural constraints. In particular, they realized that if they were to grow rapidly and enter the broad business market, they would have to deal with members of their organization who grew up under the assumption that business should involve more than just making money. They also realized that they lived too much in the present and would have to develop longer-range planning and implementation skills.

- Apple reaffirmed its assumptions about task primacy and individual responsibility by starting to articulate explicitly a philosophy of no mutual obligation between the company and its employees. When lay-offs became necessary, the company simply announced them without apology and carried them out. Apple was one of the first companies to articulate that *employment* security would gradually have to give way to *employability* security, by which they meant that an individual would learn enough during some years at Apple to be attractive to another employer if laid off. There should be no loyalty in either direction, in that employees should feel free to leave if a better opportunity came along. Where, then, would commitment and loyalty reside? In the project.

Illustration 5: Ciba-Geigy—Did the Culture Change?

This case examines a major multiyear turnaround that was designed to fix a great many problems that Ciba-Geigy had generated in the 1970s and that was viewed at the time as a real example of culture change. The story illustrates many of the mechanisms discussed in the preceding chapters but also raises some fundamental questions about whether or not real culture change took place at Ciba-Geigy.

In the earlier description of the Ciba-Geigy paradigm, I tried to show how certain deep shared assumptions related to each other, and how that pattern of assumptions explained a great deal of the day-to-day behavior of the organization. In this analysis, I also want to show how a change process revealed some of the elements of the Ciba-Geigy culture and how that culture did and did not change, even as the organization changed. In laying out the case, it will also become clearer what I mean by a clinical approach to studying culture. I will present data from Ciba-Geigy along with contrasting observations from other cases to illustrate, through concrete events, how the change process unfolds and how the consultant gets involved with it.

Initial Contact and First Annual Meeting

My involvement with Ciba-Geigy began in 1979 with a major "educational intervention" for the top management group at its annual worldwide meeting. Dr. Leupold, the manager of Ciba-Geigy's management development function, had heard me speak at a 1978 open seminar on career development and career anchors (Schein, 1978, 1993b). He suggested to his boss, Sam Koechlin, the chairman of the executive committee (the group accountable for the company's performance), that my material on career dynamics might be worth sharing with Ciba-Geigy's senior management.

Koechlin's goal for the annual meeting was to combine work on company problems with some stimulating input for the group, broadly in the area of leadership and creativity. He saw that the company was moving into a more turbulent economic, political, and technological environment that would require new kinds of responses. Koechlin was a descendant of one of the Swiss founding families of the company but had spent ten years of his career in the U.S. subsidiary and had come to appreciate that the more dynamic U.S. environment stimulated a level of creativity that he saw as lacking in the home country. His own educational background was not in science but in law. He was a good example of the kind of marginal leader who could simultaneously be in his culture, yet perceive it somewhat objectively. His bringing of various outside speakers into the annual meeting was a deliberate attempt to broaden the perception of his top management. My two days of lecturing were to be focused on leadership and creativity in the context of individual career development.

Both the topic of creativity and the approach of lecturing to the group were completely congruent with Ciba-Geigy's assumptions that (1) creativity is important in science, (2) knowledge is acquired through a scientific process, and (3) knowledge is communicated through experts in a didactic way. By way of contrast, in the pragmatic environment at DEC, it would have been inconceivable to devote two whole days of senior management time to a seminar involving primarily outside lecturers, and the topic of creativity would not have interested the senior managers—it would have been viewed as much too abstract.

In Ciba-Geigy, everything was planned to the level of the smallest detail. After Koechlin and Leupold had agreed between themselves on the general topic, it was necessary for me to meet Koechlin to see whether my general approach and personal style were compatible with what he was looking for. I was invited to spend a day and night at his house outside of Basel, where I also met his wife. Koechlin and I got along well, so it was agreed that we would go ahead with my sessions at the 1979 annual meeting in Merlingen, Switzerland.

Some weeks later, a Mr. Kunz visited me at MIT to discuss the details. Kunz was the seminar administrator responsible for the detailed agenda of the three days, and, as it turned out, also had to indoctrinate me on how to deal with this group. He had been a line manager who had moved into executive training, but, by virtue of his prior experience, was familiar with the expectations of senior line management. Kunz met with me at MIT for many hours some months prior to the seminar to plan for the materials to be used, the exercise to be designed to involve the participants, the schedule, and so on.

In this process, I observed firsthand how carefully Ciba-Geigy managers planned for every detail of an activity for which they were responsible. I had to provide a plan in writing that showed virtually minute by minute what would happen during the two days, and the company was clearly willing to commit all the time and energy it might take to design as nearly perfect a meeting as possible. Not only was Ciba-Geigy's high degree of commitment to structure revealed in this process, but, in retrospect, it also revealed how basic the assumption was about managerial turf. Kunz had clear responsibility for the conduct of the meeting, though he was two levels below the participants in the hierarchy. He had formed a review

committee, including Koechlin and some members of the executive committee, to review the seminar plan and to obtain their involvement, but
this group gave considerable freedom to Kunz to make final decisions on
seminar format. Thus, the culture was displaying itself in the manner in
which I encountered the organization, but I did not know this at the time.

The participants at the Ciba-Geigy annual meeting were the chairman of the external board, Koechlin's boss, several board members who
showed up as visitors, the nine-person executive committee, all the
senior functional and divisional managers, and the most important country managers—a total of forty-five. This group met annually for five days
or less, depending on the specific agenda to be covered.

Though I did not know it at the time, the meeting served a major integrative and communication function in that it legitimized during the meeting what culturally did not happen in day-to-day operations—a high level
of *open* and *lateral* communication. It also reflected the hierarchical emphasis, however, in that this sharing across units took place in public under the
scrutiny of the executive committee and board members. Moreover, there
was still a strong tendency to be deferential toward others and to share ideas
only when information was specifically asked for. The meeting also provided an opportunity for senior management to get a major message across
quickly to the entire organization and, as we will see, to involve the entire
organization in crisis management when that was needed.

The meeting took place at a pleasant Swiss mountain resort and, as
described earlier, always included a special recreational event that helped the
group loosen up with each other. My talks were delivered on the second and
third day, and I included in the day's activities a set of mutual interviews on
career histories to help participants to determine their "career anchors." I put
creativity into the context of innovation—especially "role innovation"—
to highlight that scientific creativity was by no means the only kind, and
that managers in any role could become more innovative in their approach.
Determining the career anchor requires pairs of people to interview each
other about their educational and career history (Schein, 2006). I asked
people to pair themselves up in any way that seemed comfortable to them
to avoid having to make up formal pairs that might bring people together
who would not be comfortable sharing with each other. The chairman of
the board enthusiastically participated, and thereby set a good tone for the

meeting. When I was not lecturing, I was encouraged to participate by getting to know more of the people and attending planning meetings.

I learned on the third day that the fun activity would be crossbow shooting. Early in the afternoon, we all boarded buses and were taken twenty-five miles to a site where crossbow shooting was being done recreationally, and each of us had to take our turn trying to learn to hit a target with this rather novel and different weapon. The activity reduced everyone to the same level of incompetence and thereby provided an opportunity for much teasing across hierarchical boundaries. Following the crossbow shooting, we were all bussed to a nearby castle where a large, informal dinner, accompanied by much wine and beer, topped off the day. At this dinner, the chairman spoke very informally and made reference to his career anchor, thereby legitimating the previous day's input, and again illustrating how ready the group was to listen to authority and use academic inputs.

Impact of First Annual Meeting.   The three major effects of this meeting, were as follows:

- The group obtained new insights and information about creativity and innovation, especially the insight that innovation occurs within a variety of careers and organizational settings and should not be confused with the pure creative process that scientists are engaged in. The assumption had crept in that only scientists are creative, so those managers who had left their technical identities behind long ago were reassured by my message that managerial role innovations in all the functions of the business were much needed in a healthy organization. This legitimized as "creative" a great many activities that had previously not been perceived as such and liberated some problem-solving energy by linking innovation to day-to-day problem solving. This insight would not have been all that important but for the fact that the group was so embedded in assumptions about science and the creative process within science. I learned later that it was Koechlin's intention all along to broaden the group's perspective and to lay the groundwork for changes that he had in mind.

- The group obtained new insights from the discussion of career anchors, which emphasized the variety of careers and the different things people are looking for in their careers. The effect was to unfreeze some of the monolithic notions about careers and the role of scientific backgrounds in careers. The chairman's humorous talk legitimized the notion of individual differences in careers, particularly since the chairman was a lawyer, not a scientist.

- The group got to know me and my style as a responsive process consultant through several spontaneous interventions that I made during the three days. In particular, I was allowed to attend Kunz's planning committee meetings to review each day's activities and found in that context a number of occasions on which my ideas for process and design facilitated the group's planning. Koechlin and other members of the executive committee were able to observe that a process consultant could be very helpful at a meeting.

During the informal times at meals and in the evening, my spontaneous responses were geared to getting out of the expert role. For example, if I was asked "what are companies doing today in the field of participative management," I would give some examples and highlight the *diversity* of what I observed rather than generalizing as I was expected to do. I had the sense that in this process I was disappointing some of the managers with whom I was speaking because I did not fit the stereotype of the scientist who is willing to summarize the state of knowledge in a field. On the other hand, my willingness to delve into the problems of Ciba-Geigy appealed to some managers, and they accepted my self-definition as a process consultant rather than an expert consultant.

Toward the end of the meeting, plans were made to institute career planning and job/role planning in broad segments of the company. Specifically, Koechlin and the executive committee decided to ask all senior managers to do the "job/role planning exercise," which involves each person rethinking his or her own job in the context of how it has changed and will continue to change as he or she projects ahead five years and analyzes the environment around the job (Schein, 1978, 1995, 2006). Koechlin also encouraged more managers to do the "career anchor interview exercise" as an input to the annual management development process and authorized the development of an adaptation of the original interview questionnaire for use specifically in the company. I was asked to work with the headquarters management development group to help implement these two activities by spending roughly ten to fifteen days during the subsequent year as a consultant. My clients were to be Leupold, the management development manager, and Koechlin; the broad mission was to increase the ability of the company to innovate.

First Year's Work: Getting Acquainted with the Culture. I visited the company several times during the year, each time for two to three days. During these visits I learned more about the management development system, met some of the members of the executive committee, and gradually got involved in what I considered to be my most important activity: the planning of the next annual meeting. From my point of view, if innovation was to take hold, the most important thing to take advantage of was the relatively more open climate of the annual meeting. My goal was to be accepted as a process consultant to the entire meeting, not as an educator coming in with wisdom for one or two days.

But the notion that I could help "on line" continued to be quite foreign to most of the managers, though at DEC I had learned the opposite lesson: unless I worked on line with real problems, the group considered me more or less useless. Initially I thought that the reactions of Ciba-Geigy's managers were simply based on misunderstanding. It was only with repeated experiences of not being invited to working meetings at Ciba-Geigy, of always being put into an expert role, and of always having to plan my visits in great detail that I realized I was up against something that could be genuinely defined as cultural. The Ciba-Geigy managers' perception of what consultants do and how they work reflected their more general assumptions about what managers do and how they work.

For example, as I mentioned in the opening chapter, I noticed that managers whom I had met on previous visits looked past me and ignored me when I encountered them in the public lobby or the executive dining room. I later learned that to be seen with a consultant meant that one had problems and needed help—a position that managers in Ciba-Geigy strongly avoided. I could only be accepted in a role that fit Ciba-Geigy's model, that of educator and expert to management as a whole. The point is important because my request to attend the next annual meeting in a process consultant role was, unbeknownst to me, strongly countercultural.

But Koechlin was intrigued, and his own innovativeness swayed other members of the planning committee to accept me in that role. Through his own behavior, he was beginning to lay the groundwork for some new ways of looking at things.

We compromised by agreeing that I would also give some lectures on relevant topics based on the events I observed at the meeting, thus legitimizing my attendance. My role as a consultant was further legitimized by my being cast as a scientist who had to be given an opportunity to get to know top management better, so that I could be more helpful in the future. Koechlin and other senior managers had a specific view of what the total group needed, and they were prepared to introduce an outsider in the consultant role to facilitate this process. I came to realize that they wanted to unfreeze the group to get it to be more receptive to the crisis message they were preparing to deliver. An outsider with new ideas was seen as helpful in this process, both as a source of feedback to the group and as an expert on the change process that was about to be launched.

Another outsider, a professor of policy and strategy who also occupied a position on the board of Ciba-Geigy, was invited as well. Our attendance at the meeting was related to a decision made by Koechlin and the executive committee that at the 1980 annual meeting a major review of company performance, division by division, would be undertaken. Such a review, they believed, would bring out the need for major change and innovation and, thereby, reverse a slide into unprofitability that had been going on but was not clearly recognized or accepted. They also planned to introduce a program of change called "the redirection project."

This business problem had been developing over several years but had not yet been identified as a crisis to be collectively shared with senior management worldwide. The major product divisions of the company were the primary profit centers, but, as I indicated before, were not likely to communicate much with each other, even though their headquarters were all in Basel. These divisions knew what their individual situations were but seemed unaware of the impact on the company as a whole of dropping profit levels in many areas. Only the executive committee had the total picture.

This situation could easily arise because of the low amount of lateral communication, permitting the manager of a division that was losing money to rationalize that his loss was easily compensated for by the profits of other divisions and that things would soon improve. The culture encouraged each manager to worry only about his own piece of the organization, not to take a broad corporate view. Although communications that had gone out to the divisions over the year had suggested a total company problem, no one seemed to take it very seriously. Therefore, much of the annual meeting was to be devoted to selling the idea that there was a total company problem and helping managers, in small group meetings, to accept and deal with those problems.

Given these goals, the planning committee saw the point of having me help in the design of the meeting and to plan lectures, as needed, on how to initiate and manage various change projects. In other words, the economic and market environment was creating a financial crisis, top management decided it was time to deal with it, and the consultation process became one piece of management's more general process of launching the redirection project.

Unfreezing at the Second Annual Meeting. The first segment of the meeting was devoted to presenting financial data, division by division, followed by small group meetings to digest and analyze the situation and formulate proposals for reversing the business decline. What made the situation complicated was that some of the divisions—those operating in mature markets—were losing money and needed major restructuring, while other divisions were growing and making good contributions to overall profit levels. The division managers from the problem divisions were embarrassed, apologetic, and overconfident that they could reverse the situation, while others said privately that the losing divisions could not possibly accomplish their goals, were not really committed to change, and would make only cosmetic alterations.

The division managers from the profitable divisions bragged, felt complacent, and wondered when top management would do something about the "losers" who were dragging others down with them. But many people from the losing divisions and from top management said privately that even the profitable divisions, although they might look good relative to others inside the company, were not performing as well as they should compared to outside competitors in their own industrial market segments. Clearly it was up to the hierarchy to fix this problem, as the divisions saw it.

During the divisional reviews and presentations, another important cultural assumption surfaced. The company had been diversifying for a number of years and was attempting to get into consumer goods via the recent acquisition in the United States of Airwick. I learned during the Airwick product review how strongly Ciba-Geigy's self-image revolved around "important" products that cured diseases and prevented starvation. Selling something only because it made money did not fit into some of their cultural assumptions about the nature of their business, and dealing with an organization whose processes were primarily geared to marketing made them uneasy. It was no surprise, therefore, when in 1987 this division was sold off even though it was profitable.

The country managers, representing subsidiary companies in the major countries of the world, acknowledged the cross-divisional issues but were actually more upset by the fact that the headquarters organization—representing such functions as research and development, finance and control, personnel, and manufacturing—had become overgrown. These managers insisted that the headquarters functional staffs should be reduced because they were an unnecessary overhead and, in many cases, an active interference in running the businesses in the countries. A high degree of centralization of research and development, manufacturing, and financial control had made sense when the company was young and small; but as it expanded and became a worldwide multinational, the small regional sales offices had gradually become large autonomous companies that managed all the functions locally.

Country heads needed their own staffs, but these staffs then came into conflict with the corporate staffs and the division staffs, who felt that they could communicate directly with their division people in each country. Because of the hierarchical nature of the organization, the headquarters groups asked for enormous amounts of information from the regions and frequently visited the regions. They felt that if they had worldwide responsibility for something, they had to be fully informed about everything at all times. Because of the lack of lateral communication, the functional staffs did not realize that their various inquiries and visits often paralyzed local operations because of the amount of time it took to answer questions, entertain visitors, get permission to act, and so on.

As the cost structure of the company came under increasing scrutiny, the country organizations were asked to reduce costs, while the headquarters organizations remained complacent, fat, and happy. The question that most worried the country managers was whether top management considered the profit erosion serious enough to warrant reductions in the headquarters functional staffs. If not, it must mean that this was only a fire drill, not a real crisis.

Inducing Survival Anxiety. By the end of the first day of the meeting, the disconfirming financial data had been presented, and groups had met to consider what should be done, but the feedback from the groups indicated neither a complete understanding nor a real acceptance of the problem. There was clearly insufficient anxiety or guilt. The planning committee met to consider what to do and decided that the other consultant could help the group recognize the seriousness of the problem if he interrogated the group members in the style of a Harvard case discussion and led them to the inevitable conclusion that a crisis really existed. He did this very effectively on the second day of the meeting in a two-hour session that proved conclusively to all present that the group could not remain profitable in the long run unless major changes were made. The result was a real sense of survival anxiety and depression. For the first time, the message had really been accepted collectively, setting the stage for the introduction of the redirection project.

Why did this work? I had the sense that, in a culture where senior managers function symbolically as parent figures, it is difficult for the parents to tell the children that the family may fail if they don't shape up. The children find it too easy to blame each other and the parents and to collectively avoid feeling responsible. There was too much of a tradition that senior managers (the parents) would take care of things as they always had. The anxiety of facing up to the "family problem" was too overwhelming, so a great deal of denial had been operating.

The outside consultant could, in this case, take the same information but present it as a problem that the family as a whole owned and had to confront and handle as a total unit. He could be much more direct and confrontational than insiders could be with each other; at the same time, he could remind the total group that everyone was in this together—the executive committee as the symbolic parents along with all the children. This recognition did not reduce the resultant panic; however, it forced it out into the open because denial was no longer possible. The group had been genuinely disconfirmed and made anxious, but not knowing how to fix problems heightened learning anxiety as well, and the group did not yet feel psychologically safe and hence felt paralyzed.

Providing Some Psychological Safety. The next problem, then, was how to reduce the learning anxiety and discouragement now present in the group. How could we provide some psychological safety that would permit the group to redefine the situation, to begin to feel capable of doing something constructive? The other consultant and I took a long walk to think this out and came up with the idea that now would be a good time to give some lectures on the nature of resistance to change and how to overcome it. He had been confrontational, so I should now come on as supportive and facilitative.

I hurriedly pulled together notes, made transparencies, and on the following morning gave lectures on (1) why healthy organizations need to be able to change; (2) why individuals and groups resist change; (3) how to analyze forces that facilitate and forces that constrain change; and (4) how to develop valid change targets for the coming year, in the context of the redirection project, with timetables, measurements of outcomes, and accountabilities. I emphasized a point that is central to change projects: that the period of change has itself to be defined as a stage to be managed, with transition managers specifically assigned (Beckhard and Harris, 1987).

These lectures had the desired effect of giving the group members a way of thinking positively, so that when they were sent back into small groups to develop priority issues for making the redirection project a success, they were able to go off to these meetings with a sense of realism and optimism. The general results of the small group meetings were quite clear. They saw the need for the unprofitable divisions to shrink and restructure themselves, and the need for profitable divisions to become more effective relative to the competition, but they stated clearly that neither of these could happen if the headquarters organization did not confront the excess people in the headquarters and the style of management that was emanating from the functional groups. The ideas were not new, but they were now shared—and with some conviction. The meeting ended with top management making a commitment to confront all of the issues identified and to create a set of task forces to deal with the problems.

Creating a Structure for the Redirection Project: Project Task Forces as a "Parallel System"   The Ciba-Geigy managers were skillful at working in groups. Koechlin and the executive committee used this skill first by creating a steering committee to organize the redirection project into thirty or so separate, manageable tasks. The steering committee met for several days following the annual meeting to think through the specific tasks to be accomplished in the redirection process and to design the entire parallel system that would implement it.

A separate steering committee was created for each task, and one member of the executive committee was made accountable for the performance of that task group. To avoid asking some of the senior managers to shrink and restructure divisions for which they had previously been responsible, responsibilities were reshuffled so that no conflicts of interest would arise, and each division would be looked at with fresh eyes.

In addition, each task group was assigned a "challenger"—a senior manager who would review and challenge the proposed solutions of that task group to ensure that they made sense and had been properly thought through. The steering committee defined the timetables and the broad targets. Each team was also given the services of an internal organizational consultant to help with the organization of the team itself, and several of the teams asked for and obtained my help on how to structure their work.

All of this was communicated clearly by top management in written form, through meetings, and through trips to various parts of the company throughout the following year. Not only the process but also the necessity for it and top management's commitment to it were highlighted in these meetings. Great emphasis was given to the particular project that would reduce the number of people in the Basel headquarters by at least one-third—no small task, as this involved laying off friends and relatives.

These structural changes in job responsibilities were major innovations implemented by the steering committee. The skillful use of groups, both at the annual meeting and in the design of the projects, struck me as paradoxical. How could a company that was so hierarchical and so concerned about individual turf be so effective in inventing groups and in operating within a group context? The answer appeared to be in the fact that the top management of the company was itself a group that had worked together for a long time and felt jointly accountable. The broader Swiss-German macroculture in which the company functioned also represented this same paradox—strong individualism with, at the same time, a strong sense of community and a commitment to working together in groups to solve problems.

We might also speculate that group work had such importance in Ciba-Geigy because it was virtually the only form of lateral communication available in the company. The sensitivities that might be operating if managers from one division offered help to or asked for help from another division could be overcome, with faces saved, if a task force consisting of members of both divisions adopted a process of taking turns reporting to each other on the progress of effective and ineffective interventions. The listener could then learn and get new ideas without either identifying himself or herself as a problem or having others identify him or her as a target of their input. Group meetings thus preserved face all the way around.

It was also recognized that groups helped to build commitment to projects even though the implementation system was essentially hierarchical. If groups had discussed the issue, the hierarchy worked more smoothly, as in the Japanese system, where consensus is sought before a decision is announced. In various ways, the redirection project was using the cultural strengths of the company and was redefining its formal procedures to deal with the business problem without changing the culture overtly.

Second Year: Consolidation of the Redirection Project

During my several visits following the second annual meeting, I worked on three important areas. First, I made myself available to any project group or group members who wished to discuss any aspect of how to proceed, with the appointment to be made at their initiative. If I learned something that would help other projects, I would summarize it and write it up for circulation to others. I was consulted by several managers on how best to think about downsizing and early retirement, especially when this had to occur in the tightly knit home community of Basel; how to get managers to think about innovative restructuring; and how to use career anchors in the management development process. I also spent a good deal of time with the executive committee member who was responsible for the whole redirection project, helping him keep his role and his leadership behavior in his project group clear and effective. He was the only member of the executive committee who consistently used me as a process consultant. Parenthetically, he was their CFO and also a lawyer. Several project managers wanted help in thinking through their roles as project chairmen and solicited my reactions to proposals prior to running them by the challengers.

Second, I became more familiar with the management development inventory and planning system and began a series of meetings with Leupold, the manager of this function, to see how it could be improved. Bringing in and developing better and more innovative managers was seen as a high-priority longer-range goal of the redirection project. It was also known that Leupold would retire within a year, and his successor might need a consultant who had learned something about the company to help him think out his program.

Third, I was asked by Koechlin and the planning group to think about the cultural assumptions operating, to interview managers about the company culture, and to figure out how the culture was aiding or hindering the redirection project. The basic idea was to be prepared to comment on the role of the culture at the third annual meeting.

Third Annual Meeting: The Culture Lecture Disaster. I had made it clear that they should think of change as a stage to be managed, with targets and assigned change managers. From this point of view, the third annual meeting provided a natural opportunity to review progress, check out what problems had been encountered, share successes and good innovations, replan some projects if necessary, and, most important, announce newly defined role relationships among executive committee members, division heads, and country heads.

The headquarters organization was too involved in the day-to-day operation of the local businesses. So as the functions were shrunk and restructured, it also appeared desirable to redefine the corporate headquarters role as more strategic, with the operating units to do more of the day-to-day management. This was possible because country managers were now willing and able to assume more responsibilities and because the executive committee increasingly recognized the importance of its strategic role.

At the opening session, I was asked to review the progress of the redirection project, based on interviews with a series of managers about their experiences with the project. This lecture was designed to remind the participants of change theory, to legitimize their individual experiences and frustrations by giving a wide range of examples, to illustrate how restraining forces had been dealt with by innovative managers, and to introduce to the group the concept of corporate culture as a force to be analyzed. Based on my observations and systematic interviews, as part of my lecture I was to review some of the major cultural assumptions operating at Ciba-Geigy.

The reaction to the culture portion of the lecture produced an important insight. Many participants said that I had stated things more or less accurately, but they clearly were not pleased that I, as an outsider, had made portions of their culture public and that I had misunderstood or misinterpreted the culture. One or two executive committee members subsequently decided that I was not a useful consultant. For me to discuss their cultural assumptions created a polarized situation. Some managers moved closer to me; others moved further away. Internal debates were launched about whether or not certain statements about their culture were correct or not. I concluded that if a consultant does not want that kind of polarization, he or she should help the group decipher its own culture rather than presenting his or her own view of that culture in a didactic manner.

Following the general presentation on culture and change, each of the projects was asked to give a brief review of its status, and small groups met to consider implications and make suggestions. The last part of the meeting—and, from the point of view of the planning group, the most difficult—concerned the problem of how to inform everyone about the new roles of the executive committee, the division heads, and the country heads. The executive committee members were not sure that their planned effort to become more strategic and to have more individual accountabilities would get across just by saying it.

We therefore planned a three-step process: (1) a formal announcement of the new roles; (2) a brief lecture by me on the implications of role realignment, emphasizing the systemic character of role networks and the need for each manager to renegotiate his or her role downward, upward, and laterally if the new system was to work; and (3) a powerful emotional speech by the CFO on the effect of this new alignment in streamlining the company for the future. The meeting ended on a high note, based on a sense of what had already been accomplished in one year, what accomplishments were in the works, and what improvements could be expected from the new role that the executive committee had taken for itself. To announce all of the changes and to ensure that the country managements would take them seriously, small groups of executive committee members visited all of the local units and personally described the changes that would be implemented.

The fact that the headquarters organization had begun to shrink through early retirements and had reduced some of its more bothersome control activities sent the clear message that top management was serious about its role in the redirection project even though the early retirement of headquarters people was an extremely painful process. The fact that people were being retired destroyed the taken-for-granted assumption that people had a guaranteed career in the company, but the highly individualized and financially generous manner in which retirements were handled reinforced another basic assumption: that the company cared very much for its people and would not hurt them if there was any way to avoid it.

Assessment During the Third Year. Most of my regular visits subsequent to the third annual meeting were devoted to working with Joe Wells, the new manager of management development. Leupold had been asked to retire as part of the headquarters restructuring. Though I continued to meet with members of the executive committee on redirection matters, the priority shifted to helping Wells think through his new role and reexamine how the entire process could be improved. Leupold was offered, as part of his retirement package, a consultantship with the company, provided he developed a research project that could be jointly conducted with me.

We proposed a study of the careers of the top 200 managers in the company, with the purpose of identifying critical success factors or problems in those careers. The project was approved by the executive committee with the condition that I was to act as technical supervisor of the project, reminding me once again that my credibility as a consultant rested heavily on my scientific reputation and that scientific validity was the ultimate decision criterion for the company. The study involved a detailed historical reconstruction of the 200 careers and revealed surprisingly little geographical, cross-functional, and/or cross-divisional movement as those careers progressed.

A presentation of these and other results was given to the executive committee by Leupold, which led to a major discussion of how future general managers should be developed. A consensus was reached that there should be more early geographic rotation and movement into and out of headquarters, but cross-functional and cross-divisional movement remained a controversial issue. The executive committee members also realized that rotational moves, if they were to be useful, had to occur early in the career. They decided that such early movement would occur only if a very clear message about the importance of career development went out to the entire organization.

This decision led to the design of a half-day segment on management development, which was inserted into the management seminars that were periodically given to the top 500 managers of the company. A new policy on early rotation was mandated, and the data from the project were used to justify the new policy. Once senior management accepted a conclusion as valid, it was able to move decisively and to impose a proposed solution on the entire company. The message was communicated by having executive committee members at each seminar, but implementation was left to local management.

During this year, Koechlin relinquished the job of chairman of the executive committee for health reasons, which raised a potential succession problem. However, the executive committee had anticipated the problem and had a new chairman and vice chairman ready. The new chairman was a scientist, but the new vice chairman was the CFO who had shown great leadership skills during the redirection project. Both of them strongly reaffirmed the scientific and technical assumptions underlying the success of Ciba-Geigy, as if to say, "We are making major changes but we are the same kind of culture as before."

By the end of the third year, the financial results were much better, and the restructuring process in the unprofitable divisions was proceeding rapidly. Each unit learned how to manage early retirements, and a measure of interdivisional cooperation was achieved in the process of transferring people who were redundant in one division into other divisions. Initial attitudes were negative, and I heard many complaints from managers that even their best people were not acceptable to other divisions. This attitude was gradually eroded because the assumption that "We don't throw people out without maximum effort to find jobs for them" eventually overrode the provincialism of the divisions. Managers who were too committed to the old strategy of running those divisions were gradually replaced with managers who were deemed to be more innovative in their approach. One of the managers of a division that needed to make major reductions and redesign its whole product line was deemed so successful in this project that he was promoted to the executive committee.

Because it had fulfilled its functions, the redirection project was officially terminated at the end of the third year. Relevant change projects would now be handled by the executive committee, and I was asked to be "on call" to line managers needing help. For example, the new head of one of the previously unprofitable divisions wanted help in restoring the morale of those managers who remained after many of their colleagues were retired or farmed out to other divisions. He sensed a level of fear and apathy that made it difficult to move forward positively. In true Ciba-Geigy fashion, he had tried to solve this problem on his own by bringing in an outside training program, but it had been unsuccessful. He then requested a meeting with me to seek alternative solutions. Given the Ciba-Geigy culture and his own commitment, it was obvious that he should build his program internally and enlist the aid of the corporate training people, who would know how to design a program that would be culturally congruent. He had never considered using the corporate training group to help him, though he knew of it and liked some of the people in it. I found myself being the broker between two parts of the organization that could have been talking to each other directly. He did follow up, and in the subsequent year, a successful in-house program was developed.

During the next two years, my involvement declined gradually. The head of the redirection project's headquarters reduction team became the chairman of the board, and the former head of the division that had needed the most downsizing became the chairman of the executive committee. Both of these managers showed their talent in the way they handled their projects. All of the changes were accomplished without any outsiders being brought into Ciba-Geigy. I continued to work with Wells on management development issues and helped him implement some of his programs. I also worked with the U.S. subsidiary on projects for which my knowledge of the culture was considered an asset. But the assumption that companies use consultants only when they have serious problems prevailed, so from 1988 on my involvement decreased to zero.

Summary and Conclusions

Based on what I observed and heard, Ciba-Geigy successfully weathered a major organizational crisis involving many elements of its culture.

- The financial trend toward nonprofitability was decisively reversed.
- Two previously unprofitable divisions restructured themselves by drastically cutting products, facilities, and people, and by reorganizing their production and marketing activities to fit the current market and economic realities. One of these divisions was considered a loser, but because of its successful restructuring under a dynamic manager, it became the company hero. The manager of this division eventually became the chairman of the executive committee.
- The functions in the corporate headquarters were reduced by 30 to 40 percent, and more line responsibility was delegated to the countries and divisions.
- The functions in the divisions were also reassessed, and their role was changed in line with headquarters' becoming more strategic.
- The profitable divisions thoroughly reassessed themselves and began programs—particularly in the pharmaceutical division—to become more competitive in their particular industries.
- Executive committee members restructured their own accountabilities so that each division, country, and function had one clear line boss whose focus was more strategic. In the previous system, these organizational units had felt accountable to the entire executive committee and were often micromanaged by headquarters people from Basel.
- A major management succession occurred and was negotiated successfully, in that the new chairman and vice chairman of the executive committee were perceived by senior management as good choices and were promoted further in recent years.
- In this whole three-year change process, many managers who were considered less effective were weeded out through early retirement, permitting the filling of key jobs by managers considered more dynamic and effective.

- Senior managers acquired insight into the ways in which their culture both constrained and helped them.

- A major cultural assumption about career stability and "lifetime employment," particularly at headquarters, was reassessed and abandoned. In that process, another major assumption about dealing with people on an individualized and humane basis was reaffirmed.

- Managerial career development was redefined in terms of required rotation both geographically and through headquarters.

- The consumer goods acquisition that did not fit was reevaluated and a decision was made to sell it. At the same time, the corporate acquisition policy was clarified to only look for companies that were based on technologies with which Ciba-Geigy felt comfortable.

- The need for more emphasis on marketing was met by recognizing those skills in the pharmaceutical and agricultural chemicals divisions and promoting more of their managers into key corporate jobs.

Most managers in Ciba-Geigy said that they had undergone some great changes and that many of their assumptions about the world and the company had changed. On the surface it looked like a clear case of major culture change. However, when we look closely, the cultural paradigm of the company had not really changed at all. There continued to be the same bias toward scientific authority; the hierarchy functioned as strongly as ever, but with redefined roles; the assumption that managers do their job best when left alone to learn for themselves was still very strong; and lateral communication was still considered mostly irrelevant. For example, there was still no regular meeting of division heads except at the annual meeting, where they met with everyone else, and there were no functional meetings across countries or divisions.

Various projects—for example, to bring in MBAs on a trial basis and to hold worldwide meetings of functional people, such as the management development coordinators from all the divisions and key countries—were proposed, but I sensed that they were only tolerated, not encouraged. On one of my visits, Wells arranged for me to meet five of the MBAs who had been hired into different parts of Ciba-Geigy to see how they were reacting to their different situations. We had a productive and constructive meeting. However, a week later, Wells was criticized by several of the bosses of the MBAs for organizing the meeting because he was stepping onto the turf of these other managers. *It turned out that they would not have given permission for such a cross-departmental group to meet.*

When the redirection project began, we all talked of culture change. To label a change as culture change enhanced the drama of what was happening, so it may have had some motivational value even if in the end it was inaccurate. At the same time, it focused people on the culture, so that they could identify both the constraints and the enhancing features of the culture. But the important thing to note is that *considerable change can take place in an organization's operations without the basic cultural paradigm changing at all.* In fact, in Ciba-Geigy, some of the assumptions could not have changed but for the even stronger action of deeper assumptions. Thus, some parts of the culture helped many of the changes to happen in other parts of the culture. Specifically, the downsizing of the headquarters organization, which clearly abandoned one cultural assumption, could not have occurred but for the deeper assumption that "we take good care of our people."

This insight leads to a further point. Many assumptions around mission, goals, means, measurement systems, roles, and relationships can be superficial within the total structure of the cultural paradigm, yet be very important for the organization's functioning on a day-to-day basis. The assumption that the headquarters functional groups had worldwide responsibility for tracking everything was not a very deep assumption within the whole Ciba-Geigy culture, but it had a major impact on business performance and managerial morale in the country companies. Changing some of these superficial assumptions and their resulting practices was crucial to Ciba-Geigy's effective adaptation.

It should also be noted that the deeper assumptions are not necessarily functional. The commitment to science continued to be manifested in commitment to scientists, especially some of the older ones who had helped the company become successful. In one extreme case, such a person was a country manager who was performing poorly in that role. A more skillful general manager had been groomed to take over this country, but the decision to give him authority was held up for two full years to let the scientist retire at his normal time. It was felt that to force him into early retirement would not only be destructive to him but would send the wrong signal to the rest of the organization.

What, then, really happened in the redirection project and why? Many in the company asked this question to understand the reasons for the success of the change effort. My own observation is that the effort was successful because the executive committee (1) sent a clear message that a change was needed, (2) involved itself fully in the change process, (3) tackled the impossible job of reducing headquarters staff as well as the power of the functional groups, and (4) thereby not only created involvement and ownership down the line in the country groups but made it clear that operational problems would increasingly be delegated down. Even though communication laterally was still minimal, the vertical channels were more opened up. Financial information was shared more than before, suggestions coming up through the project structure were listened to, and proposals that were accepted were effectively implemented through the existing hierarchy as a result of clear top-down signals.

The design of the redirection project—with an externalized steering committee that created project groups with consultants and challenger managers and provided clear goals, timetables, and time off to work on the problem—reflected skills embedded in the Ciba-Geigy culture. They knew very well how to design group projects and work in groups. In this sense, Ciba-Geigy used its cultural strength to redirect itself more rapidly than might have been possible in a less structured organization or one less sensitive to group process issues.

The driving force and the source of many of the key insights behind this change effort was Koechlin, who, as mentioned before, was the kind of leader who could step outside of his own culture and assess it realistically. The willingness of the CFO and various division managers to step outside their own subcultures and learn some new approaches also played a key role. But in the end, the culture changed only in peripheral ways by restructuring some minor assumptions. Yet such peripheral culture change is often sufficient to redesign the core business processes and thereby to fix major organizational problems.

As a postscript, Ciba-Geigy eventually merged with Sandoz to become Novartis, a larger multinational now focused more specifically on pharmaceuticals. I had occasion to ask the CEO of Novartis about this later merger and was told that it went very smoothly, even though these two companies had been competitors and "enemies" at the time of my work with them. If this merger went smoothly, it is probably because the two companies had some strong common elements—the Basel culture and the industry culture of pharmaceuticals.

Part Five

NEW ROLES FOR LEADERS AND LEADERSHIP

In the previous editions of this book I emphasized the need for leaders to become learners and culture managers. This need is now greater than ever because globalism and information technology are creating a whole new set of cultural challenges. In the previous edition, I also described what a "learning culture" might look like and applied this concept to organizational units. These ideas remain the same and will again be reviewed in this edition. But some new issues are surfacing.

What I observe now is that we need to think beyond organizations into many *new kinds of work units* such as multicultural task forces, multicultural joint ventures and partnerships, and multicultural networks. These new kinds of organizations will require a different kind of culture management because they will be *multi*cultural. What tools and processes are available to lead a task force consisting of five members from five countries working together in a sixth country? How do we help a multicultural team operating in different countries when the members have never met and yet have to work together?

Cultural analysis has also migrated into some of the major social issues and problems of today, particularly the area of "safety" in high hazard industries and in health care. As the energy needs of the world increase, the pressure for a safe nuclear industry increases as well. Occupational cultures and subcultures turn out to be a crucial factor in maximizing nuclear safety. As the costs of health care continue to skyrocket even as health care procedures become technologically more complex, the cultural issues among doctors, nurses, and administrators become foci for how to get health care under some kind of control. As the world tries to get global warming under control, the issue of how to get dozens of countries with different cultures to work together becomes central.

In these various arenas, it is not enough to exhort leaders to become innovative learners. We need to provide some concepts and tools that would show leaders how to approach cultural problems. To this end, I will first review in Chapter Twenty the characteristics of learning cultures and learning leaders. Then in Chapter Twenty-One, I will introduce the concept of the *cultural island* as a process that can help to move multicultural groups toward effective work output, and will discuss *managed dialogues* as one of the best examples of cultural islands. This material builds on a similar analysis in my 2009 book *The Corporate Culture Survival Guide*.

As a final note, growing out of the dialogue discussion, I will propose that cultural analysis should begin to focus more and more on the two archetypal issues of "authority" (how power is handled) and "intimacy" (how love is handled). In a multicultural setting, the danger is that we try to understand *all* of another culture when, in fact, only some cultural dimensions are crucial. Authority and intimacy are two such dimensions.

20

THE LEARNING CULTURE AND THE LEARNING LEADER

The various predictions about globalism, knowledge-based organizations, the information age, the bio-tech age, the loosening of organizational boundaries, networks, and so on all have one theme in common: We basically do not know what the world of tomorrow will really be like, except that it will be different, more complex, more fast fast-paced, and more culturally diverse (Drucker Foundation, 1999; Global Business Network, 2002; Schwartz, 2003; Michael, 1985, 1991).

This means that organizations, their leaders, and all the rest of us will have to become perpetual learners (Michael, 1985, 1991; Kahane, 2010; Scharmer, 2007; Senge, Smith, Kruschwitz, Laur, and Schley, 2008). When we pose the issue of perpetual learning in the context of cultural analysis, we confront a paradox. Culture is a stabilizer, a conservative force, and a way of making things meaningful and predictable. Many management consultants and theorists have asserted that "strong" cultures are desirable as a basis for effective and lasting performance. But strong cultures are, by definition, stable and hard to change. If the world is becoming more turbulent, requiring more flexibility and learning, does this not imply that strong cultures will increasingly become a liability? Does this not mean, then, that the process of culture creation is itself potentially dysfunctional because it stabilizes things, whereas flexibility might be more appropriate? Or is it possible to imagine a culture that, by its very nature, is learning oriented, adaptive, and flexible? Can we stabilize perpetual learning and change? What would a culture look like that favored perpetual learning and flexibility?

To translate that question into leadership terms, what is the direction in which the leaders of today should be pushing cultural evolution to prepare for the surprises of tomorrow? What sort of characteristics and skills must a leader have to perceive the needs of tomorrow and to implement the changes needed to survive?

What Might a Learning Culture Look Like?

The ideas spelled out in this chapter have resulted from many conversations with the late Donald Michael (1985, 1991) and with my colleagues Tom Malone (1987, 2004), Peter Senge (1990; Senge and others, 2008), and Otto Scharmer (2007) about the nature of organizations and work in the future. They have also been tested in many workshops where I have heard first hand from leaders in both the private and nonprofit sector how rapidly the world is evolving into new uncharted territory.

1. Proactivity

A learning culture must assume that the appropriate way for humans to behave in relationship to their environment is to be proactive problem solvers and learners. If the culture is built on fatalistic assumptions of passive acceptance, learning will become more and more difficult as the rate of change in the environment increases.

Learning-oriented leadership must portray confidence that active problem solving leads to learning and, thereby, set an appropriate example for other members of the organization. It will be more important to be committed to the learning process than to any particular solution to a problem. In the face of greater complexity, the leader's dependence on others to generate solutions will increase, and we have overwhelming evidence that new solutions will be more likely to be adopted if the members of the organization have been involved in the learning process (Schein, 2009a,b).

2. Commitment to Learning to Learn

The learning culture must have in its DNA a "learning gene," in the sense that members must hold the shared assumption that learning is a good thing worth investing in and that learning to learn is itself a skill to be mastered. "Learning" must include not only learning about changes in the external environment but also learning about internal relationships and how well the organization is adapted to the external changes. For example, one way of understanding the failure of DEC is to note that they were committed to continued technological innovation, but there was very little reflection or commitment to learning how their own organization was creating destructive intergroup competition.

The key to learning is to get feedback and to take the time to reflect, analyze, and assimilate the implications of what the feedback has communicated. Feedback is only useful if the learner has asked for it, so one of the key motivations of the learning leader must be to ask for help and accept it (Schein, 2009a). A further key to learning is the ability to generate new responses, to try new ways of doing things. This takes time, energy, and resources. A learning culture must therefore value reflection and experimentation, and must give its members the time and resources to do it.

3. Positive Assumptions About Human Nature (Theory Y)

Learning leaders must have faith in people and must believe that ultimately human nature is basically good and, in any case, malleable. The learning leader must believe that humans can and will learn if they are provided the resources and the necessary psychological safety. Learning implies some desire for survival and improvement. If leaders start with assumptions that people are basically lazy and passive, that people have no concern for organizations or causes above and beyond themselves, they will inevitably create organizations that will become self-fulfilling prophecies. Such leaders will train their employees to be lazy, self-protective, and self-seeking, and then they will cite those characteristics as proof of their original assumption about human nature. The resulting control-oriented organizations may survive and even thrive in certain kinds of stable environments, but they are certain to fail as environments become more turbulent and as technological and global trends cause problem solving to become increasingly more complex.

Knowledge and skill are becoming more widely distributed, forcing leaders—whether they like it or not—to be more dependent on other people in their organizations. Under such circumstances, a cynical attitude toward human nature is bound to create, at best, bureaucratic rigidity, and at the worst extreme, counter-organizational subgroups.

4. Belief That the Environment Can Be Managed

A learning culture must contain in its DNA a gene that reflects the shared assumption that the environment is to some degree manageable. The learning leader who assumes that organizations must symbiotically accept their niche will have more difficulty in learning as the environment becomes more turbulent. Adaptation to a *slowly* changing environment is also a viable learning process, but I am assuming that the way in which the world is changing will make that less and less possible. In other words, the more turbulent the environment, the more important it will be for leadership to argue for and show that some level of management of the environment is desirable and possible.

5. Commitment to Truth Through Pragmatism and Inquiry

A learning culture must contain the shared assumption that solutions to problems derive from a deep belief in inquiry and a pragmatic search for "truth." The inquiry process itself must be flexible and reflect the nature of the environmental changes encountered. What must be avoided in the learning culture is the automatic assumption that wisdom and truth reside in any one source or method. This point is especially important in that in the macrocultural world even what is considered "scientific" varies considerably, so we cannot take some of the physical science models of science as being the only way to truth.

As the problems we encounter change, so too will our learning method have to change. For some purposes, we will have to rely heavily on "normal science"; for other purposes, we will have to find truth in experienced practitioners because scientific proof will be impossible to obtain; for still other purposes, we will collectively have to experiment and live with errors until a better solution is found. Knowledge and skill will be found in many forms, and what I am calling a clinical research process—in which helpers and clients work things out together—will become more and more important because no one will be "expert" enough to provide an answer. In the learning organization, everyone will have to learn how to learn.

The toughest problem for learning leaders here is to come to terms with their own lack of expertise and wisdom. Once we are in a leadership position, our own needs and the expectations of others dictate that we should know the answer and be in control of the situation. Yet if we provide answers, we are creating a culture that will inevitably take a moralistic position in regard to reality and truth. The *only* way to build a learning culture that continues to learn is for leaders themselves to realize that there is much that they do not know and must teach others to accept that there is much that they do not know (Schein, 2009a). The learning task then becomes a shared responsibility.

I am often asked how to make someone more sensitive to culture. My short answer is "Travel more." It is through giving ourselves more varied experiences in more different kinds of cultures that we learn about cultural variation and develop cultural humility. The learning leader should make it a point to spend a lot of time outside his or her organization and travel to as many other cultures as is practical.

6. Positive Orientation Toward the Future

The optimal time orientation for learning appears to be somewhere between the far future and the near future. We must think far enough ahead to be able to assess the systemic consequences of different courses of action, but we must also think in terms of the near future to assess whether or not our solutions are working. If the environment is becoming more turbulent, the assumption that the best orientation is to live in the past or to live in the present clearly seems dysfunctional.

7. Commitment to Full and Open Task-Relevant Communication

The learning culture must be built on the assumption that communication and information are central to organizational well-being and must therefore create a multichannel communication system that allows everyone to connect to everyone else. This does not mean that all channels will be used or that any given channel will be used for all things. What it does mean is that anyone must be able to communicate with anyone else, and everyone must assume that telling the truth as best they can is positive and desirable.

This principle of "openness" does not mean that we suspend all the cultural rules pertaining to face and adopt a definition of openness as equivalent to the proverbial "letting it all hang out." There is ample evidence that *interpersonal* openness can create severe problems across hierarchical boundaries and in multicultural settings. But we must become sensitive to *task*-relevant information and be as open as possible in sharing that. One of the important roles for learning leadership is to specify, in terms of any given task, what the minimum communication system must be and what kind of information is critical to effective problem solving and learning. *More* information is not necessarily a good thing because the more we know, the more questions we develop about what we don't know. Full task-relevant information can be achieved only if the members of the group have learned to trust each other, and trust is basically built by the parties telling each other the truth as far as the rules of the social order will allow. One of the major challenges for learning leadership is how to establish trust in a network where people may not have face-to-face contact.

8. Commitment to Cultural Diversity

The more turbulent the environment, the more likely it is that the organization with the more diverse cultural resources will be better able to cope with unpredicted events. Therefore, the learning leader should stimulate diversity and promulgate the assumption that diversity is desirable at the individual and subgroup levels. Such diversity will inevitably create subcultures, and those subcultures will eventually be a necessary resource for learning and innovation.

For diversity to be a resource, however, the subcultures or the individuals in a multicultural task group must be connected and must value each other enough to learn something of each other's culture and language. A central task for the learning leader, then, is to ensure good cross-cultural communication and understanding. Some ideas of how this can be accomplished will be covered in the next chapter. Creating diversity does not mean letting diverse parts of the system run on their own without coordination. Laissez-faire leadership does not work because it is in the nature of subgroups and subcultures to protect their own interests. To optimize diversity therefore requires some higher-order coordination mechanisms and mutual cultural understanding.

9. Commitment to Systemic Thinking

As the world becomes more complex and interdependent, the ability to think systemically, to analyze fields of forces and understand their joint causal effects on each other, and to abandon simple linear causal logic in favor of complex mental models will become more critical to learning. The learning leader must believe that the world is intrinsically complex, non-linear, interconnected, and "overdetermined" in the sense that most things are multiply caused. This has come to be a central issue in the analysis of safety issues in high hazard industries and in health care.

10. Belief That Cultural Analysis Is a Valid Set of Lenses for Understanding and Improving the World

In a learning culture, leaders and members believe that analyzing and reflecting on their culture is a necessary part of the learning process. Cultural analysis reveals important mechanisms by which groups and organizations function in completing their tasks. Without cultural analysis, it is difficult to understand how groups are created, how they become organizations, and how they evolve throughout their existence.

Case Example: SAAB Combitech

An excellent example of cultural intervention in the service of organizational learning was the 1997 seminar run by Saab Combitech, the R&D arm of the Saab Company, and its leader Per Risberg. Combitech consisted of seven separate research units working with different technologies such as developing complex training systems, military hardware, marine electronics, aerospace technology, and space exploration technology. These units had created their own subcultures based on their tasks, technologies, and the occupations of their employees. The units were friendly to each other but did not understand each other well enough to discover that they could all improve if they shared more of their technological and organizational insights.

Risberg recruited me to help him design an intervention that would teach the hundred or so members of these groups about culture and help them to become more familiar with each other's cultures. Risberg and I designed a three-day workshop and asked the groups to read

(Continued)

portions of my culture book before the meeting. Each group was asked to write me a letter in which they were to compare themselves to DEC and Ciba-Geigy and write out some observations on their own culture.

On the first day of the workshop, I introduced the culture model, gave them more examples, and briefly reviewed their self-analyses. We then had each group volunteer two of its members to become "anthropologists" who would go into one other group to learn what its culture was like. I provided some dimensions of the sort covered in Chapters Five through Nine and gave them several hours to visit, observe, and inquire about the group's artifacts, espoused values, and tacit assumptions. On the second day, these observations were then reported in a plenary session so that each group heard how it was perceived by its two anthropologists. Through this process, we all became highly aware of both the communality of assumptions and diversity of assumptions across the groups. Groups were encouraged to ask each other questions and explore further each other's cultures.

The third day was devoted to a systematic exploration of the ways in which the research units were interdependent and how they could help each other by sharing more of their technology and know-how. That evening, Risberg invited the attendees and their spouses to a final banquet, which began with formal cocktails and a sit-down dinner at long tables. It was very awkward because many of the Combitech people did not know each other very well; the spouses were uncomfortable, and we all chafed at the prospect of a long dull evening.

However, after the first course, Risberg asked us all to go to our rooms and follow instructions that we would find there. We found a box with some new clothing—tie-dyed shirts, loose pants, slippers, and headbands! We were to put on these clothes and report to the parking lot, where we found a huge audio setup. We were then instructed to line up for "dance lessons" provided by an instructor—several simple steps that all of us could master. The leader then played some rhythmic music, and we practiced our steps until we were able to really do the dance and enjoy it. We could feel ourselves relaxing and getting to know each other at this more primitive level, so that by the time we had danced for twenty minutes and were instructed to go back into dinner, we were all chatting amicably.

Dinner was a big Indian buffet that required much moving around and further loosening up. By the end of the evening there was laughter, backslapping, exchanges of cards, and commitments to get together in the future. Risberg had created a "cultural" event that reinforced beautifully his intention of having his research groups get to know each other and work more with each other. Not only did the group learn about culture as a concept, but the design of the workshop used culture creatively by having the groups play at being "anthropologists."

Having us all change into informal "hippie clothes" and dancing together was similar in intent to what Ciba-Geigy did when we all had to shoot cross-bows or engage in some other sport that brought us all down to the same level. Risberg had realized that even though his organization had existed for many years, the members were not well acquainted with each other and needed some event to build commonality. He had produced "cultural islands," a concept that will be explored in more detail in the next chapter.

Why These Dimensions?

Many other dimensions could be analyzed as being relevant to learning. I have chosen to ignore those where the conclusion as to what would aid learning seemed unclear. For example, with respect to the dimension of individualism versus groupism, the best prescription for learning is to accept the notion that every system has both elements in it, and the learning culture will be the one that optimizes individual competition and collaborative teamwork, depending upon the task to be accomplished. A similar argument can be made around the dimension of task versus relationship orientation. An optimal learning system would balance these as required by the task rather than opting for either extreme.

With respect to degree of hierarchy, autocracy, paternalism, and participation, it is again a matter of the task, the kind of learning required, and the particular circumstances. In the Alpha Power example, we saw that knowledge of environmental hazards and how to deal with them was initially learned in a very autocratic, top-down training program, but as experience in the field accumulated, the learning process shifted to local innovation, which was then circulated to the rest of the organization. Innovative solutions to environmental, health, and safety issues were captured in videotapes and circulated throughout the organization. Monthly award lunches were held, at which successful teams met with senior management and each other to share "how they did it" and to communicate solutions to other teams.

In the end, we have to recognize that even the concept of *learning* is heavily colored by cultural assumptions and that learning can mean very different things in different cultures and subcultures. The dimensions I listed previously reflect only my own cultural understanding and should therefore be taken only as a first approximation of what a learning culture should emphasize.

The role of learning-oriented leadership in a turbulent world, then, is to promote these kinds of assumptions. Leaders themselves must first hold such assumptions, become learners themselves, and then be able to recognize and systematically reward behavior based on those assumptions in others.

Learning-Oriented Leadership

Having described the generic characteristics of a learning culture and the implications in general for the learning leader, it remains to examine briefly whether learning-oriented leadership varies as a function of the different stages of organizational evolution.

Learning Leadership in Culture Creation

In a rapidly changing world, the learning leader/founder must not only have vision but also be able both to impose it and to evolve it further as external circumstances change. Just as the new members of an organization arrive with prior organizational and cultural experiences, a common set of assumptions can only be forged by clear and consistent messages as the group encounters and survives its own crises. The culture creation leader therefore needs persistence and patience, yet as a learner must be flexible and ready to change.

As groups and organizations develop, certain key emotional issues arise: those having to do with dependence on the leader, with peer relationships, and with how to work effectively. At each of these stages of group development, leadership is needed to help the group identify the issues and deal with them. During these stages, leaders often have to absorb and contain the anxiety that is unleashed when things do not work as they should (Hirschhorn, 1988; Schein, 1983, Frost, 2003). The leader may not have the answer, but he or she must provide temporary stability and emotional reassurance while the answer is being worked out. This anxiety-containing function is especially relevant during periods of learning, when old habits and ways must be given up before new ones are learned. And, if the world is becoming more changeable, such anxiety may be perpetual, requiring the learning leader to play a perpetual supportive role.

The difficult learning agenda for founder leaders is how to be simultaneously clear and strong in articulating their vision and yet open to change as that very vision becomes maladaptive in a turbulent environment.

Leadership in Organizational Midlife

Once the organization develops a substantial history of its own, its culture becomes more of a cause than an effect. The culture now influences the strategy, the structure, the procedures, and the ways in which the group members will relate to each other. Culture becomes a powerful influence on members' perceiving, thinking, and feeling, and these predispositions, along with situational factors, will influence the members' behavior. Because it serves an important anxiety-reducing function, culture will be clung to even if it becomes dysfunctional in relationship to environmental opportunities and constraints.

Midlife organizations show two basically different patterns, however. Some, under the influence of one or more generations of leaders, develop a highly integrated culture even though they have become large and diversified; others allow growth and diversification in cultural assumptions as well and, therefore, can be described as culturally diverse with respect to their business, functional, geographical, and even hierarchical subunits. How leaders manage culture at this stage of organizational evolution depends on which pattern they perceive and which pattern they decide is best for the future.

Leaders at this stage need, above all, the insight and skill to help the organization evolve into whatever will make it most effective in the future. In some instances, this may mean increasing cultural diversity, allowing some of the uniformity that may have been built up in the growth stage to erode; in other instances, it may mean pulling together a culturally diverse set of organizational units and attempting to impose new common assumptions on them. In either case, the leader needs to (1) be able to analyze the culture in sufficient detail to know which cultural assumptions can aid and which ones will hinder the fulfillment of the organizational mission, and (2) have the intervention skills to make desired changes happen.

Most of the prescriptive analyses of how to bring organizations through this period emphasize that the leader must have certain insights, clear vision, and the skills to articulate, communicate, and implement the vision, but they say nothing about how a given organization can find and install such a leader. In U.S. organizations in particular, the outside board members probably play a critical role in this process, but if the organization has had a strong founding culture, its board may be composed exclusively of people who share the founder's vision. Consequently, real changes in direction may not become possible until the organization gets into serious survival difficulties and begins to search for a person with different assumptions to lead it.

Leadership in Mature and Declining Organizations

In the mature organization, if it has developed a strong unifying culture, that culture now defines even what is thought of as "leadership," what is heroic or sinful behavior, how authority and power are allocated and managed, and what the rules of intimacy are. Thus, what leadership has created now either blindly perpetuates itself or creates new definitions of leadership, which may not even include the kinds of entrepreneurial assumptions that started the organization in the first place. The first problem of the mature and possibly declining organization, then, is to find a process to empower a potential leader who may have enough insight and power to overcome some of the constraining cultural assumptions.

Leaders capable of such managed culture change can come from inside the organization, if they have acquired objectivity and insight into elements of the culture. However, the formally designated senior managers of a given organization may not be willing or able to provide such culture change leadership. If a leader is imposed from the outside, he or she must have the skill to diagnose accurately what the culture of the organization is, which elements are well adapted, which elements are problematic for future adaptation, and how to change that which needs changing.

Leadership conceived of in this way is, first of all, the capacity to surmount your own organizational culture, to be able to perceive and think about ways of doing things that are different from what the current assumptions imply. Learning leaders therefore must become somewhat marginal and must be somewhat embedded in the organization's external environment to fulfill this role adequately. At the same time, learning leaders must be well connected to those parts of the organization that are themselves well connected to the environment—the sales organization, purchasing, marketing, public relations, and legal, finance, and R&D. Learning leaders must be able to listen to disconfirming information coming from these sources and to assess the implications for the future of the organization. Only when they truly understand what is happening and what will be required in the way of organizational change can they begin to take action in starting a culture learning process.

Much has been said of the need for vision in leaders, but too little has been said of their need to listen, to absorb, to search the environment for trends, to seek and accept help, and to build the organization's capacity to learn (Schein, 2009a). Especially at the strategic level, the ability to see and acknowledge the full complexity of problems becomes critical. The ability to acknowledge complexity may also imply the willingness and emotional strength to admit uncertainty and to embrace experimentation and possible errors as the only way to learn (Michael, 1985). In our obsession with leadership vision, we may have made it difficult for the learning leader to admit that his or her vision is not clear and that the whole organization together will have to learn. And, as I have repeatedly argued, vision only helps when the organization has already been disconfirmed, and members feel anxious and in need of a solution. Much of what the learning leaders must do occurs before vision even becomes relevant.

Leadership and Culture in Mergers and Acquisitions

When the management of a company decides to merge with or acquire another company, it usually checks carefully the financial strength, market position, management strength, and various other concrete aspects pertaining to the "health" of the other company. Rarely checked, however, are those aspects that might be considered "cultural": the philosophy or style of the company, its technological origins, its structure, and its ways of operating, all of which might provide clues as to its basic assumptions about its mission and its future. Yet, if culture determines and limits strategy, a cultural mismatch in an acquisition or merger is as great a risk as a financial, product, or market mismatch (Buono & Bowditch, 1989; COS, 1990; McManus & Hergert, 1988).

For example, at one point in its history, General Foods (GF) purchased Burger Chef, a successful chain of hamburger restaurants. Despite ten years of concerted effort, GF could not make the acquisition profitable. First of all, GF did not anticipate that many of the best Burger Chef managers would leave because they did not like the GF philosophy. Then, instead of hiring new managers with experience in the fast-food business, GF assigned some of its own managers to run the new business. This was its second mistake because these managers did not understand the technology of the fast-food business and hence were unable to use many of the marketing techniques that had proved effective in the parent company. Third, GF imposed many of the control systems and procedures that had historically proved useful for it, driving Burger Chef's operating costs up too high. The GF managers could never completely understand franchise operations and hence could not get a "feel" for what it would take to run that kind of business profitably. Eventually GF sold Burger Chef, having lost many millions of dollars over the course of a decade.

Another example highlights the clash of two sets of assumptions about authority. A first-generation company, run by a founder who injected strong beliefs that success resulted from stimulating initiative and egalitarianism, was bought by another first-generation company, which was run by a strong autocratic entrepreneur who had trained his employees to be highly disciplined and formal. The purchasing company wanted and needed the new talent it acquired, but within one year of the purchase, most of the best managers from the acquired company had left because they could not adapt to the formal autocratic style of the parent company. The autocratic entrepreneur could not understand why this had happened and had no sensitivity to the cultural differences between the two companies. What is striking in both of these cases is the acquiring company's lack of insight into its own unconscious assumptions about how a business should be run.

In a third example, we see a case of cultural misdiagnosis. A U.S. company realized that it was about to be acquired by a larger British firm. The company conducted an internal audit of its own culture and concluded that being taken over by the British company would be highly unpalatable. It therefore instituted a set of procedures that made them unattractive (such as poison pills) and waited for a situation that looked more promising. A French company came onto the scene as a potential buyer and was perceived to be a much better cultural match, so the company allowed itself to be bought. Six months later, the French parent sent over a management team that decimated the U.S. company and imposed all kinds of processes that were much less compatible than anything the U.S. company had imagined. But it was too late.

After mergers, acquisitions, or diversifications have run into trouble, managers frequently say that cultural incompatibilities were at the root of it, but somehow these factors rarely get taken into account during the initial decision-making process. What then is the role of leadership in these situations? Four critical tasks can be identified:

1. Leaders must understand their own culture well enough to be able to detect where there are potential incompatibilities with the culture of the other organization.

2. Leaders must be able to decipher the other culture to engage in the kinds of activities that will reveal to them and to the other organization what some of its assumptions are.

3. Leaders must be able to articulate the potential synergies or incompatibilities in such a way that others involved in the decision process can understand and deal with the cultural realities.

4. If the leader is not the CEO, she or he must be able to convince the CEO or the executive team to take the cultural issues seriously.

Members of planning groups or acquisition teams often develop the cross-cultural insights necessary to make good decisions about mergers and acquisitions but lack the skills to convince their own senior managers to take the culture issues seriously. Or, alternatively, they get caught up in political processes that prevent the cultural realities from being attended to until after the key decisions have been made. In any case, cultural diagnosis based on marginality and the ability to surmount one's own culture again surfaces as the critical characteristic of learning leaders.

Leadership and Culture in Partnerships, Joint Ventures, and Strategic Alliances

Joint ventures and strategic alliances require cultural analysis even more than mergers and acquisitions because in today's rapidly globalizing world, cross-*national* boundaries are increasingly involved. Deciphering differences between two companies in the same national culture is not as difficult as deciphering both national and company differences when engaging in a partnership or joint venture across national boundaries (Salk, 1997). One of the special difficulties is to determine whether the differences that are perceived are attributable to national or organizational cultures, yet it is important to make this determination because the likelihood of changing national or other macrocultural characteristics is very low.

The role of learning leadership in these situations is much the same as in mergers and acquisitions, except that leaders must even surmount their national identities. For example, Essochem Europe, the European subsidiary of Exxon, could never find local managers to put on their board because they were all "too emotional." They never came to terms with their own stereotype of managers as intrinsically unemotional sorts of people and never realized or accepted that this was based on assumptions of the U.S culture. Many organizations make international assignments a requirement for a developing general manager, with the explicit notion that such experiences are essential if potential leaders with broader outlooks are to surface. In other words, the learning leader must become marginal not only with respect to the organizational culture but even with respect to national and ethnic culture.

Implications for the Selection and Development of Leaders

What, then, is really needed to exercise learning leadership that will stimulate cultural learning?

1. Perception and Insight

The learning leader must be able to perceive the problem, to have insight into the culture and its dysfunctional elements. Such boundary-spanning perception can be difficult because it requires leaders to see their own weaknesses, to perceive that their own defenses not only help in managing anxiety but can also hinder their efforts to be effective. Successful architects of change must have a high degree of objectivity about themselves and their own organizations. Such objectivity results from spending portions of their careers in diverse settings that permit them to compare and contrast different cultures. In the development of future leaders, many organizations are therefore emphasizing international experience.

Individuals often are aided in becoming objective about themselves through counseling and psychotherapy. Learning leaders could benefit from comparable processes, such as training and development programs that emphasize *experiential* learning and self-assessment. From this perspective, we should also note that one of the most important functions of outside consultants or board members is to provide the kind of counseling that produces cultural insight. It is therefore far more important for the consultant to help the leader figure himself or herself out than to provide recommendations on what the organization should do. The consultant also can serve as a "cultural therapist," helping the leader figure out what the culture is and which parts of it are more or less adaptive.

To become learning oriented, leaders also need to acknowledge their own limitations. As the world becomes more turbulent, it will be more and more difficult to develop clear visions. Instead, leaders will have to admit to not knowing the answer, to admit to not being in control, to seek help even from subordinates, to embrace trial-and-error learning, and to become supportive of the learning efforts of others. As I have argued in a recent book, the leader must be able to seek help from others, even the subordinates, and must develop the skill of "humble inquiry" (Schein, 2009a).

2. Motivation

Learning leaders require not only insight into the dynamics of the culture but also the motivation and skill to intervene in their own cultural process. To change any elements of the culture, leaders must be willing to unfreeze their own organization. Unfreezing requires disconfirmation, a process that is inevitably painful for many. The leader must find a way to say to his or her own organization that things are not all right and must, if necessary, enlist the aid of outsiders in getting this message across. Such willingness requires a great ability to be concerned for the organization above and beyond the self, to communicate dedication or commitment to the group above and beyond self-interest.

If the boundaries of organizations become looser, a further motivational issue arises in that it is less and less clear where a leader's ultimate loyalty should lie—should it be with the organization, the industry, the country, or with a professional community whose ultimate responsibility is to the globe and to humanity in some broader sense?

3. Emotional Strength

Unfreezing an organization requires the creation of psychological safety, which means that the leader must have the emotional strength to absorb much of the anxiety that change brings with it and must also have the ability to remain supportive to the organization through the transition phase, even if group members become angry and obstructive. The leader is likely to be the target of anger and criticism because, by definition, he or she must challenge some of what the group has taken for granted. This may involve such powerful symbolic acts as closing down a division in the company that was the original source of the company's growth and the basis of many employees' source of pride and identity. It may involve laying off or retiring loyal, dedicated employees and old friends. Worst of all, it may involve the message that some of the founder's most cherished assumptions are wrong in the contemporary context. It is here that dedication and commitment are especially needed to demonstrate to the organization that the leader genuinely cares about the welfare of the total organization even as parts of it come under challenge.

4. Ability to Change the Cultural Assumptions

If an assumption is to be given up, it must be replaced or redefined in another form, and it is the burden of learning leadership to make that happen. In other words, leaders must have the ability to induce "cognitive redefinition" by articulating and selling new values and concepts or creating the conditions for others to find these new values and concepts. They must be able to bring to the surface, review, and change some of the group's basic assumptions. In Ciba-Geigy, this process had only begun in the redirection program project described in the previous chapter. Many managers were beginning to doubt that the organization's commitment to science-based technical products could sustain the company in the long run. The eventual merger with Sandoz and the concentration on pharmaceuticals clearly stimulated this redefinition.

5. Ability to Create Involvement and Participation

A paradox of learning leadership is that the leader must be able not only to lead but also to listen, to involve the group in achieving its own insights into its cultural dilemmas, and to be genuinely participative in his or her approach to learning and change. The leaders of social, religious, or political movements can rely on personal charisma and let the followers do what they will. But in an organization, the leader has to work with the group that exists at the moment because he or she is dependent on the people to carry out the organization's mission. The leader must recognize that, in the end, cognitive redefinition must occur inside the heads of many members of the organization, and that will happen only if they are actively involved in the process. The whole organization must achieve some degree of insight and develop motivation to change before any real change will occur, and the leader must create this involvement. All of what has been said so far becomes more complicated when macrocultures become involved and when the work units become multicultural.

Another way of saying this is that the leader must have the process skills to manage relationships and groups across macrocultural boundaries and across hierarchical and occupational boundaries.

Summary and Conclusions

I have tried to articulate in this chapter the characteristics of what we might call a "learning culture" and the implications for leadership of the realities of creating such a culture in an increasingly turbulent and unpredictable world. I reviewed the culture change issues at the major stages of organizational development and focused on the leadership role in developing strategy, in mergers and acquisitions, and in joint ventures and strategic alliances.

Learning and change cannot be imposed on people. Their involvement and participation is needed in diagnosing what is going on, in figuring out what to do, and in the actual process of learning and change. The more turbulent, ambiguous, and out of control the world becomes, the more the learning process will have to be shared by all the members of the social unit doing the learning. To this end, we need to next explore the concept of *cultural islands*, which are culturally oriented dialogues.

21

CULTURAL ISLANDS: MANAGING MULTICULTURAL GROUPS

In the previous chapter, I outlined what a learning culture and learning leadership must be. It is easy to specify these requirements; it is very hard to fulfill them. In particular, it is not at all clear how cultural insight and mutual understanding can be achieved in *multicultural* settings, groups, and organizations when several national and occupational macrocultures are involved. Multicultural task forces and projects will not only be more common but they have even acquired a new name—"collaborations." Such groupings are described in an article within the *Handbook of Cultural Intelligence* (Ang and Van Dyne, 2008):

> Participants in a collaboration may come together on a one-time basis, without anticipating continued interaction. A core set of members may remain involved for an extended period of time, but other participants may float on and off the effort, working only on an "as needed" sporadic basis. Further, collaborations may have periods of intensely interdependent interaction, but may otherwise consist of quite independent actors. Many are not embedded in a single organizational context, but represent either cross-organizational cooperation or participants may not have any organizational affiliation at all. Participants may feel as though they share a common purpose for the duration of a given project, yet may not view themselves as a "team." Collaborators may never meet face-to-face, may be geographically dispersed, and may be primarily connected by communication technology. Thus collaborations are more loosely structured, more temporary, more fluid, and often more electronically enabled than traditional teams. (Gibson and Dibble, 2008, pp. 222–223)

The two prototype situations to consider are (1) a task force in which every member comes from a different nationality, and (2) a team such as a surgical team in which every member comes from a different occupational culture with hierarchical differences within the team. The unique factor in these kinds of groups is that we are dealing both with national and status differences. From a culture management and learning leadership perspective, how are such groups to be created and made effective?

In each of these cases, the group must undergo some experiences that enable the members to discover essential cultural characteristics of the other members, to overcome the rituals of deference and demeanor that curtail open communication across status levels, to develop some amount of understanding and empathy, and to find some common ground. In particular, they must discover the norms and underlying assumptions that deal with *authority* and *intimacy* because common ground in those areas is essential to developing feasible working relationships. This task is made especially difficult because each culture's social order has norms about "face" that make it difficult and dangerous to talk about these areas openly. Rules of politeness and fear of offending make it very likely that members will not easily reveal their deeper feelings about authority and intimacy.

We are not talking about how to manage a merger or joint venture when only two cultures are involved and where some formal mutual education might work. Instead we are now talking about how an Arab, an Israeli, a Japanese, a Nigerian, and an American, for example, can be shaped into a functioning work group even if they share some knowledge of English. Briefing the group on where each country stands on the Hofstede dimensions would do little to foster understanding or empathy. Or consider how a surgeon, an anesthesiologist, several nurses, and technicians who have to implement a new surgical technique can become a successful team (Edmondson, Bohmer, and Pisano, 2001). Add the possibility that in this medical team, three of the members are from different countries and received their training in those countries; how would they find common ground? Lecturing to such a group about the culture of doctors and the different culture of nurses would only scratch the surface if the members need to collaborate constructively. What kind of education or experience would enable such groups to develop working relationships, trust, and task-relevant open communications? That is the puzzle to be solved.

It is necessary to remember that the *social order* and its norms of politeness, tact, and face saving is an *essential* component of culture, designed to make society possible. Every macroculture develops a social order, but the actual norms differ from culture to culture. For example, in the United States, face-to-face criticism is acceptable; in Japan it is not. In some cultures, hiring relatives is the only way to get trusted employees; in other cultures, it is called nepotism and is forbidden. In some cultures, trust is established with a handshake; in others, it can only be established with pay-offs and bribes (and even the word "bribe" is culturally loaded). Differences across occupational boundaries might not be as extreme, but they are just as important if teams that cut across hierarchical boundaries and occupations have to function together.

Cultural Intelligence

One approach to solving multicultural issues of this sort is to educate each member about the norms and assumptions of each of the cultures involved. I have already indicated that this approach would not only be cumbersome because of the number of different cultures involved but also would have to be so abstract that the learners would not know how to apply what they have been told.

A second approach is to focus on cultural capacities and *learning skills*, what is increasingly being called *cultural intelligence* (Thomas and Inkson, 2003; Earley & Ang, 2003; Peterson, 2004; Plum, 2008; Ang and Van Dyne, 2008). Because there are very many macrocultures in the world, to learn their content appears to be a much less feasible approach than to develop the learning skills to quickly acquire whatever knowledge is needed of the cultures that are involved in a particular situation. The basic problem in multicultural situations is that the members of each macroculture may have opinions and biases about "the others," or may even have some level of understanding of the "the others" but operate by the premise that their own culture is the one that is "right." Getting multicultural organizations, projects, and teams to work together, therefore, poses a much larger cultural challenge than how to evolve or manage cultural change within a single macroculture such as was discussed in the previous two chapters.

The concept of *cultural intelligence* introduces the proposition that to develop understanding, empathy, and the ability to work with others from other cultures requires four capacities: (1) actual knowledge of some of the essentials of the other cultures involved, (2) cultural sensitivity or mind-fulness about culture, (3) motivation to learn about other cultures, and (4) behavioral skills and flexibility to learn new ways of doing things (Earley and Ang, 2003; Thomas and Inkson, 2003). For multicultural teams to work, therefore, implies that certain individual characteristics have to be present to enable cross-cultural learning.

In their *Handbook of Cultural Intelligence* (2008), Ang and Van Dyne present a set of papers that both describe the development of a cultural intelligence scale and show that teams with members that score higher on this measure perform better than lower scoring groups. There are clearly individual differences in cultural sensitivity and learning capacity, and there is a vast psychological literature on what makes people more or less culturally competent, but *selecting* people for this capacity does not address two problems. First, in many work situations, we do not have choices in whom to assign because of limited resources in the technical skills needed to do the work. Second, if a leader decides to *increase* the cultural com-petence of employees, what kind of experiences should they have? What should the leader do by way of designing learning processes that will stimu-late such competence regardless of the initial state of cultural intelligence of the participants? The goal in this chapter is to begin to describe such a process.

Because culture is so deeply embedded in each of us, this process must confront the fundamental reality that each member of each culture begins with the assumption that what he or she does is the right and proper way to do things. We each come from a social order into which we have been socialized and, therefore, take its assumptions for granted. Intellectual understanding of other cultures may be a start in granting that there are other ways to do things, but it does little to build empathy and does not enable us to find common ground for working together. More likely we begin by noting how the "other processes or positions won't work or are wrong."

To achieve a sufficient level of empathy and a context in which the group is motivated to engage in a mutual search for common ground requires a temporary suspension of some of the rules of the social order. We must be brought to the point of being able to reflect on our own assumptions and consider the possibility that some other assumptions may be just as valid as our own. This process starts with questioning ourselves, not with becoming convinced of the rightness of others. How is this to be done? What kind of social process has to be created to achieve such a state of reflection?

The Concept of a Temporary Cultural Island

A *cultural island* is a situation in which the rules of having to maintain face are temporarily suspended so that we can explore our self-concepts and thereby our values and tacit assumptions, especially around authority and intimacy. The first use of this term in the organizational domain was in Bethel, Maine where Human Relations Training groups met for several weeks to learn about leadership and group dynamics (Bradford, Gibb, and Benne, 1964; Schein and Bennis, 1965). The essence of this training process was described in detail in Chapter Twelve and is based on the theory that this kind of learning has to be "experiential" in the sense that group members would learn from their own efforts to become a group. The groups were deliberately composed in such a way that all members would be strangers to each other so that no one had to maintain a particular identity vis-à-vis the others in the group. At the same time, the "trainers" or staff members of these T-groups (training groups) deliberately withheld any suggestions for the agenda, working method, or structure, thus forcing members to invent their own social order, their own norms, and ways of working together. The main impact of this kind of learning was that people confronted their own assumptions and observed how these differed from the assumptions of others.

As was described in Chapter Twelve, the problems of authority, intimacy, and identity had to be confronted immediately through personal experimentation and observation of an individual's impact on others. Members became acutely aware that there was no one best way to do things, that the best way had to be discovered, negotiated, and ratified, leading eventually to strong group norms that created a microculture in each T-group. Members also discovered that they did not have to *like* each other to work together, but they had to have sufficient empathy to be able to *accept* others and work with them. Microcultures often formed within a day or two in these groups and were viewed by each group as the best way to do things—"we are the best group."

What made T-group experiential learning possible was that the learning took place under conditions where members could relax the need to defend their own cultural assumptions because they were strangers to each other, were in a situation defined as "learning" rather than performing, and had the time and staff resources to develop their own learning skills. In terms of the change model described in Chapter Seventeen, they were in a psychologically safe situation.

It is my proposition that for multicultural collaborations to work, the members must first learn about each other in a temporary cultural island. The leaders and managers who create such groups must therefore develop the skills to create temporary cultural island experiences for the members to enable them to work effectively. How would a leader design such a situation? Exhibit 21.1 shows the essential conditions that are needed for this learning process to be successful.

Several of the points in the exhibit are deliberately general and abstract because how they are implemented will vary with the purpose of establishing the cultural island in the first place. But the basic logic is that to truly understand the deep assumptions of the macrocultures involved in the group, we must create a microculture that personalizes those assumptions and makes them available for reflection and understanding. I can be told that as an American, we have fairly "low power distance" in U.S. culture, and that my Mexican team member comes from a culture with "higher power distance," but this will mean nothing to me until we can concretize these generalizations in our own behavior and feelings. I need to discover

Exhibit 21.1.   Conditions for a Temporary Cultural Island for a Multicultural Work Group.

- Participants must be motivated and committed to new learning.
- Participants must be physically isolated from their work situation.
- Authority figures must adopt egalitarian norms and emphasize that learning is a mutual responsibility.
- Authority figures must become facilitators and process managers.
- Facilitators must define the goals and working rules to enable the participants to feel psychologically safe to suspend some of the rules of the social order.
- Facilitators must define the main learning focus as authority and intimacy.
- The process must involve talking about concrete experiences and feelings.

within myself how I relate to people in authority, and I need to listen with empathy to how my Mexican teammate feels about his relationship to authority. If there are more than two of us, we must each develop some understanding and empathy for each other.

Cultural islands that attempt to facilitate this level of mutual understanding are created when we send teams to Outward Bound kinds of training, when we put teams in simulations, in role playing situations, in post-mortems or After Action Reviews where a review of operations or experiences deliberately tries to minimize hierarchy and open communication to lower status participants (Conger, 1992; Darling and Parry, 2001; Mirvis, Ayas, and Roth, 2003). What these situations and programs have in common is that they put participants into the cultural island, but then what they do within the cultural island setting varies widely according to the purpose of the exercise. To focus the activity within the cultural island on obtaining multicultural insight and empathy, the participants must create a conversation in a dialogue format.

Focused Dialogue as a Cultural Island

Dialogue is a form of conversation that allows the participants to relax sufficiently to begin to examine the assumptions that lie behind their thought processes (Isaacs, 1999; Schein, 1993). Instead of trying to solve problems rapidly, the dialogue process attempts to slow down the conversation to allow participants to reflect on what comes out of their own mouths and what they hear from the mouths of others. The key to initiating dialogic conversation is to create a setting in which participants feel secure enough to *suspend* their need to win arguments, clarify everything they say, and challenge each other every time they disagree. In a dialogue, if someone has just said something that I disagree with, *suspension* would mean that I would hold back voicing my disagreement and, instead, silently ask myself why I disagree and what assumptions I am making that might explain the disagreement.

This form of dialogue is a low-key "talking around the campfire," allowing enough time for and encouraging reflective conversation, rather than confrontational conversation, discussion, or debate. Talking "to the campfire" is an important element of this dialogue process because the *absence* of eye contact makes it easier to suspend reactions, disagreements, objections, and other responses that might be triggered by face-to-face conversation. The purpose is not just to have a quiet, reflective conversation; rather, it is to allow participants to begin to see where their deeper levels of thought and tacit assumptions differ. Paradoxically such reflection leads to better listening in that if I identify my own assumptions and filters first, I am less likely to mishear or misunderstand the subtle meanings in the words of others. I cannot understand another culture if I have no insight into my own.

For this to work, all of the parties to the dialogue have to be willing to suspend their impulses to disagree, challenge, clarify, and elaborate. The conversational process imposes certain rules such as not interrupting, talking to the symbolic campfire instead of to each other, limiting eye contact, and, most important of all, starting with a "check-in." Checking in at the beginning of the meeting means that each member in turn will say something to the group as a whole, the campfire, about his or her present mental state, motivation, or feelings. Only when all of the members have checked in, is the group ready for a more free-flowing conversation. The check-in ensures that everyone has made an initial contribution to the group and, thereby, has helped to *create* the group.

An example of discovering our own culture typically arises immediately around the instruction to talk to the campfire and avoid eye contact. For some people, this is very easy, but for others, for example, American human resource professionals, this is very difficult because in U.S. culture looking at each other is considered "good communication," and this is reinforced by the professional norms in the human resource field that eye contact is necessary to make the other feel that you are really listening.

Talking to the symbolic campfire serves several important functions. First of all it encourages group members to become more reflective by not getting distracted by how others look and respond. Second, it preserves the sense of being one whole group by symbolically contributing each comment to the center not to one or two other members, even though the comment may have been triggered by them. For example, if I have a specific question based on what member A has said, there is a consequential difference between my saying directly to A, "What did you mean by . . . ?" versus saying to the campfire, "What A has just said makes me want to ask. . . ."

The second way of saying it raises the issue for the group as a whole. Third, the campfire avoids the common phenomenon of two members getting into a deep discussion while the rest of the group becomes a passive audience. The goal is to suspend as many of the assumed rules of interaction coming from all the different cultural social orders and create a new container within which members can talk more openly and can verbalize their reflections.

Dialogue as a Cultural Island for Multicultural Exploration

The norms created in a dialogue group lend themselves to the explorations of critical cultural differences. The dialogue process allows the articulation of macrocultural differences at a personal level so that the participants not

---

Case Example

A group of ten MIT MBA students from different countries wanted to explore cultural differences within their group. They all spoke English but had a sense that they did not understand each other well enough to be able to work together on a joint task. We agreed to meet for a two-hour session to explore cultural differences.

Step 1. Setting Up the Dialogue Rules

As the faculty facilitator, I explained the concept of dialogue and the basic rules that we would speak only to the "campfire," not to each other; that we did not have to respond to questions; that we would not at any time interrupt each other; and that we would begin with a "check-in" by each answering two questions about ourselves.

Step 2. First Check-In Question: Focus on Authority Issues

I asked each person to think for a moment about a past situation in which their boss or someone else in a position of authority was about to do something wrong in relation to the task they were engaged in. I then asked each person, in order and without being interrupted or questioned, to tell *the campfire* what they did or would do in that situation and give as much personal detail as possible. I emphasized that I did not want general comments about "their culture" but personal stories so that we would experience the culture through the personal experiences. Later

(Continued)

we could follow up with general questions about each culture. I then turned to the person on my right and asked him or her to begin. When that person was finished, I asked the next person to talk to the campfire and so on until everyone had told their story. I enforced the rule of no questions or interruptions and kept the group members talking in order.

If someone was not sure what I meant, I kept emphasizing that we wanted to hear from each member about an actual incident or, if they had no actual experience, their account of what they think they would do if a boss was about to make a mistake or do something wrong. The goal is to push down the abstraction ladder, to get some concrete examples. I also emphasized that we needed to hear what they would do, not what someone in their culture might do because we needed to get acquainted with the person in the room, not some abstract representative of the culture.

Step 3. Reflection and Open Conversation

When everyone had told their stories, I asked for a few minutes of silent reflection on what variations we had heard and what common ground there seemed to be among the stories. I then asked for comments, observations, and questions but with the ground rule that we kept looking at and talking to the campfire. This was awkward at first but the group learned within a few minutes that it was easier to say what was on their minds if they did not look at a particular other group member even if the question was directed to him or her. If the group included members of obviously different rank or status, I asked for reflection on the implications of what they had heard for this group. This conversation went on for about fifteen to thirty minutes. I then introduced the second questions.

Step 4. Second Check-In Question: Focus on Intimacy and Trust

I said we would now again go in order to each talk about a situation in which the person had to decide whether or not he or she could trust a coworker, and how they made the decision. What kinds of behavior would they look for in the other person to determine whether or not that person could be trusted? What criteria did they use in deciding whether to trust the person, and how did it work out? Again, each person, in order and without interruption, was to tell the campfire his or her story of how this worked out.

Step 5. Open Conversation to Reflect on Intimacy and Trust Stories

Here again I imposed the rule of talking only to the campfire as the group explored differences and similarities in what they heard from each other. I asked the group to reflect on the implications of what they had heard for this group's ability to work together. At an appropriate point, I shifted the conversation to the next step.

Step 6. Exploration of How the Dialogue Format Had Influenced Members' Understanding of Themselves and Each Other

The learning goal was to show members that cross-cultural understanding can be achieved through a dialogue process, and that they can set up such a process whenever they get stuck in the future. I emphasized the importance of getting personal experiences from everyone on how the specific problems of authority and intimacy were handled by them in their culture. Other dimensions of the macrocultures could come into the discussion, but the critical issues for the group to be able to work together were authority and intimacy.

The logic of this format is to surface reliable personal information about how each member of this multicultural group feels about and handles authority and intimacy because those are the crucial areas in which a working consensus is needed for the group to function on a task. The goal is not to learn about cultures in general but to enable the members of this team to learn enough about each other to be able to work together.

only learn how macrocultures differ at a general level but can experience those differences immediately in the room. This learning is achieved by using the check-in to focus on the critical issues of authority and intimacy. The process is illustrated in the case and could be varied according to the actual circumstances that a given leader faces.

How to Set Up a Dialogue

The case example involved students in a learning situation. How a comparable process would be set up in a multicultural task force or a surgical team depends very much on the actual situation and the goals that the leader is trying to accomplish. Ideally the group will have already decided to move physically out of the work setting to make the creation of the cultural island atmosphere easier. However, the dialogue format can create the cultural island atmosphere on its own if the ground rules are followed. In fact, the power of the dialogue format is that it stimulates the cultural island norms through its process even if it is done in a work setting. Exhibit 21.2 lays out the process if you desire to run your own dialogue session.

If the new organization is a multicultural group or a collaboration, the same process is used but the initial questions for the check-in might be something specific that highlights cultural differences in relation to the task but always deals with authority and intimacy. For example, if the group is a safety committee in a multinational company such as Schlumberger, you might ask each member to, say, "What would you do if you saw your boss

---

Exhibit 21.2.   How to Set Up a Dialogue.

1. Identify the group that needs to explore intercultural relationships.

2. Seat everyone in a circle or as near to it as possible.

3. Lay out the purpose of the dialogue: "to be able to listen more reflectively to ourselves and to each other, to get a sense of the similarities and differences in our cultures."

4. Start the conversation by having the members in turn check in by introducing who they are and answering the relevant question about authority relations as they see them, for example, "What do you do when you see your boss doing something wrong?" Ask each person to talk to the campfire, avoid eye contact, and prohibit any questions or comments until everyone has checked in.

5. After everyone has checked in, launch a very general question, such as, "What differences and commonalities did anyone notice?" Ask members to continue to talk to the campfire even if they are addressing a particular member. Encourage an open conversation on what everyone has just heard without the constraints of proceeding in order or having to withhold questions and comments.

6. When the topic runs dry or the group loses energy, introduce the second question, for example, "How do you know whether or not you can trust one of your coworkers?" Again, have everyone in turn give an answer before general conversation begins.

7. Let the differences and commonalities emerge naturally; don't try to make general statements because the purpose is mutual understanding and empathy, not necessarily clear description or conclusions.

8. After this topic runs dry, ask the group to poll itself by asking each person in turn to share one or two insights about his or her own culture and any other cultures that he or she has heard about during the dialogue.

9. Ask the group to identify common ground and what, if any, problems they see in working together, given what they have heard about authority/power and intimacy/trust.

10. Ask the group what next steps they feel they need to work together.

---

about to do something that you consider to be unsafe?" And for the second round, you might ask, "What would you do if a coworker whom you don't know is about to do something that you consider to be unsafe?"

Again, the goal is to avoid one-on-one conversations, questions, or arguments, stimulating instead a listening climate such that members will be less self-conscious and less worried about self-presentation. Talking to the campfire is crucial because the campfire does not talk back.

When and Why to Use Dialogue and Other Forms of Cultural Islands

I have been arguing throughout this fourth edition that the world is changing toward more cultural diversity. Cultural diversity breeds more communication problems, especially at hierarchic boundaries because the rules of deference and demeanor are so highly variable around the world and across occupations. My own organizational experience tells me that communication is a problem even within a given culture, so the trend toward cultural diversity will exacerbate this problem.

For example, in the arena of safety in high hazard industries such as nuclear power, airlines, and health care, the biggest inhibiter to effective performance is the failure of *upward* communication. It is sad to see how many fatal accidents over the years have resulted from communication failures that have cultural roots. In the NASA space program in both the Challenger and Columbia cases, there were engineers who were unable to communicate with managers, clear examples of subcultural differences that did not get resolved (Gerstein, 2008). In the power industry as exemplified by the Alpha case reviewed in this book, it has become increasingly clear that the day-to-day performance of the entire organization rests on the skill and commitment of the hourly employees. If supervisors and their managers fail to create a climate of psychological safety that stimulates upward communication, both safety and overall organizational effectiveness will be compromised. To minimize this risk, most committees have both union and management on the committee and trained facilitators to run the meetings. Though they do not use the formal dialogue model presented here, they create cultural islands through their training center programs and through very thorough accident investigations that deemphasize blame. The surgical teams referred to before went away for training in a cultural island setting and went through various interpersonal exercises and simulations to establish open communication lines.

When it comes to multinational groups, the problems are, of course, worse because there may not even be a common language with which to have a dialogue. In such a situation, the actual learning of a common language can itself be a facilitative cultural island. As Gladwell (2008) points out in his reconstruction of the Colombian airlines disaster in 1990, that at the root of it was (1) the failure of the Colombian co-pilot to understand that the JFK controllers did not translate "we are low on fuel" into "EMERGENCY," and (2) that the co-pilot did not know that being put at the head of the line for landing only occurred if you declared an emergency. He further notes that the Korean Airline had a series of disasters in the 1990s because of communication failures across rank levels within the cockpit and that this eventually was only ameliorated by shifting the cockpit language to English. The change in language provided the cultural island that permitted the introduction of new rules that led to better communication in the cockpit.

Along these same lines, "procedures" and "checklists" are devices that can function as cultural islands in the sense that going through the list is a culturally neutral process. The subordinate is licensed to ask challenging questions of the more senior person if it is a checklist item without thereby threatening the senior person's face. Checklists and procedures have been very helpful in the medical context in that they neutralize the dangerous status gap between nurses and technicians on the one hand and doctors on the other hand. The checklist or procedure can become a superordinate authority that puts the doctor, nurse, and technician on an equal level as they go through the procedure. Insisting that dialogue conversations be "to the campfire" in a multinational group serves the same neutralizing function in implying that each culture is of equal rank and validity. Face-to-face implies comparison, which at this stage of exploration, is undesirable.

Summary and Conclusions

The analysis of safety issues in high hazard industries and in the health care field has revealed several important facts that will serve as conclusions to this analysis. Let me put these into a sequential logic:

1. Many failures in the safety arena could have been prevented if there had been better communication across cultural boundaries.

2. Some of these boundaries are technical where people did not understand the jargon and subtle meanings, and hence either failed to understand or misunderstood.

3. Some of these boundaries are rank levels where communication breaks down because of cultural norms of deference and demeanor, leading to face protection rather than open sharing of task-relevant information.

4. Some of these boundaries are macrocultural reflecting either national or occupational norms and values that lead either to not communicating things in the first place or dismissing communications from culture members who are viewed as "wrong" or "not knowing" or "having the wrong values."

5. These three kinds of cultural boundary problems are highly visible in multicultural groups that involve either nations or major occupational groups, but they operate just as much in organizations within a given national culture because of the subcultures built around ranks and functions.

6. Theories of organizational effectiveness emphasize the importance of open communications vertically and laterally, but they fail to acknowledge that such communications occur across cultural boundaries and, therefore, require cultural island settings to ensure understanding and empathy. Exhorting the surgeon and the nurse to be open with each other is not enough; they have to have some kind of mutual cultural island experience that builds common ground and mutual understanding.

7. A cultural perspective that acknowledges the existence of national and occupational macrocultures, functional subcultures, and subcultures based on rank and common experience is therefore an essential component of organizational leadership.

8. The organizational leader must therefore become aware of when and how to create temporary cultural islands to enable various members of the organization to communicate with each other more openly.

9. When and how this is done is itself a function of the macroculture in which the organization and the leaders are operating. For example, a culture in which time is measured in very short units and is considered a key to productivity might have to speed up some version of the dialogue process. The important point is not how long it takes but the creation of the climate of neutrality and temporary suspension of the rules of the social order.

As organizations become more multicultural, new ways of doing this will have to be invented, but some form of temporary cultural island will always be needed to improve communication across cultural boundaries. As organizations become more decentralized and electronically connected, some version of cultural islands will have to be invented to enable people who have not and may not ever meet each other to develop understanding and empathy. It is quite possible that the dialogic format can work well in a network if the participants tell their own stories of authority and intimacy to each other by e-mail, Facebook, or whatever technology is extant at the time.

The world is changing rapidly, but the issues of how we treat each other and how we handle status and authority remain remarkably stable. Perhaps more dialogues around these issues will stimulate some new ideas on how to get along better.

A Final Word

We have examined organizational cultures, microcultures, macrocultures, and subcultures. The details and content of what goes on varies enormously, but the fundamental cultural dynamics are much the same at every level. If we remember that culture is our learned solution to making sense of the world, to stabilizing it, and to avoiding the anxiety that comes with social chaos, then we have taken the first important step toward deeper cultural understanding.

References

Adizes, I. (1990). *Corporate life cycles*. Englewood Cliffs, NJ: Prentice-Hall.

Adorno, T. W., Frenkel-Brunswick, E., Levinson, D. J., & Sanford, R. N. (1950). *The authoritarian personality*. New York: Harper & Row.

Aldrich, H. E., & Ruef, M. (2006). *Organizations evolving* (2nd ed.). London: Sage.

Allan, J., Fairtlough, G., & Heinzen, B. (2002). *The power of the tale*. London: Wiley.

Allen, T. J. (1977). *Managing the flow of technology*. Cambridge, MA: MIT Press.

Ancona, D. G. (1988). Groups in organizations. In C. Hendrick (Ed.), *Annual review of personality and social psychology: Group and intergroup processes*. Beverly Hills, CA: Sage.

Ancona, D. G., & Chong, C. L. (1996). Entrainment: Pace, cycle, and rhythm in organizational behavior. In B. M. Staw, & L. L. Cummings (Eds.), *Research in organizational behavior* (Vol. 18, pp. 251–284). Greenwich, CT: JAI.

Ang, S. & Van Dyne, L. (Eds.). (2008). *Handbook of cultural intelligence*. Armonk, NY: M. E. Sharpe.

Argyris, C. (1964). *Integrating the individual and the organization*. New York: Wiley.

Argyris, C. (1976). *Increasing leadership effectiveness*. New York: Wiley-Interscience.

Argyris, C., & Schon, D. A. (1974). *Theory in practice: Increasing professional effectiveness*. San Francisco, CA: Jossey-Bass.

Argyris, C., & Schon, D. A. (1978). *Organizational Learning*. Reading, MA: Addison-Wesley.

Argyris, C., & Schon, D. A. (1996). *Organizational learning II*. Reading, MA: Addison-Wesley.

Argyris, C., Putnam, R., & Smith, D. M. (1985). *Action science*. San Francisco: Jossey-Bass.

Ashkanasy, N. M., Wilderom, C. P. M., & Peterson, M. F. (Eds.). (2000). *Handbook of organizational culture and climate*. Thousand Oaks, CA: Sage.

Bailyn, L. (1978). Accommodation of work to family. In R. Rapoport, & R. N. Rapoport (Eds.), *Working couples*. London: Routledge & Kegan Paul.

Bailyn, L. (1982). The apprenticeship model of organizational careers: A response to changes in the relationship between work and family. In P. A. Wallace (Ed.), *Women in the workplace*. Boston: Auburn House.

Bailyn, L. (1985). Autonomy in the industrial R&D lab. *Human Resource Management, 24*, 129–146.

Bailyn, L. (1992). Changing the conditions of work: Implications for career development. In D. H. Montross and C. J. Shinkman (Eds.), *Career development in the 1990s: Theory and practice* (pp. 373–386). Springfield, IL: Charles C. Thomas.

Bailyn, L. (1993). *Breaking the mold*. New York: Free Press.

Barley, S. R. (1984a). The professional, the semi-professional, and the machine: The social implications of computer-based imaging in radiology. Unpublished doctoral dissertation, Sloan School of Management, MIT.

Barley, S. R. (1984b). Technology as an occasion for structuration: Observations on CT scanners and the social order of radiology departments. Cambridge, MA: Sloan School of Management, MIT.

Barley, S. R. (1988). On technology, time, and social order. In F. A. Dubinskas (Ed.), *Making time* (p. 145). Philadelphia: Temple University Press.

Barley, S. R., & Kunda, G. (2001). Bringing work back in. *Organization Science, 12*, 76–95.

Bartlett, C. A., Ghoshal, S., & Birkinshaw, J. (Eds.). (2004). *Transnational management*. New York: McGraw-Hill Irwin.

Bartunek, J. (1984). Changing interpretive schemes and organizational restructuring: The example of a religious order. *Administrative Science Quarterly, 29*, 355–372.

Bartunek, J. M., & Louis, M. R. (1996). *Insider/outsider team research*. Thousand Oaks, CA: Sage.

Bass, B. M. (1981). *Stogdill's handbook of leadership* (Rev. ed.). New York: Free Press.

Bass, B. M. (1985). *Leadership and performance beyond expectations*. New York: Free Press.

Beckhard, R., & Dyer, W. G. Jr. (1983a). Managing continuity in the family-owned business. *Organizational Dynamics*, Summer, 5–12.

Beckhard, R., & Dyer, W. G. Jr. (1983b). Managing change in the family firm: Issues and strategies. *Sloan Management Review, 24*(3), 59–65.

Beckhard, R., & Harris, R. T. (1987). *Organizational transitions: Managing complex change*. Reading, MA: Addison-Wesley.

Bennis, W., & Nanus, B. (1985). *Leaders*. New York: Harper & Row.

Bennis, W. G., & Shepard, H. A. (1956). A theory of group development. *Human Relations, 9*, 415–437.

Berg, P. O., & Kreiner, C. (1990). Corporate architecture: Turning physical settings into symbolic resources. In P. Gagliardi (Ed.), *Symbols and artifacts* (pp. 41–67). New York: Walter de Gruyter.

Bion, W. R. (1959). *Experiences in groups.* London: Tavistock.

Blake, R. R., & Mouton, J. S. (1964). *The managerial grid.* Houston: Gulf.

Blake, R. R., & Mouton, J. S. (1969). *Building a dynamic organization through grid organization development.* Reading, MA: Addison-Wesley.

Blake, R. R., Mouton, J. S., & McCanse, A. A. (1989). *Change by design.* Reading, MA: Addison-Wesley.

Bluedorn, A. C. (1997). Primary rhythms, information processing, and planning: Toward a strategic temporal technology. *Technology Studies, 4,* 1–36.

Bluedorn, A. C. (2000). Time and organizational culture. In N. M. Ashkanazy, C. P. M. Wilderom, & M. F. Peterson (Eds.), *Handbook of organizational culture and climate* (pp. 117–128). Thousand Oaks, CA: Sage.

Bradford, L. P, Gibb, J. R., & Benne, K. D. (Eds.). (1964). *T-group theory and laboratory method.* New York: Wiley.

Buono, A. F., & Bowditch, J. L. (1989). *The human side of mergers and acquisitions.* San Francisco: Jossey-Bass.

Bushe, G. R. (2009). *Clear leadership* (Rev. ed.). Mountain View, CA: Davis-Black.

Cameron, K. S., & Quinn, R. E. (1999). *Diagnosing and changing organizational culture.* Reading, MA: Addison-Wesley.

Cameron, K. S., & Quinn, R. E. (2006). *Diagnosing and changing organizational culture.* San Francisco: Jossey-Bass.

Castaneda, C. (1968). *The Teachings of Don Juan.* New York: Pocket Books.

Castaneda, C. (1972). *Journey to Ixtlan.* New York: Simon & Schuster.

Chandler, A. D., Jr. (1962). *Strategy and structure.* Cambridge, MA: MIT Press.

Ciampa, D. (1992). *Total quality: A user's guide for implementation.* Reading, MA: Addison-Wesley.

Coghlan, D. (1996). Mapping the progress of change through organizational levels. *Research in Organizational Change and Development, 9,* 123–150.

Coghlan, D., & Brannick, T. (2005). *Doing action research in your own organization.* Thousand Oaks, CA: Sage.

Conger, J. A. (1989). *The charismatic leader.* San Francisco: Jossey-Bass.

Conger, J. A. (1992). *Learning to lead.* San Francisco: Jossey-Bass.

Cook, S. D. N., & Yanow, D. (1993). Culture and organizational learning. *Journal of Management Inquiry, 2*(4), 373–390.

Cooke, R. A., & Szumal, J. L. (1993). Measuring normative beliefs and shared behavioral expectations in organizations: The reliability and validity of the Organizational Culture Inventory. *Psychological Reports, 72,* 1299–1330.

Corlett, J. G., & Pearson, C. S. (2003). *Mapping the organizational psyche.* Gainesville, FL: Center for Application of Psychological Type.

COS (Centre for Organizational Studies). (1990). *Mergers and acquisitions: Organizational and cultural issues*. Barcelona: COS/Foundation Jose M. de Anzizu, 1990.

Coutu, D. L. (2002). The anxiety of learning (interview of Ed Schein). *Harvard Business Review*, March.

Dalton, M. (1959). *Men who manage*. New York: Wiley.

Dandridge, T. C., Mitroff, I. I., & Joyce, W. (1980). Organizational symbolism: A topic to expand organizational analysis. *Academy of Management Review*, 5(1), 77–82.

Darling, M. J., & Parry. C. S. (2001). After-action reviews: Linking reflection and planning in a learning practice. *Reflections*, 3(2), 64–72.

Davis, S. M. (1984). *Managing corporate culture*. Cambridge, MA: Ballinger.

Davis, S., & Davidson, B. (1991). *2020 vision*. New York: Simon and Schuster.

Deal, T. E., & Kennedy, A. A. (1982). *Corporate cultures*. Reading, MA: Addison-Wesley.

Deal, T. E., & Kennedy, A. A. (1999). *The new corporate cultures*. New York: Perseus.

Denison, D. R. (1990). *Corporate culture and organizational effectiveness*. New York: Wiley.

Denison, D. R. & Mishra, A. K. (1995). Toward a theory of organizational culture and effectiveness. *Organizational Science*, 6(2), March-April.

Denison, D. R., Haaland. S., & Goelzer, P. (2003). *Corporate culture and organizational effectiveness: Is there a similar pattern around the world?* (pp. 205–227) Greenwich: Jai Press.

DiBella, A. J. (1993). The role of assumptions in implementing management practices across cultural boundaries. *Journal of Applied Behavioral Science*, 29(3), 311–332.

Donaldson, G., & Lorsch, J. W. (1983). *Decision making at the top*. New York: Basic Books.

Dougherty, D. (1990). Understanding new markets for new products. *Strategic Management Journal, 11*, 59–78.

Douglas, M. (1986). *How institutions think*. Syracuse, NY: Syracuse University Press.

Drucker Foundation, Hesselbein, F., Goldsmith, M., & Somerville, I. (Eds.). (1999). *Leading beyond the walls*. San Francisco: Jossey-Bass.

Dubinskas, F. A. (1988). *Making time: Ethnographies of high-technology organizations*. Philadelphia, PA: Temple University Press.

Dyer, W. G., Jr. (1986). *Culture change in family firms*. San Francisco: Jossey-Bass.

Dyer, W. G., Jr. (1989). Integrating professional management into a family-owned business. *Family Business Review*, 2(3), 221–236.

Earley, P. C., & Ang, S. (2003). *Cultural intelligence: Individual interactions across cultures*. Stanford, CA: Stanford University Press.

Edmundson, A. C., Bohmer, R. M., & Pisano, G. P. (2001). Disrupted routines: Team learning and new technology implementation in hospitals. *Administrative Science Quarterly, 46*, 685–716.

England, G. (1975). *The manager and his values*. Cambridge, MA: Ballinger.

Etzioni, A. (1975). *A comparative analysis of complex organizations*. New York: Free Press.

Evans, P., Pucik, V., & Barsoux, J-L. (2002). *The global challenge*. New York: McGraw-Hill Irwin.

Fadiman, A. (1997). *The spirit catches you and you fall down*. New York: Farrar, Strauss & Giroux.

Festinger, L. A. (1957). *Theory of cognitive dissonance*. New York: Harper & Row.

Frost, P. J. (2003). *Toxic emotions at work*. Boston: Harvard Business School Press.

Gagliardi, P. (Ed.) (1990). *Symbols and artifacts: Views of the corporate landscape*. New York: Walter de Gruyter.

Gagliardi, P. (1999). Exploring the aesthetic side of organizational life. In S. R. Clegg, & C. Hardy (Eds.), *Studying organization: Theory and method* (pp. 311–326). Thousand Oaks, CA: Sage.

Geertz, C. (1973). *The interpretation of cultures*. New York: Basic Books.

Gersick, C. J. C. (1991). Revolutionary change theories: A multilevel exploration of the punctuated equilibrium paradigm. *Academy of Management Review, 16*, 10–36.

Gerstein, M. (2008). *Flirting with disaster*. New York: Union Square.

Gerstein, M. S. (1987). *The technology connection: Strategy and change in the information age*. Reading, MA: Addison-Wesley.

Gerstner, L. V. (2002). *Who says elephants can't dance*. New York: Collins.

Gibson, C. F., & Ball, L. D. (1989). Executive mindscapes and information technology. *Indications* (Index Group Inc.), 6(6).

Gibson, C. B., & Dibble, R. (2008). Culture inside and out: Developing a collaboration's capacity to externally adapt. In S. Ang, & L. Van Dyne (Eds.), *Handbook of cultural intelligence*. Armonk, NY: M. E. Sharpe.

Gladwell, M. (2008). *Outliers*. New York: Little Brown.

Global Business Network. (2002). *What's next? Exploring the new terrain for business*. Cambridge, MA: Perseus Books.

Goffee, R., & Jones, G. (1998). *The character of a corporation*. New York: Harper Business.

Goffman, E. (1959). *The presentation of self in every day life*. New York: Doubleday.

Goffman, E. (1961). *Asylums*. New York: Doubleday Anchor.

Goffman, E. (1967). *Interaction ritual.* Hawthorne, NY: Aldine.

Goldman, A. (2008). Company on the couch: Unveiling toxic behavior in dysfunctional organizations. *Journal of Management Inquiry, 17*(3), 226–238.

Greiner, L. E. (1972). Evolution and revolution as organizations grow. *Harvard Business Review, 76*(3), 37–46.

Greiner, L. E., & Poulfelt, L. (Eds.). (2005). *Management consulting today and tomorrow.* New York: Routledge.

Grenier, R., & Metes, G. (1992). *Enterprise networking: Working together apart.* Maynard, MA: Digital Press.

Hall, E. T. (1959). *The silent language.* New York: Doubleday.

Hall, E. T. (1966). *The hidden dimension.* New York: Doubleday.

Hall, E. T. (1977). *Beyond culture.* New York: Doubleday.

Hamilton B. A. (2003) Carl Bertelsmann–Preis 2003: Unternehmens profile unpublished study, Gütersloh: Bertelsmann Stiftung.

Hampden-Turner, C. M., & Trompenaars, A. (1993). *The seven cultures of capitalism.* New York: Doubleday Currency.

Hampden-Turner, C. M., & Trompenaars, A. (2000). *Building cross-cultural competence.* New York: Wiley.

Handy, C. (1978). *The gods of management.* London: Pan Books.

Harbison, F., & Myers, C. A. (1959). *Management in the industrial world.* New York: McGraw-Hill.

Harrison, R. (1979). Understanding your organization's character. *Harvard Business Review, 57*(5), 119–128.

Harrison, R., & Stokes, H. (1992). *Diagnosing organizational culture.* San Francisco: Pfeiffer.

Hassard, J. (1999). Images of time in work and organization. In S. R. Clegg, & C. Hardy (Eds.), *Studying organization* (pp. 327–344). Thousand Oaks, CA: Sage.

Hatch, M. J. (1990). The symbolics of office design. In P. Gagliardi (Ed.), *Symbols and Artifacts.* New York: Walter de Gruyter.

Hatch, M. J., & Schultz, M. (Eds.). (2004). *Organizational identity: A reader.* Oxford, UK: Oxford University Press.

Havrylyshyn, B. (1980). *Road maps to the future.* Oxford, UK: Pergamon Press.

Henderson, R. M., & Clark, K. B. (1990). Architectural innovation: The reconfiguration of existing product technologies and the failure of established firms. *Administrative Science Quarterly, 35,* 9–30.

Herzberg, F. (1968). One more time: How do you motivate employees? *Harvard Business Review,* January-February, 53–62.

Hirschhorn, L. (1988). *The workplace within: Psychodynamics of organizational life.* Cambridge, MA: MIT Press.

Hofstede, G. (1991). *Cultures and organizations*. London: McGraw-Hill.

Hofstede, G. (2001). *Culture's consequences (2nd ed.)*. Beverly Hills, CA: Sage. (Original work published 1980.)

Hofstede, G., & Bond, M. H. (1988). The Confucius connection: From cultural roots to economic growth. *Organizational Dynamics, 16*(4), 4–21.

Holland, J. L. (1985). *Making vocational choices* (2nd ed.). Englewood Cliffs, NJ: Prentice-Hall.

Homans, G. (1950). *The human group*. New York: Harcourt Brace Jovanovich.

Hughes, E. C. (1958). *Men and their work*. Glencoe, IL: Free Press.

Isaacs, W. (1999). *Dialogue and the art of thinking together*. New York: Doubleday.

Jaques, E. (1982). *The forms of time*. London: Heinemann.

Jaques, E. (1989). *Requisite organization*. Arlington, VA: Cason Hall.

Johansen, R., Sibbet, D., Benson, S., Martin, A., Mittman, R., & Saffo, P. (1991). *Leading business teams*. Reading, MA: Addison Wesley.

Jones, G. R. (1983). Transaction costs, property rights, and organizational culture: An exchange perspective. *Administrative Science Quarterly, 28*, 454–467.

Jones, M. O., Moore, M. D., & Snyder, R. C. (Eds.). (1988). *Inside organizations*. Newbury Park, CA: Sage.

Kahane, A. (2010). *Power and love*. San Francisco: Berrett-Koehler.

Kets de Vries, M. F. R., & Miller, D. (1984). *The neurotic organization: Diagnosing and changing counterproductive styles of management*. San Francisco: Jossey-Bass.

Kets de Vries, M. F. R., & Miller, D. (1987). *Unstable at the top: Inside the troubled organization*. New York: New American Library.

Kilmann, R. H., & Saxton, M. J. (1983). *The Kilmann-Saxton culture gap survey*. Pittsburgh: Organizational Design Consultants.

Kleiner, A. (2003). *Who really matters*. New York: Doubleday Currency.

Kluckhohn, F. R., & Strodtbeck, F. L. (1961). *Variations in value orientations*. New York: Harper & Row.

Koprowski, E. J. (1983). Cultural myths: Clues to effective management. *Organizational Dynamics*, Autumn, 39–51.

Kotter, J. P., & Heskett, J. L. (1992). *Culture and performance*. New York: The Free Press.

Kunda, G. (1992). *Engineering culture*. Philadelphia: Temple University Press.

Lawrence, P. R., & Lorsch, J. W. (1967). *Organization and environment*. Boston, MA: Harvard Graduate School of Business Administration.

Leavitt, H. J. (1986). *Corporate pathfinders*. Homewood, IL: Dow Jones-Irwin.

Lewin, K. (1947). Group decision and social change. In T. N. Newcomb, & E. L. Hartley (Eds.), *Readings in Social Psychology* (pp. 459–473). New York: Holt, Rinehart and Winston.

Lewis, G. (1988). *Corporate strategy in action: The strategy process in British road services*. London: Routledge.

Likert, R. (1967). *The human organization*. New York: McGraw-Hill.

Lorsch, J. W. (1985). Strategic myopia: Culture as an invisible barrier to change. In R. H. Kilmann, M. J. Saxton, R. Serpa, *Gaining control of the corporate culture*. San Francisco: Jossey-Bass.

Louis, M. R. (1980). Surprise and sense making. *Administrative Science Quarterly, 25*, 226–251.

Louis, M. R. (1981). A cultural perspective on organizations. *Human Systems Management, 2*, 246–258.

Louis, M. R. (1983). Organizations as culture bearing milieux. In L. R. Pondy, P. J. Frost, G. Morgan, & T. C. Dandridge et al. (Eds.), *Organizational Symbolism*. Greenwich, CT: JAI Press.

Malone, T. W. (2004). *The future of work*. Boston: Harvard Business School Press.

Malone, T. W., Yates, J., & Benjamin, R. (1987). Electronic markets and electronic hierarchies. *Communications of the ACM, 30*, 484–497.

Marshak, R. J. (2006). *Covert processes at work*. San Francisco: Berrett-Koehler.

Martin, J. (1982). Stories and scripts in organizational settings. In A. Hastorf, & A. Isen (Eds.), *Cognitive social psychology* (pp. 255–305). New York: Elsevier.

Martin, J. (1991). A personal journey: From integration to differentiation to fragmentation to feminism. In P. Frost, L. F. Moore, M. Reis Louis, C. C. Lundberg, & J. Martin (Eds.), *Reframing organizational culture*. Newbury Park, CA: Sage.

Martin, J. (2002). *Organizational culture: Mapping the terrain*. Newbury Park, CA: Sage.

Martin, J., & Powers, M. E. (1983). Truth or corporate propaganda: The value of a good war story. In L. R. Pondy, P. J. Frost, G. Morgan, & T. C. Dandridge (Eds.), *Organizational symbolism*. Greenwich, CT: JAI Press.

Maruyama, M. (1974). Paradigmatology and its application to cross-disciplinary, cross-professional, and cross-cultural communication. *Dialectica, 28*, 135–196.

Maslow, A. (1954). *Motivation and personality*. New York: Harper & Row.

McGregor, D. M. (1960). *The human side of enterprise*. New York: McGraw-Hill.

McManus, M. L., & Hergert, M. L. (1988). *Surviving merger and acquisition*. Glenview, IL: Scott-Foresman.

Merton, R. K. (1957). *Social theory and social structure* (Rev. ed.). New York: Free Press.

Michael, D. N. (1985). *On learning to plan—and planning to learn*. San Francisco: Jossey-Bass.

Michael, D. N. (1991). Leadership's shadow: The dilemma of denial. *Futures*, Jan./ Feb., 69–79.

Miller, D.(1990). *The Icarus paradox*. New York: Harper.

Mirvis, P., Ayas, K. & Roth, G. (2003). *To the desert and back*. San Francisco: Jossey-Bass.

Mitroff, I. I., & Kilmann, R. H. (1975). Stories managers tell: A new tool for organizational problem solving. *Management Review*, 64(7), 18–28.

Mitroff, I. I., & Kilmann, R. H. (1976). On organizational stories: An approach to the design and analysis of organizations through myths and stories. In R. H. Kilmann, L. R. Pondy, & L. Sleven (Eds.), *The Management of Organization Design*. New York: Elsevier.

Neuhauser, P. C. (1993). *Corporate legends and lore*. New York: McGraw-Hill.

O'Donovan, G. (2006). *The corporate culture handbook*. Dublin: Liffey Press.

O'Reilly, C. A. III, & Chatman, J. A. (1996). Culture as social control: Corporations, cults and commitment. In B. M. Staw, & L. L. Cummings (Eds.), *Research in organizational behavior* (Vol. 18, pp. 157–200). Greenwich, CT: JAI.

O'Reilly, C. A., III, Chatman, J. A., & Caldwell, D. F. (1991). People and organizational culture. *Academy of Management Journal, 34*, 487–516.

Onken, M. (1999). Temporal elements of organizational culture and impact on firm performance. *Journal of Managerial Psychology, 14*, 231–243.

Oshry, B. (2007). *Seeing systems*. San Francisco: Berrett-Koehler.

Ouchi, W. G., & Johnson, J. (1978). Types of organizational control and their relationship to emotional well-being. *Administrative Science Quarterly, 23*, 293–317.

Ouchi, W. G. (1981). *Theory Z*. Reading, MA: Addison-Wesley.

Packard, D. (1995). *The HP way*. New York: Harper Collins.

Parsons, T. (1951). *The social system*. New York: Free Press.

Pascale, R. T., & Athos, A. G. (1981). *The art of Japanese management*. New York: Simon & Schuster.

Pava, C. H. P. (1983). *Managing new office technology*. New York: Free Press.

Pedersen, J. S., & Sorensen, J. S. (1989). *Organizational cultures in theory and practice*. Aldershot, UK: Gower Publishing Co.

Peiperl, M., & Jonsen, K. (2007). Global careers. In H. Gunz, & M. Peiperl (Eds.), *Handbook of career studies* (pp. 350–375). Thousand Oaks, CA: Sage.

Perin, C. (1991). The moral fabric of the office. In S. Bacharach, S. R. Barley, & P. S. Tolbert (Eds.), *Research in the Sociology of Organizations* (special volume on the professions). Greenwich, CT: JAI Press.

Perin, C. (2005). *Shouldering risks*. Princeton, NJ: Princeton University Press.

Peters, T. J. (1987). *Thriving on chaos*. New York: Knopf.

Peters, T. J., & Waterman, R. H., Jr. (1982). *In search of excellence*. New York: Harper & Row.

Peterson, B. (2004). *Cultural intelligence.* Boston: Intercultural Press.

Pettigrew, A. M. (1979). On studying organizational cultures. *Administrative Science Quarterly, 24,* 570–581.

Plum, E. (2008). *CI: Cultural intelligence.* London: Middlesex University Press.

Pondy, L. R., Frost, P. J., Morgan, G., & Dandridge, T. (Eds.). (1983). *Organizational symbolism.* Greenwich, CT: JAI Press.

Porras, J., & Collins, J. (1994). *Built to last.* New York: HarperBusiness.

Redding, S. G., & Martyn-Johns, T. A. (1979). Paradigm differences and their relation to management, with reference to Southeast Asia. In G. W. England, A. R. Neghandi, & B. Wilpert (Eds.), *Organizational Functioning in a Cross-Cultural Perspective.* Kent, OH: Comparative Administration Research Unit, Kent State University.

Ritti, R. R., & Funkhouser, G. R. (1987). *The ropes to skip and the ropes to know* (3rd ed.). Columbus, OH: Grid.

Rockart, J. F., & DeLong, D. W. (1988). *Executive support systems.* Homewood, IL: Dow Jones-Irwin.

Roethlisberger, F. J., & Dickson, W. J. (1939). *Management and the worker.* Cambridge, MA: Harvard University Press.

Sackman, S. A. (2006). *Success factor: Corporate culture.* Guetersloh, Germany: Bertelsman Stiftung.

Sahlins, M. (1985). *Islands of history.* Chicago: University of Chicago Press.

Sahlins, M., & Service, E. R. (Eds.). (1960). *Evolution and culture.* Ann Arbor, MI: University of Michigan Press.

Salk, J. (1997). Partners and other strangers. *International Studies of Management. and Organization, 26*(4), 48–72.

Savage, C. M. (1990). *Fifth generation management: Integrating enterprises through human networking.* Maynard, MA: Digital Press.

Scharmer, C. O. (2007). *Theory U.* Cambridge, MA: Society for Organizational Learning.

Schein, E. H. (1961a). *Coercive persuasion.* New York: Norton.

Schein, E. H. (1961b). Management development as a process of influence. *Industrial Management Review (MIT), 2,* 59–77.

Schein, E. H. (1964). Personal change through interpersonal relationships. In W. G. Bennis, E. H. Schein, D. E. Berlew, & F. I. Steele (Eds.), *Interpersonal Dynamics* (pp. 357–394). Homewood, IL: Dorsey.

Schein, E. H. (1968). Organizational socialization and the profession of management. *Industrial Management Review, 9,* 1–15.

Schein, E. H. (1969). *Process consultation: Its role in organization development.* Reading, MA: Addison-Wesley.

Schein, E. H. (1971). The individual, the organization, and the career: A conceptual scheme. *Journal of Applied Behavioral Science, 7,* 401–426.

Schein, E. H. (1972). *Professional education: Some new directions.* New York: McGraw Hill.

Schein, E.H. (1975). In defense of theory Y. *Organizational Dynamics,* Summer, 17–30.

Schein, E. H. (1978). *Career dynamics: Matching individual and organizational needs.* Reading, MA: Addison-Wesley.

Schein, E. H. (1980). *Organizational psychology* (3rd ed.). Englewood Cliffs, NJ: Prentice-Hall. (Original work published 1965; 2nd ed. published 1970.)

Schein, E. H. (1983). The role of the founder in creating organizational culture. *Organizational Dynamics,* Summer, 13–28.

Schein, E. H. (1987a). *The clinical perspective in fieldwork.* Newbury Park, CA: Sage.

Schein, E. H. (1987b). *Process Consultation. Vol. 2: Lessons for Managers and Consultants.* Reading, MA: Addison-Wesley.

Schein, E. H. (1987c). Individuals and careers. In Jay W. Lorsch (Ed.), *Handbook of organizational behavior* (pp. 155–171). Englewood Cliffs, NJ: Prentice-Hall.

Schein, E. H. (1988). *Process consultation. Vol. 1: Its role in organization development* (2nd ed.). Reading, MA: Addison-Wesley.

Schein, E. H. (1990). Innovative cultures and adaptive organizations. *Sri Lanka Journal of Development Administration,* 7(2), 9–39.

Schein, E. H. (1992). The role of the CEO in the management of change. In T. A. Kochan, & M. Useem (Eds.), *Transforming Organizations* (pp. 80–96). New York: Oxford University Press.

Schein, E. H. (1993a). On dialogue, culture, and organizational learning. *Organizational dynamics,* Autumn, *22,* 40–51.

Schein, E. H. (1993b). *Career anchors* (Rev. ed.). San Diego: Pfeiffer.

Schein, E.H. (1993c). How can organizations learn faster? The challenge of entering the green room. *Sloan Management Review, 34,* 85–92.

Schein, E. H. (1995). *Career survival.* San Francisco: Jossey-Bass.

Schein, E. H. (1996a). Three cultures of management: The key to organizational learning. *Sloan Management Review, 38*(1), 9–20.

Schein, E. H. (1996b). *Strategic pragmatism: The culture of Singapore's Economic Development Board.* Cambridge, MA: MIT Press.

Schein, E. H. (1999a). *Process consultation revisited.* Englewood Cliffs, NJ: Prentice-Hall (Addison-Wesley).

Schein, E. H. (1999b). *The corporate culture survival guide.* San Francisco: Jossey-Bass.

Schein, E. H. (2001). Clinical inquiry/research. In P. Reason, & H. Bradbury (Eds.), *Handbook of action research* (pp. 228–237). Thousand Oaks, CA: Sage Press.

Schein, E. H. (2003). *DEC is dead; Long live DEC.* San Francisco: Berrett/Kohler.

Schein, E. H. (2004). *Organizational culture and leadership* (3rd ed.). San Francisco: Jossey Bass.

Schein, E. H. (2006). *Career anchors* (3rd ed.). San Francisco: Jossey-Bass/Pfeiffer.

Schein, E. H. (2008). Clinical inquiry/research. In P. Reason, & H. Bradbury (Eds.), *Action research* (2nd ed.) (pp. 266–279). Thousand Oaks, CA: Sage.

Schein, E. H. (2009a). *Helping.* San Francisco: Berrett/Koehler.

Schein, E. H. (2009b). *The corporate culture survival guide* (2nd ed.). San Francisco: Jossey-Bass.

Schein, E. H., & Bennis, W. G. (1965). *Personal and organizational change through group methods.* New York: Wiley.

Schneider, B. (Ed.). (1990). *Organizational climate and culture.* San Francisco: Jossey-Bass.

Schultz, M. (1995). *On studying organizational cultures.* New York: De Gruyter.

Schwartz, P. (2003). *Inevitable surprises.* New York: Gotham Books.

Scott-Morton, M. S. (Ed.). (1991). *The corporation of the 1990s.* New York: Oxford University Press.

Senge, P. M. (1990). *The fifth discipline.* New York: Doubleday Currency.

Senge, P., Roberts, C., Ross, R.B., Smith, B. J., & Kleiner, A. (1994). *The fifth discipline field book.* New York: Doubleday Currency.

Senge, P., Smith, B., Kruschwitz, N., Laur, J., & Schley, S. (2008). *The necessary revolution.* Cambridge, MA: Society for Organizational Learning.

Shrivastava, P. (1983). A typology of organizational learning systems. *Journal of Management Studies, 20,* 7–28.

Sithi-Amnuai, P. (1968). The Asian mind. *Asia,* Spring, 78–91.

Smircich, L. (1983). Concepts of culture and organizational analysis. *Administrative Science Quarterly, 28,* 339–358.

Snook, S. A. (2000). *Friendly fire.* Princeton, NJ: Princeton University Press.

Sorensen, J. B. (2002). The strength of corporate culture and the reliability of firm performance. *Administrative Science Quarterly, 47,* 70–91.

Steele, F. I. (1973). *Physical settings and organization development.* Reading, MA: Addison-Wesley.

Steele, F. I. (1981). *The sense of place.* Boston: CBI Publishing.

Steele, F. I. (1986). *Making and managing high-quality workplaces.* New York: Teachers College Press.

Tagiuri, R., & Litwin, G. H. (Eds.). (1968). *Organizational climate: Exploration of a concept.* Boston: Division of Research, Harvard Graduate School of Business.

Thomas, R. (1994). *What machines can't do.* Berkeley, CA: University of California Press.

Thomas, D. C., & Inkson, K. (2003). *Cultural intelligence.* San Francisco: Berrett/Kohler.

Tichy, N. M., & Devanna, M. A. (1987). *The transformational leader*. New York: Wiley, 1986.

Trice, H. M., Beyer, J. M. (1984). Studying organizational cultures through rites and ceremonials. *Academy of Management Review, 9*, 653–669.

Trice, H. M., & Beyer, J. M. (1985). Using six organizational rites to change culture. In R. H. Kilmann, M. J. Saxton, & R. Serpa, *Gaining Control of the Corporate Culture* (pp. 370–399). San Francisco: Jossey-Bass.

Trice, H. M., & Beyer, J. M. (1993). *The cultures of work organizations*. Englewood Cliffs, NJ: Prentice-Hall.

Turquet, P. M. (1973). Leadership: The individual and the group. In G. S. Gibbard, J. J. Hartman, & R. D. Mann (Eds.), *Analysis of groups: Contributions to theory, research, and practice*. San Francisco: Jossey-Bass.

Tushman, M. L., & Anderson, P. (1986). Technological discontinuities and organizational environments. *Administrative Science Quarterly, 31*, 439–465.

Tyrrell, M. W. D. (2000). Hunting and gathering in the early Silicon age. In N. M. Ashkanasy, C. P. M. Wilderom, & M. F. Peterson (Eds.), *Handbook of organizational culture and climate* (pp. 85–99). Thousand Oaks, CA: Sage.

Van Maanen, J. (1973). Observations on the making of policemen. *Human Organization, 4*, 407–418.

Van Maanen, J. (1976). Breaking in: Socialization at work. In R. Dubin (Ed.), *Handbook of work organization and society*. Skokie, IL: Rand McNally.

Van Maanen, J. (1979a). The fact of fiction in organizational ethnography. *Administrative Science Quarterly, 24*, 539–550.

Van Maanen, J. (1979b). The self, the situation, and the rules of interpersonal relations. In W. Bennis, J. Van Maanen, E. J. Schein, & F. I. Steele, *Essays in interpersonal dynamics* (pp. 43–101). Homewood, IL: Dorsey Press.

Van Maanen, J. (1988). *Tales of the field: On writing ethnography*. Chicago: University of Chicago Press.

Van Maanen, J., & Schein, E. H. (1979). Toward a theory of organizational socialization. In B. M. Staw, & L. L. Cummings (Eds.), *Research in organizational behavior* (Vol. 1). Greenwich, CT: JAI Press.

Van Maanen, J., & Barley, S. R. (1984). Occupational communities: Culture and control in organizations. In B. M. Staw, & L. L. Cummings (Eds.), *Research in organizational behavior* (Vol. 6). Greenwich, CT: JAI Press.

Van Maanen, J., & Kunda, G. (1989). Real feelings: Emotional expression and organizational culture. In B. Staw (Ed.), *Research in organizational behavior* (Vol. 11). Greenwich, CT: JAI Press.

Vroom, V. H., & Yetton, P. W. (1973). *Leadership and decision making*. Pittsburgh: University of Pittsburgh Press.

Watson, T. J., Jr., & Petre, P. (1990). *Father, son & co.: My life at IBM and beyond*. New York: Bantam Books.

Weeks, J. (2004). *Unpopular culture*. Chicago: University of Chicago Press.

Weick, K. (1995). *Sensemaking in organizations*. Thousand Oaks, CA: Sage.

Weick, K., & Sutcliffe, K. M. (2001). *Managing the unexpected*. San Francisco: Jossey-Bass.

Wilderom, C. P. M., Glunk, U., & Maslowski, R. (2000). Organizational culture as a predictor of organizational performance. In N. M. Ashkanasy, C. P. M. Wilderom, & M. F. Peterson (Eds.), *Handbook of organizational culture and climate*. Thousand Oaks, CA: Sage, pp. 193–209.

Wilkins, A. L. (1983). Organizational stories as symbols which control the organization. In L. R. Pondy, P. J. Frost, G. Morgan, & T. Dandridge (Eds.), *Organizational symbolism*. Greenwich, CT: JAI Press.

Wilkins, A. L. (1989). *Developing corporate character*. San Francisco: Jossey-Bass.

Williamson, O. (1975). *Markets and hierarchies, analysis and anti-trust implications: A study in the economics of internal organization*. New York: Free Press.

Womack, J. T., Jones, D. T., & Roos, D. (2007). *The machine that changed the world*. New York: Free Press.

Zuboff, S. (1984). *In the age of the smart machine*. New York: Basic Books.

Index

Page references followed by *t* indicate a table; followed by *fig* indicate an illustrated figure; followed by *e* indicate an exhibit.

A

Acceptance, 149
Acculturation process, 19–20
Achievement oriented typology, 166
Achievement status, 153
Adaptability cultural dimension, 169
Adaptive capacity, 284
Adhocracy cultural dimension, 168
Adizes, I., 275
Adorno, T. W., 120
Aggression management, 149
Aggressive/Defensive Styles, 170
Agilent, 183, 231
Airwick, 66, 77, 183, 348
Airwick France, 66
Alcoa, 237
Aldrich, H. E., 275
Allan, J., 255
Allen, T. J., 140
Alpha Power Company: cultural reinforcers used at, 253, 254; example of espoused/actual rewards at, 248–249; how culture illuminates situation example at, 10–11; introduction of cell phones for employees at, 285; job safety program of, 237, 248–249; polychronic time approach used by, 129; scandal and cultural change at, 291; subculture differentiation by product, market, or technology, 267; successful cultural change process at, 311–312; taking cultural perspective to understand situation at, 12; unfreezing process by employees at, 302
Amoco: blaming culture of, 109; cognitive restructuring by employees of, 308; how culture illuminates situation example at, 10; taking cultural perspective to understand situation at, 12; unfreezing to learn new reward and control system at, 302
Ancona, D. G., 134, 167
Anderson, P., 275, 295
Ang, S., 15, 387, 388
Apollo (The Role culture), 166
Apple Computer: cultural assessments done at, 321–322; cultural differences between other companies and, 182, 183; cultural influence of founders at, 229–230; John Scully's leadership at, 230, 288; organizational culture change at, 335–339; return of Steve Jobs to, 282; space symbolism used at, 138
Argyris, C., 15, 27, 28, 144
Artifacts: Apple Computer assessment identifying, 321–322; Ciba-Geigy, 44–48; DEC (Digital Equipment Corp.), 36–38; description of, 23–25; group self-assessment eliciting descriptions of, 319–320; as level of culture, 24*e*; specifying, 20
Ascription status, 153
Ashkanasy, N. M., 15, 236

Assumptions: cultural, 115–123; distortions of unconscious, 29, 30–32; double-loop learning or frame breaking new, 28; how leaders embed culture with their values and, 235–250; inferring culture through, 20; learning-oriented leadership ability to change, 382; management using human nature, 30; microcultures of shared, 67; rapid deciphering of, 316–317, 321–323; Theory X, 145–146, 155, 165; Theory Y, 145, 155, 165, 367. *See also* Basic assumptions; Deeper macroculture assumptions

Athena (The Task culture), 166

Athos, A. G., 15

Australian collectivism, 151

Authority relationships: building new norms around, 207–209; coercive organizations and, 163, 164, 165; culture formation and dealing with assumptions about, 204–211; group reality testing on, 209–211; managing internal integration through, 101–104; normative organizations and, 164; organizational management of, 69; utilitarian organizations and, 163, 164, 165. *See also* Leadership; Management; Power

Ayas, K., 391

B

Bailyn, L., 29, 131, 132

Bank Wiring Room (Hawthorne studies), 14

Barley, S. R., 15, 56, 100, 111, 132, 133, 184, 193, 261, 285

BART (San Francisco Bay Transit Authority), 62

Bartunek, J., 28, 188

"Basel Aristocracy" (Ciba-Geigy), 76, 99–100

Basic assumptions: characteristics and applications of, 28–32; Ciba-Geigy company paradigm and, 48–53, 76; as cultural level, 24e; DEC paradigm and, 40–44, 76; description of, 23, 27–28; engineering/design subculture, 61e; executive subculture, 63e–64; on external adaptation issues, 73–92; learning-oriented leadership ability to change, 382; on managing internal integration, 93–113; microcultures of shared, 67; operator subculture, 58e; rapid deciphering to identify shared, 321–323; subcultures created by shared, 55–56. *See also* Assumptions

Basic values, 23

Bass, B. M., 165

Beckhard, R., 105, 350

Behavior change: intervention to change DEC microculture, 11; resistance to, 8. *See also* Culture change

Behavioral regularities: common types of cultural, 14–16; inferring culture through, 20

Behaviors: inferring culture through, 20; organizational culture to understand, 11–13; power distance control over someone's, 151–152; resistance to change, 8; two central assumptions about human, 322

Being orientation, 147

Being-in-becoming orientation, 147–149

Beliefs. *See* Espoused beliefs and values

Bell System, 304

Benne, K. D., 198, 389

Bennis, W. G., 198, 205, 235, 293, 300

Berg, P. O., 128

Bertelsman Stiftung, 171

Beta Service Company, 329–331

Bethel "cultural island," 198

Beyer, J. M., 14, 16, 17, 253

Bhopal chemical explosion, 291

Bion, W. R., 204, 207, 213

Blake, R. R., 167, 285

Blake's Managerial Grid, 167, 285
Blame culture, 109
Bluedom, A. C., 129, 134
BMW Group, 172
"Boat people," 109
Body language, 139
Bohmer, R. M., 386
Bond, M. H., 126
Booz Allen Hamilton, 171
Bowditch, J. L., 377
Bradford, L. P., 198, 389
Brannick, T., 188
Breadth of culture, 17
British Petroleum Company (BP),
    102–103, 109, 120, 139, 290
Buono, A. F., 377
Burger Chef, 377
Bushe, G. R., 29, 119
Business decisions: different assumptions of
    reality impacting, 118; dominant belief
    system used to make, 270; information
    used to reach, 121–123; Ken Olsen's
    philosophy on, 226; resource allocation,
    245–246; shared social reality needed to
    make, 118–119

C

Cambridge-at-Home: how
    culture illuminates situation
    example at, 10; taking cultural
    perspective to understand situation
    at, 12
Cameron, K. S., 168
Career movement dimensions, 99–100
Castaneda, C., 117
Celebrations, 16
Centre d'Etudes Industrielle
    (Geneva), 187
CEOs: culture change through outside,
    287–289; executive subculture
    assumptions applying to, 63e–64;
    occupational identification of, 65;
    similar subcultures created among, 57;

succession of, 280–284, 287–289. See
    also Leadership; Management
Challenger space shuttle, 291, 397
Chandler, A. D., Jr., 275
Change. See Culture change
Charismatic leaders, 235–236
Chatman, J. A., 278
Chong, C. L., 134
Ciampa, D., 285
Ciba-Geigy: artifacts of, 44–48;
    assumptions on reality and truth at,
    116–117; background information
    on, 44; "Basel Aristocracy" of, 76,
    99–100; basic assumptions and company
    paradigm of, 48–53, 76; challenge of
    collecting data on, 183; collectivistic
    and hierarchical culture of, 152;
    comparing subcultures of DEC and,
    65–66; cultural evolution at, 280;
    cultural reinforcers used at, 252–253,
    254; culture change process at, 339–362;
    debate over "valuable" products, 77; on
    employee loyalty, 146; espoused beliefs
    and values of, 48; founding and early
    growth of, 274; geographical subculture
    differentiation in, 264–265; how
    culture illuminates situation example
    at, 10; lessons of internal analysis of,
    189–190; as low-context culture, 119;
    macrocultures of, 55, 70; moralistic
    culture of, 121; norms on achieving
    goals, 82; organizational culture
    change at, 339–357; primary type and
    treatment of employee of, 57, 249, 250;
    self-guided cultural evolution at, 277;
    subculture differentiation by product,
    market, or technology, 266–267; taking
    cultural perspective to understand
    situation at, 12. See also DEC/Ciba-
    Geigy comparison; Macrocultures;
    Organizational culture case studies
Ciba-Geigy culture change: assessment
    during the third year, 355–357;
    background information on, 339–340;

creating "parallel system" for, 351–352; getting acquainted with the culture, 345–347; impact of first annual meeting on, 343–345; inducing survival anxiety, 349–350; initial contact and first annual meeting, 340–352; providing some psychological safety, 350; second year of consolidation of redirection project, 352–357; summary and conclusions about, 358–362; third annual meeting and culture lecture disaster, 353–355; unfreezing at the second annual meeting, 347–349

Ciba-Geigy/Sandoz merger, 44, 45, 149, 362

Clan cultural dimension, 168

Clark, K. B., 15

Clear Leadership (Bushe), 119

Climate: as cultural artifact, 24; description of, 15

Coaching: creating psychological safety through, 306; leader role of, 246–247

Coercive organizations, 163, 164, 165

Coghlan, D., 188

Cognitive clarity, 149

Cognitive restructuring: imitation/identification vs. scanning/trial-and-error learning, 300e, 310–311; learning new concepts and new meanings, 300e, 309–310; progress of culture change through, 300e, 308–309

Collaborations. *See* Multicultural groups

Collectivism, 150–151

Collins, J., 75

Colombian airlines disaster (1990), 397–398

Columbia space shuttle, 291, 397

Common language/category systems, 93–97

Communal culture, 167

Communication: airline disasters caused by poor, 397–398; body language, 139; creating conceptual categories/common language for, 93–97; emotional outbursts as, 239–241; "jargon" used in, 97; learning culture commitment to task-relevant, 369–370; new group creation of norms for, 200–202; primary embedding mechanisms and forms of, 236e–250; secondary articulation and reinforcement mechanisms forms of, 250–257. *See also* Dialogue

Communication technology: culture change through new, 285; impact on time and space, 140–141; limitations of, 141

Compaq Corporation, 9, 36, 229, 231, 294–295

Conflict: clarifying assumptions about, 96; creating common language/categories to resolve, 93–97; DEC norm of hostile, 37, 39–40, 131, 214, 240–241; leader's inconsistent signals as source of, 241–243; "the other" as defined during, 143. *See also* Human relationships

Conger, J. A., 235, 391

Consistency cultural dimension, 169

Constructive Styles, 170

Cook, S.D.N., 15, 81, 84, 105

Cooke, R. A., 162, 170

Corlett, J. G., 162, 167

Corporate culture, 1, 2e. *See also* Organizational culture

Corporate Culture Survival Guide, 2d Ed. (Schein), 315, 364

COS, 377

Coutu, D. L., 307

Creator archetype, 167

Critical incidents, 243–245

Cultural assumptions: about appropriate human activity, 146–149; being aware of differences in, 115; consensus on what is information, 121–123; differences in macroculture, 116e; high-context and low-context, 119–120; about human nature, 143–146; moralistic and pragmatic, 120–121; about nature of human relationships, 149–154; about nature of reality and truth, 116–119; about nature of space, 135–142; possible criteria for determining truth, 121e; about time, 125–134

Cultural DNA: belief that environment can be managed as part of, 368; DEC (Digital Equipment Corporation), 42–44; employee surveys tapping into the, 160; group norms as critical to, 104; "learning gene" as part of, 366–367

Cultural evolution: general, 275–276; hybrids for managed, 279–280; insight used for self-guided, 277–279; through new technology, 284–287; specific, 276

Cultural intelligence, 387–389

Cultural islands: focused dialogue on topic of, 391–393; multicultural exploration through dialogue of, 393–395; starting dialogue on, 395–397; temporary, 389–391; when and why to use dialogue for, 397–398

Cultural levels: artifacts, 20, 23–25, 36–38; basic underlying assumptions, 23, 24e, 27–32; espoused values, 15, 23, 24e, 25–27

Cultural reinforcers: design of space, facades, and buildings as, 255; formal statements of philosophy, creeds, and charters, 256–257; organizational design and structure as, 251–252; organizational systems and procedures as, 252–253; rites and rituals of the organization as, 14, 16, 101, 139, 253–255; secondary articulation/ reinforcement mechanisms as, 250–251; stories about important events and people, 255–256

Culture: artifacts of, 20, 23–25, 36–38, 44–48, 319–322; behavioral regularities of, 14–16, 20; business value of understanding, 4–5; categories of, 1–2e; connection between leadership and, 3–4; differentiated and/or fragmented, 18; emergence in new groups, 197–218; as empirically based abstraction, 13–16; formal definition of, 18; group as foundation of strength and stability of, 197; high-context and low-context, 119–120; how leaders embed their values and assumptions in, 235–250; identifying elements and dimensions of, 74; individualism and collectivism in, 150–151; learning, 366–383; observable events and underlying forces of, 14–16; power distance, 151–152; process of forming, 73; social order created through, 3, 103–104, 197, 365, 386–387; social and organizational situations from, 7; socialization or acculturation to, 19–20; structural analysis of, 69–70; understanding phenomena by understanding, 9. See also Organizational culture

Culture assessment: Ciba-Geigy's, 355–357; identifying culture elements that need changing, 325–326; rapid deciphering approach to, 315–325

Culture change: Ciba-Geigy, 339–362; conceptual model for, 300e–311; culture assessment component of, 315–326; founding and early growth, 273t, 274–280; mechanisms listed, 273t; organizational maturity and potential decline, 273t, 289–295; principles in regard to, 311–313; psycho-social dynamics of organizational, 299–300; resistance to, 8, 303–305; succession problems and transition to midlife, 273t, 280–289; through technological seduction, 284–287. See also Behavior change

Culture change case studies: Apple Computer, 335–339; Beta Service Company, 329–331; Ciba-Geigy, 339–362; MA-COM, 331–334; U.S. Army Corps of Engineers, 334–335

Culture change model: stage 1: unfreezing/ disconfirmation, 300e–307; stage 2: cognitive restructuring for learning, 300e, 308–311; stage 3: refreezing to internalize new learning, 300e, 311

Culture characteristics: breadth, 17; depth, 16; patterning or integration, 17; structural stability, 16

Culture content: challenges of measuring, 70–71; leadership creating organization's, 71; social psychology and group dynamics to identify, 73

Culture formation: defining boundaries and identity for, 94e, 97–100, 202; founder/leader actions and beginnings of, 203–204, 219–233; how individual intensions become group consequences, 200–202; originating and marker events of, 198–204; through sharing perceptions/articulating feeling, 202–203; stages of, 204–218

Culture formation stages: 1: dealing with assumptions about authority, 204–211; 2: building norms around intimacy, 211–216; 3: group work and functional familiarity, 216–217; 4: group maturity, 217–218

Culture studies: conceptual approach to, 2–5; forces influencing, 4e

Customer service, 241

D

Dalton, M., 60, 177
Dandridge, T., 16
Darling, M. J., 391
Data: information versus, 122; researcher's process for collecting, 180–183; validity of clinically gathered, 185–186. See also Information
Deal, T. E., 15, 16, 253
DEC (Digital Equipment Corporation): artifacts of, 36–38; background information on, 35–36; basic assumptions and DEC paradigm, 40–44, 76; "boot camps" for new employees at, 278; challenge of collecting data on, 181, 182–183, 184; cultural DNA of, 42–44; cultural evolution in, 276, 277–280; cultural reinforcers used at, 252, 253, 254, 256; employee promotion/excommunication at, 249–250; engineering subculture dominance at, 65–66; espoused beliefs and values of, 38–40; failure to learn new concepts at, 309–310; founding and early growth of, 226, 274; as high-context culture, 119; hostile conflict norm at, 37, 39–40, 131, 214, 240–241; how culture illuminates situation example at, 9; inconsistent leadership messages impact on, 242; incorrect research analysis of, 187; individualistic but reduced power distance at, 152; intervention to change microculture of, 11; lack of learning culture at, 367; leader inferences on what was/was not important, 241; macrocultures of, 55, 70; myth created at, 112; norms on achieving goals, 82–83; organizational crises approach taken by, 244; pragmatic culture of, 120–121; primary type of employee of, 57; process for determining truth used at, 123; resistance to changing market by, 289–290; resource allocation approach taken by, 245–246; Robert Palmer leadership changing culture of, 295; self-guided cultural evolution at, 277–279; subculture differentiation in, 265–266, 267, 269; as Theory Y driven organization, 146; "Woods meetings" held at, 254. See also Macrocultures; Olsen, K.; Organizational culture case studies
DEC Is Dead: Long Live DEC (Schein), 41, 43
DEC/Ciba-Geigy comparison: in assumptions about space, 137; basic

assumptions and environment, 50–52; consultation experience, 345; cultural artifacts, 45–46, 47; different types of employees, 57, 76; distributing power, authority, and status, 101–104; in employee self-development encouragement, 148–149; espoused beliefs and values, 48; on goals derived from mission, 78–80; high-context vs. low-context culture, 119; hiring process, 98–100; in human relationships, 153; macrocultures of, 55, 70; on means of measurement, 87–88; on means to achieve goals, 82–83; moralistic versus pragmatic culture, 120–121; national cultural differences, 54; in organization versus individual importance, 146; planning and development time, 130; on remedial and repair strategies, 89–90; reward and punishment allocations, 108; rules for relationships, 106–107; subcultures, 65–66; on symbolism of space, 138–139; time horizons, 131; on what to measure for results, 84, 87

Deciphering organizational cultures: categories of research for, 181t–183; ethical issues in, 186–191; from the outside, 178e–179; reasons for, 177–178; researcher role in, 179–186

Decision making. *See* Business decisions

Deeper macroculture assumptions: about appropriate human activity, 146–149; consensus on what is information, 121–123; high-context and low-context cultures and, 119–120; about human nature, 143–146; moralism and pragmatism, 120–121; about nature of human relationships, 149–154; about nature of reality and truth, 116e–119; about nature of space, 135–142; possible criteria for determining truth, 121e; rapid deciphering to identify, 321–323; about time, 125–134. *See also* Assumptions

Degree of emotionality, 153

Degree of specificity vs. diffuseness, 153

Degree of status ascription vs. achievement, 153

Degree of universalism vs. particularism, 153

DeLong, D. W., 122

Denison, D. R., 159, 162, 169

Depth of culture, 16

Designers. *See* Engineering/design subculture

Deutsche Lufthansa, 172

Devanna, M. A., 293

Development time, 130

Dialogue: exploring cultural islands through focused, 391–393; how to begin a cultural island, 395–397; multicultural exploration through, 393–395; when to explore cultural islands through, 397–398. *See also* Communication

Dibble, R., 385

Dickson, W. J., 144

Differentiated cultures, 18

Diffuseness vs. Specificity, 153

Dionysus (The Existential culture), 166

Distance: flight, 137; intimacy, 135–136; intrusion, 137; personal, 136; public, 136; social, 136

"Distinctive Skills," 167

Diversity: learning culture commitment to, 370; subculture, 283–284. *See also* Multicultural management

Divisionalization differentiation, 268–270

Dogma, 121e

Doing orientation, 146–147

Dominance-establishing rituals, 101

Don Juan (Indian shaman), 117

Donaldson, G., 75, 220, 245, 270

Double-loop learning, 28

Dougherty, D., 56, 122

Douglas, M., 15, 29

Drucker Foundation, 365

Dubinskas, F. A., 125, 129

Dyer, W. G, Jr., 105, 281, 287

E

Earley, P. C., 387, 388
Eastman, G., 282
Economic crisis (2009), 244, 292
Edmondson, A. C., 386
EDS (Electronic Data Systems), 289
Embedded skills, 15
Embedding mechanisms: deliberate role modeling, teaching, and coaching, 236e, 246–247; how leaders allocate resources, 236e, 245–246; how leaders allocate rewards and status, 236e, 247–249; how leaders select, promote, and excommunicate, 236e, 249–250; listed, 236e; reactions to critical incidents/ organizational crises, 236e, 243–245; what leaders pay attention to, measure, and control, 236e, 237–243. See also Secondary articulation/reinforcement mechanisms
Emotional outbursts, 239–241
Emotionality, 153
Employee motivation: to answer surveys honestly, 160; assumptions on human nature and, 144–146; reward and punishment used for, 107–110; Theory X and Theory Y on, 145–146, 155, 165
Employee surveys: possible negative consequences of, 161; problems in the use of, 159–161; when to use, 161–163
Employees: Ciba-Geigy and DEC's response to laying off, 277–279; DEC "boot camps" for new, 278; learning rules of the game, 15; managing internal integration of, 93–113; new communication technology provided to, 285; process used for hiring, 98–100; resistance to change by, 8, 303–305; rewarding and punishing, 107–110; self-development of, 148–149; socialization or acculturation of, 19–20; socialized embedded skills of, 15. See also Human relationships; Learners; Organizational culture; Subordinates

Engineering/design subculture: assumptions of the, 61e; characteristics of, 60–62; Ciba-Geigy's strong, 66; DEC dominance of, 65–66; human factor mistakes recognized by, 61–62; misalignment between executives and, 62
England, G., 120
Enron scandal, 292
Espoused beliefs and values: Ciba-Geigy, 48; company's ideology conflicting with, 27; on cultural analysis as valid, 371; as cultural level, 24e; DEC (Digital Equipment Corporation), 38–40; description of, 15; group learning and transformation of, 25–26; how leaders embed culture with their, 235–250; myths supporting, 112, 290–291; rapid deciphering for identifying, 320–321; social validation confirmed through, 26–27. See also Value assumptions
Essochem, 148
Essochem Europe, 380
Ethical research issues: professional obligations of the culture analyst, 190–191; risks of an analysis for research purposes, 186–188; risks of an internal analysis, 188–190
Ethnographers, 184. See also Researchers
Etzioni, A., 163
European time value, 127–129
Everyperson archetype, 167
Evolution. See Cultural evolution
Executive subculture: assumptions of, 63e; characteristics of, 63–67; misalignment between engineering/design and, 62; undervalued DEC, 66
Explorer archetype, 167
External adaptation issues: goals derived from mission, 78–80; means to achieve goals, 80–83; measuring results and correction mechanisms, 83–88; problems faced by organizations, 74e; remedial and repair strategies, 88–91;

shared assumptions about mission, strategy, and goals, 74–78
External physical reality, 117
Exxon, 148, 380
Eye contact, 139

F

Fairtlough, G., 255
Feedback: creating psychological safety through, 306; emotional resistance to giving, 103–104; HP's global policy on, 269–270
Festinger, L. A., 117, 308
The Fifth Discipline (Senge), 285
"Fight or flight," 207, 212–213
Fiorina, C., 231
Flight distance, 137
The Ford Motor Co., 281
Formal philosophy, 15
Formal rituals, 16
Founding and early growth: culture change mechanisms listed, 273t; incremental change through evolution, 275–276; managed evolution through hybrids, 279–280; self-guided evolution through insight, 277–279. *See also* Leaders/founders
Fragmented culture, 167
Fragmented cultures, 18
Frame breaking, 28
Fred Smithfield Enterprises, 224–225, 280
Freud, S., 105
Frost, P. J., 16, 180, 242, 374
Functional/occupational subculture: description of, 260–261; differentiation of, 261–263
Funkhouser, G. R., 15
Fusion assumption: group intimacy and, 212–213; reality testing of, 213–214

G

Gagliardi, P., 16, 24, 138, 255
Geertz, C., 15

General Doriot, 226
General Foods (GF), 77–78, 89, 108, 377–378
General Motors, 289
Geographical subculture differentiation, 263–266
Gersick, C.J.C., 275, 295
Gerstein, M. S., 285, 291, 303, 397
Gerstner, L., 230, 326
Gibb, J. R., 198, 389
Gibson, C. B., 385
Gladwell, M., 7, 56, 397
Global Business Network, 365
Goals: measuring results and correction mechanisms for reaching, 74e, 83–88; meeting individual, 149; remedial and repair strategies for reaching, 74e, 88–91; setting, T group, 199–200; shared assumptions about means to achieve, 74e, 80–83; shared assumptions on mission-derived, 74e, 78–80. *See also* Needs
Goffee, R., 167, 168
Goffman, E., 14, 101, 103, 104, 137, 138, 139, 154, 165
Goldman, A., 146, 180
Greiner, L. E., 165, 275
Grenier, R., 140, 285
Group formation: defining boundaries during, 94e, 97–100, 202; how individual intensions become group consequences, 200–202; leadership intervention and role in, 203–204; originating and marker events of, 198–204; setting T group goals for, 199–200; through sharing perceptions/articulating feeling, 202–203; stages of, 204–218
Group formation stages: 1: dealing with assumptions about authority, 204–211; 2: building norms around intimacy, 211–216; 3: group work and functional familiarity, 216–217; 4: group maturity, 217–218

Group norms: built around authority relationships, 207–209; built around intimacy, 211–216; as critical to cultural DNA, 104; DEC hostile confrontation, 37, 131, 214, 240–241; description of, 14; developed for relationships, 94e, 104–107; new groups creation of communication, 200–202; operator subculture, 60

Group self-assessment: eliciting descriptions of artifacts during, 319–320; identifying espoused values during, 320–321; meeting to explain purpose of, 319; selecting appropriate setting for, 318; selecting groups for, 317–318; short lecture on how to think about culture prior to, 319

Groups: acceptance and intimacy within, 149; airing/discussing learning problems in support, 306–307; allocating rewards and punishment within, 94e, 107–110; as culture strength and stability source, 197; defining boundaries and identity of, 94e, 97–100, 202; developing rules for relationships within, 94e, 104–107; emergence of culture in new, 197–218; "fight or flight" response by, 207, 212–213; information training of members of, 306; managing multicultural, 385–400; managing the unmanageable/explaining the unexplainable within, 110–112; power, authority, and status distributed in, 94e, 101–104; survival anxiety and fear of losing membership in, 304. See also T-groups

Grundfos, 172

H

Hall, E. T., 119, 127, 135, 137
Hampden-Turner, C. M., 126, 128, 153, 168
Handbook of Cultural Intelligence (Ang & Van Dyne), 385, 388

Handy, C., 166
Harbison, F., 165
Harris, R. T., 350
Harrison, R., 166
Hassard, J., 125, 127
Hatch, M. J., 16, 29, 77, 112, 137
Havrylyshyn, B., 150
Hawthorne studies, 14, 144
Heinzen, B., 255
Henderson, R. M., 15
Henkel, 172
Hergert, M. L., 377
Hero archetype, 167
Herzberg, F., 145
Heskett, J. L., 75, 293
Hewlett, B., 230
Hewlett-Packard: Compaq acquired by, 36, 294–295; compared to DEC, Apple cultures, 182–183; example of misunderstanding at macrocultural level at, 269–270; "HP Way" of, 15, 27, 231, 264; myths reaffirming self-image of, 112, 290; switch to computer technology by, 230–231; team player norm of, 106
Hierarchy cultural dimension, 168
Hierarchy of needs, 144–145
Hierarchy. See Organizational hierarchy
High-context culture, 119–120
Hilti, 172
Hiring procedures, 98–100
Hirschhorn, L., 374
Hofstede, G., 15, 120, 126, 150
Holland, J. L., 261
Homans, G., 14, 144
Hospital radiology departments, 111
"HP Way" (Hewlett-Packard), 15, 27, 231, 264
HSBC, 172
Hughes, E. C., 60
Human activity: the being orientation, 147; the being-in-becoming orientation, 147–149; the doing orientation of, 146–147
Human factor mistakes, 61–62

Human nature: assumptions about, 143–146; hierarchy of needs, 144–145

Human relationship assumptions: individualism and collectivism, 150–151; joint effect of time, space, and, 154; "pattern variables" of role relationships, 152–154; power distance, 151–152

Human relationships: assumptions about nature of, 149–154; authority-related, 69, 101–104, 163–165, 204–211; group norms of interaction and, 14; managing internal integration and, 93–113; observed behavioral regularities during interactions, 14; problems to resolve in, 149–150. See also Conflict; Employees

Human synergistics International, 170

"Humble inquiry" skill, 381

I

I-Chat camera, 230

I-Pod, 230

I-Touch phone, 230

IBM, 20, 36, 230, 326

IBM PC, 256

"Ideal sphere," 135–136

Identity: defining group boundaries and, 94e, 97–100, 202; power and, 149; survival anxiety due to fear of losing, 304. See also Status

Incompetence fear, 304

Individual reality, 118

Individualism, 150–151

Influence, 149

Information: business decisions based on, 122–123; consensus on defining what is, 121–122; inherent ambiguity of, 122; psychological safety tendency to deny conflicting, 302–303; unfreezing or disconfirmation of, 300–303. See also Data

Information technology (IT): communication aspects of, 140–141; seduction of revolution of, 286–287; subculture of, 261–263. See also Technology

Inkson, K., 387

Innocent archetype, 167

Integrating symbols, 15–16

Integration (or patterning): as cultural characteristic, 17; cultural formation through, 18

Integration perspective bias, 175

Internal integration: allocating rewards and punishment for, 107–110; creating common language and conceptual categories for, 93–97; defining group boundaries and identity for, 97–100; developing rules for relationships for, 104–107; distributing power, authority, and status for, 101–104; managing the unmanageable/explaining the unexplainable, 110–112; problems related to, 94e

Intimacy: building norms around, 211–216; fusion assumption of, 212–213; group and acceptance and, 149; organizational culture typology of authority and, 163–166; pairing to create, 213

Intimacy distance, 135–136

Intrusion distance, 137

Involvement cultural dimension, 169

J

Japanese kamikaze pilots, 150–151

Jaques, E., 130, 131, 132

"Jargon," 97

Jester archetype, 167

Jobs, S., 229–230, 282

Johansen, R., 140, 285

Joint venture leadership, 379–380

Jones, D. T., 285

Jones, G. R., 14, 165, 167, 168

Jungian archetypes, 167

K

Kahane, A., 365
Kamikaze pilots, 150–151
Kennedy, A., 15, 16, 253
Kets de Vries, M.F.R., 146, 242, 243
Kilmann, R. H., 14
Kleiner, A., 15, 287
Kluckhohn, F. R., 28, 126, 143, 146, 148, 150, 152
Kodak Eastman, 282
Koechlin, S., 45, 49, 52, 340, 341, 342, 344, 345, 346, 353, 356, 361
Korean Airlines disasters (1990s), 398
Kotter, J. P., 75, 293
Kreiner, C., 138
Kruschwitz, N., 365
Kunda, G., 20, 40, 100, 177, 184, 193, 278
Kunz, Mr., 341–342, 344

L

Latin cultures: polychronic time valued in, 128; status displayed in, 129
Laur, J., 365
Lawrence, P. R., 130
Leaders/founders: articulation of new vision by, 305–306; charismatic, 235–236; conflict caused by inconsistent signals sent by, 241–243; emotional outbursts by, 239–241; espoused beliefs and values coming from, 39–40; examining new roles for, 363–364; group culture formation role of, 203–204, 219–233; how they embed their beliefs, values, and assumptions, 235–250; inferences from what they don't pay attention to, 241; reactions to critical incidents/organizational crises by, 243–245; rewards and status allocation by, 247–249; role modeling, teaching, and coaching by, 246–247; secondary articulation and reinforcement mechanisms by, 250–257; succession of, 280–284, 287–289; understanding

how culture changes, 273t–296. See also Founding and early growth
Leadership: connections between culture and, 3–4; culture content created by, 71; culture formation and assumptions about, 204–211; examining new roles for, 363–364; executive subculture of, 63e–67; key dimensions for successful, 171fig; learning-oriented, 374–383; obtaining culture change commitment by, 317; organizational "midlife" and changing role of, 259–271. See also Authority relationships; CEOs; Management; Organizational hierarchy
Learners: cognitive restructuring by, 300e, 308–311; formal training and involvement of, 306; psychological safety of, 300e, 302–303, 305–307; refreezing by, 300e, 311; survival anxiety by, 300e, 302, 303–305; unfreezing or disconfirmation by, 300e–307. See also Employees
Learning: airing/discussing problems to support, 306–307; cognitive restructuring for new, 300e, 308–311; double-loop, 28; espoused beliefs and values on group, 25–26; imitation/identification vs. trial-and-error, 300e, 310–311; within organizational culture typologies, 158; rules of the game by employees, 15; unfreezing or disconfirmation of old, 300e–307
Learning culture: assumptions of a, 373; characteristics of a, 366–371; implications for selection/development of leaders, 380–383; learning-oriented leadership of, 374–380; SAAB Combitech example of a, 371
"The Learning Organization," 285
Learning-oriented leadership: ability to change cultural assumptions, 382; ability to create involvement and participation, 382–383; culture creation and role of, 374; emotional strength of, 381–382;

during mergers and acquisitions, 377–379; motivation required of, 381; in organizational midlife, 374–375; in partnerships, joint ventures, and strategic alliances, 379–380; perception and insight required of, 380–381

Leavitt, H. J., 235, 293

Leupold, J., 44, 45, 46, 49, 50, 340, 341

Lewin, K., 186, 299, 301

Likert, R., 165

"Linear time" concept, 128

Litwin, G. H., 15

Lorsch, J. W., 75, 130, 220, 245, 270

Louis, M. R., 19, 188

Lover archetype, 167

Low-context culture, 119–120

M

MA-COM, 331–334

McCanse, A. A., 285

McGregor, D. M., 30, 145, 165, 237–238

McManus, M. L., 377

McNeill, P., 237

Macro context, 55

Macrocultures: appropriate human activity in, 146–149; assumptions about human nature in, 143–146; consensus on what is information, 121–123; cultural agreements maintaining, 103; description of, 1–2e, 20–21; dynamic nature of, 3; globalization impacting, 4–5; high-context and low-context, 119–120; individualism and collectivism in, 150–151; managing the unmanageable/explaining the unexplainable, 110–112; moralism and pragmatism, 120–121; nature of human relationships in, 149–154; about nature of reality and truth, 116e–119; about nature of space, 135–142; possible criteria for determining truth used by, 121e; social order developed by, 3, 103–104, 197, 365, 386–387; about time, 125–134; unconscious assumptions

forming the core of, 29, 30–32. See also Ciba-Geigy; DEC (Digital Equipment Corporation)

Madoff, B., 292

Magician archetype, 167

Malone, T., 366

Management: Anglo-Saxon cultural tradition of, 96–97; articulation of new vision by, 305–306; assumptions about human nature and, 30; distortions of unconscious assumptions and, 29, 30–32; emotional resistance to giving feedback by, 103–104; executive subculture of, 63e–67; multicultural, 385–400; similar subcultures created among, 57; Theory X and Theory Y on, 145–146, 155, 165; U.S. norm of unemotional, 148. See also Authority relationships; CEOs; Leadership; Organizational hierarchy

Management of aggression, 149

Management of intentions and will, 149

Management of love, 149

Managerial Grid, 167, 285

Managing internal integration: allocating rewards and punishment, 107–110; creating common language and conceptual categories, 93–97; defining group boundaries and identity, 97–100; developing rules for relationships, 104–107; distributing power, authority, and status, 101–104; managing the unmanageable/explaining the unexplainable, 110–112; problems related to, 94e

Market cultural dimension, 168

Market subculture differentiation, 266–267

Marshak, R. J., 206

Martin, J., 18, 160, 175, 255

Martyn-Johns, T. A., 126

Maruyama, M., 119

Maslow, A., 144

Mature organizations. See Organizational maturity/decline

Measuring results: consensus on means of measurement, 87–88; consensus on what to measure, 84–87; shared assumptions on, 83–84

Mercenary culture, 167

Mergers and acquisitions (M&Q): culture change through, 294–295; learning-leadership role in, 377–379; Sandoz and Ciba-Geigy, 44, 45, 149, 362

Merton, R. K., 75

Metes, G., 140, 285

Michael, D. N., 118, 120, 365, 366, 377

Microcultures: examples of, 67; intervention used to change DEC, 11; shared assumptions of, 67; temporary cultural islands formed in, 389–391

Midlife organizations: differentiation by hierarchical level, 270–271; differentiation by product, market, or technology, 266–267; divisionalization differentiation of subcultures in, 268–270; functional/occupational differentiation of subcultures in, 260–263; geographical differentiation of, 263–266; learning-oriented leadership in, 374–375; organizational maturity and potential decline, 273t, 289–295; recognizing growth process of, 259–260; succession problems and transition to, 273t, 280–289. See also Organizations

Miller, D., 146, 242, 243

Mirvis, P., 391

Mishra, A. K., 162

Mission: multifunctional issue of core, 76; obtaining shared understanding of, 74e–78; relationship between strategy and, 76–77; shared assumptions about goals derived from, 74e, 78–80

Mission cultural dimension, 169

MIT Sloan Fellows Program, 80–81

Monochronic time, 127–129

Moralistic cultural dimension, 120–121

Morgan, G., 16

Motivation: to answer surveys honestly, 160; assumptions on human nature and, 144–146; learning-oriented leadership, 381; reward and punishment used for, 107–110; Theory X and Theory Y on, 145–146, 155, 165

"Motivational Faith," 166

Mouton, J. S., 167, 285

Multicultural groups: cultural intelligence of, 387–389; description and challenges of, 385–387; using dialogue to explore cultural islands in, 391–398; temporary cultural island concept applied to, 389–391

Myers, C. A., 165

Myths: culture change through explosion of, 291–292; DEC (Digital Equipment Corporation) created, 112; espoused beliefs and values supported by, 290–291; organizational creation of superstitions and, 110–112; reaffirming HP self-image, 112, 290. See also Storytelling

N

Nanus, B., 235, 293

NASA space program, 397

National Cash Register Company, 230

National Training Laboratories, 198

Needs: hierarchy of, 144–145; meeting individual, 149. See also Goals

Networked culture, 167

Neuhauser, P. C., 255

Normative organizations, 164

Norms. See Group norms

Novartis, 44, 45, 149, 362

Novo Nordisk, 172

NUMMI, 289

O

Occupational cultures: macrocultures of, 3, 4–5, 20–21; subcultures creating within, 56–57; varying structures of, 3

O'Donovan, G., 172

Olsen, K.: communicating what is important to him, 238–239, 245; company-wide influence of, 277–278; comparing Packard's managerial style with, 231; cultural reinforcers used by, 252, 253; DEC culture influenced by, 76, 89, 152, 225–229; DEC founding by, 35; DEC norm of conflict determined by, 37, 39–40, 131, 214, 240–241; emotional outbursts by, 239–241, 244; firing of, 295; high-context culture reaffirmed by, 119; human factor recognized by, 61; informal measures taken by, 87; as licenses pilot, 38; "paternal" centralized control of, 242; reaffirming company's dedication to technical values, 112; resource allocation approach taken by, 245–246; role modeling, teaching, and coaching by, 246; stories told about, 256. *See also* DEC (Digital Equipment Corporation)

"Operational autonomy," 131

Operator subculture: assumptions of the, 58*e*; characteristics of, 58–60; norms developed in, 60; "practical drift" of, 60; "work to rule" process of, 59

O'Reilly, C. A., III, 278

Organizational climate, 15, 24

Organizational crises, 243–245

Organizational culture: anomalies explained by differences in, 7–8; artifacts of, 20, 23–25, 36–38; behavioral regularities of, 14–16, 20; blaming, 109; characteristics of a healthy, 173*fig*–174*fig*; content of, 18–20; deciphering, 177–193; description of, 1, 2*e*; emergence in new groups, 197–218; example of situations in context of, 9–11; founder/leadership role in creating, 219–233; on goals derived from mission, 78–80; how leaders embed beliefs, values, and assumptions into, 235–250; integration perspective bias in study of, 175; key dimensions for successful, 171*fig*;

learning, 366–383; on means to achieve goals, 80–83; on measuring results/correction mechanisms, 83–88; on mission, strategy, and goals of, 74–78; observable events and underlying forces of, 14–16; practical applications of understanding, 4–5; on remedial/repair strategies, 88–91; resistance to, 8, 303–305; socialization or acculturation to, 19–20; stabilizing function of, 365; typologies of, 70, 157–176; understanding organizational behaviors through, 11–13; variations in, 3. *See also* Corporate culture; Culture; Employees; Organizational culture typologies

Organizational culture case studies: Ciba-Geigy basics, 10, 12, 44–53; DEC (Digital Equipment Corp.) basics, 9, 11, 35–44. *See also* Ciba-Geigy; DEC (Digital Equipment Corporation); Organizational culture change case studies

Organizational culture change: conceptual model for, 300*e*–311; culture assessment component of, 315–326; founding and early growth, 273*t*, 274–280; mechanisms listed, 273*t*; organizational maturity and potential decline, 273*t*, 289–295; principles in regard to, 311–313; psycho-social dynamics of organizational, 299–300; succession problems and transition to midlife, 273*t*, 280–289; through technological seduction, 284–287

Organizational culture change case studies: Apple Computer, 335–339; Beta Service Company, 329–331; Ciba-Geigy, 339–362; MA-COM, 331–334; U.S. Army Corps of Engineers, 334–335. *See also* Organizational culture case studies

Organizational culture change model: stage 1: unfreezing/disconfirmation, 300*e*–307; stage 2: cognitive restructuring for learning, 300*e*,

308–311; stage 3: refreezing to internalize new learning, 300e, 311

Organizational culture characteristics: breadth, 17; depth, 16; patterning or integration, 17; structural stability, 16

Organizational culture examples: Alpha Power, 10–11; Amoco, 10; Cambridge-at-Home, 10; Ciba-Geigy, 10; DEC (Digital Equipment Corporation), 9

Organizational culture typologies: of authority and intimacy assumptions, 163–166; characteristics of a healthy, 173fig–174fig; example of using priori criteria for evaluating, 171fig–172; integration perspective bias introduced by, 175; issues of using, 70, 157–159; learning within, 158; lists of different, 166–169; problems in use of surveys of, 159–161; survey-based profiles of, 169–171; when to use surveys to measure, 161–163. See also Organizational culture; Organizations

Organizational hierarchy: authority relationships in, 69, 101–104; body language rituals used to reinforce, 139; differentiation of subculture by, 270–271; distributing power, authority, and status through, 101–104; subcultures of given levels within, 56. See also Leadership; Management; Status

Organizational maturity/decline: culture changes through process of, 289–295; destruction and rebirth, 295; learning-oriented leadership during, 376–377; mergers and acquisitions, 294–295; scandal and explosion of myths, 291–292; turnarounds by, 293–294

Organizations: basic time orientation of, 126–127; being orientation of, 147; being-in-becoming orientation, 147–149; challenges of measuring culture content in, 70–71; changing role of leadership in "midlife," 259–271; coercive, 163, 164, 165;

doing orientation of, 146–147; external adaptation issues faced by, 74e–91; formal statements of philosophy, creeds, and charters, 256–257; founding and early growth of, 273t, 274–280; macro context of, 55; managing internal integration, 93–113; maturity and potential decline of, 289–295, 376–377; MIT Sloan Fellows Program exercise to build an, 80–81; monochronic and polychronic time in, 127–128; normative, 164; rites and rituals of, 14, 16, 101, 139, 253–255; secondary articulation and reinforcement mechanisms by, 250–257; superstitions and myths formed in, 110–112; three dimensions of career movement in, 99–100; utilitarian, 163, 164, 165. See also Midlife organizations; Organizational culture typologies; Strategies

Oshry, B., 270

"The other," 143

Ouchi, W. G., 15, 112, 168, 244

Outliers (Gladwell), 7–8

P

Packard, D., 27, 230, 282

Pairing, 213

Palmer, R., 295

Parry, C. S., 391

Parson, T., 152

Particularism vs. universalism, 153

Partnership leadership, 379–380

Pascale, R. T., 15

Passive/Defensive Styles, 170

"Pattern variables," 152–153

Patterning (or integration): as cultural characteristic, 17; cultural formation through, 18

Pava, C.H.P., 294

Pearson, C. S., 162, 167

PepsiCo, 230

Performance appraisal, emotional resistance to, 103–104

Perin, C., 29, 303

Personal distance, 136

Peters, T. J., 15

Peterson, B., 387

Peterson, M. F., 236

Petre, P., 230, 282

Pettigrew, A. M., 112

Pisano, G. P., 386

Planning time, 129–130

Plum, E., 387

Polychronic time, 127–129, 140

Pondy, L. R., 16

Porras, J., 75

Poulfelt, L., 165

Power: distribution of, 101–104; needs for influence and, 149; survival anxiety due to fear of losing, 303. See also Authority relationships

Power distance, 151–152

Power oriented typology, 166

Powers, M. E., 255

"Practical drift," 60

Pragmatic cultural dimension, 120–121

Predictability validity criteria, 185

Primary embedding mechanisms: concluding observations about, 250; deliberate role modeling, teaching, and coaching, 236e, 246–247; how leaders allocate resources, 236e, 245–246; how leaders allocate rewards and status, 236e, 247–249; how leaders select, promote, and excommunicate, 236e, 249–250; listed, 236e; reactions to critical incidents/organizational crises, 236e, 243–245. See also Secondary articulation/reinforcement mechanisms

"Prince Albert" syndrome, 281

Process analysis, 204

Products: Ciba-Geigy debate over "valuable," 77; discretionary time horizons in developing, 130–132; MIT Sloan Fellows Program exercise on, 80–81; subculture differentiation related to, 266–267; subculture variations in planning and development of, 129–130

Promotion: organizational approach to, 249–250; systematically and from selected subcultures, 283–284

Psychological safety: Ciba-Geigy and process of providing, 350; denial of conflicting information to maintain, 302–303; how to create, 305–307; unfreezing process and importance of, 300e, 302

Public distance, 136

Punishment: organizational systems for, 107–110; survival anxiety and fear of, 304. See also Reward systems

Putnam, R., 28

Q

Quinn, R. E., 168

R

R&D (research & development): differing time horizons of, 130–132; planning and development time by, 129–130; task forces to communicate with sales/marketing, 263

Radiology technology, 132–133, 285

Rapid deciphering process: description of, 315–316; identifying culture elements that need changing with, 325–326; key assumptions for, 316–317; steps in, 317–325

Rapid deciphering steps: 1: obtaining leadership commitment, 317; 2: selecting groups for self-assessment, 317–318; 3: selecting appropriate setting for group self-assessment, 318; 4: explaining purpose of the group meeting, 319; 5: short lecture on how to think about culture, 319; 6: eliciting descriptions of the artifacts, 319–320; 7: identifying espoused values, 320–321; 8: identifying shared underlying assumptions, 321–323; 9: identifying cultural aids and hindrances, 323–324; 10: decisions on next steps, 324–325

Reality: different assumptions related to, 116–117; external physical, 117; incremental change to adapt to new, 279–280; individual, 118; moralism vs. pragmatism approach to, 120–121; possible criteria for determining truth and, 121e; reaching a consensus on, 118–119; social, 117–119. *See also* Truth

Reality testing: of fusion assumption and intimacy, 213–215; by group on authority relationships, 209–211

Redding, S. G., 126

Relationships: assumptions about nature of human, 149–154; group norms of interaction and, 14; joint effect of time, space, and, 154; managing internal integration and, 93–113; observed behavioral regularities during interactions, 14; "pattern variables" of role, 152–154. *See also* Authority relationships

Religious beliefs, 110

Remedial/repair strategies: comparing DEC and Ciba-Geigy approach to, 89–90; consensus for external adaptation of, 88–91

Replication validity criteria, 185

Research ethical issues: professional obligations of the culture analyst, 190–191; risks of an internal analysis, 188–190; risks of analysis for research purposes, 186–188

Researchers: consultant/helper role of, 183–185; contacting and negotiating with organization, 179–180; data collection by, 180–183; deciphering organization from the outside, 178e–179; levels of involvement by, 183t; professional obligations of, 190–191; validity of clinically gathered data, 185–186. *See also* Ethnographers

Resistance to change: managerial response to, 8; stages of responses, 304–305; survival anxiety and, 303–304

Resource allocation, 245–246

Revolutionary archetype, 167

Reward systems: allocation of, 107–110, 247–249; consistency of culture change with, 307; leadership attention focused on, 237–238. *See also* Punishment; Status

Ritti, R. R., 15

Rituals: behavioral regularities of, 14; body language used as, 139; celebrations and formal, 16; as cultural reinforcers, 253–254; dominance-establishing, 101

Roberts, C., 15

Rockart, J. F., 122

Roethlisberger, F. J., 144

Role modeling: creating psychological safety through, 306; by founders and leaders, 246–247; psychological identification with, 308

Role oriented typology, 166

Role relationships, 152–154

Roos, D., 285

Root metaphors, 15–16

Rosie the Riverter posters, 147

Ross, R. B., 15

Roth, G., 391

Ruef, M., 275

Ruler archetype, 167

Rules of the game, 15

S

SAAB Combitech, 371–372

Sackman, S. A., 171, 172

Sage archetype, 167

Sahlins, M., 185, 275

Salk, J., 379

San Francisco Bay Transit Authority (BART), 62

Sandoz/Ciba-Geigy merger, 44, 45, 149, 362

Saturn division, 289

Savage, C. M., 285

Saxton, M. J., 14

Scandals, 291–292

Scharmer, C. O., 365, 366

Schein, E. H., 2, 15, 19, 35, 41, 42, 43, 52, 62, 64, 89, 99, 127, 139, 144, 145, 165, 172, 184, 198, 220, 246, 261, 281, 285, 294, 299, 300, 307, 316, 340, 342, 344, 366, 369, 374, 377, 381

Schley, S., 365

Schlumberger, 395

Schneider, B., 15, 236

Schon, D. A., 15, 27

Schultz, M., 16, 29, 77, 112

Schwartz, P., 365

Scully, J., 230, 288

Secondary articulation/reinforcement mechanisms: as cultural reinforcers, 250–251; design of space, facades, and buildings as, 255; formal statements of philosophy, creeds, and charters, 256–257; organizational design and structure as, 251–252; organizational systems and procedures as, 252–253; rites and rituals of the organization as, 14, 16, 101, 139, 253–255; stories about important events and people, 255–256. See also Primary embedding mechanisms

Senge, P., 15, 285, 365, 366

"Sensory screening," 137

Service, E. R., 275

Shared cognitive frames, 15

Shared meanings, 15

"Shared Vision," 166

Shepard, H. A., 205

Shrivastava, P., 165

Sithi-Amnuai, P., 128

Slavery justification, 143

Smircich, L., 15

Smith, B. J., 15, 365

Smithfield Enterprises, 224–225, 280

Smithfield, F., 224–225, 238

Snook, S. A., 60, 291

Social distance, 136

Social interactions: assumptions about nature of human, 149–154; group norms of, 14; managing internal integration and, 93–113; observed behavioral regularities during, 14

Social needs, 144–145

Social order: cultural rules maintaining, 3, 103–104, 197, 365, 386–387; manners and morals as essential rules of, 103, 365

Social reality: description of, 117–118; reaching a consensus on, 118–119

Social validation, through espoused values, 26–27

Socialization process, 19–20

Space: assumptions about nature of, 135–142; body language, 139; cultural reinforcement through design of physical, 255; distance and relative placement of, 135–137; interaction between time and, 140–141; joint effect of relationship assumptions, time, and, 154; symbolism of, 137–139

Specificity vs. diffuseness, 153

Stakeholders: consensus on measuring results and correction mechanisms, 74e, 83–88; consensus on remedial and repair strategies, 74e, 88–91; shared assumptions about means to achieve goals, 74e, 80–83; shared concept of survival problem by, 74e–78

Status: ascription vs. achievement, 153; differentiation of subculture by, 270–271; distribution within groups, 94e, 101–104; leader allocation of, 247–249; survival anxiety due to fear of losing, 303; symbolism of space to indicate, 138–139; time concepts used to define, 129. See also Identity; Organizational hierarchy; Reward systems

Steele, F. I., 137, 138, 140, 255

Steinberg, S.: communicating what was important to him, 238–239; cultural reinforcers used by, 252; customer service importance to, 241;

family ownership promoted by, 105; inconsistent messages from, 242; lack of concern for subordinates by, 244; leadership approach taken by, 220–224; role modeling, teaching, and coaching by, 246–247

Stokes, H., 166

Storytelling, 255–256. *See also* Myths

Strategic alliance leadership, 379–380

Strategies: for measuring results and correction mechanisms, 83–88; relationship between mission and, 76–77; remedial and repair, 88–91. *See also* Organizations

Strodtbeck, F. L., 28, 126, 143, 146, 148, 150, 152

Structural stability, 16

Subculture differentiation: divisionalization, 268–270; functional/occupational, 260–263; geographical, 263–266; by hierarchical level, 270–271; by product, market, or technology, 266–267

Subcultures: description of, 2e; differentiation and growth of, 260–271; diversity of, 283–284; engineering/design, 60–62, 65–66; executive, 63e–67; within given levels within a hierarchy, 56; occupational communities, 56–57; operator, 58e–60; shared assumptions creating, 55–56; systematic promotion from selected, 283–284; three generic types of, 57–67; variations in planning and development time, 129–130

Subordinates: conflict from inconsistent leader messages to, 241–243; emotional outbursts directed to, 239–241; emotional resistance to giving feedback to, 103–104; HP's global policy on giving feedback to, 269–270; motivation of, 107–110, 144–146, 155, 160, 165; selection, promotion, and excommunication of, 249–250. *See also* Employees

Succession issues: infusion of outsiders, 287–289; midlife organizations facing, 280–283; "Prince Albert" syndrome of, 281; systematic promotion from selected subcultures for, 283–284

Suicide bombers, 151

Supermarket bar code technology, 222

Superstitions, 110–112

Support oriented typology, 166

Survey-based culture profiles, 169–171

Surveys: possible negative consequences of, 161; problems in the use of, 159–161; when to use, 161–163

Survival anxiety: Ciba-Geigy and induced, 349–350; creation of, 300e, 302; learning anxiety versus, 303–305; responses to, 304–305; two principles to understand about, 305

Sutcliffe, K. M., 15, 300

Symbolism: body language and gestures, 139; of space, 137–139

Systemic thinking commitment, 371

"Systems Dynamics," 285

Szumal, J. L., 162, 170

T

T-groups: differences due to personalities of members, 214–215; process analysis by members of, 204; setting goals for, 199–200; stages of culture formation of, 204–218. *See also* Groups

Tagiuri, R., 15

"Tall poppy syndrome," 151

Task-relevant communication, 369–370

Tasks: differing time horizons for completing, 130–132; interaction between time and space during, 140–141; planning and development time for, 129–130; technology to improve pacing of radiology, 132–133, 285; temporary symmetry of, 132–134

Teaching by leaders, 246–247

Technology: culture change through new, 284–287; HP's switch to computer,

230–231; impact on communication time and space, 140–141, 285; improving pacing of radiology, 132–133, 285; subculture differentiation related to, 266–267; supermarket bar code, 222. *See also* Information technology (IT)

Technology seduction: culture change through, 284–287; example of employee's rethinking identity through, 286; examples of communication and social, 285; of IT revolution, 286–287

Temporary incompetence fear, 304

Temporary symmetry, 132–134

Terrorist suicide bombers, 151

Theory X, 145–146, 155, 165

Theory Y, 145, 155, 165, 367

Thomas, D. C., 387

Thomas, R., 56, 62

Three Mile Island, 291

Tichy, N. M., 293

Time: assumptions about, 125–134; cultural basic orientations toward, 126–127; discretionary time horizons/ degree of accuracy, 130–132; interaction between space and, 140–141; joint effect of relationship assumptions, space, and, 154; "linear time" concept of, 128; monochronic and polychronic, 127–129, 140; new technology changing pace of radiology tasks, 132–133, 285; subculture variations in planning and development, 129–130; summary on main aspects of, 134; temporal symmetry, pacing, and entrainment of, 132–134

Time horizons, 130–132

Total Quality Management, 285

Toyota recall (2009), 88

Training programs, 306

Transformative change. *See* Culture change

Trice, H. M., 14, 16, 17, 253

Trompenaars, A., 126, 128, 153, 168

Truth: criteria used to determine, 121e; DEC's process for determining, 123; learning culture commitment to, 368–369. *See also* Reality

Turnarounds, 293–294

Turquet, P. M., 212

Tushman, M. L., 275, 295

2001: A Space Odyssey (film), 256

Typologies. *See* Organizational culture typologies

Tyrell, M.W.D., 286

U

Unconscious assumption distortions, 29, 30–32

Unfreezing/disconfirmation: Ciba-Geigy process of, 347–349; progress of culture change through, 300e–303; psychological safety during, 300e, 302–303, 305–307, 350–352; survival anxiety versus learning anxiety during, 300e, 302, 303–305, 347–350

Unilever, 20

United Nations health team, 4

United States: constitutional individual rights in the, 150; doing orientation of business ideology in the, 147; economic crisis (2009) of the, 244, 292; eye contact norm in the, 139; individualistic culture of, 151; monochronic time valued in the, 127–129

Universalism vs. particularism, 153

U.S. Army Corps of Engineers, 334–335

U.S. Defense Department, 267

U.S. Department of Defense, 337

U.S. Food and Drug Administration, 265

U.S. Navy cooks/servers, 100

U.S. Shell Oil Company, 85

Utilitarian organizations, 163, 164, 165

V

Value assumptions, 23. *See also* Espoused beliefs and values

Van Dyne, L., 15, 387, 388

Van Maanen, J., 14, 15, 19, 20, 56, 60, 118, 135, 139, 154, 177, 184, 185, 193, 261
Victoria, Queen, 282
Vision, 305–306
Vroom, V. H., 165

W

"Wander the halls," 109
Waterman, R. H., Jr., 15, 244, 281
Watson, T. J., Jr., 230, 281, 282
Weeks, J., 193
Weick, K., 15, 17, 300
Whirlwind, 226
Whiting, J., 95
Wikipedia, 123

Wilderom, C.P.M., 236
Wilkins, A. L., 112, 166, 255
Williamson, O., 168
Womack, J. T., 285
"Woods meetings" (DEC), 254
"Work to rule," 59
Wozniak, S., 229–230

Y

Yanow, D., 15, 81
Yetton, P. W., 165

Z

Zeus (The Club culture), 166
Zuboff, S., 59, 285